This book makes an enormous contribution tc
many individuals and communities across the
of this much-needed volume illustrates the po
of reconciliation and the multi-faceted peace
given his church.

Dr Peter Rowan
National Director OMF (UK)

This book combines personal testimony, therapeutic expertise, and biblical exegesis in a way that is as rare as it is useful. Written by Christians from a variety of cultures with experience in helping trauma victims, many of these essays will prove enormously helpful to pastors, therapists, and survivors as they think through strategies for recovery from a biblical and Christian perspective.

Frank Thielman, PhD
Presbyterian Professor of Divinity,
Beeson Divinity School, Birmingham, Alabama, USA

In the UK today the word "trauma" is often debased by overuse and application to trivial events. This book lays bare the scope and depth and impact of real trauma, and combines profound scriptural truth, painful testimony, and reports of almost unimaginable suffering, both individual and communal. It offers wise practical advice as to Christian response and action. Surely, the heart of God asks us to weep and mourn with those who suffer, to listen and learn, but then to bring by word and deed his love and grace that is the only source of real healing. Sober, painful reading, but a biblical tool in our hands for our hurting world.

Rose Dowsett
Author, Missiologist, Speaker
Member of OMF International
Member of Lausanne Cape Town Commitment Team
Former Vice-Chair, WEA Mission Commission

A strength of this book is the unique combination of Scripture with personal narrative and experience, as well as more clinical- and evidence-based information about trauma. I'm encouraged to see pastoral leadership willing to engage with this difficult topic and desiring to be informed about these things to better lead and serve. It is of the utmost importance to emphasize that pastors (and all engaging in trauma work) need a processing space and accountability for secondary trauma. It is difficult to see how holding the trauma of others impacts our own hearts, minds, and bodies; and it is important to gain perspective on individual cases to most wisely proceed in providing care and counsel.

Jen Scofield
Licensed Graduate Social Worker
Mental Health Practitioner

Tackling Trauma

Tackling Trauma

Global, Biblical, and Pastoral Perspectives

General Editor

Paul A. Barker

Published 2019 by Langham Global Library
An imprint of Langham Publishing
www.langhampublishing.org

Langham Publishing and its imprints are a ministry of Langham Partnership

Langham Partnership
PO Box 296, Carlisle, Cumbria, CA3 9WZ, UK
www.langham.org

ISBNs:
978-1-78368-481-6 Print
978-1-78368-482-3 ePub
978-1-78368-483-0 Mobi
978-1-78368-484-7 PDF

In chapter 6, unless marked otherwise, Scripture quotations are the author's own.

British Library Cataloguing-in-Publication Data
A catalogue record for this book is available from the British Library

ISBN: 978-1-78368-481-6

Cover & Book Design: projectluz.com

CONTENTS

Preface

Our world is traumatic. Natural disasters, tsunamis, genocide, wars, terrorism, persecution, abuse, tragedy, bereavement, injustice, deep sadness. People suffer; Christians suffer.

For some, the tragedy in our world confronts faith in God, challenges our ideas of a loving and merciful God. Some abandon faith, yet others keep trusting God.

How do we make sense of a traumatic world? How do we love and offer hope in a traumatic world?

This book is a diverse range of essays that explores biblical and theological approaches to trauma as well as pastoral responses. The essays are grounded both in the Scriptures as well as in reality and experience. The essays come from writers who are from, or have worked in, various countries of Africa, Asia, the Middle East and Eastern Europe. The essays vary in style and approach but we see them as complementary, thought-provoking, worthy of reflection and discussion, all with the aim of bringing benefit to people throughout this suffering world. Truly this is a global collection of essays.

The contexts of the authors differ, but just as Christians read the Psalms into their own contexts and find help and solace though their situations differ from the original psalmist, so these articles have relevance across a range of contexts and experiences. Some authors have written out of the genocide of Rwanda, poverty and natural disaster in the Philippines, war in the Ukraine, and numerous other major traumas. Some essays are more pastoral, others more theological. We need a variety of tools to be equipped to deal with the trauma of our world. The wisdom and grace of our writers shines through in the essays that follow.

This book is compiled with pastors around the world in mind. We hope that among these essays will be some at least that help, equip, and encourage pastors who are preaching, teaching and exercising care for people who face potential trauma or indeed have experienced trauma.

We are grateful for funding from First Fruit, Inc. to enable this work to be undertaken. We canvassed a wide range of experts across the globe to contribute. Then some of the contributors met together in Addis Ababa to review the articles, suggest revisions, and get an overall feel for the project. I am grateful for the fellowship and expertise at that gathering of Sam

Thielman, Rolex Cailing, Isaac Mbabazi, Annabel Manalo, John Steward and Muhindo Isesomo.

Langham Partnership, under whose auspices this project has been implemented, seeks to equip the church in the Majority World with literature and resources, as well as scholarships and preaching training, to grow the church in depth under the word of God. We pray this project will be effective for those purposes also.

This book is dedicated to those across the globe who have suffered, and continue to suffer, major trauma in a world that needs to know Jesus more and more.

Bishop Paul A. Barker, Editor
Anglican Diocese of Melbourne
Formerly Asian Regional Coordinator for Langham Preaching and Langham Scholar Care

1

Joseph and Trauma Recovery

John Steward

For this is the wonder of God, that when we walk in the light of his countenance, the very shadows of our life are charged with healing power. –Hugh Redwood

Background

In a practical and general sense, trauma is a widely used term to describe hurtful and challenging events that threaten to cause setbacks in our life. It may be an unexpected situation of calamity, loss or abuse that confronts us and impacts our body, mind and spirit. Often overwhelming and unpleasant, the energy of trauma usually stays within us and affects how we think, feel, choose and behave.

If any Old Testament character knew trauma and how to live through it, Joseph son of Jacob stands out. Brought up as a long-awaited child of Jacob's favorite wife, Rachel, Joseph had a special place in the affections of his parents. As a favorite son born to parents in their old age, who already had many other children in their clan, Joseph benefited from what his parents had come to realize – their need to encourage each child's giftedness. By the time he was a teenager, Joseph was a confident, communicative young man. His older siblings considered him to be quite brash and arrogant.

A Flood of Trauma

Joseph was born into a family of immense complexity. His first experience of trauma came when he suffered the loss of his mother during the birth of his brother, Benjamin, which occurred "on the road" (Gen 35:16–18).[1]

Because the motherless Joseph was adored by his aged father and probably indulged by his clan aunties, he became a target for derision from his half-brothers. The Middle Eastern traditions of community support, known in Africa as *Ubuntu*, began to break down. By the time Joseph had become a proud dreamer who went about showing his father's love by wearing his special coat, he had earned a rebuke from his father, and his stepbrothers had begun to envy and then loathe him. They demonstrated their abrasive and growing intolerance at every opportunity, marking the second experience of trauma in Joseph's life (37:2–11).

Joseph's older brothers resented his special treatment, and so they began to conspire and abuse him. First, they plotted to kill him when he came to find them as they were pasturing their father's flock (37:18–20). When his eldest brother Reuben intervened, the other brothers agreed to throw him into a pit and leave him there, without any water (37:21–24). Then, at brother Judah's suggestion, they hardened their hearts and rejected Joseph completely by selling him into slavery when he was seventeen years old (37:25–28). Years later, the brothers admitted, "we saw the anguish of his soul . . . and we would not hear" (42:21 JUB). Joseph's complete rejection by his brothers and his loss of freedom marks the third experience of trauma in his life.

To cover up what they had done, the brothers had to deceive their father. Judah paid for this deception with his own personal experiences of trauma (see ch. 38). This illustrates the fact that *trauma, when unresolved, is like an eagle which spreads its wings and catches others in its claws.*

Joseph's arrival in Egypt marks his fourth experience of trauma, for he had to live as a refugee and a slave in another culture with a foreign religion and new dialect (37:36). Though this may be a common adventure for modern youth, it was traumatic for Joseph because it confirmed the loss of his family and community.

While in Egypt, Joseph did well by using his natural gifts, but then his handsome appearance and appealing demeanor led his employer's wife to try to seduce him. When Joseph refused, she tried to trap him, and when Joseph

1. Some writers would put this second and start with the attitude of the brothers, because the time of the birth of Benjamin is difficult to determine.

refused again, she lay the blame at Joseph's feet (39:1–18). This double-blow marks Joseph's fifth experience of trauma.

Because Joseph was employed by Potiphar, an officer of Pharaoh, he was thrown into prison and placed in a dungeon (39:19–20). Psalm 105:18 (NASB) reminds us how he suffered there:

> They afflicted his feet with fetters,
> He himself was laid in irons.

The dungeon must have reminded Joseph of the desert hole, where he had been abandoned by his brothers, and from where he had been cast away into a foreign land. Being rejected and held captive because of a false accusation marks the sixth experience of trauma in Joseph's life.

Ironically, Joseph was not alone in the prison, and he enjoyed a sympathetic audience as he conversed with others, describing his life journey (40:15) and listening as they shared their stories. Once more, Joseph used his natural gifts and prospered in the prison. He found favor with the prison keeper (39:21–23) and used his spiritual gift to interpret the dreams of two fellow prisoners, a butler and a baker (40:9–19). But when the butler, whose dream Joseph had interpreted favorably, was released, he did not remember Joseph and failed to speak out on his behalf, though Joseph had asked him to do so (40:14). The butler's failure to remember Joseph intensified his previous traumas of betrayal, rejection and imprisonment. For many of us, the failure of a friend, whom we have greatly assisted but who does not return the favor, might easily become 'the final straw' that breaks us.

Two years later, the tide turned unexpectedly when Pharaoh desperately wanted to understand his dream, but his wise men and diviners could not help him (41:1–8). The restored butler heard about Pharaoh's frustration and recalled how Joseph had interpreted his dream while he had been in prison, and so he spoke up and recommended Joseph (41:9–13). Then Pharoah called for Joseph, who stressed that this dream announced what God was about to do throughout Egypt: there would be seven years of great abundance followed by seven years of severe famine (41:14–37).

Joseph's clarity, honesty and generosity were rewarded, for Pharaoh granted him a new beginning of hope and deep responsibility (41:38–44). Joseph was also given a beautiful wife and an indigenous name, Zaphenath-Paneah, which means "the god speaks and he [the one named] lives" (41:45). The gift of a new identity and vocation confirmed Joseph's new citizenship and reflected the impact of his witness. During the seasons of plenty, the couple had two sons: Ephraim and Manasseh (41:50–52).

In the first thirty years of Joseph's life, he suffered six major traumas: first, his mother died in childbirth; second, his half-brothers plotted to kill him but then threw him in a pit; third, in order to make a profit, his half-brothers disowned him and sold him into slavery; fourth, he became a refugee in another culture; fifth, his employer's wife tried to seduce him and lied about his behavior; sixth, her accusation caused him to be thrown into prison, where he helped a man who later forgot to speak on Joseph's behalf after being released.

What enabled Joseph to cope with all this trauma? Now, to be clear, we cannot simply "cope" or "get over" trauma, for we must process our trauma, or else it will remain a wound of the heart that continues to affect our spirits, minds and bodies. Using a story from my own family life, I will explore some of the ways in which Joseph was able to process his numerous experiences of trauma.

I come from Australia, a country that sent hundreds of thousands of men to war during the 1920s and 1940s. These men suffered immensely, and *if* they returned home, they brought their trauma with them and continued to carry it in their bodies, minds, spirits, attitudes and behaviors. Many of these former soldiers were ordered to keep their experiences secret for fifty years, and so most returnees said little about what they had seen and experienced. Yet their lives and functioning suggested that carrying such deep hurts had changed them, for many remained troubled for years afterwards. Though the emotional impact was suppressed, it was passed onto the generations that followed.

My father was a medical orderly in the war from 1941 to 1945, and he faced many dangers in the Middle East and Papua New Guinea. Trauma, including shock treatment, and ill health (malaria and dysentery) forced him to need hospitalization and eventually early discharge. In 2014 – nearly seventy years after he returned to Australia – I asked him to talk about his experiences in the war, which he did for almost three hours. He was very thankful for our conversation, which was the only open and frank discussion we'd ever had about how the war had affected him, both positively and negatively. Over the years, he had gained new insights about his suffering – such as how God had been with him and that what he had learned had opened later doors of service in Indonesia and with Asian students in Australia.

My dad's long silence about his traumatic experiences was not unique, because denial is a typical response after we experience painful events. Denial enables us to continue living in the hope that whatever bad we experienced will not affect our lives. We may pretend some traumatic experience did not happen, or we may decide to ignore it and just get on with our lives, or we may know that we have been affected but not know what to do about it. In each of these denials, the bad energy remains within us – from which a bitter root may grow (Heb 12:15) until it is brought into the open for healing.[2] Joseph overcomes this hindrance by following a pathway of both survival and recovery.

Joseph's Survival and Recovery

In pondering Joseph's experiences, we might ask the following questions: *Are there situations and events that helped Joseph overcome the effects of his traumatic experiences? What reasons do we find for his success in saving Egypt and restoring unity to his own clan?*

In reflecting on these questions, we can make several observations about how Joseph transcended the pain he experienced because of the hurtful actions and moral failures of others. First, he learned from the example of his ancestors and parents. Second, he did not deny the bad things that happened to him. Third, he experienced healing and restoration. Fourth, he returned good for evil, thus overcoming the negative effects of trauma for himself by practicing love for God, self and others. Fifth, when Joseph faced his grief, he mourned. In the following discussion, we will look more closely at each of these five aspects.

First, Joseph followed the example of his ancestors and parents, especially his father, Jacob. Jacob had endured a long and stressful series of setbacks after falling in love with Rachel. To be able to marry Rachel, he had to serve her father, Laban, for seven years – and then Laban tricked Jacob into marrying his elder daughter Leah, and so Jacob had to serve Laban for another seven years (29:18–30). After these long years of testing, Rachel remained barren while Leah had four boys, and then the maids of Rachel and Leah had four boys, and then Leah had a fifth and sixth son, followed by a daughter (29:31–30:21). When Rachel finally gave birth to her firstborn, she named him Joseph, which means "may God add [posterity]" (30:22–24). This name connotes openness and hope. Through the gift of this long-awaited child, Jacob and Rachel saw their hope in God fulfilled, and this was a healing experience for them.

Then Laban's sons began to influence their father against Jacob, and so he had to flee with his wives and family (31:1–2). In preparing for his secret departure, Jacob told Rachel and Leah, "your father has cheated me by changing my wages ten times. However, God has not allowed him to harm me" (31:7 NIV). In a dream, God confirmed his favor to Jacob and then told him to return to the land of his birth (31:10–13). Thus Jacob acted on this dream, just as he did earlier in Genesis 28.

2. See ch. 15 in this collection, "By His Wounds I Am Healed to Love," also by John Steward.

Now because Joseph grew up in a community with a custom of storytelling, he would have heard all these stories as the family ate their meals or sat around the fire by night. He also would have heard the stories about his great-grandfather Abraham and his grandfather Isaac – how God had visited, led, tested and provided for them while promising them a great future. He also would have witnessed how his father and mother embraced the importance of a godly perspective on everything that had happened to their forebears, both the good and the bad.

Thus many years later, when harm came to Joseph, he behaved as if he believed his father's words – that God would not let harm come to him. Jacob's faith was a significant heritage for young Joseph, and he followed in his father's footsteps and eventually became a master of dream interpretation. We, too, can learn from the good and bad experiences of our ancestors and their heritage. Their faith can help form our faith, and their confidence in God can inform our trust.

Second, Joseph did not deny that bad things had happened to him, nor did he become a victim and let those bad things define him. For each of his traumatic experiences, Joseph made conscious responses, and these became a kind of antidote to his pain. He kept his love alive for his father; he did not seek revenge on his brothers; he honored God in all of his decisions; he fled temptation; he remained generous, strong and patient. Although his life never returned to normal, and he described Egypt as "the land of my affliction" (Gen 41:52), he accepted his circumstances and made the most of his life by settling in and becoming active in his new culture and the country of his adoption.

In brief, Joseph restrained himself despite his pain, and he never seemed to give into anger or self-recrimination. He may have remembered his losses every day, but they did not poison his spirit or disable his work. He was able to stay above the dirty and undesirable actions of his brothers and those who forgot him, cheated him or accused him falsely.

Each time Joseph's social status improved, the narrator of Genesis reminds us that it was because of God's auspices. God's faithful presence enabled Joseph to live with a pattern of behavior based on trust and obedience to God. What are our patterns of responding to difficulties? Do we tend to see ourselves as victims, survivors or victors? Do we face our difficulties and setbacks? Do we seek instruction and value in our suffering as we follow in the footsteps of Jesus the Christ?

Third, Joseph experienced healing, and so he did not remain a hostage to the pain of his past. Joseph loved to talk, which greatly annoyed his brothers when he was young, for he was not easily suppressed, and he was not afraid to speak out. This trait was important after he arrived in Egypt, for he had numerous conversations that influenced his fate: Potiphar and his household, the chief jailor, his fellow prisoners, the priest of On, his wife Asenath, and so on.

As Fr Michael Lapsley of South Africa is fond of quoting in his reconciliation workshops: "Every person has a story to tell and every story needs a listener." Each time Joseph shared his stories of loss with others, his inner pain lessened a bit. But when we cannot share our stories, we can become stuck in the pain of our past.

A clear indication of Joseph's healing from pain and bitterness is revealed when he and his Egyptian wife named their first child "Manasseh," which means "forget." Much later, when the elder son asked, "Why did you give me that name?" Joseph would have answered, "I have chosen to live my life in freedom, and so I am living now as if I have forgotten the bad things of the past." Joseph would have gone on to tell Manasseh that because of forgiveness, those painful events did not shape him or poison his spirit.

Joseph and Asenath named their second son "Ephraim," which means "to be fruitful." When Ephraim asked about his name, Joseph would have pointed out the connection with his own name, "may God add . . ." He would have gone on to tell Ephraim that he had found contentment by welcoming God's provision of offspring and believing that God had blessings in store for him – even through life's challenging experiences. Joseph's faith was alive. Rather than being chained to a painful past, he let go of his bitterness and lived with hope for the future.

Trauma binds us to the past and makes it difficult to live in the present – let alone look ahead. But Joseph lived to an old age and looked far ahead. Paul's letter to the Hebrews traces the nature of Joseph's forward-looking faith: "By faith Joseph, when his end was near, spoke about the exodus of the Israelites from Egypt and gave instructions concerning the burial of his bones" (Heb 11:22 NIV). Yet it took 430 years before Joseph's bones were taken and buried in the land of his ancestors (see Gen 50:25–26; Exod 12:40)!

As Jesus said in another context: "your faith has made you well [whole]" (Mark 5:34; Luke 17:19; Matt 9:22 NIV). What pains and hurts still hold us back? How can we tell our stories in a safe and trusting space? Have we surrendered the bitterness and poison from our wounds? Does our faith enable us to accept the weight of our past while looking forward in hope toward "the glory that will be revealed in us"? (Rom 8:18 NIV)

Fourth, Joseph returned good for evil. While he did not ignore what had happened to him, he did not hold grudges, and he never sought revenge. Some tend to look negatively at Joseph's treatment of his brothers during their visits to Egypt. However, the way Joseph played out the drama is consistent with a Rwandan principle, which is "do not forgive too soon or too readily." In *The Interpreter's Dictionary of the Bible,* Wintermute observes that "A mistreated person needs to test the reliability of the mistreat-ers before restoring them. So Joseph devised a series of tests to do this."[3]

In Genesis 42–44, Joseph tested his brothers without demeaning them, which suggests that he bore no malice towards them. By challenging them, he invited them to reflect on their actions, and slowly honesty began to emerge in them. Through this exchange, Joseph overcame the negative effects of his trauma as he extended love to those who had hurt him.

In Genesis 44, Joseph offered peace and grace to his former tormenters. Later, when his brothers feared that he would turn against them after their father died, they asked forgiveness for their crime and flung themselves at his feet (50:15–18). They offered to become his slaves, but Joseph responded with kindness: "Have no fear . . ." (50:19). His "tough love" became gentle.

When a perpetrator seeks forgiveness, it opens the possibility for reconciliation. Joseph took that opportunity. Reconciliation reflects healing for both the victim and perpetrator, but because such an outcome is relatively rare, stories that hold this hope are important for our congregations, children and communities.

The word "forgive" is first used in Genesis by Joseph's brothers in 50:17. The Hebrew word is broad, general and common, and it is mostly translated as "take away, bear, carry." This term is not used in the Old Testament for divine forgiveness, as that is a rarely used word that means "pardon" and is used only for God. Thus the brothers' plea to Joseph implored him to bear the pain and consequences of their actions without recriminations. This is a realistic description of forgiveness from one who has been wronged by someone else.

Yet when Joseph's brothers prostrated themselves before him, it is clear that he had already forgiven them. For Joseph invoked the name of God twice in his response: "Am I in the place of God? You intended to harm me, but God intended it for good . . ." (50:19–20 NIV). Throughout the unpleasant seasons of his life, Joseph held onto faith and hope in God, just as his ancestors had before him. Rachel, his mother, spoke of her faith in God (30:6, 23–24; 31:16), and his father spoke of his various experiences with God and angels (28:16–22; 31:5, 9, 11, 13). Joseph had to suffer and be tested before his heart could be

---

3. O. S. Wintermute, "Joseph, Son of Jacob," *The Interpreters Dictionary of the Bible* (New York: Abingdon, 1962), 2, 983.

described as steadfast and open to God (39:9; 41:52; 42:18). His trust in God is clearly revealed through his understanding of dreams, which he regarded as messages from God (40:8; 41:16, 25, 28, 32, 37).

Inner healing is essential for someone to forgive from the heart, and it is equally necessary for someone to ask for forgiveness. Though healing may remove the poison, it does not take away the wound, for a scar remains. When we bear a grudge or have the desire to abuse someone else with our power, that is a sign that we are bearing hurts that have not been healed. When we forgive, the sting of the pain begins to fade. As the scar from our wounds begins to heal, it no longer breaks open as readily.

Fifth, as Joseph faced his grief, he mourned. The narrative tells us several times that Joseph wept (see 42:24; 43:30; 45:14; 46:29; 50:1). As an adult he had learned the need for and value of open and appropriate expression of emotions. In the early stages of meeting his brothers in Egypt, he tried to hide it, but by the end, he no longer tried to prevent his tears. His farewell to his father involved seventy days of mourning in Egypt and seven days in Canaan. Joseph felt pain and learned to express it freely in a healthy way. His emotions were in balance. He no longer feared his brothers even though they were afraid of him.

In a healing workshop I led for church leaders from the South Pacific region, a participant burst into tears and began to wail. The group was comprised of mostly male pastors, and they all quickly moved away from the woman while three females drew near her. I also moved towards her and said, "It is okay to keep crying, something important is happening, let your tears continue." After she calmed down, she talked about what had happened to release her tears and the cries of agony. She had been revisiting the painful moment when her brother was executed, which she witnessed through a stand of trees where she was sheltering. As the memory of that trauma re-surfaced, she began to grieve the loss once more.

A few hours later, the woman told me: "Something has happened since I wept today – a physical problem I have had since my brother's death has disappeared. The pain in my joints has gone, my immovable limb is now free." Expressing the pain of her grief and loss, which she had carried for some years, opened the possibility for healing in her body, mind and spirit. Whenever painful memories return, we need to grieve again, but each time we grieve, the pain diminishes. Telling our stories also lessens the sting of trauma.

In many places in the world, weeping openly is not regarded as "manly." Yet tears help us sincerely express our grief. Mourning steadies us and opens up a reflective space, where we do not have to pretend that "all is well." Mourning is a gift from God that enables us to express deep feelings of loss, which helps prevent further harm to ourselves and others. As John Bradshaw says in his book *Homecoming*, "You cannot heal what you cannot feel."[4]

Applying Joseph's Story to Our Own Lives

Pharaoh spoke highly of Joseph (Gen 41). His father, Jacob, gave him an amazing tribute (Gen 49), and he is included in Moses's great blessing in Deuteronomy 33. Joseph died at a good age of 110, and his importance and progeny is acknowledged in Numbers 1 and 36 as well as Psalms 80, 81 and 105.

Joseph suffered, survived, settled and served in Egypt for eighty years. Throughout that time, he spoke of his trust in God. He lived his life to the fullest and participated in life-giving work. His traumatic experiences neither defined nor inhibited him, for as he said, "God has made me fruitful in the land of my suffering" (41:52). He was like a healthy tree that flourishes in its surroundings and bears fruit in the right season (Ps 1:3) because he tended to the needs of his tree rather than neglecting them. Throughout his long life, Joseph kept his heart open to the presence and power of Almighty God.

As we look into our lives and own the signs of our trauma, we can reflect on Joseph's life and appreciate how his trauma shaped his character. We can also benefit from the way he responded to his traumatic experiences as well as the steps he took towards recovery, which were made possible through healing and forgiveness.

We may feel that trauma isolates us, but Joseph shared his story in prison and gained a new family and a community. *We can share our story of pain and struggle and gain friends and community.*

We may feel that trauma paralyses us, but Joseph made good decisions and acted upon them. *We can make good choices and act upon them.*

We may feel that trauma weakens us, but Joseph resolved to be strong and to hold onto the good. *We can choose to grow and serve others.*

We may feel that trauma will make us bitter, but Joseph kept his faith alive and honored God. *We can trust in God and stay tenderhearted.*

We may feel that trauma will cloud our minds, but Joseph continued to look ahead. *We can plan for the future in hope.*

We may feel that trauma is nurturing anger within us, but Joseph chose to be reunited with his brothers rather than to seek revenge. We can forgive and turn our anger into strength. We can act strongly but not severely.

---

4. John Bradshaw, *Homecoming* (Bantam Books, 1990), 80.

We may feel that trauma is filling us with negative feelings, but Joseph's tears washed away his bad feelings. We can express our feelings rather than suppressing them. We can recognize that our feelings help us realize that there is something which needs our attention.

We may feel that trauma will bring about intense dreams, but Joseph respected the insights and messages of hope that his dreams conveyed. *We can listen to our dreams for God's guidance, correction and encouragement.*

2

Praying the Psalms

From Trauma to Resilience

Samuel B. Thielman

Traumatic events affect people in a variety of ways, and some people, for unclear reasons, develop long-lasting psychological symptoms as a result of a traumatic event. However, the outcome is not always negative. Many people, whether or not they experience long-lasting psychological changes, also experience posttraumatic growth.[1] The ability to bounce back after a trauma has been the focus of widespread research and reflection in the last two decades, and researchers have identified certain factors that promote resilience. Such factors include the ability to find meaning in adversity, gratitude,[2] the ability

1. J. Tsai et al., "Longitudinal Course of Posttraumatic Growth among U.S. Military Veterans: Results from the National Health and Resilience in Veterans Study," *Depression and Anxiety* (2015).

2. Robert A. Emmons and Michael E. McCullough, "Counting Blessings Versus Burdens: An Experimental Investigation of Gratitude and Subjective Well-Being in Daily Life," *Journal of Personality and Social Psychology* 84, no. 2 (2003): 377–389.

to forgive,[3] a willingness to seek social support, and a capacity to follow one's own inner moral compass.[4]

These resilience factors, in particular, would seem to be things that are part of a faithful Christian life. Indeed, "religion," as understood in the literature of medicine and psychology, frequently promotes posttraumatic growth.[5] Prayer and "trust based beliefs" also seem to promote resilience and factors related to resilience.[6]

Studies of trained disaster workers suggest that they have lower rates of posttraumatic stress than others, in part because of their training.[7] One study of persecuted Chinese pastors found that they coped through preparing to suffer, letting go and surrendering, worshiping and reciting scripture, experiencing God's presence, identifying with Christ's suffering, and believing in a greater

---

3. E. L. Worthington, Jr. et al., "Forgiveness, Health, and Well-Being: A Review of Evidence for Emotional Versus Decisional Forgiveness, Dispositional Forgivingness, and Reduced Unforgiveness," *Journal of Behavioral Medicine* 30, no. 4 (2007): 291–302; Jeanette M. Walters and Jungmeen Kim-Spoon, "Are Religiousness and Forgiveness Protective Factors for Adolescents Experiencing Peer Victimization?," *Journal of Aggression, Maltreatment & Trauma* 23, no. 10 (2014):1090–1108; C. V. Witvliet et al., "Posttraumatic Mental and Physical Health Correlates of Forgiveness and Religious Coping in Military Veterans," *Journal of Traumatic Stress* 17, no. 3 (2004): 269–273.

4. S. Southwick et al., "Resilience: An Update," *PTSD Research Quarterly* 25, no. 4 (2015):1 ; Steven M. Southwick and Dennis S. Charney, *Resilience: The Science of Mastering Life's Greatest Challenges* (New York: Cambridge University Press, 2012).

5. A. Shaw, S. Joseph, and P. A. Linley, "Religion, Spirituality, and Posttraumatic Growth: A Systematic Review," *Mental Health, Religion, and Culture* 8, no. 1 (2005): 1–11; L. G. Calhoun et al., "A Correlational Test of the Relationship between Posttraumatic Growth, Religion, and Cognitive Processing," *Journal of Traumatic Stress* 13, no. 3 (2000): 521–527; Amy L. Ai et al., "Character Strengths and Deep Connections Following Hurricanes Katrina and Rita: Spiritual and Secular Pathways to Resistance among Volunteers," *Journal for the Scientific Study of Religion* 52, no. 3 (2013): 537–356; Amy L. Ai et al., "Hope, Meaning, and Growth Following the September 11, 2001, Terrorist Attacks," *Journal of Interpersonal Violence* 20, no. 5 (2005): 523–548.

6. Neal Krause and R. David Hayward, "Prayer Beliefs and Change in Life Satisfaction over Time," *Journal of Religion and Health* 52, no. 2 (2013): 674–694; Amy L. Ai, Paul Wink, and Marshall Shearer, "Fatigue of Survivors Following Cardiac Surgery: Positive Influences of Preoperative Prayer Coping: Prayer Coping and Vitality after Cardiac Surgery," *British Journal of Health Psychology* 17, no. 4 (2012): 724–742; P. Possel et al., "Do Trust-Based Beliefs Mediate the Associations of Frequency of Private Prayer with Mental Health? A Cross-Sectional Study," *Journal of Religion and Health* 53, no. 3 (2014): 904–916.

7. Ya-Jun Guo et al., "Posttraumatic Stress Disorder among Professional and Non-Professional Rescuers Involved in an Earthquake in Taiwan," *Psychiatry Research* 127, no. 1 (2004): 35–41; C. S. North et al., "Psychiatric Disorders in Rescue Workers after the Oklahoma City Bombing," *American Journal of Psychiatry* 159, no. 5 (2002): 857–859.

purpose – all elements of coping with suffering.[8] So there is good reason to believe that preparing spiritually can help people live through difficult times. Such preparation helps a survivor feel more in control of an otherwise chaotic situation, and this sense of control is a key component in the psychological notions of "hardiness" and "resilience," ideas that have applicability across many cultures. This paper proposes the Christian practice of using the book of Psalms devotionally to promote post-trauma resilience.

The idea of "trauma" is not really a concept addressed by the Bible itself, since the discussion of trauma, medically speaking, goes back only to the 1860s when John E. Erichsen (1818–1896), a surgeon and professor of surgery at University College, London, published his book *Railway and Other Injuries of the Nervous System* (1866) in which he described the manner in which railway accidents led to mental shock.[9] His book is considered to be the first medical discussion of phenomena we now think of as traumatic stress. Around the same time, others were writing on similar topics. In France, Jean Martin Charcot (1825–1893) wrote about "traumatic hysteria" (1877), and in Berlin, Herman Oppenheim (1858-1919) wrote about "traumatic neuroses" (1888).[10]

The nineteenth-century notion of "nervous shock" is picked up in the twentieth century by physicians and psychologists dealing with soldiers affected by the horrific fighting of the First World War.[11] Brave, experienced soldiers were stunned and refusing to return to the battlefield. Because they were not simply cowards, another explanation was called for, and the notion of "shell shock" emerged.[12] Psychotherapy cures were attempted, consistent with the early twentieth century notions of therapy, and continued to evolve through World War II. By the late twentieth century the trauma experienced by Vietnam veterans led American psychiatrists to add the diagnosis of posttraumatic stress

8. Rachel Sing-Kiat Ting and Terri Watson, "Is Suffering Good? An Explorative Study on the Religious Persecution among Chinese Pastors," *Journal of Psychology and Theology* 35 (2007): 202–210.

9. R. Harrington, "The Railway Accident: Trains, Trauma, and Technological Crises in Nineteenth-Century Britain," in *Traumatic Pasts: History, Psychiatry, and Trauma in the Modern Age, 1870–1930*, ed. M. Micale (Cambridge, UK: Cambridge University Press, 2001), 31–56.

10. Edward Shorter, *A Historical Dictionary of Psychiatry* (New York: Oxford University Press, 2005), 223–226.

11. P. Lerner and M. S. Micale, "Trauma, Psychiatry, and History: A Conceptual and Historigraphical Introduction," in *Traumatic Pasts: History, Psychiatry, and Trauma in the Modern Age, 1870–1930*, ed. M. Micale (Cambridge, UK: Cambridge University Press, 2001), 1–27; H. Merksey, "Shell Shock," in *150 Years of British Psychiatry, 1841–1991*, ed. G.E. Berrios and H. Freeman (London: Gaskell, 1991), 245–267; M. Stone, "Shellshock and the Psychologists," in *The Anatomy of Madness: Essays in the History of Psychiatry*, ed. W. F. Bynum, R. Porter, and M. Shepherd (Abingdon-on-Thames: Routledge, 1985), 242–271.

12. Merksey, "Shell Shock," 250.

disorder (PTSD) to their official diagnoses in 1980. Since then, PTSD and the psychology of trauma have become part of the medical and psychological knowledge base in many parts of the world.[13]

A separate issue, however, is how are these very recent concepts to be understood spiritually? I believe they do have relevance to the Christian life, and that, although they are not ancient, such concepts are not very far from Christian experience through the ages. Regardless of terminology, it is self-evident that people in the ancient world reacted with surprise and horror at unexpected disastrous events. The traumatic events of the ten plagues of Exodus and the Babylonian captivity are etched in the collective memory of the ancient Jews, something recognized by scholars from a variety of theological perspectives.[14] The poetry of the Jews, especially of the Psalms, appropriated so thoroughly and wonderfully by the church since its beginning, gives us a language for speaking to God about the difficulties of human experience at every level. An older generation saw Psalms as a work "present[ing] the anatomy of all parts of the human soul."[15]

The Psalms have been part of personal and group worship since the early centuries of the church.[16] Psalms are prayed in their entirety weekly or monthly by Christians who practice their faith in religious orders. The role of psalms in shaping prayer has been acknowledged by the church since early days. As early as the fourth century, St Athanasius (ca. 295–373) observed:

> In the Psalter . . . you learn about yourself. You find depicted in it all the movements of your soul, all its change, its ups and downs, its failures and recoveries. Moreover, whatever your particular need or trouble, from this same book you can select a form of words to fit it, so that you do not merely hear and then pass on, but learn the way to remedy your ill.[17]

13. Roberto Lewis-Fernández and Neil Krishan Aggarwal, "Culture and Psychiatric Diagnosis," *Advances in Psychosomatic Medicine* 33 (2013): 15–30.

14. Martin O'Kane, "Trauma and the Bible: The Artist's Response," *Interpretation: A Journal of Bible and Theology* 69, no. 1 (2015): 49–62; David Aberbach, "Trauma and Abstract Monotheism: Jewish Exile and Recovery in the Sixth Century B.C.E," *Judaism: A Quarterly Journal of Jewish Life and Thought* 50, no. 2 (2001): 211; Aiton Birnbaum, "Collective Trauma and Post-Traumatic Symptoms in the Biblical Narrative of Ancient Israel," *Mental Health, Religion & Culture* 11, no. 5 (2008): 533–546.

15. Rowland E. Prothero, *The Psalms in Human Life* (London: John Murray, 1907), 1.

16. Robert F. Taft, *The Liturgy of the Hours in East and West: The Origins of the Divine Office and Its Meaning for Today*, 2nd ed. (Collegeville, MN: Liturgical Press, 1993).

17. Quoted in B. D. Wayman, *Make the Words Your Own: An Early Christian Guide to the Psalms* (Brewster, MA: Paraclete Press, 2014), xv.

St Jerome, writing in the early centuries of the church, talked about the fact that even non-clerical people in his world recited the Psalms. He talks about the farmer of Palestine who, "while he handles of the plow, sings Alleluia; the tired reaper [who] employs himself in the Psalms; and the vine dresser [who] while lopping off the vines with his curved hook, sings something of David."[18]

Today many devout Christians are less familiar with the Psalms than Christians in earlier eras, though the pressures on modern Christians are as great as at any time in the past. To take full advantage of the Psalms as a resource, familiarity is essential. Christians believe that there is particular spiritual value in praying the psalms corporately as well as individually, so recitation of psalms in groups that meet for prayer and Bible study can foster some familiarity. The Anglican Book of Common Prayer includes a Psalter divided into portions that make it possible to read through the book of Psalms completely within one month. (Psalm 119, because of its length, is divided into portions so it can be read over three days.) Other plans could undoubtedly be substituted, the key notion being to familiarize oneself with the Psalms and thereby have them as part of our Christian thinking when trauma hits.

There's no need to convert the Psalms to therapy. They have a therapeutic dimension, but this is not their purpose. They are God's poetic gift to us that has a powerful therapeutic dimension when prayed in the light of Christian faith. Looking at a few of the psalms that may be helpful to Christians in times of traumatic stress, this chapter will focus on how praying from the book of Psalms before, during and after times of extreme stress might support resilience. It will provide an overview of how the Psalms point to a Christian way of coping by (1) giving voice to stress and distress, (2) channeling our thoughts toward God during times of distress, (3) showing us how to find meaning in adversity, (4) engendering hope and gratitude, and (5) developing the Christian character trait of endurance. What follows is an exploration of several psalms that can be helpful to Christians in times of distress.

---

18. J. M. Neale and Richard Frederick Littledale, *A Commentary on the Psalms: From Primitive and Mediaeval Writers; and from the Various Office-Books and Hymns of the Roman, Mozarabic, Ambrosian, Gallican, Greek, Coptic, Armenian, and Syriac Rites*, vol. 1., 4th ed. (New York: J. Pott, 1884), 5.

Voicing the Unutterable

Following a traumatizing event, people often experience the world as disordered, unhinged, and unreal.[19] The traumatized person benefits from having a routine, from emotional calm, and from interacting with others who understand their emotional reactions and can offer credible reassurance. A major curative aspect of psychotherapy is its ability to help patients construct a meaningful narrative and to give shape to seemingly indescribable events. From a psychological standpoint, praying the Psalms can help reconstruct and de-traumatize the painful experience of catastrophic events. This redone narrative points to ultimate victory over a seemingly irrational and difficult to face world, the mental world that many traumatized individuals experience. The Psalms, which show such deep understanding of emotional distress, can be part of a program of healing of the traumatic experience.

Among the Psalms that may be helpful in providing a way to voice the unutterable are Psalms 22, 38, 39, 69, and 88.[20] In Psalm 38, the psalmist tells God he is speechless in his distress:

> I am like a deaf man; I do not hear,
>   like a mute man who does not open his mouth.
> I have become like a man who does not hear
>   and in whose mouth are no rebukes. (vv. 13–14)

In Psalm 39, the psalmist is troubled, and like the traumatized person who has done things regretted in a catastrophic time, says:

> I was mute and silent;
>   I held my peace to no avail,
> and my distress grew worse.
>   My heart became hot within me.
> As I mused, the fire burned . . . (Ps 39:2–3a)

Then he prays to the Lord asking for the Lord's perspective on his situation:

---

19. A classic reference describing the change of worldview that can happen in the wake of a traumatic event is J. Herman, *Trauma and Recovery: The Aftermath of Violence – from Domestic Abuse to Political Terror* (New York: Basic Books, 1997), see especially ch. 3.

20. For understanding the Psalms from a scholarly and church history perspective, I have relied primarily on: Allen P. Ross, *A Commentary on the Psalms* (Grand Rapids, MI: Kregel Academic & Professional, 2011–2016); Derek Kidner, *Psalms 1–72: An Introduction and Commentary on Books I and II of the Psalms*, Tyndale Old Testament Commentaries (London: InterVarsity Press, 1973); *Psalms 73–150: A Commentary on Books III–V of the Psalms*, 1st ed., Tyndale Old Testament Commentaries (London: InterVarsity Press, 1975); Neale and Littledale, *Commentary on the Psalms*; Claus Westermann, *Praise and Lament in the Psalms* (Atlanta, GA: Westminster John Knox Press, 1981).

O LORD, make me know my end
and what is the measure of my days . . . (v. 4)

In Psalm 69 David again puts words to feelings that many traumatized people also express:

Reproaches have broken my heart,
so that I am in despair.
I looked for pity, but there was none,
and for comforters, but I found none. (Ps 69:20)

But then moves to a hopeful conclusion:

For the LORD hears the needy
and does not despise his own who are prisoners. (v. 33)

Psalm 88, the most downbeat of psalms, is the prayer of someone who has no strength (v. 4), who feels like he has died and is in the grave (v. 5), who feels he has been put there by God and abandoned:

O LORD, why do you cast my soul away?
Why do you hide your face from me? (v. 14)

But even this psalm, though it concludes on a low note, contains a glimmer of hope in its beginning where in faith he prays, "O LORD, God of my salvation" (v. 1).

When distressed and traumatized Christians are familiar with these psalms, they can find words for feelings that seem unutterable. This is clear when Christ prayed Psalm 22 when he was on the cross, setting an example for us when he was in distress. He himself used the psalms to voice his terrible feeling, crying out with the psalmist, "My God, my God, why have you forsaken me?" (Ps 22:1). Jesus suffered extreme physical and mental pain on the cross. Earlier in the Garden of Gethsemane, he had asked God to remove this cup from him (Matt 26:39; Mark 14:36; Luke 22:42), but it was not to be. As he was dying, he was drawing from the Psalms to voice his prayer of distress to God.

Psalm 22 continues:

Why are you so far from saving me, from the words of my groaning?
O my God, I cry by day, but you do not answer,
and by night, but I find no rest. (vv. 1b–2)

Yet later, as he neared his death, Jesus prayed a prayer of confidence in the Father as he prayed Psalm 31:5: "Into your hand I commit my spirit . . ." Significantly, this verse continues in a victorious vein: ". . . you have redeemed me, O LORD, faithful God" (v. 5b). Christ provided the example of praying psalms in distress. Through many centuries, Christians wanting to follow Jesus's example have used his last words for themselves as they were dying. Well-known Christians who have died saying this prayer include Basil the Great, Charlemagne, Thomas Becket, John Hus, and many others.[21] They are words that can be confidently appropriated by traumatized individuals when other words fail.

Presenting Unacceptable Feelings and Thoughts to God

The use of the Psalms in prayer also helps to validate feelings of discouragement, anger, disappointment, and abandonment because the psalm writers describe similar feelings. For someone who has been traumatized, the psalmists' honest words can reduce a sense of isolation and alienation. They remind believers of their Christian heritage, promote social contact when prayed corporately, and facilitate natural healing. The Psalms show us that our feelings and thoughts of depression can be presented to God, and that the writers of the Bible also had periods of spiritual lowness. When part of Christian prayer, Psalms facilitate connectedness to a spiritual dimension, opening up untapped spiritual resources.

Psalm 61 finds the Psalmist praying to God from a distance, like the person who has faced disaster or personal assault:

> Hear my cry, O God,
> listen to my prayer;
> from the end of the earth I call to you
> when my heart is faint. (vv. 1–2a)

Help seems far away and God's help is desperately needed:

> Lead me to the rock
> That is higher than I,
> For you have been my refuge,
> a strong tower against the enemy. (vv. 2a–3)

Then there is this anticipation of protection from God.

> Let me dwell in your tent forever!
> Let me take refuge under the shelter of your wings!

21. Prothero, 18, 71, 76, 116.

> For you, O God, have heard my vows;
> you have given me the heritage of those who fear your name.
> (vv. 4–5)

Those who trust in God, who have committed themselves to him, can know that God has heard – and they are beneficiaries of "the heritage of those who fear [God's] name." This passage also points us to the community of believers, those present with us and those now with God, who are a heritage that supports us in our distress.

Psalm 44 also talks about the heritage of stories describing God's past deliverance of his people:

> We have heard with our ears, O God;
> our ancestors have told us
> what you did in their days,
> in days long ago. (v. 1 NIV)

Indeed, the Hebrews of old, like Christians now, were shaped by the story of God's deliverance. Yet God did not deliver the Hebrews by empowering them, but by extending his own powerful hand in love:

> It was not by their sword that they won the land,
> nor did their arm bring them victory;
> it was your right hand, your arm
> and the light of your face, for you loved them. (v. 3 NIV)

And they were proud of God's favor:

> In God we make our boast all day long, and we will praise your name forever. (v. 8 NIV)

But then, God's favor seems to have passed: ". . . now you have rejected and humbled us" (v. 9 NIV). They had to retreat before their adversaries (v. 10), and worse, "you sold your people for a pittance" (v. 12 NIV) and "you have made us a byword among the nations" (v. 14 NIV). The writer's face is covered with shame at the taunts he is receiving (v. 15) and everything that has happened, even though the people "had not forgotten [God] or been false to [his] covenant" (v. 17 NIV).

Here is a righteous person who is being taunted and crushed, and he is disappointed. There is nothing of the victorious declaration such as the one in Psalm 91:7, that "a thousand may fall at your side, ten thousand at your right hand, but it will not come near you" (NIV). Clearly such a declaration does not hold for all circumstances, even for the righteous. This declaration means something important, but it can't mean we're invincible. The larger context of the Psalms won't allow us to think that, and the writer of Psalm 44 is experiencing a time of puzzlement in defeat:

> Yet for your sake we face death all day long;
> we are considered as sheep to be slaughtered.
> Awake, O Lord! Why do you sleep?
> Rouse yourself and do not reject us forever.
> Why do you hide your face?
> Why do you forget our misery and oppression? (vv. 22–24 NIV)

Many Christians facing the aftermath of trauma or extreme stress feel that they should be happy in the face of the adversity (and in fact there are many reasons for hope). But this psalm, like others, lets us know that feelings of discouragement and even abandonment by God can be part of the experience of believers. If we have been traumatized, or if we've had friends injured, beaten, killed – unfairly, randomly, brutally – we can ask with the psalmist, "Why do you hide your face? Why do you forget our affliction and oppression?"

Psalm 44 also shows us the pathway our thought should take when it concludes: "Rise up and help us; rescue us because of your unfailing love" (v. 26 NIV). Our grasp of what God intends for us to understand relies not only on our personal reading of the psalm, but also on understanding how to read the psalm through the lens of the gospel, reading it, "in Christ." This very psalm, which ends asking God to rise up, is picked up and used by Paul in an unexpected way in Romans chapter 8:

> If God is for us, who can be against us? He who did not spare his own son but gave him up for us all – how will he not also, along with him, graciously give us all things? . . . Who shall separate us from the love of Christ? Shall trouble or hardship or persecution or famine or nakedness or danger, or sword? (Rom 8:31b–32, 35 NIV)

Then, quoting Psalm 44, Paul says:

> As it is written,
> "For your sake we are being killed all the day long;
> we are regarded as sheep to be slaughtered." (Rom 8:36)

In Psalm 44, the psalmist continues differently, with a sort of protest to the Lord, saying, "Awake! Why are you sleeping, O Lord?" (v. 23). But Paul stops his Psalm 44 quotation here and continues in a very different voice of resilience and endurance:

> No, in all these things we are more than conquerors through him who loved us. For I am sure that neither death nor life, nor angels nor rulers, nor things present nor things to come, nor powers, nor height nor depth, nor anything else in all creation, will be able to separate us from the love of God in Christ Jesus our Lord. (Rom 8:37–39)

Paul takes Psalm 44:22, used to talk about martyrs for God's cause, and points out that whatever we face, we ultimately conquer through Christ. In times of trauma, even if we find ourselves in the mindset of the psalmist more than that of Paul, we can rest assured that when we are suffering in Christ, our suffering is known to God. It is not the meaningless suffering envisioned by those who have no reference point beyond themselves.

Reading and praying at the right time and in the right frame of mind, we can find solace in the Psalms, but the reading must be a faith oriented, believing reading, one that can take in what the Psalmist is asserting and even transform it in New Testament ways. Not only do the Psalms help us express things we cannot ourselves express, but they show us that our thoughts of despair can be presented to God just as they are.

One of the most troubling aspects of a traumatic event can be thoughts about something that a person did or didn't do during a crisis. Something is weighing the person down, something that's wrong, that's unspeakable – perhaps something done in the heat of the moment, or under pressure, and that is contrary to the person's view of their own identity. In the last several years, a number of researchers have talked about the impact of such thoughts as "moral injury."[22] Moral injury has been described as "damage or harm received to one's moral center as a result of things experienced, seen, and done in the war zone."[23] The research on moral injury often refers to military veterans, but moral injury can be suffered by anyone who has been in a catastrophic situation, such as in the Rwandan genocide or the South Sudan conflict.

---

22. Harold G. Koenig et al., "Rationale for Spiritually Oriented Cognitive Processing Therapy for Moral Injury in Active Duty Military and Veterans with Posttraumatic Stress Disorder," *The Journal of Nervous and Mental Disease* 205, no. 2 (2017): 147–153; Warren Kinghorn, "Combat Trauma and Moral Fragmentation: A Theological Account of Moral Injury," *Journal of the Society of Christian Ethics* 32, no. 2 (2012): 57–74.

23. Kent Drescher and D. Foy, "When They Come Home: Posttraumatic Stress, Moral Injury, and Spiritual Consequences for Veterans," *Reflective Practice: Formation and Supervision in Ministry* 28 (2008): 85–102, 91.

Christians sometimes suffer from guilt after a traumatic experience, and several psalms are very helpful for praying in such circumstances. Psalm 32, one of the seven penitential Psalms, gives voice to such feelings:[24]

> I kept it secret and my frame was wasted.
> I groaned all day long
> for your hand, by day and by night, lay heavy upon me.
> Indeed, my strength was dried up as by the summer heat.
> To you I have acknowledged my sin;
> my guilt I did not hide.
> I said "I will confess my transgressions to the Lord."
> And you have forgiven the guilt of my sin. (vv. 3–5 RGP)
>
> Many sorrows has the wicked,
> but loving mercy surrounds
> one who trusts the Lord. (v. 10 RGP)

The one who can pray this psalm can take comfort because here is a prayer that can be used by one experiencing moral injury.

Finding Meaning in Adversity

Finding meaning in adversity is a well-known resilience factor that promotes recovery from trauma. For Christians, praying and closely reading the Psalms offers a pathway for identifying meaning in adversity. And sometimes the Psalms can help with meaning transformation.

Adversity in the Psalms comes from many sources, not only from sin, but also from an enemy, from within us, or from uncertain sources. The traumatized person, however, is often in the position of trying to understand an event that just doesn't make sense. So many questions come: why did I survive? Why did this happen to me? What if I had done something different? Did I bring this on myself?

Psalm 77 is an example of a psalm that shows the transformation of discouragement over a horrific defeat into something better. The Psalm opens:

> In the day of my distress I seek the Lord.

24. For Psalms 32 and 77, I prefer poetic but accurate rendering in Benedictine Monks of Conception Abbey, *The Revised Grail Psalms: A Liturgical Psalter* (Chicago: GIA, 2010). RGP is a Roman Catholic translation, and verse numbers begin with the superscript and so are different than the verse numbering in the ESV.

In the night, my hands are raised unwearied;
my soul refuses comfort. (v. 3 RGP)

In the subsequent verses he talks about the fact that he can't sleep or speak, and he thinks about times past:

Will the Lord reject us forever?
Will he show us his favor no more?
Has his mercy vanished forever?
Has his promise come to an end? (vv. 8–9 RGP)

Then comes a very profound worry, one shared by many traumatized individuals:

I said, "This is what causes my grief:
that the right hand of the Most High has changed." (v. 11 RGP)

The writer of this Psalm poses the question as to whether or not his distress and unanswered prayers indicate that God is unwilling, or even unable, to help. Then, abruptly, the tone changes and gives a great strategy for the Christian dealing with traumatic memories:

I remember the deeds of the LORD,
I remember your wonders of old. (v. 12 RGP)

So what does he do? He meditates on all God's work (v. 13). He remembers God is holy (v. 14). He remembers God's power (v. 15). He remembers God's faithfulness to his ancestors (v. 15–16). And he thinks of God's power and control as demonstrated in nature (vv. 17–20).

He is thinking about what God has done and about God's power. Like Job, he is saying that in this life he is unable to understand God's ways. He cannot draw conclusions about God's disfavor from the circumstances he is experiencing. Then the Psalmist thinks about nature, about God's power in thunder, lightning, the whirlwind, the sea (vv. 19–20), and the fact that:

Your way was through the sea,
Your path through the mighty waters,
But the trace of your steps was not seen. (v. 20 RGP)

The psalmist has not identified a meaning in the traumatic circumstances themselves, rather, he has looked beyond his current situation to the larger context of the whole of creation history. He remembers that God is both holy and powerful; he is faithful, and he is in control. I see this as a way the Psalmist is finding meaning in his otherwise unanswerable and undecipherable set of circumstances. He is reassuring himself that God is actively working in his life, even if he cannot see God's activity in the immediate present.

Psalm 74 has a similar set of observations, opening with the question:

> O God, why do you cast us off forever?
> Why does your anger smoke against the sheep of your pasture? (v. 1)

The Psalmist asks in verses 10–11:

> How long, O God, is the foe to scoff?
> Is the enemy to revile your name forever?
> Why do you hold back your hand, your right hand?
> Take it from the fold of your garment and destroy them!

Once again, the Psalmist begins to reflect on God's prior faithfulness and draws reassurance from this. He ends the Psalm praying to God to "arise . . . defend your cause! Remember how the foolish scoff at you all the day" (v. 22).

Psalm 102 is particularly useful in this regard. In the superscript, the Psalm is described as "a prayer of an afflicted man when he is faint and pours out his lament to God."

> . . . for you have taken me up and thrown me down.
> My days are like an evening shadow;
> I wither away like grass. (vv. 10–11)

The Psalmist here feels overwhelmed, unsettled, and fragile. In fact, much of the Psalm consists of the words of someone whose experiences coincide with our present-day concept of depression:

> I lie awake;
> I am like a lonely sparrow on the housetop. (v. 7)

His spirit has withered, and he forgets to eat (v. 4). Here, God has given us a way to identify with the Psalmist when we ourselves feel overwhelmed by the physical manifestations of discouragement of the spirit that trauma can bring.

The Psalmist does not let things rest in this negative emotional place, but instead begins to think on who God is:

> But you, O LORD, are enthroned forever;
> you are remembered throughout all generations. (v. 12)

He expresses his conviction that God will indeed deliver:

> You will arise and have pity on Zion;

> It is the time to favor her;
> the appointed time has come. (v. 13)

And then he reflects on God, yesterday, today and forever:

> Of old you laid the foundation of the earth,
> and the heavens are the work of your hands.
> They will perish, but you will remain;
> they will all wear out like a garment.
> You will change them like a robe, and they will pass away,
> but you are the same, and your years have no end.
> The children of your servants shall dwell secure;
> their offspring shall be established before you. (vv. 25–28)

As in Psalm 77, the Psalmist gives us an example of a style of thinking that may help refocus our thoughts on something other than our immediate difficult situation. This passage is also quoted in Hebrews 1:10–12, referring to Christ who is creator of the earth and who can re-create us in our distress, a resilient prayer for Christians in distress.

So, as we survey the wreckage of a life as it exists after trauma, the Psalm shows us a way to find the possibility of hope extended to us in God, though we may not be able to feel happy and may be in distress. Our suffering has meaning when seen in the light of God's power and unchanging nature. We may or may not survive our present circumstances, but we can ask, and hope, for God to deliver us, and we can know that if we are trusting in him, we are part of his everlasting kingdom, "for the children of your servants shall dwell secure; their offspring shall be established before you" (v. 28).

The Psalms and Gratitude

The Psalms show a way to offer gratitude during times of distress. Psalms 42 and 43 are psalms expressing a longing for God during times of opposition and are psalms Christians can find reassuring during difficult periods. Most commentators believe that these two psalms can be seen as a single psalm in two parts, so I've read them that way.

Psalm 42 begins:

> As the deer pants for flowing streams,
> so pants my soul for you, O God. (v. 1)

This is the prayer of a devout believer, someone who yearns for the washing of God. And yet, like the traumatized person, he is not where he longs to be with God. "When shall I come and appear before God?" (v. 2). The person who has been through a traumatic event is often emotionally numb and unable to feel God's presence in a time of need. Augustine observed that Psalm 42 was sung for those coming into the church to arouse a longing for the "fountain of forgiveness for their sins."[25] It is the prayer of someone yearning for God.

The repeated refrain of the psalm is "Why are you cast down, O my soul, and why are you in turmoil within me?" (42:5; 42:11; 43:5). And yet, he points the way toward praise and gratitude. "Hope in God; for I shall again praise him" (42:5b). His soul is cast down, so he remembers God from the land of Jordan and of Hermon, from Mount Mizar (v. 6). God's song is in him (v. 8) and yet he says to God, his rock, "why have you forgotten me?" (v. 9). He is downcast, overcome with questions; he tells himself: "Hope in God; for I shall again praise him, my salvation and my God" (v. 11).

Again, as the prayer of the psalms continues into Psalm 43, he says in verse 2, "For you are the God in whom I take refuge," yet he follows this statement with a question: "Why have you rejected me? Why do I go about mourning because of the oppression of the enemy? (v. 2). These two contradictory thoughts weigh on his mind. This devout believer, this person panting for God, feels rejected by God, yet he knows he is still in God's universe. He is in God's world. He asks for God's guidance: "Send out your light and your truth; let them bring me to your holy hill and to your dwelling! Then I will go to the altar of God, to God my exceeding joy" (vv. 3–4a).

Psalms 42 and 43 record feelings of isolation and abandonment by God, yet they also point the way to thankfulness and praise. They are psalms that capture the mindset of many who have experienced traumatic stress and demonstrate a way to continue to hope in God.

Regular use of the Psalms puts a person in touch with many psalms of gratitude and praise which make no reference to difficult times, but proclaim the glory and power of God, especially psalms such as 19 ("The heavens declare the glory of God"), and Psalms 144–150. Psalm 145 has particular relevance for the concept of resilience, for in the middle of the psalm, the psalmist declares to God:

> Your kingdom is an everlasting kingdom,
> and your dominion endures throughout all generations.
> [The LORD is faithful in all his words
> and kind in all his works.]

25. Augustine, *Expositions on the Book of Psalms, vol. 2, Psalms 37–52* (Oxford: John Henry Parker, 1847), 239.

The LORD upholds all who are falling
and raises up all who are bowed down. (Ps 145:13–14)

Despite the injustices of the present world and the totalitarian forces that attempt to squeeze us into their mold, it is God's kingdom that is the everlasting kingdom, and he is helping us when we are struggling to deal with oppressive events.

The Psalms and Endurance

Praying the Psalms can, I believe, enhance our resilience, and resilience can help us with a much more deeply rooted biblical notion, that of endurance. Endurance means persisting despite adversity. It is "holding out," standing fast, and enduring evil. It involves "courageous active resistance" to persecution.[26] In classical Christian literature, endurance is part of the cardinal virtue of "fortitude."[27] So when we are subjected to a traumatic event, one that tests our faith, endurance comes into play. When we find ourselves asking with the psalmist in Psalm 13, "How long, O Lord," endurance is the character trait we need in order to, by God's grace, carry on.

The Greek word for endurance is *hypomonḗ*, and it is a word that crops up in important places in the New Testament. In Luke's account of the parable of the sower, Jesus says that the seeds that fell in the good soil are "the ones who, when they hear the word, hold it fast in an honest and good heart, and bear fruit with patient endurance (*hypomonḗ*)" (Luke 8:15 NRSV). In the first chapter of the book of Revelation, John the apostle speaks of himself as "your brother who share[s] with you in Jesus the persecution and the kingdom and the patient endurance (*hypomonḗ*)" (Rev 1:9 NRSV). And Paul, writing in the letter to the Romans says, ". . . We rejoice in our sufferings, knowing that suffering produces endurance (*hypomonḗ*) and endurance produces character, and character produces hope, and hope does not put us to shame, because God's love has been poured into our hearts through the Holy Spirit who has been given to us" (Rom 5:3–5).

So endurance, *hypomonḗ*, is very important for Christians undergoing suffering and experiencing trauma. Praying the Psalms and using them

---

26. Gerhard Kittel, *Theological Dictionary of the New Testament*, trans. G. W. Bromiley (Grand Rapids, MI: Eerdmans, 1967) v. 4, 581.

27. Josef Pieper, *The Four Cardinal Virtues: Prudence, Justice, Fortitude, Temperance*, 1st ed. (New York: Harcourt, 1965), 117–141.

devotionally sustains us in our endurance. As Paul indicates in Romans, endurance and hope are tightly linked.

In fact, there are many ways in which praying the Psalms instills hope. Psalms encourage openly in many ways. Most interestingly, they talk about hiding in God: hiding under his wings, in his shadow, and in him as our rock. Psalm 17:6–9 contains the image of hiding under God's wings. The psalmist tells God that he will call on God, and God will answer him. He asks God to hide him in the shadow of God's wings. In Psalm 36, the psalmist says, "how precious is your steadfast love, O God! The children of mankind take refuge in the shadow of your wings" (v. 7).

Psalm 57, which like Psalm 142, is attributed to David during the time he was hiding from Saul in the cave says,

> Be merciful to me O God, be merciful to me,
> for in you my soul takes refuge;
> in the shadow of your wings I will take refuge,
> till the storms of destruction pass by. (v. 1)

This prayer is followed by a declaration that points the way for us during traumatic times. "I cry out to God most high, to God who fulfills his purpose for me (v. 2). This psalm takes on particular significance when seen as a follow-on to Psalm 142 where David says: ". . . There is none who takes notice of me; no refuge remains to me; no one cares for my soul" (Ps 142:4). This notion that we can hide in God in times of distress helps us build our Christian endurance.

Psalm 91 offers another image of God's protection where the psalmist declares, "He who dwells in the shelter of the Most High will abide in the shadow of the Almighty" (v. 1). He goes on to make some assertions that can be confusing to those suffering from traumatic stress, for it tells us, "A thousand may fall at your side . . . but it will not come near you" (v. 7), and similar protections are declared in verses 10, 12, and 13. And truly, God does protect us, sometimes in remarkable ways. These verses can be misapplied, however, as they were by Satan when he tempted Jesus in the desert (Matt 4:6 and Luke 4:11). Jesus's reply shows us how to understand these verses, for God is faithful and will preserve us in him, but there is no guarantee against suffering. Quite the opposite is true (Heb 13:12–13), but he will shelter us in his wings despite difficult circumstances. "For he will hide me in his shelter in the day of trouble; he will conceal me under the cover of his tent; he will lift me high upon a rock" (Ps 27:5).

For the Christian suffering trauma, God will be our shelter, though we may not always feel his presence or understand his way in the near term. As the

American preacher Sam Shoemaker once wrote, "He did not promise that we would not have trouble; instead, he promised triumph over trouble – which is something far more glorious."[28] The Psalms, with their nuanced account of the soul in distress and their many expressions of the meaningfulness of life in God, of gratitude, and of transforming reflection on God's goodness in the past, provide a vocabulary that can help us come back after a traumatic assault and help us endure in our faith in God.

Application and Summary

1. The Psalms are the prayer book of the Bible, and there is ample precedent in the New Testament and the life of the church to indicate that, in Christ, we can make these prayers our own.

2. If we make these inspired prayers our own prayers, we can find words to describe our feelings and frustrations if we become psychologically overwhelmed by trauma. Psalms 22, 38, 39, 69, and 88 all contain prayers that a traumatized Christian may find helpful.

3. The Bible, in its use of the Psalms, shows us how to use these prayers to find meaning in adversity. An example is the way Paul used Psalm 44 in Romans 8 to point out that God's love follows us everywhere.

4. Psalms 42 and 43 give us examples of gratitude during a time of hardship.

5. Praying the Psalms helps us increase our resilience and enhance our endurance as Christians, pointing out ways to take shelter in God, and to persist in our work for the everlasting kingdom described in Psalm 145:13.

Bibliography

Aberbach, David. "Trauma and Abstract Monotheism: Jewish Exile and Recovery in the Sixth Century B.C.E." *Judaism: A Quarterly Journal of Jewish Life and Thought* 50, no. 2 (2001): 211.

Ai, Amy L., T. Cascio, and L. K. Santangelo. "Hope, Meaning, and Growth Following the September 11, 2001, Terrorist Attacks." *Journal of Interpersonal Violence* 20, no. 5 (2005): 523–548.

28. Samuel M. Shoemaker, *Under New Management* (Grand Rapids, MI: Zondervan, 1966), 34.

Ai, Amy L., R. Richardson, C. Plummer, C. G. Ellison, C. Lemieux, T. N. Tice, and B. Huang. "Character Strengths and Deep Connections Following Hurricanes Katrina and Rita: Spiritual and Secular Pathways to Resistance among Volunteers," *Journal for the Scientific Study of Religion* 52, no. 3 (2013): 537–356.

Ai, Amy L., Paul Wink, and Marshall Shearer. "Fatigue of Survivors Following Cardiac Surgery: Positive Influences of Preoperative Prayer Coping: Prayer Coping and Vitality after Cardiac Surgery." *British Journal of Health Psychology* 17, no. 4 (2012): 724–742.

Birnbaum, Aiton. "Collective Trauma and Post-Traumatic Symptoms in the Biblical Narrative of Ancient Israel." *Mental Health, Religion & Culture* 11, no. 5 (2008): 533–546.

Calhoun, L. G., A. Cann, R. G. Tedeschi, and J. McMillan. "A Correlational Test of the Relationship between Posttraumatic Growth, Religion, and Cognitive Processing." *Journal of Trauma Stress* 13, no. 3 (2000): 521–527.

Drescher, Kent, and D. Foy. "When They Come Home: Posttraumatic Stress, Moral Injury, and Spiritual Consequences for Veterans." *Reflective Practice: Formation and Supervision in Ministry* 28 (2008): 85–102.

Emmons, Robert A., and Michael E. McCullough. "Counting Blessings Versus Burdens: An Experimental Investigation of Gratitude and Subjective Well-Being in Daily Life." *Journal of Personality and Social Psychology* 84, no. 2 (2003): 377–389.

Guo, Ya-Jun, C. H. Chen, M. L. Lu, H. K. Tan, H. W. Lee, and T. N. Wang. "Posttraumatic Stress Disorder among Professional and Non-Professional Rescuers Involved in an Earthquake in Taiwan." *Psychiatry Research* 127, no. 1 (2004): 35–41.

Harrington, R. "The Railway Accident: Trains, Trauma, and Technological Crises in Nineteenth-Century Britain." In *Traumatic Pasts: History, Psychiatry, and Trauma in the Modern Age, 1870–1930*, ed. M. Micale, 31–56. Cambridge, UK: Cambridge University Press, 2001.

Herman, J. *Trauma and Recovery: The Aftermath of Violence – from Domestic Abuse to Political Terror.* New York: Basic Books, 1997.

Kidner, Derek. *Psalms 1–72: An Introduction and Commentary on Books I and II of the Psalms*. Tyndale Old Testament Commentaries. London: InterVarsity Press, 1973.

———. *Psalms 73–150: A Commentary on Books III–V of the Psalms*, 1st ed. Tyndale Old Testament Commentaries. London: InterVarsity Press, 1975.

Kinghorn, Warren. "Combat Trauma and Moral Fragmentation: A Theological Account of Moral Injury." *Journal of the Society of Christian Ethics* 32, no. 2 (2012): 57–74.

Kittel, Gerhard. *Theological Dictionary of the New Testament*, trans. G. W. Bromiley. Grand Rapids, MI: Eerdmans, 1967.

Koenig, Harold G., N. A. Boucher, R. J. Oliver, N. Youssef, S. R. Mooney, J. M. Currier, and M. Pearce. "Rationale for Spiritually Oriented Cognitive Processing Therapy for Moral Injury in Active Duty Military and Veterans with Posttraumatic Stress Disorder." *The Journal of Nervous and Mental Disease* 205, no. 2 (2017): 147–153.

Krause, Neal, and R. David Hayward. "Prayer Beliefs and Change in Life Satisfaction over Time." *Journal of Religion and Health* 52, no. 2 (2013): 674–694.

Lerner, P., and M. S. Micale. "Trauma, Psychiatry, and History: A Conceptual and Historigraphical Introduction." In *Traumatic Pasts: History, Psychiatry, and Trauma in the Modern Age, 1870–1930*, edited by M. Micale, 1–27. Cambridge, UK: Cambridge University Press, 2001.

Lewis-Fernández, Roberto, and Neil Krishan Aggarwal. "Culture and Psychiatric Diagnosis." *Advances in Psychosomatic Medicine* 33 (2013): 15–30.

Merksey, H. "Shell Shock." In *150 Years of British Psychiatry, 1841–1991*, edited by G. E. Berrios and H. Freeman, 245–267. London: Gaskell, 1991.

Neale, J. M., and Richard Frederick Littledale. *A Commentary on the Psalms: From Primitive and Mediaeval Writers; and from the Various Office-Books and Hymns of the Roman, Mozarabic, Ambrosian, Gallican, Greek, Coptic, Armenian, and Syriac Rites*, vol. 1. 4th ed. New York: J. Pott, 1884.

North, C. S., L. Tivis, J. C. McMillen, B. Pfefferbaum, E. L. Spitznagel, J. Cox, S. Nixon, K. P. Bunch, and E. M. Smith. "Psychiatric Disorders in Rescue Workers after the Oklahoma City Bombing." *American Journal of Psychiatry* 159, no. 5 (2002): 857–859.

O'Kane, Martin. "Trauma and the Bible: The Artist's Response." *Interpretation: A Journal of Bible and Theology* 69, no. 1 (2015): 49–62.

Pieper, Josef. *The Four Cardinal Virtues: Prudence, Justice, Fortitude, Temperance*, 1st ed. New York: Harcourt, 1965.

Pössel, P., B. S. Winkeljohn, A. C. Bjerg, B. D. Jeppsen, and D. T. Wooldridge. "Do Trust-Based Beliefs Mediate the Associations of Frequency of Private Prayer with Mental Health? A Cross-Sectional Study." *Journal of Religious Health* 53, no. 3 (2014): 904–916.

Prothero, Rowland E. *The Psalms in Human Life.* London: John Murray, 1907.

Ross, Allen P. *A Commentary on the Psalms.* Grand Rapids, MI: Kregel Academic & Professional, 2011–2016.

Shaw, A., S. Joseph, and P. A. Linley. "Religion, Spirituality, and Posttraumatic Growth: A Systematic Review." *Mental Health, Religion, and Culture* 8, no. 1 (2005): 1–11.

Shoemaker, Samuel M. *Under New Management.* Grand Rapids, MI: Zondervan, 1966.

Shorter, Edward. *A Historical Dictionary of Psychiatry.* New York: Oxford University Press, 2005.

Southwick, Steven. "Resilience: An Update." *PTSD Research Quarterly* 25, no. 4 (2015): 1.

Southwick, Steven, and Dennis S. Charney. *Resilience: The Science of Mastering Life's Greatest Challenges.* New York: Cambridge University Press, 2012.

Stone, M. "Shellshock and the Psychologists." In *The Anatomy of Madness: Essays in the History of Psychiatry*, edited by W. F. Bynum, R. Porter, and M. Shepherd, 242–271. Abingdon-on-Thames: Routledge, 1985.

Taft, Robert F. *The Liturgy of the Hours in East and West: The Origins of the Divine Office and Its Meaning for Today*, 2nd ed. Collegeville, MN: Liturgical Press, 1993.

Ting, Rachel Sing-Kiat, and Terri Watson. "Is Suffering Good? An Explorative Study on the Religious Persecution among Chinese Pastors." *Journal of Psychology and Theology* 35 (2007): 202–210.

Tsai, J., L. M. Sippel, N. Mota, S. M. Southwick, and R. H. Pietrzak. "Longitudinal Course of Posttraumatic Growth among U.S. Military Veterans: Results from the National Health and Resilience in Veterans Study." *Depression and Anxiety* 33, no. 1 (January 2016): 9–18.

Walters, Jeanette M., and Jungmeen Kim-Spoon. "Are Religiousness and Forgiveness Protective Factors for Adolescents Experiencing Peer Victimization?" *Journal of Aggression, Maltreatment & Trauma* 23, no. 10 (2014):1090–1108.

Wayman, Benjamin D. *Make the Words Your Own: An Early Christian Guide to the Psalms.* Brewster, MA: Paraclete Press, 2014.

Witvliet, C. V., K. A. Phipps, M. E. Feldman, and J. C. Beckham. "Posttraumatic Mental and Physical Health Correlates of Forgiveness and Religious Coping in Military Veterans." *Journal of Traumatic Stress* 17, no. 3 (2004): 269–273.

Worthington, E. L. Jr., C. V. Witvliet, P. Pietrini, and A. J. Miller. "Forgiveness, Health, and Well-Being: A Review of Evidence for Emotional Versus Decisional Forgiveness, Dispositional Forgivingness, and Reduced Unforgiveness," *Journal of Behavioral Medicine* 30, no. 4 (2007): 291–302.

3

Facing Trauma in Proverbs 24:13–22

Cultivating Virtue Ethics amidst Evil and Wickedness

Shirley S. Ho

Proverbs is a book on the art and science of living well as human beings, not only for those in ancient times but also in our modern and complex age. It espouses practical and constructive wisdom for dealing with everyday human situations. Yet evil, wickedness and calamity are realities for every human being, and they cause trauma in various forms, either through humans or through natural disasters. Most discourses about facing trauma are engaged through the disciplines of sociology, psychology, counseling and ethics. While such approaches are insightful and helpful, a biblical and theological approach is necessary in order to ground this profoundly important theme.

This essay explores how the wisdom tradition of Proverbs can help us face the pressing challenge of human-made trauma against the righteous people of God. The cluster of aphorisms in Proverbs 24:13–22 offers eschatological[1] hope to victims of evil and wicked perpetrators by establishing a dialectical synergy between God's eschatological work of retributive justice and human beings' cultivation of the virtue ethics of resilience, tranquility and reverence

1. "Eschatology" is a biblical and theological concept that concerns the imminent and distant future fate of human life and the world.

for God and human authorities. Responding to evil and wickedness with virtue ethics makes eschatological hope for the traumatized possible.

The essay begins with a justification for the selection of this series of proverbial sayings as a literary cluster. This is followed by an exploration of the sage's proposal of virtue ethics as a wise response when facing evil and wickedness. Then I discuss three specific virtues that are advocated in these proverbial sayings: (1) resilience and tenacity, (2) tranquility, (3) reverence for the Lord and king. Finally, I outline the teleological purpose for cultivating virtue ethics amidst evil and wickedness.

Proverbs 24:13–22 as a Literary Cluster

> My child, eat honey, for it is good,
> and the drippings of the honeycomb are sweet to your taste.
> Know that wisdom is such to your soul;
> if you find it, you will find a future,
> and your hope will not be cut off.
> Do not lie in wait like an outlaw against the home of the righteous;
> do no violence to the place where the righteous live;
> for though they fall seven times, they will rise again;
> but the wicked are overthrown by calamity.
> Do not rejoice when your enemies fall,
> and do not let your heart be glad when they stumble,
> or else the LORD will see it and be displeased,
> and turn away his anger from them.
> Do not fret because of evildoers.
> Do not envy the wicked;
> for the evil have no future;
> the lamp of the wicked will go out.
> My child, fear the LORD and the king,
> and do not disobey either of them;
> for disaster comes from them suddenly,
> and who knows the ruin that both can bring? (NRSV)

One of the challenging tasks in an exegesis of the book of Proverbs is interpreting its terse two-line aphorisms. Insofar as they are aphorisms,[2] there are two difficulties. First, each aphorism is succinct and atomistic, making

2. An aphorism may be defined as a short and concise statement of wise instruction, expression or adage.

clarity elusive. Second, each aphorism stands alone, and therefore lacks discernible literary context for interpretation. However, the latest trend in Proverbs research recognizes that even though each aphorism may come out of different socio-historical contexts, its placement in the book of the Proverbs, at compositional level, provides the literary context. This literary context helps resolve the problem of clarity.

Norman Whybray and Knut Martin Heim have done an in-depth study on the compositional approach to Proverbs.[3] Heim recognizes that the individual proverb originated from its own oral context and speaks of a "proverb performance" between a speaker and hearer.[4] As such, a proverb's use and function orally is different from reading a collection. Heim maintains that a reader turns to a proverb collection to find general guidelines in matters of faith and practice. He argues that "For such a strategy, proverb collection readers rely on two fundamental assumptions comparable to those made by proverb hearers: (i) that the compilers of proverb collections had a communicative intention and (ii) that the sequences of collection are therefore contextually related."[5] This essay builds on Heim's analysis to discern general guidelines within the book of Proverbs about how to face trauma caused by evil and wicked people.

Apart from Heim's argument for the communicative intent regarding the arrangement of the proverbs in a collection, he also underscores the criteria of delimitation. He speaks of "linking devices" rather than "boundary markers" as literary keys in delimiting proverbial clusters. He argues that repetition is a linguistic feature that links and combines aphorisms. He also argues that

---

3. R. N. Whybray, *The Composition of the Book of Proverbs*, JSOT Supp 168 (Sheffield: Sheffield Academic Press, 1994); Daniel C. Snell, *Twice-Told Proverbs and the Composition of the Book of Proverbs* (Winona Lake: Eisenbrauns, 1993).

4. Heim agrees with M. Harnish on the goals of oral proverb performance: "(1) intends to allude to a common truth and (2) intends to offer that common truth as a reason for that situation (explanation), or for the hearer's action (guiding action), the reason to hold a certain attitude (inducing an attitude). (3) The speaker intends the hearer to apply the recovered common truth to the situation at hand, and determine either: what the purported explanation of the situation is, or what action in the situation is being counseled and why, or what attitude towards the situation the hearer is intended to adopt, and why." Knut Martin Heim, *Like Grapes of God Set in Silver*, BZAW 273 (Berlin: Walter de Gruyter, 2001), 69. Quoted from R. M. Harnish, "Communicating with Proverbs," *Communication & Cognition* 25 (1993): 265–290, especially 273.

5. Heim, *Like Grapes of God*, 75.

sound and sense (consonants, word roots, words, synonyms) are material for deciphering compositional strategy.[6]

Employing Heim's clustering principle in Proverbs 24:13–22, the linguistic linking features are noticeable: "cut off" (kārát) in verse 14 and "snuff out" (dā'ak) in verse 20 are synonymous; "stumble" (kāšál) in verses 16–17 and "fall" (nāṕál) in verses 16–17 are repetitious; "future" ('aḥărît) and "hope" (tikwâ) in verses 14 and 20 can be read as both synonymous and repetitious; "arise" (qûm) in verses 16 and 22 is repetitious. This literary linking points to the purposeful arrangement of these aphorisms as a cluster, and so they can be understood as contextually related.

Lastly, the use of "my son" in verses 13 and 21, which mark the beginning and ending of this cluster, functions as "literary framing." The two interrogative questions in verse 12 function as a strategic rhetorical ending to the previous section. Additionally, the subtitle at the beginning of verse 23, "These also are the sayings of the wise," separates verse 22 from verse 23 and the following verses. Hence, Proverbs 24:13–22 is a distinct literary unit.[7]

Virtue Ethics in Proverbs 24:13–22

Within this proverbial cluster, we can observe three general linguistic and conceptual ideas.

First, the cluster is comprised of a string of admonition clauses and corresponding motivation clauses, which are expressed through "because/for" (*ki*) in verses 16, 20, 22 and "lest" (*pen*) in verse 18. This use of admonition and corresponding motivation clauses is characteristically proverbial, but it is important to observe that the motivations have didactic and logical goals. As one commentator observes, "It helps the listener to discover the truth and worth of instruction."[8] These motivations are organic to these aphorisms, for wisdom involves moral reasoning to guide one's attitude and behavior. Wisdom is not pontifical nor simply a sundry list of one instructions without rationale. Wisdom, unlike legal laws (such as most of the Mosaic Law), requires good reasoning.

6. Heim, 107. Bruce Waltke names this cluster as "Prohibitions against involvement with the wicked" in Bruce Waltke, *The Book of Proverbs 15–31*, NICOT (Grand Rapids: Eerdmans, 2005), 278. Koptak labels the cluster as "Trust, Hope, Not Violence or Gloating" in Paul Koptak, *Proverbs*, NIVAC (Grand Rapids: Zondervan), 562.

7. Knut Martin Heim, *Poetic Imagination in Proverbs: Variant Repetitions and the Nature of Poetry*, Bulletin for Biblical Research Supplement 4 (Winona Lake, IN: Eisenbrauns, 2013), 351.

8. Philip Johannes Nel, *The Structure and Ethos of the Wisdom Admonitions in Proverbs*, BZAW 158 (Berlin/New York: Walter de Gruyter, 1982), 85.

Second, this cluster uses seven negative constructions: "do not lie in wait" (v. 15), "do no violence" (v. 15), "do not rejoice" (v. 17), "do not let your heart be glad" (v. 17), "do not fret" (v. 19), "do not envy" (v. 19) and "do not disobey" (v. 21). The negative syntactical construction is purposeful and rhetorically more powerful than positive expression. This literary device presupposes that the opposite practice is true. Thus, the seven negative advices are dialogical responses or reactions to a particular existential custom.

Third, the aphorisms are not instructions regarding physical actions, such as: "do not kill," "do not steal," "do not slap," or "do not injure." Linguistically, the verbs employed are stative verbs[9] that refer to the condition, state of being and emotions of a person. Thus the human heart is the primary target of this proverbial cluster. The focus on the human heart is theologically significant, for it is an explication of Proverbs 4:23: "Above all else, guard your heart, for everything you do flows from it." For the sage, the human heart is the source of all human behavior.

In *The Nicomachean Ethics,* Aristotle introduces virtue ethics. Although operating from a different philosophical and ethical framework, his work is helpful in understanding the book of Proverbs. He introduces two kinds of virtues: intellectual and moral. He unpacks the various elements involved in the complex discipline of virtue ethics, which include: right action, habit, right principle, emotion and feeling, disposition, motive, choice, avoidance, means, excess and deficiency, pleasure and pain.[10] In his discussion, he defines virtue as "the quality of acting in the best way in relation to pleasures and pains, and that vice is the opposite."[11] His discussion of emotions and feelings as factors in virtue ethics resonates well with the focus of Proverbs 24:13–22, which is the state of human heart. The proverbial cluster highlights the weightiness of human emotions in the midst of pain and trauma, which will result in further pain and regrets if left unchecked. Conversely, when positive emotions are cultivated, virtuous character will be applauded, and a life of hope will be bestowed.

But it is easier to discipline human actions than human emotions. Theoretically, we could tie our hands so that we can't slap someone in the face, or lock someone up to prevent a murder, or put duct tape over someone's mouth to restrain lies. But negative emotions are hard to curtail, and physical

9. Stative verbs refer to a state of being (mental, emotional or physical condition) as opposed to dynamic verbs of action.

10. Aristotle, *The Nicomachean Ethics*, trans. Harris Rackham (Wordsworth, 1996).

11. Aristotle, 36.

and external mechanisms tend to be ineffective in nurturing positive virtues. Accordingly, N. T. Wright says that "moral muscles" need to be exercised when developing character. He observes that "Character is a slowly forming thing. You can no more force character on someone than you can force a tree to produce fruit when it isn't ready to do so. The person has to choose, again and again, to develop the moral muscles and skills which will shape and form the fully flourishing character."[12] Aristotle uses the language of "ethos" and "habit" to describe internal character. In the language of Christian doctrine and New Testament discourse, virtue ethics are the work of the Holy Spirit in Christians rather than human fleshly instinct. Galatians 5:22–23 identifies these virtues as "the fruit of the Spirit [which] is love, joy, peace, patience, kindness, generosity, faithfulness, gentleness, and self-control." To be sure, some find developing virtues easier than others. But "those who belong to Christ Jesus have crucified the flesh with its passions and desires" (Gal 5:24). Thus these virtues are a Christians' second nature or new nature in Christ.

Virtues to Cultivate when Facing Evil and Wickedness

The wisdom tradition, particularly the book of Proverbs, divides human beings into two categories. Instead of using ethnic categories, such as Israel and the foreign nations (which are characteristically found in the Pentateuch, Deuteronomistic History and Prophets), Proverbs describes human beings in bipolar moral categories: the righteous and the wicked. While this taxonomy may be considered reductive, these categories are designed to depict the cosmic and social moral order of Proverbs: the ideal and worst human beings.

The Virtue of Resilience and Tenacity: Proverbs 24:15–16

Proverbs 24:15–16 introduces these two moral personalities: the righteous and wicked. Its placement near the beginning of the cluster sets the context and scene for both the evil intent and the evil action of the wicked. It prefaces the cluster with the evil person's preoccupation to attack the righteous.

> Do not lie in wait like an outlaw against the home of the righteous;
> do no violence to the place where the righteous live;

12. N. T. Wright, *After You Believe: Why Christian Character Matters* (New York: HarperCollins, 2010), 35.

for though they fall seven times, they will rise again;
but the wicked are overthrown by calamity. (Prov 24:15–16 NRSV)

Verse 15 depicts an image of the wicked's attempt to break and enter the house of the righteous. The attacker is rendered as a lurker (one who is lying "in wait"), whose aggression is undoubtedly premeditated. The second line of verse 15 describes the actual behavior, concretizing the warning against the wicked not to destroy the dwelling place of the righteous. The overall image describes a house burglar. Against the backdrop of the great violence around the world, a house burglar may seem to be the least evil that could happen, but nevertheless it would cause trauma to the victim.[13] The sage of Proverbs is not naïve, but presupposes a human world full of evil and dangers, particularly for the innocent righteous.[14] The image of house burglar is *pars pro toto,* for it represents any evil man who is determined to harm the well-being of another person.

In the theology of Proverbs, wisdom is interested in creating and maintaining the creation order: cosmic, moral and social. However, wicked people's behavior against the innocent has disturbed the moral and social order in human relationship. Hence, wisdom is the art and science of living in order to reorder the disturbance: to triumph over evil and wickedness.

This proverb addresses the culprit, ordering him not to strike the righteous because his evil intention to crush the righteous will never succeed. Note that the righteous may be temporarily struck down but will rise again. Indeed, although the righteous may fall down seven times, they will rise again seven times. The word "seven" cannot be ignored, for it refers to the Hebraic notion of fullness and constancy. In the creation account of Genesis 1, the heavens and the earth were completely created in seven days. In Matthew 18:22, Jesus teaches about the forgiveness granted to the sinner – not only seven times but seventy-seven times. Seven is a numerological figure that describes the ingrained character of the righteous as resilient and tenacious. Despite many attempts to bring down the righteous, either physically, emotionally, mentally or verbally, the resilience of the innocent guarantees that evil intention and action will not triumph. On the contrary, the wicked will be overcome by calamity – conceivably by one single strike! The righteous are resilient but the

13. W. R. Monfalcone, "Trauma," in *Dictionary of Pastoral Care and Counseling*, ed. Rodney Hunter (Nashville: Abingdon, 1990), 1287.

14. The book of Proverbs presupposed the presence of slanderers, prostitutes, deceivers, violent men, the arrogant, the slothful, hypocrites, the hot-tempered, the dishonest, liars, bandits, etc. in the social and moral order of the book.

wicked are weak. Thus resilience distinguishes the righteous from the wicked. Resilience is a marker of the people of God. The reason for this resilience is unpacked in the following verses.[15]

The Virtue of Tranquility: Proverbs 24:17–20

The second virtue worthy of cultivation is tranquility. Tranquility is easily misunderstood as a disposition of passivity, apathy and resignation. However, Proverbs 24:17–20 demonstrates that tranquility stems from inner strength and true knowledge about reality. There are two aphorisms within these four verses, each with its own motive clause. Following is the first aphorism:

> Do not rejoice when your enemies fall,
>   and do not let your heart be glad when they stumble,
> or else the LORD will see it and be displeased,
>   and turn away his anger from them. (Prov 24:17–18 NRSV)

Proverbs employs the label "enemies" as an appellation to refer to the wicked and unrighteous. These enemies may be ethnically Jewish or non-Jewish. "Enemies" in Proverbs are stereotypically characterized as those who do not fear God and disobey God's commandments. Contextually, the antecedent of "enemies" in these verses refers to the wicked intending to harm the righteous, as described in verses 15–16.

Because proverbial sayings are terse, they inevitably lack detailed information. First, there is no information about how the enemies fell or stumbled. Second, there is no information about who caused the enemies to stumble. Regardless of this paucity of information, the righteous are clearly not responsible for the fall of the enemies, as that would render this instruction meaningless.[16] It may be inferred that the enemies fell because of a third agent, either someone who was more wicked than the enemies, or because of a natural calamity. For this cluster, I am inclined to read a natural calamity as the cause.

The wisdom's advice to the righteous is "not to rejoice" when enemies fall. But a better translation might be "do not revel" over the downfall of enemies, even if they are your greatest enemies. Reveling leads to gloating, which is synonymous with self-righteousness. Thus the advice to refrain from gloating

---

15. Imagine resilience as a punching bag that a boxer punches when he is training. The boxer can hit the bag countless times, left punch or right punch, but the bag rebounds back and is not destroyed. When punching a water bag or a pillow, however, one single punch might break the bag.

16. If the righteous is the culprit, the wise instruction could have been, "Do not attack your enemies."

is the essence of the virtue of tranquility, for it is the absence of excitement towards evil or calamity. The admonition to renounce gloating discourages malicious excitement over the misery of enemies. Although the fall of enemies may seem fitting and may constitute a form of justice and vindication, Aristotle's recommended virtue in this type of situation is "righteous indignation."[17] In the New Testament, Paul's letter to the Philippians says pointedly: "Finally, brothers and sisters, whatever is true, whatever is noble, whatever is right, whatever is pure, whatever is lovely, whatever is admirable – if anything is excellent or praiseworthy – think about such things" (4:8 NIV). The sage is enthralled with preserving the human heart from any form of pernicious contamination (Prov 4:23). A vicious heart breeds heinous actions, and so Wisdom admonishes us not to allow the seed of malice to grow in our heart so that it becomes a poisonous tree.

Turning to verse 18, the conjunction "or else" (*pen*) provides the rationale for tranquility. The anthropomorphic language of the Lord having eyes that "will see" is telling. Rather than seeing the misery of the righteous, the Lord sees the gloating of the righteous victim. This imagery suggests the Lord's clear vision. He cannot be fooled by human pretensions. Other human beings cannot see the condition of the human heart and mind, but the Lord sees our innermost and deepest emotions. Because the Lord sees gloating as evil, he turns his anger away from the enemies.

Admittedly, the second half of verse 18, "turn away his anger from them," is vague. The deflected recipient of the Lord's anger is not easily discernible. Is the deflected recipient of the Lord's anger the one who gloats or some third party? Or is the Lord withholding his anger from afflicting people?[18] I suggest that the Lord's anger shifts to the one who gloats, since gloating mirrors the same evil action of the enemies. It is wrong for the evil to take pleasure when the righteous are afflicted or suffer calamity, and so it is morally wrong for the righteous to take pleasure in the demise of their enemies. Proverbs 24:18 maintains that the righteous draw the Lord's anger from the enemies to themselves. Because the Lord is the God of justice, evil and malice will not go unpunished.

This phenomenon is compatible with the message of the book of Obadiah, where the prophet pronounces punishment against the Edomites because they gloated when Judah fell into the hands of Babylon. Instead of comforting Judah,

---

17. Aristotle, *Nicomachean Ethics*, 32.

18. Christine Yoder, *Proverbs*, Abingdon Old Testament Commentaries (Nashville: Abingdon Press, 2009), 241.

Edom took advantage of Judah's misery (i.e. looting, gloating, apathy) under the Babylonians (Obad 1:11–14). Edom and Judah were enemies because of the sibling rivalry between Jacob and Esau. The Edomites were from the genealogy of Esau, and the hostile relationship began when the Edomites refused to let the Israelites pass through their land to go to the Land of Canaan. Tranquility does not delight in the triumph of evil and wickedness.

If tranquility in verses 17 and 18 refers to the absence of excitement towards evil and calamity, the tranquility in these two verses indicates the absence of agitation.

> Do not fret because of evildoers.
> Do not envy the wicked;
> for the evil have no future;
> the lamp of the wicked will go out. (Prov 24:19–20 NRSV)

Tranquility is being undisturbed by evil and wickedness. The righteous are admonished not to fret because of evildoers or envy the wicked. To be tranquil is to be sober emotionally, spiritually, mentally and physically, to remain unruffled and firm in one's stance, one's faith, joy and life. To be tranquil is to let the negative emotions of anxiety, hatred, humiliation and bitterness lose their grip over our hearts. Envy and fretting so easily slip into vengeance, and the wisdom tradition maintains that vengeance is God's sole prerogative (which will be discussed in Prov 24:21–22).[19]

The motivation for this warning comes in verse 20, which paints the image of a lamp. Ancient Near Eastern lamps required oil to burn. The lamp symbolizes the life of the wicked, and though their lamp might be shining bright now, in the fullness of time, the oil will eventually be consumed, which is to say that the wicked will eventually cease. Whatever triumph or happiness the evildoers' experience is only temporary and fleeting, for the wicked have no future (v. 20a).

The Virtue of Reverence for the Lord and King: Proverbs 24:21–22

> My child, fear the LORD and the king,
> and do not disobey either of them;[20]

19. Prov 20:22; 24:29; Lev 19:18; Deut 32:35; Ps 94:1–2; Rom 12:19; 1 Pet 3:9; 1 Thess 5:15.

20. This verse is problematic. The MT reads "do not associate with those who change [differ]," but this article has opted to use the NRSV's rendering, which follows the LXX.

for disaster comes from them suddenly,
and who knows the ruin that both can bring? (Prov 24:21–22 NRSV)

The placement of this virtue at the end of this cluster suggests its message, as it functions as the theological rationale for the previous aphorisms. Although these last verses are foundational to the above virtue ethics, these verses are full of textual ambiguities.

First, the literary construction in the Hebrew Bible differs from modern translations.[21] In the Hebrew Bible, the object of "fear" is "the Lord," which is interrupted by the appellation, "my son," and then followed by the conjunction, "and," and then by the definite noun, "the king." A more literal translation would be, "Fear the Lord, my child, and the king."

The Hebrew syntactical construction may be understood as nuancing the logical priority of the Lord over the human king. Regardless of the literary form in the original Hebrew, the human king in ancient Israel was the vicegerent of the Lord. The human king was to govern and judge in accordance with the Lord's instruction. Yet in the history of ancient Israel, this was never the case. Israel's kings always deviated from the instructions of the Lord as prescribed in the Torah, with few exceptions.[22] Nevertheless, in the political worldview of the wisdom tradition, the Lord and king represent the authority in heaven and earth respectively. The goal of this authority and leadership is to uphold order and justice on earth as it is in heaven. The Lord and the king have the supreme authority over both the wicked and the righteous.

While the natural result of physical and emotional trauma is fear and anxiety, the instruction of the sage is to "fear" and "not to disobey" these authorities. Needless to say, the "fear of the Lord" (not "fear of the king") is an important recurring theme in the book of Proverbs.[23] Moreover, it is unmistakable that the instruction "Fear the Lord and king" is the *only* positive advice in this cluster amidst seven negative ones. It suggests observance of the rule of law, order and justice. Civil disobedience is discouraged. The temptation to usurp their authority is repudiated. The wicked's attack against

21. The issue here concerns the word order, which most English translations have taken the liberty to rearrange for target language. The NIV writes, "Fear the Lord and the king, my son." The ESV writes, "My son, fear the Lord and the king." The NRSV writes, "My child, fear the Lord and the king."

22. Israel violated the instructions on idolatry, offerings and sacrifices, alliance with foreign nations and wives, etc.

23. Proverbs scholars talk about the emotional, cultic, ethical, pious and epistemological understanding of "fear of the Lord" (*yir'at Yahweh*).

the righteous victim is deemed a destruction to the creation order of the Lord, creating "chaos" in human relationships. Hence, "the fear of the Lord and the king" is a wisdom call to submit to the Lord's authority to restore the creation order in human relationships. Vengeance and personal vendetta against the perpetrator is disallowed as they are behaviors contrary to the above aphorisms on resilience and tranquility. Both the Lord and king will bring about "sudden disaster" which may mean divine wrath. The rhetorical question, "and who knows the ruin that both can bring?" speaks of the absolute authority of the Lord and king. No ordinary citizen knows how and when the judgment in the form of disaster will come about. Only the capricious Lord and unpredictable king have full knowledge and power. "The disaster wrought by the Lord and king as utterly unpredictable – with regard to timing ('suddenly') and scope ('Who knows?')."[24] The synergy between the Lord and the king find its ultimate and perfect expression in God the father and Jesus Christ the king in the New Testament. The Lord judges the righteous and the wicked through Jesus Christ in the fullness of time.

Lastly, while these three virtues may easily be perceived as three parallel advices without clear logical relationships, this essay argues that they are building blocks with the third virtue as the critical foundation. Fear and reverence toward the Lord and king alone will make the righteous victim muster strong resilience and unwavering tranquility. It is entrusting the injustice and evil into the supreme authority of the Lord and king. The sage's message is clear: only the Lord and the king, the creator of the creation order, can restore the disorder in human relationships caused by the wicked against the righteous.

The Telos of Virtue Ethics

What is the purpose of responding to the trauma of evil and wickedness with virtue ethics? The sage asserts that the telos[25] of virtue ethics makes eschatological hope viable for the righteous victim.

> My child, eat honey, for it is good,
>   and the drippings of the honeycomb are sweet to your taste.
> Know that wisdom is such to your soul;

24. Yoder, *Proverbs*, 241.

25. Telos comes from the Greek word τέλος, which means "to accomplish an activity," "purpose or aim," "make perfect" (Bauer, Arndt, Gingrich and Danker, "τέλος," *BDAG*, 996–997).

> if you find it, you will find a future,
> and your hope will not be cut off. (Prov 24:13–14)

These two verses are set apart from the succeeding verses due to their diverse thematic and linguistic characteristics. They serve as the prelude for the three virtue ethics, which are espoused in the subsequent eight verses. This subsection begins with Proverb's characteristic hortatory call to the son, "My child." Here the son is urged to eat honey because it is good and sweet. This honey is immediately compared to wisdom. Just as honeycomb is sweet, wisdom is also sweet – not only to one's tastebud, but also to one's life or soul.[26] Honey is known to be a therapeutic, healing agent. Absorbing wisdom heals the pain of wickedness against the righteous. Forti writes, "Wisdom, just as honey, provokes pleasant feelings; the contents of learning and the teaching processes are compared to the intake, swallowing and digesting of honey that leaves its sweet taste upon the palate."[27] Parenthetically, while wisdom is sweet like honey, the law of the Lord is comparatively sweeter than honey (Pss 19:10; 119:103).

There are two important Hebrew words in the second line of verse 14: אחרית (*ʾaḥărît,* future) and תקוה (*tiqwâ*, hope). Although these two words are used in two different sentences, the construction may be a combination of two figures of speech: hendiadys and merism. When these two nouns are conjoined, they form "future hope," or even better, "eschatological hope."[28] The verb used with "future" is "find" and the verb used for "hope" is "not be cut off." Although these constructions are both positive and negative, the parallelism enhances the idea that wisdom anticipates eschatological hope.

This eschatological hope is unpacked in the aphorisms discussed above. Hope includes retributive justice for the wicked along with the vindication of the righteous victim. The fate of the wicked is described as being brought down by a calamity (v. 16), falling (v. 17) and as those who have no hope (v. 20a) and are like a snuffed-out lamp (v. 20b). The cumulative effect of these descriptions depicts a brief life, a premature death for the wicked.

On the other hand, verse 16 describes the eschatological hope of the righteous victim as "rising seven times." Although there is only one description of the righteous in this cluster, that paucity does not undermine its value. This description may be understood in two ways. First, the righteous will outlast the

26. Lucas has correctly observed that "soul" (*nefesh*) also means "appetite." Ernest C. Lucas, *Proverbs,* The Two Horizons Old Testament Commentary (Grand Rapids: Eerdmans, 2015), 160.

27. Tova L. Forti, "Bee's Honey – From Realia to Metaphor in Biblical Wisdom Literature," *Vetus Testamentum* 56, no. 3 (2006): 335.

28. Stephen R. Spencer, "Hope," in *Dictionary for Theological Interpretation of the Bible,* ed. Kevin J. Vanhoozer (Grand Rapids: Baker, 2005), 305–307.

wicked. His life will not be cut short, and he will see and experience vindication. Thus the righteous victim's practice of virtue ethics will outlast the wicked's practice of evil.[29] Second, "rising seven times" reflects the resilience that will become a habit for the righteous, "an abiding quality in a person that inclines one to act in a good manner."[30]

In practicing virtue ethics, the innocent victim will never be cut off from future hope, whereas "Hopelessness refuses to wait for God's promises, insisting 'now or never.'"[31] Eschatological hope is a doctrine that sees and evaluates human life and existence not only from the past or present perspectives but also from the future perspective. The intent is to envision a future of divine retributive justice, which promises to bring sense and meaning to tragedy and suffering. The telos of virtue ethics is not only to deal with the present trauma but also to have a forward-looking perspective. Thus the virtues espoused in Proverbs 24:13–22 are not merely a mechanism for facing present suffering and pain, for they guide us beyond the present and towards the future. As we face trauma caused by evil and wickedness, eschatological hope is as sweet as honey to our soul, for it brings us comfort and consolation, and it enables us to see and experience a future that is different from our present circumstances.

Conclusion

Human beings are easily corrupted by pain and trauma. Generally, our natural and fleshly emotional response to trauma goes in two different directions. On the one hand, we may respond with despondence, hopelessness and collapse. On the other hand, we may respond with anger, hatred, envy and vengeance. All these responses invite unnecessary trouble, self-destruction and premature death. But the righteous victim is exhorted to practice virtue ethics. As we practice and choose wisdom, Wisdom sagaciously reorders our moral and relational disturbances, helping us look beyond our present circumstance of evil and wickedness toward a future of vindication and justice.

---

29. It may be argued that this imagery is Proverbs' unique grammar to speak of the New Testament concept of "life after death" or "eternal life."

30. William C. Mattison III, *Introducing Moral Theology: True Happiness and the Virtues* (Grand Rapids: Brazos Press, 2008), 61.

31. Spencer, "Hope," 307.

Bibliography

Aristotle, *The Nicomachean Ethics, with an Introduction by Stephen Watt*. Translated with Note by Harris Rackham. Hertfordshire: Wordsworth, 1996.

Estes, Daniel K. *Hear, My Son: Teaching and Learning in Proverbs 1–9*. NSBT. Grand Rapids: Eerdmans, 1997.

Forti, Tova L. "Bee's Hoey – From Realia to Metaphor in Biblical Wisdom Literature." *Vetus Testamentum* 56, no. 3 (2006): 327–341.

Harnish, R. M. "Communicating with Proverbs." *Communication & Cognition* 25 (1993): 265–290.

Heim, Knut Martin. *Like Grapes of God Set in Silver*. BZAW 273. Berlin: Walter de Gruyter, 2001.

———. *Poetic Imagination in Proverbs: Variant Repetitions and the Nature of Poetry*. Bulletin for Biblical Research Supplement 4. Winona Lake, IN: Eisenbrauns, 2013.

Koptak, Paul E. *Proverbs*. The NIV Application Bible. Grand Rapids: Zondervan, 2003.

Longman, Tremper III. *Proverbs*. Baker Commentary on the Old Testament: Wisdom and Psalms. Grand Rapids: Baker Academic, 2006.

Lucas, Ernest C. *Proverbs*. The Two Horizons Old Testament Commentary. Grand Rapids: Eerdmans, 2015.

Mattison, William C. III. *Introducing Moral Theology: True Happiness and the Virtues*. Grand Rapids: Brazos Press, 2008.

Monfalcone, W. R. "Trauma." In *Dictionary of Pastoral Care and Counseling*, edited by Rodney Hunter, 1287. Nashville: Abingdon, 1990.

Nel, Philip Johannes. *The Structure and Ethos of the Wisdom Admonitions in Proverbs*. BZAW 158. Berlin/New York: Walter de Gruyter, 1982.

Schwáb, Zoltán S. *Toward an Interpretation of the Book of Proverbs: Selfishness and Secularity Reconsidered*. Journal of Theological Interpretation Supplement 7. Winona Lake, IN: Eisenbrauns, 2013.

Snell, D. C. *Twice-Told Proverbs and the Composition of the Book of Proverbs*. Winona Lake: Eisenbrauns, 1993.

Spencer, Stephen R. "Hope." In *Dictionary for Theological Interpretation of the Bible*, edited by Kevin J. Vanhoozer, 305–307. Grand Rapids: Baker, 2005.

VanGemeren, Willem A. "Proverbs." In *A Biblical-Theological Introduction to the Old Testament: The Gospel Promised*, edited by Miles V. Van Pelt, 373–398. Wheaton, IL: Crossway, 2016.

Waltke, Bruce. *The Book of Proverbs 15–31*. The International Commentary on the Old Testament. Grand Rapids: Eerdmans, 2005.

Westberg, Daniel A. *Renewing Moral Theology: Christian Ethics as Action, Character and Grace*. Downers Grove: IVP Academic, 2015.

Whybray, R. N. *The Composition of the Book of Proverbs*. JSOTSupp 168. Sheffield: Sheffield Academic Press, 1994.

Wright, N. T. *After You Believe: Why Christian Character Matters*. New York: HarperCollins, 2010.

Yoder, Christine. *Proverbs*. Abingdon Old Testament Commentaries. Nashville: Abingdon Press, 2009.

4

A Trauma Observed

Biblical Reflections on Safety, Control and Fragmentation

Ida Glaser

This is not a paper on how to assist traumatized people, but a very personalized case study written from within a world of Post-Traumatic Stress Disorder (PTSD). It is how a particular individual with a particular history of personal, family and ethnic experience of trauma has been reading Scripture. The careful reader may observe characteristics of a traumatized mind, as different segments of the subject are dealt with in discrete sections, and as I allow my reflective, academic mind to converse with my personal experience. This reflects a classic "coping" mechanism of dealing with life in manageable fragments – both by fragmenting my story, and by separating the rational process from the emotions. In order to assist the reader, I have put some of my personal story in *italics*, and I have organized the material, but I have not made everything fit together. I am journeying towards accepting myself and my history as a continuous whole, but, in my world, everything does not yet fit together.

Most of the paper represents reflections from different stages of my own journey. My journey through PTSD began in 2006, when a head injury triggered traumatic memories from a car accident in 1966, in which fifteen-year-old Ida and her thirteen-year-old brother survived while their parents and grandfather were killed. *So similar was the 2006 head injury to the head injury which I sustained in that accident that my spectacles were scratched and bent in the same way. It was four months before a therapist helped me to make the connection, but I can remember vividly the sense of déjà vu and the "Oh no! Not again!" feeling as my head hit the pavement and again as I looked at my damaged spectacles.*

The reflections on communal trauma are based on decades of learning to cope with being the daughter of a Jew who took two years to travel from Czechoslovakia to the UK during the Second World War, and with bearing the name of his mother, who died at Auschwitz. It may help the reader to know that most people from this sort of background feel that they are fighting for the very right to exist. Hitler's "final solution" was certainly a denial of the right of Jewish people to exist; but to this must be added centuries of having lived under the rule of Christians who could not fit us into their worldview. *Some of my ancestors fled to Bohemia in the fifteenth century, because there was no survival for Jews as Jews at that time in Spain. I can see an interplay between the fight for the right to exist, the fear of non-existence and the pain of accepting existence as I re-read this paper.*

In retrospect, I understand that I cannot divide the "communal" experience from the "personal" experience, and that my traumatized responses did not begin with the emergence of crippling symptoms in 2006. But one needs some sort of analysis to sort out the chaos of an inner world which has collapsed into fragments. The analyses offered below should not be read as generalized analyses of PTSD, but as my own attempts to reach a biblical understanding of my journey. The central portion of this paper is a slightly edited version of material written a decade ago, when I was just beginning to function after months of being so traumatized that I had difficulty in walking, thinking, speaking and even eating. I was trying to make sense of the experience, and so, as a Christian missionary theologian, I had been turning to the Bible. I was invited to write a paper for a conference on "mission and migration," and this was the result.[1]

Now, a decade later, the world seems to be full of people fleeing from catastrophic situations; and many are deeply wounded. My biblical analysis of my own experience has proved more relevant than I could have imagined, and I have begun to think that the traumatization was one of the best things that ever happened to me. Not only has it enabled me to deal afresh with the

1. This was a conference of the British and Irish Association for Mission Studies. See Stephen Spencer, ed., *Mission and Migration: Papers Read at the Biennial Conference of the British and Irish Association for Mission Studies at Westminster College, Cambridge, 2nd–5th July 2007* (Sheffield: Cliff College, 2008). My paper, being rather unusual, was not included in the book, but an edited version was published by itself as *Trauma, Migration and Mission: Biblical Reflections from a Traumatised Hebrew*, Crowther Centre Monograph No. 2 (Oxford: Church Mission Society, 2008).

underlying childhood trauma (I no longer suffer from clinical depression) and opened my understanding of other people, of the Bible and of God himself; it is, even more than all my academic qualifications, my major qualification for working on the Muslim–Christian interface in today's troubled world.

"*This paper is part of my own movement towards 'reconnection as a survivor' – my celebration of survival not as a diminished thing still suffering from traumatic symptoms and with a 'working memory' a shadow of its former self, but as an augmented person, with something new to offer to the Body of Christ. I can see the trauma as preparation for the next stage of the mission to which God has called me. Perhaps I am not alone. Perhaps a measure of trauma, or, at least, the experience of traumatic events, is a necessary equipment for mission,*" I wrote at the end of my original paper. Ten years on, I want to change the "perhaps" to "certainly."

Over the past ten years, I have learned a great deal by living with the ongoing effects of Post Traumatic Stress Disorder. Through the help of another therapist, I eventually discovered that many of my problems were due to "dissociation": the final section of this paper dates to 2017, and shares a key stage in learning to accept myself as a coherent created being.

Getting Started

Trauma is a Greek word, meaning "wound." The one place it appears in the New Testament is in Jesus's exposition of the commandment to love our neighbors: it was into the *trauma* of the beaten Jew that the Good Samaritan poured his oil and wine (Luke 10:34). The word also appears as a verb, *traumatizo*, twice: first, in the parable of the wicked tenants who *traumatize* the third emissary from their master (Luke 20:12), and second in Acts 19:16, when the sons of Sceva are *traumatized* by the man with the evil spirit. The world, it seems, is a dangerous place, one where human beings can wound us if we do our mission in God's way, and evil powers can wound us if we do it in our own way. We are called to minister to the traumatized, but our shared humanity means that we are also in danger of trauma, and our ministry may increase the danger.

It is not surprising, then, that all the Synoptic Gospels record Jesus preparing his disciples for coming catastrophic events in both the near and the distant future – the fall of Jerusalem; the wars, famines and natural disasters of the end times; and the persecutions that will beset his followers throughout (Matt 24; Mark 13; Luke 21). One of the results of such events is that some people become refugees: Jesus even advises his disciples to do so (Matt 24:16;

Mark 13:14; Luke 21:21). Embedded in these chapters are key statements on mission:

- This gospel of the kingdom will be preached in the whole world as a testimony to all nations, and then the end will come (Matt 24:14 NIV).
- The gospel must first be preached to all nations. . . . say whatever is given you at the time, for it is not you speaking, but the Holy Spirit (Mark 13:10–11 NIV).
- And so you will bear testimony to me (Luke 21:13 NIV).

When everything is mixed up in your mind, you need to find some order. So I searched for some categories to give me a framework for re-ordering my thought world. The invitation to write a paper on the theme of "migration and mission" turned me to the juxtaposition of catastrophic events, flight and mission in Matthew 24, Mark 13 and Luke 21. It enabled me to begin to make sense of what was happening to me as having great potential for ministry. For me, things can make sense if they can bear fruit. I realize that, from the age of sixteen, I have only been able to cope with suffering as I have offered it to the Lord to be used in his mission to his world.[2]

I developed three frameworks as I began to reorganize my world. First, I tried to understand PTSD; second, I looked for something in the Bible which might parallel the car accident which was so central to my experience; and, third, I identified some key concepts which would direct me to relevant biblical material.

Framework 1: Understanding Trauma[3]

In English, and particularly in medicine and psychology, the word "trauma" has developed specific meanings. I want now to explore the understanding of trauma as a state resulting from an experience that combines extreme danger with utter helplessness. *PTSD is frightening. It's so strange to be aware of what is going on, but to be able to make no sense of it. Why am I jumping at the slightest sound? Why do I keep slowing down so that I can't function? Why can I sometimes not even find my own name in my confused mind? I am so thankful*

2. Col 1:24–29; Phil 1:21–25; and Phil 3:10 have been key passages for me.

3. This section owes much of its understanding of the dynamics of trauma to Judith Herman, *Trauma and Recovery: The Aftermath of Violence – from Domestic Abuse to Political Terror* (New York: Basic Books, 1992).

for the therapist who identified this as "trauma." The label began the journey towards understanding.

I will distinguish between "trauma" and "traumatic events." By "trauma," I shall mean a kind of wounding that can result from experiencing, witnessing or even hearing about "traumatic events": that is, situations of acute danger which a person is powerless to resist. Such events usually result in loss and consequent grief for all; but the occurrence, nature and extent of trauma as defined below depends on numerous factors.

Trauma has physiological as well as psychological dimensions, because of the way that the body responds to danger: it produces adrenalin. It seems that the combination of danger and helplessness can lead to the adrenalin being unable to find its normal release, so something gets stuck. Instead of the mind and body processing the horrible event in the normal way,

- The body, through the autonomic nervous system, gets stuck in its responses to stimuli associated with the event – summarized as fight, flight or freeze. *In my case, my body tries to "freeze" in response to anything it associates with traveling in a car! It's a response I have no control over, like blinking when someone shines a light in my eye.*
- The mind keeps repeating the memory – whether at a conscious or subconscious level. You see the thing happening again and again in dreams or in "flashbacks," and, when it's really acute, it's like living in it – *for me, like living in a car that's just about to crash and kill everyone around me and maybe me too.*
- Mind and body are constantly anticipating a repeat of the events. The body can be in a state of constant arousal, which may be evidenced in "startle responses" – uncontrollable jerks in response to any stimulus that suggests the original traumatic situation.

In summary, we might say that the event is experienced in the present (in repeated memories) and in the future (in constant anticipation of a repeat) instead of, as is normal with memories, in the past. Through it all is the sense of *danger* and *helplessness*. There is likely to be a constant struggle for safety and control to compensate for these feelings. There may also be a variety of physical and mental symptoms – sleeplessness, weight change, nausea, irritability, and feelings of dissociation, fragmentation and disconnection. Very common is what is sometimes called "survivor guilt" – feeling that you are somehow responsible for what happened or for not averting it, or that you rather than others should have died. Some people even feel that they have died, or no longer exist.

All this applies very widely, consciously or unconsciously, at both personal and communal levels: the children of refugees who live with an edge of fear, and whose reactions are dominated by "fight," "flight" or "freeze," or the communities feeling under threat, playing the "terrorist outrage" over and over on TV. Again and again in traumatized communities, we see desperate "it must never happen again" attempts to escape danger, and fighting to convince ourselves that we are not really helpless.

Such trauma is often resistant to ordinary talk-based counseling techniques. It cannot effectively be dealt with until whatever has been stuck gets unstuck. There are various strategies that can be used to access the memories so that they can be processed and the experience can move into the past.[4] The body can then be retrained to change its responses to the remembered stimuli.

Herman[5] proposes three stages on the journey to recovery which must, she says, take place within the context of relationships, and must involve the recognition that recovery does not depend on someone else putting things right.[6]

- Establishing a sense of safety;
- Recovering and processing memories;
- Reconnecting with the world as a survivor.

These three stages can be discerned in the biblical material explored below. The importance of healing relationships, which can be offered by the church, the missionary and, most importantly, by God himself through Christ, is assumed.

Framework 2: Seeking Trauma in the Bible

I have found analyzing trauma along two axes a helpful starting point for seeking relevant biblical material:

---

4. See, for example, Francine Shapiro and Margot Silk, *EMDR: The Breakthrough Therapy for Overcoming Anxiety, Stress and Trauma* (New York: Basic Books, 1997); Laurence Heller and Diane Heller, *Crash Course: Auto Accident Recovery Breakthrough* (Berkeley, CA: North Atlantic Books, 2001).

5. Herman, *Trauma and Recovery.*

6. This is a logical progression, but the stages are not discrete: they can be variously traversed in time.

Axis 1: Between Trauma Caused by Events Originating in Human Sin, and Trauma Caused by Events Originating in the Natural Order

In Matthew 24, events originating in human sin would include persecutions and wars. Events originating in the natural order would include earthquakes and famines. There are numerous other places in the Bible that deal with either "natural disaster" or human atrocities. There is, however, a spectrum here. We now recognize that many apparently natural disasters have been aggravated or even caused by human agency – whether by environmental damage, by factors leading to the vulnerability of the victims, or by deliberate or accidental mishandling of the aftermath of the events.

Where does a car crash fit along this axis? On the one hand, we call it an "accident," implying an uncontrollable chance and therefore, perhaps, a "natural" event. On the other hand, my father was driving the car when he was tired, and someone had left a lorry parked in the wrong place. It seems to me that such an event is therefore situated right at the center of the axis, along with events caused by other man-made devices that unwittingly let loose the destructive powers of nature. The greatest potential for trauma is when human attempts to control the natural order are directed towards evil ends; but there can also be enormous damage when human beings find their attempts loosing powers beyond their control.

Axis 2: Between Individual and Ethnic Trauma

There is **individual trauma**: each person's experience is different, and such specific trauma symptoms as referred to above depend on particular experiences. *For example, although my brother also survived the car crash, the head injury with the resultant memory loss and the recent similar injury that triggered the lost memories were mine alone.*

There is **trauma that affects families** – nuclear and extended. Even a trauma that apparently affects only one person – for example, a rape that is not spoken of – affects family and friends because it affects the person's relationships with them. *In our case, the deaths of my father and mother resulted in the immediate emigration of his sister and her children from the Czech Republic. In addition to the shock of loss was the change of place, culture and language for the emigrating family, and the change of language and culture within the home for the receiving family.*

There is **trauma that affects whole communities and ethnic groups**. *For example, the "Holocaust" has affected not only our family but also all Jews, whether or not their families were directly involved, and to whichever post-*

Holocaust generation they belong. To this can be added the whole history of Jewish experience under hostile rule.

There is **trauma with worldwide effects**. This can be through media coverage, or simply because the events are so extensive that they affect the course of history and/or are so terrible that many countries and peoples get involved. There are obvious recent examples, but I would also include the "Holocaust" here, with its lasting heritage of publicity and guilt, and the political ramifications of seeking security for future generations.

The Bible deals with individual trauma in, for example, Job, various psalms, and stories of individuals. However, all this is embedded in the history of Israel and in the documents of the early Christian community. This paper arises out of immediate individual trauma, but it has the background of family and communal contexts, and is undergirded by the conviction that family and community are fundamental to dealing with individual trauma as with everything else.

A key biblical resource is the often traumatic experience of the Jewish people. The word "Hebrew" may or may not have originated as a somewhat derogatory term for slaves and migrants, but the condition of exile and humiliation has been a frequent one in Jewish history – in both biblical and post-biblical times. I have written elsewhere of the use of Psalm 137 as a place for processing memories of peoples traumatized by conflict and land loss.[7] The psalm invites readers into the experience of Israel, thus normalizing the trauma and dealing with consequent grief, anger and isolation. Often a feeling of isolation and difference is part of the condition of trauma: hence the importance of sufferers understanding that they share the experience with others.

Framework 3: Key Concepts

Key Concept 1: The Normality of Trauma

Our twenty-first-century Western world breeds the myth that safety is the normal human condition, which occasionally gets violated by dangers that someone ought to avert. Biblically, there is a measure of truth in this, in that God created a good and safe world, so this is what we long for. However, safety disappeared very rapidly as sin appeared, and the hard facts are that danger is now normal, and that we are often powerless to counter it. It is

7. "We Sat Down and Wept: Biblical Resources for Conflict Situations," in *The Round Table: The Commonwealth Journal of International Affairs* 382 (2005): 641–652.

not only that such feelings as expressed in Psalm 137 are normal responses to violence and exile: it is also that traumatic events are, since the "fall," the regular human experience.

So, in Matthew 24, Mark 13 and Luke 21, Jesus tells his disciples to be ready for traumatic events. He prepares them both for traumatic events due to human sin and for traumatic events due to natural causes. The teaching can be applied by individuals, but it is addressed to a group. In summary, Jesus taught that

- Traumatic events are to be expected.
- They are meaningful – in terms of mission, of judgment, and of the eschaton, which is the ultimate aim of the world.
- They are limited – both in intensity and in duration.
- In the midst of them, there is something that will never pass away.
- Therefore the person who endures to the end will be *safe*.

Underlying it all is the assurance that, despite all appearances, God and only God is in control. He and only he knows (Matt 24:36).

There are two corollaries here for mission.

First, it offers a resource for ministry to people involved in traumatic events. The acknowledgment of the commonality and normality of trauma can help to deal with the disconnection, isolation and anger that so often follow traumatic experience. The assurances of meaning and limitation give hope. The vision of something permanent offers a fixed point of reference in an apparently chaotic world. Safety and control are, as we shall see, crucial.

Second, if we take this teaching seriously and prepare ourselves to face such events, they will become for us opportunities for witness (Luke 21:13), for sharing in the proclamation of the kingdom of God (Matt 24:14). How? In the place of helplessness, we will find the Holy Spirit, the promised Helper, speaking through us (Mark 13:11). The place of trauma becomes the place of mission.

Key Concept 2: Safety and Control

> The core experiences of psychological trauma are disempowerment and disconnection from others. Recovery, therefore, is based upon the empowerment of the survivor and the creation of new connections.[8]

8. Herman, *Trauma and Recovery*, 133. This section owes much of its understanding of the dynamics of trauma to Herman.

The biblical resources explored in the following sections take up the themes of empowerment and reconnection. However, there is a prerequisite: Herman's first stage of recovery is establishing a place of safety. The books tell us that, in order to start processing the traumatic memory and let it recede into the past,

- the feeling of danger needs to be countered by being in a place of safety;
- the feeling of helplessness needs to be countered by being in control.

From a biblical perspective, these are forlorn efforts: the world is fallen and therefore not a safe place; and trying to be in control is the original sin. I want to agree that safety and control are of key importance in dealing with a condition rooted in danger and helplessness, but to insist that God is the only one who can safely be in control, and that the only ultimate safety is in God himself – and that is a safety that can face even the dreaded repeat of the traumatic event, because it lasts beyond death. Of course, finding as much physical safety as possible, and the realization that one is responsible for one's own recovery and not a helpless victim, are still necessary. However, the recognition of God as the place of safety and control both offers ultimate security and puts self-control into perspective.

There is a mass of biblical material on God as the author of safety (related words are often translated in terms of "salvation") in both this world and the next. Here, I want to focus briefly on God as a place of safety, before going on to the next section which takes up the theme of God in control. As the song says, quoting Proverbs 18:10, "The name of the LORD is a strong tower: the righteous run into it and they are safe."

One of the rabbinic names for God is *Ha Maqqom* – "The Place." The idea is explored in the Midrash[9] on Genesis 28:11, where Jacob, setting out for Haran, "came to a certain place." In the understanding of this midrash, Jacob met the *shekinah*, and it is to the *shekinah* that the Torah refers with the word "place." Why? Because God is the Place of the world. The train of thought then moves to the "place near God" in the cleft of the rock, where Moses could safely stand as the glory passed (Exod 33:21–22), and to God as dwelling place (*ma'on*) in Deuteronomy 33:27 and Psalm 90:1. The question underlying this midrash is whether God is the dwelling place of the world, or the world the dwelling place of God; and the conclusion is that the world is in God, and not vice versa. The Christian might move further, to the *shekinah* dwelling in the world in Christ, and recall that *Yeshua*, the Hebrew name for "Jesus," can be translated "safety."

9. *Genesis Rabbah* 48:9.

One of the techniques for processing traumatic memories is to repeatedly return to an envisaged place of safety. The idea of God as The Place in which the world dwells, and therefore as the dwelling place of God's people and of the individual, offers a truly safe place.

Midrash often gathers together references to similar ideas from different parts of the Bible. Before the discussion of *Ha Maqqom*, the Midrash here applies Proverbs 3:23 to Jacob, and puts Psalm 121 into his mouth.[10] As Jacob comes to lie down in the Place, God's promise to those who observe his wisdom is applied to him: "You will go your way safely and not injure your feet. When you lie down you will be unafraid; you will lie down and your sleep will be sweet. You will not fear the sudden terror or the disaster that comes upon the wicked, for the Lord will be your trust; He will keep your feet from being caught" (JPS Tanakh translation). Jacob responds with the assurance that, helpless though he is in himself, God is his helper and his protector from all that he fears. His sense of helplessness is not countered by a sense of his being in control, but by the assurance that help will come from the Lord who is in control.

It is crucial to the above understanding that God's control is, ultimately, safe.[11] In fact, God is the only one who can safely take control because he is the only one who has both complete goodness and complete wisdom. His control deals with both ends of our first trauma spectrum: he made the natural order, and his management of potentially destructive forces is without the weakness of human limitation or the taint of human sin.

It is this God who is the safe Place, the Helper of the helpless.

Biblical Resources 1: Empowerment – God in Control

The corollary of the above, and the thesis that underlies what follows, is that empowerment must be rooted in perception of God's control, and of his infinite goodness and wisdom. It is not an empowerment dependent on achieving safety, or on struggling to take control over the dangerous thing. It is based on the hard acknowledgment that there really are areas in which we are helpless, but there is a Helper, one who can help us stand on our own two feet and move forward. It is an empowerment found in trust, in the acceptance both of our

---

10. *Genesis Rabbah* 48:1–2.

11. The rabbis recognize that this is not always apparent, and that it often appears that the righteous suffer more than the wicked. *Genesis Rabbah* 48:5 notes the apparent ease of Esau and suffering of Jacob at this time, and observes: "Thus we learn that the Holy One, blessed be He, hastens the happiness of the wicked and delays that of the righteous."

limitation and of our value as his image, in knowing forgiveness of sin, and in accepting the help of the Holy Spirit.

The idea of this God being in control has been the single most important idea helping me through my journey. Here follow three biblical resources that have helped me to know the God who is in control as my Helper.

Noah

There can be few worse experiences than having the whole world and its peoples destroyed around you; but I have found the flood story an essential foundation, because it shows God in control both of human sin and of the natural order.

- God is in control of nature. In fact, he is able to un-make and re-make it all, because he is its creator. In particular, he is in control of the waters, which represented fearful forces of destruction to the peoples of the time.
- God is in control of human wickedness. The Noah story can be read as Genesis's response to the question of human evil.

This would be terrifying if it were presented as God's normal mode of action – he would be the author of trauma. But the point of the Noah story is that God has covenanted never to destroy like this again. God's control is subject to the promise of preservation of the natural order until the eschaton.

There is, of course, a problem here. What does it *mean* that God is in control of a world that contains traumatic events? Were the people who did unspeakable things to my grandmother somehow doing God's will? Was my family particularly under God's judgment? I am not going to try to solve such problems, but rather offer some pointers that I have found helpful in living with the questions. Essentially, the flood and the covenant together sum up God's response to human wickedness. It is most important here to notice how the Genesis writer locates both the decision to destroy and the decision to preserve in the very heart of God. In both chapter 6 (v. 5) and chapter 8 (v. 21), we read that the human heart is thoroughly wicked. In both verses, God reflects in his heart. The first time, he decides to destroy; the second, because of the aroma of Noah's sacrifice, he covenants never to do so again.

The decision to preserve is linked with the aroma of the sacrifice. Christians recognize this as an early pointer to the cross – the place where human wickedness was dealt with by God himself, so that human beings can find forgiveness and, as it were, an ark in which to find safety from the flood.

Here is good news for the many who, whether because of religious teaching or because of personal reactions, fear that the traumatic event was a judgment; and also for those who feel guilty about their responses to it, or for whom self-blame is one of the "stuck" responses to trauma triggers. Any real guilt can be forgiven.

Noah and his family were saved in the ark by God's grace (6:8): Noah says nothing but simply obeys God. Here are two helpful pictures for those who are, or feel, surrounded by danger: an ark in which to live safely through the storm, and an oasis of quiet obedience in the midst of a tumultuous world.

The decision to judge comes not out of a detached or angry desire to destroy, but out of a heart of *grief* (6:6). The word translated "pain" or "grief" is *'itsvon*. The root of this is used to mean "The most intense form of human emotion, a mixture of rage and bitter anguish."[12] It is used of God elsewhere in the Old Testament only in Psalm 78:40 and Isaiah 63:10, to describe God's agonizing over the rebellion of his beloved Israel. Its intensity can be seen from its use in relation to human beings: Dinah's brothers, when they heard of her rape (Gen 34:7); Joseph's brothers, confronted with the brother they had wronged (Gen 45:5); Jonathan, when Saul wanted to kill David (1 Sam 20:34); David, when he heard of Absalom's death (2 Sam 19:2); and a deserted wife (Isa 54:6).

The root has already been used four times in Genesis – in 5:29; 3:16 (twice); and 3:17. In each case, it refers to the pain that both women and men suffer because of the fall. Genesis 3:16 and 17 are part of the "curses," and 5:29 tells of the longing of Noah's father to have some relief from the painful toil of the very long lives lived by his ancestors.

Putting all this together, we can suggest both that the divine heart mirrors the pain and grief experienced by his image as a result of sin, and that our sense of grief and outrage at traumatic events can mirror God's own response to them. Rabbinic comment on Genesis 6:6 sees Ecclesiastes 2:21–22 as describing God's grief over the way that humans have handled his creation, and underlines this by citing Genesis 7:10 and the use of 'itsvon to describe David's grief for Absalom as evidence that God took the full seven days of mourning for a near relative over his creation before sending the flood.[13] The pain in the heart of the God who is in control and who accepts the sacrifice is what, for me, makes the existence of trauma bearable.

12. Gordon Wenham, *Genesis 1–15* (Waco, TX: Word Books, 1987), 144.

13. *Genesis Rabbah* 27:1–4; 32:7.

Psalm 46 offers a helpful meditation on some of these ideas. Natural disasters are dealt with in verses 2–3: we need not fear if the waters are raging again, and the earth appears to be falling apart. Human-caused disasters are dealt with in verses 6 and 8–10: it is God who judges, who ends warfare, and who says, "Desist! I dominate the nations! I dominate the earth!" (JPS Tanakh translation). In the center of the psalm is a reflection on this God being in the midst of his people; the first and last verses declare him to be a refuge, a stronghold and a haven. For the traumatized, overwhelmed by helplessness, perhaps the most telling verses are 1 and 5. God, being "very near" and "in the midst," is the help in trouble, the One coming to help. Our God is the God of Jacob.

The more common translation of verse 10 is also telling: "Be still, and know that I am God." It is not only that the nations should heed God and stop fighting, but that the wounded can be still in the knowledge that God is the one fighting the battles. This is an invitation into the ark of safety in God's presence, but also a challenge to endure the long, slow journey through the incapacity caused by the trauma.

Job

The book that most obviously explores individual trauma is Job: and the tragedies that beset him apparently originated both with human beings (the Sabaeans and Chaldeans who attacked his oxen, donkeys and camels) and with natural disaster (the fire that destroyed the sheep and shepherds, and the wind that killed his children). Thus Job deals with both ends of our trauma spectrum as well as with Job's own personal discomfort.

Most of the book deals with Job's agonies and questionings, and with the inadequacy of human response. I want to focus here on something that Job found totally adequate: God's speaking to him out of the whirlwind. There are doubtless many ways of hearing God's response to Job. Until recently, I had found it easy enough to identify with Job's laments, but had tended to hear the same harsh tones in God's words as in those of the "comforters." It is only through my experience of trauma that I have begun to understand how Job could have been satisfied with both the manner and the content of God's response.

Job had been speaking to his friends, and they to him, for thirty-five chapters. He had been through suicidal despair to anger, tried to make sense of it all, argued about justice, glimpsed a possible resolution after death, and then turned to lamenting his losses. But, by the end of all this, his distress was undiminished. This was not only because his friends were insensitive counselors, or because they got their theology wrong. The LXX uses *trauma (or "wound")* to translate *k'eb* in Job 16:6:

> If I speak, my pain [trauma] is not assuaged,
> and if I forbear, how much of it leaves me?

Job thinks that he could comfort the comforters were their positions reversed (16:1–6), but there is something in his own pain that cannot be reached by speaking. The passage goes on to describe the agony of feeling that God is the enemy who is tearing him apart; and Job's final words in 31:35–40 are a plea for something more than words. Elihu offers more words: God's response in chapters 38–41 is satisfactory because it goes far beyond mere speech.

Most obviously, this is **a direct encounter with God**. A key here is 42:5: Job is at last able to rest because he has received an answer direct from God, which is what he wanted all along. The "comforters" had already told him about God's control, but, as chapter 16 suggests, his knowledge that God was in control was a major part of Job's problem. Telling Job that God was in control just made matters worse: he needed to hear God for himself. The personal encounter allows him to hear what we may not hear by reading chapters 38–40: the tone of God's voice, as it were. Where the "comforters'" exposition of God's control was one of judgment, God's own voice spoke affirmation as well as challenge, and reminded Job of his human dignity (38:3; 40:7). The outcome was also much more than speech – it was a total reversal of his condition.

For the traumatized, a key observation is that God spoke to Job **out of the whirlwind**. The scene is an approaching storm, with a background of rumbling thunder (37:2). Elihu is telling Job that God is in control of the weather – for judgment and for blessing. Given his previous experience, this was not something that Job needed to be told. If he was traumatized by the wind's destruction of his children, then the approach of the wind must have triggered a sense of impending doom. Together with Elihu's message of judgment, it would have been terrifying. However, we find that it is out of the very destructive forces that caused the trauma that God speaks. Facing the terror and meeting God there is the key to unlocking the trauma.

- Facing the terror is necessary to "unsticking" whatever got stuck in the original traumatic event. Only then can the memories begin to be processed.
- Meeting God there gives an experience of positive survival in the face of the danger. It is a step on the way to "desensitization" – to retraining the system so that it responds more positively to what have hitherto been trauma triggers.

- For Job, the meeting with God culminated in his being given a job – praying for his friends – and in restoration of what had been lost. The whole negative experience was limited in time, and had a positive outcome.

Job did not realize it, but the gathering storm was a sign of God's coming. Henceforward, he would be able to perceive the wind as a herald of God rather than of disaster.

To turn my attention to God in the face of my various trauma triggers – to find THERE *a security in his greatness and my smallness, to heed* THERE *the call to stand straight in my human dignity, is an ongoing challenge; but it is a great help in the long journey of desensitization. What can God say to me in traffic noise? I have heard him say, "You survived! You are here! You are here because I want you here: I didn't let you die or even be critically injured."*

This morning, after meditating on Psalm 46 in preparation for writing this paper, I heard an ambulance siren. Usually, sirens and/or flashing lights flash me back into a helplessly concussed and confused fifteen-year-old that I had long forgotten and can still scarcely remember, standing beside a wrecked car, with unknown people milling around and cars whizzing past in the darkness, not knowing what had happened or what to do or where to go. Today, I turned my attention to God, and suddenly realized that the emergency services were coming to HELP. *Here is my journal entry:*

> *Sirens: This is not a signal that disaster is all around me, but the sound of someone coming to* HELP. *God is my helper in time of trouble – very near (Ps 46:1). Can I hear him coming to help in the sirens? I may be the helpless victim beside the smash, but here is my Helper coming. The help may have been delayed* THEN, *but he will come at the right time* NOW. *It may have been inappropriate* THEN, *but God knows just how to treat the wounds.*

Of course, it's taken months to get to this point. First, the sirens were just one among a bundle of things that distressed me. Then they came especially to my notice during a stay near a fire station. I became particularly distressed by them, and I went into "freeze" mode every time I heard one. Next, I began to consciously "flash back" into the after-crash situation. It was only then that I asked the question of how I might hear God in them.

Finally, **what did God say to Job?** The main message is loud and clear: it is the message that I have suggested is so crucial to the traumatized – that God is in control of both human evil and the natural order. Chapters 38–41 speak first of the weather and then of the animals, but also of judging human beings. The control over weather and animals in chapters 38 and 39 serves the preliminary purpose of stilling Job: he sees how big God is and how small[14] he is, and can be quiet and listen (40:4). The declaration of God's justice and the demonstration of the limitations of human justice, with its implications of the ineffectiveness of human anger in 40:8–14, followed by the poem of God's control over the monsters, enables Job to worship (42:6).

It is interesting that the *form* of this message is that of God questioning Job. Trauma calls everything into question, so it is not surprising that, hitherto, Job has been questioning God, his friends and everything around him. But the deepest pain, underlying the rage and confusion, is likely to be that trauma calls the self into question. The experience disrupts my whole way of being, and leaves me feeling disconnected and fragmented. So Job's encounter with God turns into a call to encounter himself. "Who is this?" (38:2) may refer to Elihu, who "darkens my counsel with words without knowledge," but Job refers it to himself in 42:3. By the end, he realizes that his problems will not be solved by reforming his comforters, but by his own humble acceptance of whatever God permits. He knew that in the beginning (1:20–21), but now he knows it in a whole new way.

God's only instruction to Job, repeated in 38:3 and 40:7, is to stand up as a human being in order to hear God's questions. Before he is reminded of God's greatness, Job is reminded that, as a human being made in God's image, he can stand and meet God. It is thus, standing, that God gives him, as it were, a tour of creation, and he knows himself as a small creature. At last, he sees God greatness and accepts his own limitations, and that is why he can stop his agonized but ineffective speech.

There is relief in acknowledging my smallness. The world is NOT going to collapse if I am too traumatized to function. I'm not in charge – God is. So it doesn't matter too much if I don't understand what's going on. All I really need to know is that God is in control, and he is good.

There is joy in understanding myself in the context of creation – in having survived to see its beauty, in recognizing that God cares for it and controls it, and in knowing that he values me, small as I am, more than the sparrows.

There is liberation in knowing that my path to wholeness depends on myself before God, and not on any other human being. It does not depend on anyone who has wronged me making amends, or on any "comforter" getting things right.

---

14. This is the root meaning of the word translated "unworthy" (NIV) or "of small account" (ESV).

It is myself I need to meet, and I can do that as I meet God, accept all that has happened to me, and offer it back to him.

Revelation

Much of the New Testament is written out of or into situations of migration, persecution or even famine. The book that deals most explicitly with such issues is, perhaps, Revelation: it is written from enforced exile and, like Jesus in Matthew 24, Mark 13 and Luke 21, it focuses both on opposition to discipleship and on the traumatic events of the end times. And, as in these chapters, the accomplishment of the mission to the nations is embedded in the treatment of these concerns (e.g. 5:9; 7:9; 11:9; 14:6; 15:4; 17:15; 21:24; 22:2). It is not surprising, then, that the main features of Jesus's teaching relating to traumatic events can also be traced in Revelation.

Revelation picks up much Old Testament imagery, so it is also not surprising that it mirrors both Noah and Job. The final universal judgment mirrors the first universal judgment, and, like Genesis 6–9, emphasizes God's control of both human wickedness and the natural order.[15] The imagery of storms is frequent: for example, Jesus has a voice like mighty waters (1:15), the throne emits thunder and lightning (4:5) but is encircled by a rainbow (4:3).

Throughout, Revelation reassures of God's control and of the ultimate safety of his people. It is important that these two areas are the focus of worship for both human beings and the heavenly hosts throughout. The vision of God's throne (chs. 4 and 5), which is foundational to the whole book, indicates God's control over both the natural order and human sin. In chapter 4, God is worshiped for his supremacy in creation (4:11). In chapter 5, the slain Lamb appears beside the throne, and receives worship because his death has dealt with sin (5:9–10). It is this dealing with human wickedness that offers safety and empowerment to those who believe. It follows that, to be assured of safety in the midst of cosmic upheaval, we need to know that the rule of God, which supersedes all earthly rule, is also the rule of his Christ (11:15); and that the "Lord of lords and King of kings" who is the judging warrior who puts a final

15. It is interesting to compare the two judgments. One has the salvation of one family in the ark: the other the salvation of countless thousands through the blood of Christ. One is a single cataclysm that destroys all: the other a series of deliberately limited judgments that offers opportunity for repentance. One is followed by the re-creation of the world to accommodate wickedness and death: the other culminates in a new creation which excludes wickedness and death.

end to human wickedness (19:16) is also the Lamb who has made safe the faithful (17:14).

There is, then, much in Revelation that speaks into traumatic experience. Here, I shall offer some brief pointers structured around the themes of Jesus's teaching in Matthew 24, Mark 13 and Luke 21.

Traumatic Events Are to Be Expected

Revelation certainly normalizes trauma. It reassures the church that these things will happen, and that we need to be prepared for them in order to stand through them. Like Job, Revelation gives much space to natural disasters, and deals with questions of justice and of the worthiness and worship of God. Like the Noah story, it has to do with God's un-making and re-making his world in response to human wickedness.

Traumatic Events Are Meaningful

Like Job, Revelation addresses the question of trauma on earth in the light of what is going on in heaven. In particular, it recognizes the dimension of Satanic activity. It represents Satan as the enemy of humans, especially of believers, and also as the enemy of God. It goes much further than Job, seeing Satan's activity in terms of warfare, and announcing his ultimate defeat. The believer's part in this warfare is potentially martyrdom, but certainly witness (12:11; cf. 1:9). As in Jesus's teaching, the traumatic events find their meaning in relation to the establishment of the kingdom of God. An added focus of Revelation is that the events are associated throughout with humans and angels worshiping the King.

As Job's comforters asserted, and as in the flood, the traumatic events are also seen as judgments. They are part of the sovereign Lord's cleaning up of his creation, and it is this aspect of them that provokes the grand worship of chapter 19. As is clear from chapter 16, the seven "bowls of God's wrath" (16:1) are also a call to repentance, but, sadly, one that is not heeded (16:9, 11).

Traumatic Events Are Limited

Like Job, Revelation climaxes with the appearance of God. While Job has only the voice of God in the whirlwind, Revelation has, quite literally, heaven coming down. While Job's personal suffering comes to an end after his encounter with God, all suffering comes to an end as heaven comes down and every tear is wiped away (21:4). From beginning to end, there is assurance that the end will come "soon" (1:1; 22:20). Two thousand years on, we may wonder what "soon" means; but at least it indicates that God's timing will be right.

There Is Something That Will Never Pass Away

Like Job, Revelation takes us to the throne of God. Behind all the events on earth is the sovereign God in heaven, and the Alpha and Omega who is alive for evermore. The vision of God's throne in chapters 4 and 5 is helpful here. We note the potentially destructive and terrifying thunder and lightning that has its origin in the throne itself (4:5), but that is preceded by the rainbow that surrounds the throne and reminds us of God's covenant with Noah (4:3). The traumatic events described in the later chapters are not only under God's control, but also subject to his commitment to humankind.

It is not surprising, then, that we find in these chapters both the sacrifice and the pain in the heart of God. The elder informs John that the Lion of Judah has conquered: John looks and sees the Lamb – the symbol of sacrifice; and this Lamb has been slain. The slaying, the wounding, of the Lamb is stated three times (5:6, 9, 12). It is the slaying that makes him worthy to open the scroll and to be worshiped. It is also the slaying that opens the mission to all tribes and peoples. Here is the completion of the Noah story.

Those Who Endure to the End Will Be Safe

Revelation declares that there is ultimate safety available for those who persevere through the trauma, as well as for those who repent in response to it. The saints who go through the traumatic events will be safe in the presence of God (7:15–17). The survivors of the earthquake of chapter 11 are terrified, but they praise God (11:13).

The corollary, often unwelcome to Western Christian ears, is that those who do not endure, or who do not repent, will not be safe. As observed above, one of the purposes of the traumatic events is to give a final call to repentance. In trying to avoid the errors of Job's comforters, we may stop people, including ourselves, from hearing this call, and forget that Job's route to peace included repentance (Job 42:6). The exact meaning here is difficult to ascertain, but the symbolism of "dust and ashes" certainly implies a measure of humbling, and of learning to see himself in a right perspective (cf. Gen 18:27). As the letters to the churches in Revelation 2 and 3 make clear, traumatic events can be calls to change for believers as well as for unbelievers.

Biblical Resources 2: Reconnection

Job Again

Reconnection is hard, because it is a re-introduction of oneself to the world, and the self has been through disconnection and fragmentation. There are two implications here. First, the reconnecting self is not quite the same as the self that the world knew before. She functions differently, looks at the world differently, and relates to God in a whole new way. Perhaps the most challenging and painful aspect of reconnection is that she understands herself differently, and it can take a long time for others to recognize the person she now thinks she is. Second, as has already been observed, the three stages of recovery are not discrete. The person attempting to reconnect with the outside world is likely to be still going through the process of reconnecting the inner fragments. She is therefore still needing to process memories, and vulnerable to any response from the world that her being may interpret as linked with the trauma. Reconnecting with the world can feel like returning to a place of great danger.

Most of my attempts at reconnection require me to go outside the house, where there is TRAFFIC. *In order to get to the office, or to church, I have to get the bus to the place of my recent head injury. So, before I even start relating to the people, I have to negotiate the triggers of the physical trauma.*

The last chapter of Job is instructive here. The book has spent forty chapters on Job's reconnection with God and with himself: now **God helps Job to reconnect to others**. Having faced himself and his troubles in his meeting with God, he is not just left to sort out his relationships with comforters, friends and family, and to re-establish his business. God does it for him.

- God speaks to the comforters, and vindicates Job.
- He sends the comforters to Job, rather than making Job take the difficult step of confronting them.
- He gives Job an important task, and then honors it.
- He restores what has been lost.

I shall always be grateful for the people who helped my father to make connections in the UK, and who were, for us, the extended family that we would not otherwise have had.

The book of Job has a happy ending in this life – the happiest ending that the writer could imagine at that stage in history. But I do not think that reconnection was finished with the restoration of Job's fortunes. The final stage was the writing of the story, leaving a public record for all to see. This final stage is important in that it affirms Job's being and the value of his experience. The memory matters. It is also the way in which future generations, like us, can receive its blessing: the passing on of the story gives it a significance for all time which makes the whole experience worthwhile.

Celebrating Survival

> Then Moses said to the people, "Remember this day in which you came out from Egypt, out of the house of slavery, for by a strong hand the LORD brought you out from this place." (Exod 13:3)

A key to recovery from trauma is recognition that you have survived, and that survival is good. Both of these can be problematic for those who suffer "survivor guilt." The Bible's celebrations of survival can be of great help here.

I have found myself singing, "I'm alive, I'm alive, I'm alive for evermore – Jesus is risen from the dead!" and it's some years since I concluded that the single most significant theological insight on the Holocaust is that the "final solution" failed – and we are here to prove it.

At the heart of Christian identity is the celebration of the resurrection, which is not only Jesus's survival of crucifixion but also the proof that his trauma was eternally worthwhile. Revelation rings with the assurance that Jesus was dead, but is alive for evermore (1:18). The resurrection offers the believer personal assurance of eternal survival, even if the horror of "it happening again" should occur.

At the heart of Jewish identity is the celebration of the Passover, which is not only the history of the formation of a people, but also a celebration of survival and migration. The very first thing Moses is recorded as saying to the Israelites after they leave Egypt is "Remember this day." They are still in a state of extreme danger – more than 600,000 people in the desert, with limited provisions (Exod 12:39), and Pharaoh is about to send his troops after them; but Moses stops to tell them, "Remember this day." He adds an educational program for coming generations (Exod 13:8, 9, 14, 16). Remembrance, it seems, takes priority over provision and even escape for flourishing after survival. Remembrance of what? Of *this* day – the day of freedom, and not the centuries of bondage. Of course, the Passover festival continues to recount the trauma, but, for the long term, the identity that is being established prioritizes survival over trauma: "We were slaves . . . this is what we suffered . . . but God brought us out."

A second biblical festival, Purim also celebrates the survival of a migrant people, this time of a minority threatened with violent extinction.[16] If we may stray outside the Bible, we might add Hanukkah, with its dimension of survival in the face of a political and cultural domination that threatened worship.[17] These three festivals ritualize the regular processing of communal traumatic memories, giving them meaning and enabling the community to place them in the past without losing them, thus allowing them to form identity in a positive manner.

This suggests to me that Scripture is teaching us to transform memories of trauma into celebrations of survival.

Iconic for me personally is Holocaust Memorial Day – 27 January – which happens to be my birthday. I have always tried to avoid the lugubrious media reminders of the horrors, which tend but to revive the agony, but can I make the day instead into a celebration of my, and our, existence? It is, after all, the anniversary of the liberation of Auschwitz.

Revelation makes me pause here and ask whether I am being too Jewish. It has no celebration of a particular people, but of all peoples together around the throne of God. Perhaps the US's "melting pot" model is nearer to this than the UK's "salad bowl" which celebrates ethnic distinction. But the gathered nations around the throne still have their languages, and the Americans are a gathering of migrant peoples, many with traumatic histories. They are liberated slaves, escapees from threatened destruction and political oppression . . . all with a history of survival to celebrate.

But peoples come and go. Does the history of peoples really matter in eternal terms? If, as I believe, Israel is an icon of humanity, the answer has to be "Yes." God chose to work through a family and a people rather than through, say, a series of prophets. Israel is special, and not all peoples have four thousand years of memories to celebrate, but all have something they have survived.

Journeying On

"The structure lacked overall cohesion, making it difficult to discern meaningful connections between her story, the biblical narrative, and the overall theme of trauma recovery. There were also difficulties in terms of narrative distance/

16. Purim celebrates the defeat of Haman's plot to destroy the Jews at the time of King Ahasuerus (see Esth 3–9).

17. Hanukkah, sometimes called "The Festival of Lights," marks the rededication of the temple after its desecration by Antiochus Epiphanes and its liberation by the Maccabees (165 BC). It is mentioned in John 10:22.

stance (where Glaser was in relation to the events she was tracing) and narrative time (where we were located along the arc of Glaser's recovery journey)" – so commented one reader of this paper. I take this as a huge compliment: the paper has effectively communicated from inside a traumatized mind, difficult though that may be for the reader. The experience of trauma is one of a world which has lost cohesion, and where nothing feels connected. And I am not ready to tell my story even to myself as a single coherent narrative. It does not matter if the reader does not know exactly where the reflections fit with the journey, or if there is no discernible arc of "recovery." In fact, I no longer think of this as "recovery," but as an onward journey into the unknown. Some aspects of PTSD can be overcome, but one does not get traumatized and then recover in the sense of returning to an untraumatized state. Rather, one learns to incorporate the trauma (and other traumas) into one's whole life journey. This section reflects on the decade following the writing of the previous sections: it was written as I was going through the Psalm 139 journey herein described.

"Reconnection is hard, because it is a re-introduction of oneself to the world, and the self has been through disconnection and fragmentation," I wrote a decade ago (see above). Reconnection has been harder than I had ever imagined, and the disconnection and fragmentation was much greater than my fragmented being could have thought. It was not, as everyone seemed to think, my head injury that was at the root of my difficulties in absorbing information, in thinking coherently, in performing complex tasks and in keeping a focus on what was going on around me: it was what my recent therapist called "dissociation."

I used to describe my head injury as having upset the filing cabinet of my mind. I knew that everything was there, but I couldn't find things, and no longer knew how they related to each other. I could do one task at a time, but not two, so I had to break complex tasks down and do one simple task at a time. For example, making a cup of tea used to be one task, but it was too complex to face. So I broke it down: first, boil the water. Still too complex: first, fill the kettle. Still too complex: first, take the kettle to the tap. Still too complex: first, pick up the kettle. Yes! I can do that! And so on . . . Gradually, things began to join up as I re-learned how to function.

My understanding now is that my coping strategy had broken down. The strategy was the common one of splitting life into "copeable" pieces. In particular, if you can't cope with the loss, you split off the present from the past, so that you don't have to face the difference between life before and after the traumatic event. If it's too much to cope with life at home and life at school, you switch home off when you go to school, and you switch school off when you go home. And so on. It was done unconsciously, and it seemed to work very well for four decades, but then, suddenly, it was stretched to breaking point, and everything shattered. I couldn't cope with anything. Even when the initial acute stage eased, I was regularly switching out of the present into a dream (or, more likely, nightmare) state and generally living in a state of being not quite in contact with present reality. The journey has been one of trying to put my life back together. It was six years after writing the initial paper that the "dissociation" was identified, and it took eighteen months of therapy before I woke up one morning and thought, "The world suddenly feels real again."

What do I do with this biblically? Therapy has helped me to identify what has been going on, and processing some of the unbearable realities which caused the underlying splitting has greatly eased the fragmentation. But the journey towards wholeness – towards being able to live with myself as a single being – is a long one, and I wonder whether any of us reaches the destination in this life. How can the Bible guide me on the way?

My first year's reflections have continued to feed my thinking and to undergird my relationships with God and with others, and they will continue to do so. God's good control as seen in Job and Revelation has been my lifeline, and knowing that he sees and loves and can cope with all the parts of my broken being is an essential foundation. The pain of God in Genesis 6:6 has become an organizing center for much of my biblical theology,[18] and it continues to give meaning to every step of the way. God alone has been my safe place through intensive and demanding trauma therapy, and I know that it is he who is the place where my fragments can safely be united.

But what in the Bible can help me to understand this fragmentation? Characters like King Saul and the man possessed by "Legion" might be seen as "fragmented," and as indicating the potential for damage to both others and the self. It is instructive to study Saul's deterioration as he refuses to repent, and encouraging to see the possessed man returned to himself and sitting at Jesus's feet, but they are specific cases and hence of limited application.[19] I want to focus here on a resource that addresses something which, I think, underlies the fragmentation.

---

18. It is a key idea throughout my (with Hannah Kay) *Thinking Biblically about Islam: Genesis, Transfiguration, Transformation* (Carlisle: Langham, 2016).

19. In particular, both have elements of demonic involvement: although I acknowledge the need to be aware of possible demonic dimensions, it can be destructive to approach the very human phenomenon of Post-Traumatic Stress Disorder on that basis.

Psalm 139: No Escape!

I identified Psalm 139 as a key resource by re-reading Job with my "dissociation" questions in mind. What immediately resonated was the passionate desire to escape – from the very existence of self and from God's omnipresent and heavy hand. The explosion of words in Job 3 is not so much a desire for death as a rebellion against existence. Death ends life: it does not end existence. Job's anguish is not only that he was born, but that he was even conceived (Job 3:3–10) – he is cursing his very being. Only then does he go on to wishing that he had not been born, and then – seeing that he was born – that he could die. The anguish of not being able to escape from God is expressed in Job's second complaint (chs. 6 and 7). Job 6:8–9 expresses the terrifying prayer that God would "crush me . . . let loose his hand and cut me off"; 7:11–21 complains about what God is doing, and pleads, "leave me alone!" (7:16). Job eventually proceeds from this to complaint, to demanding justice, to longing to meet God and to actual encounter with him, but the expression of the desire to escape is the essential starting point.

I have described origins of trauma as situations of danger and helplessness: another way of saying this is that there are unbearable places which allow no escape. The "splitting" strategy can then be seen as an (unconscious) attempt to escape from an unbearable situation by mentally cutting off part of my existence. What I see reflected in Job is a deep refusal to accept part of my being, together with a longing to rewrite my life – to escape from the reality of what is happening or what has happened – which is, in the final analysis, a longing to escape from something which God has permitted, from the idea that God is in control, and even (and this is frightening if God is in fact the only safe place) from God himself.

So here I read Psalm 139 with both Job's predicament and my own in mind.[20] This affirms a reading of verses 1–12 as describing an oppressive rather than a peaceful setting for the psalm; and there is evidence for this reading within the psalm. The most obvious evidence is the prayer against "the wicked" in verses 19–22: why should the psalmist be praying in this way if he is not being oppressed by these wicked people? There is also evidence in the language[21] of verses 1–12: the word translated by the ESV and the NIV as

20. There are many parallels to Job in Ps 139. See N. B. Albright, "Was David Familiar with the Book of Job: The Enigma of Psalm 139," *Edge Induced Cohesion* (blog), 10 August 2011, https://edgeinducedcohesion.blog/2011/08/10/was-david-familiar-with-the-book-of-job-the-enigma-of-psalm-139/.

21. I am indebted to my colleague, Danny Crowther, for insights into the Hebrew of Ps 139.

"you hem me in" in verse 5 (*tsartānī*) is most often used to describe siege or even enmity. The picture is not, then, the assuring presence and guidance of Psalm 23, but of God as the enemy from whom there is no escape. Yet, just as Job moves from wanting to escape God to wanting to meet him, so the psalmist will move from describing God's unsettling searching, oppressive knowledge and intrusive leading to praying that God will further search him, know him and lead him (vv. 23–24). What enables the journey?

He Recognizes That There Is No Escape

The psalmist, like Job, sees his situation as being not only known by God but also sent by God: it does not matter what he does or where he goes, or even if he seeks death (v. 8) or oblivion (v. 11), God will be there. Gerard Manley Hopkins, struggling with despair,[22] declares his resolve to "not choose not to be": this psalm tells us that there is no option "not to be." Even suicide will not help. One cannot escape if God is the besieger.

I could not have made this step a decade ago, as I did not realize that I was trying to escape. The mere recognition that this is going on begins a journey towards accepting that there are some things which are inescapable, and hence to accepting the reality of those things and to dealing with them. The psalm takes us further: albeit painfully, it gives us words to acknowledge that God knows all the inescapable fragments of our beings – even those of which we are ourselves unconscious because we are in such refusal of their existence.

He Accepts His Created Body

Not only does God besiege the psalmist: it is God who is responsible for his very existence. Verse 13 states the fact: God made him as a single being, "knit together" in his mother's womb; and God owns his inner being.[23] This is of key importance. However many fragments there may be in my mind, there is one nonnegotiable and inescapable reality which unites them: my body. Whether or not I can face it, the fact is that there is continuity between Ida-before-the-trauma, Ida-during-the-trauma and Ida-after-the-trauma because there is continuity in the one body of one Ida. Perhaps that is why Job was so rebellious about his existence: he objected to being trapped in his body. But, for the psalmist, the acknowledgment of his body as a nonnegotiable creation is a turning point. He can now deliberately accept the necessity of existence and thank God for the very thing that he sought to escape: his created being.

22. In the poem "Carrion Comfort" (1885–1887).

23. Literally, his kidneys.

He Acknowledges That God's Knowledge Is Beyond His Understanding

The psalmist has sung of God's knowledge, which is just too much for him (v. 6). Now, here is something that he does know: that God's work is not only fearful but also wonderful (v. 14). He returns to his theme of God's knowledge, and even to God's ordering of his life (vv. 15–16), but he is now positive. God's thoughts are "precious,"[24] and they are more numerous than he can imagine (vv. 17–18). An implication is that God knows something bigger than the trauma: that, in God's larger perspective, even the bits of his existence from which the psalmist wants to escape can join together for good purposes.

And so he comes to the end of his escape attempt: he "awakes," and realizes that he has not escaped (v. 19). It is not that God is still chasing him, but that he is still with God; and the subsequent verses affirm that this is a good thing. We are not so wrong to go back and read the first part of the psalm as a celebration of God's presence, and even a hymn of thankfulness that he was unable to escape.

> *"Awakening" is a helpful metaphor for emerging from dissociation. It can feel like moving out of a nightmare state into contact with the present, and the two states can be as different and as disconnected as sleeping and waking.*

He Subjects His Anger to God's Anger

The "awakening" takes the psalmist back to his situation, but with a difference. If, as I am suggesting, he began with a Job-like rejection of his own existence, he has now accepted his existence and is turning to face the external problem: that of the evil in the world, and of the people who perpetrate it. We might say that, instead of directing his anger at himself and then at God, he is directing it at the people who caused his problems.

We could pause here to reflect on the importance of appropriate direction of anger; but I want, rather, to draw three observations from the psalm.

First, the psalmist does not speak here in terms of anger but in terms of hatred, and he describes his hatred as "perfect" (KJV) or "complete" (ESV) (v. 22). The Hebrew root is *klh*, and denotes completion, fulfillment or finishing. The NIV translates, "I have nothing but hatred for them." There is, of course, a question here about how this sort of hatred might relate to God's love for all and desire to save all; but there is also something important about a discerning

24. NIV and ESV. The literal meaning is "expensive."

anger which is able first to see evil for what it is, and then to move towards a complete hatred of that evil.

Second, the psalmist recognizes that the evil directed against him is also directed against God. While he was "asleep," he had thought that God was his enemy. Now that he is "awake," he can see that God is good, and that whoever perpetrates evil against human beings is also attacking God.

Third, the psalmist puts dealing with evil into God's hands. For himself, he dismisses the evil people: "Away from me, you bloodthirsty men!" (v. 19). It is for God to punish them. Perhaps, we may speculate, the psalmist himself and those of us who use his words may eventually be able to pray for God to have mercy on the enemies, to bring them to repentance and to save them; but the first step is recognizing that God is the judge, and that God's hatred of evil is purer and more complete than ours can ever be.

> *I find myself worshiping God for his holy and magnificent anger. If I hate evil, how much more does he? If I am angry at the causes of my trauma, how much more is he? His huge and righteous anger burns up my puny anger: his omnipotent and wise hatred can deal with the evil that angers me, and can also purify me to my inmost being.*

He Comes to See That God Is the Safe Place

And so, finally, the psalmist turns back to God with confidence, and asks him to continue the work of searching and knowing which he found so difficult (v. 24; cf. v. 1). In particular, he wants God to seek out any "grievous way" in him (v. 25, ESV; cf. NIV, "offensive"). The word translated "grievous" has the same root as the word describing God's pain in Genesis 6:6. God's showing him the painful/sorrowful way inside him is then linked to God's leading him into the "everlasting" way. It seems that he has understood that he can safely ask God to do this, because God is the one who is able to show him himself, and to lead him on from there to the place of eternal safety.

> *Lord, are there still fragments of my being which I need to face? Show me! Lead me! I am so glad that you made me and that you know them all!*

The Turning Point: Worship

What turns the psalmist from his desire to escape to his desire for God? The pivot is the first word of verse 14, which stands by itself in the traditional Hebrew text: "I praise you/give thanks to you."

And so we return to the theme of worship. I have said that we cannot tell, from the book of Job, the tone of the voice from the whirlwind; but we do know that Job was satisfied and worshiped. Revelation makes things much clearer: from the first vision of Jesus, through the worship around the throne, and to the final vision of heaven, we see the wounded and risen Messiah at the heart of God. It is he who is the first revelation to the exiled John, and who says, "Do not be afraid" and "I know . . . I know . . . I know . . . I know . . . I know . . . I know . . . I know" (1:17; 2:2, 9, 13, 19; 3:1, 8, 15). It is he, who is both missionary and survivor, who is in control (1:5).

The traumatized are invited, then, to worship. It is not enough to know that God is in control: we are invited to be glad that he is in control, to address him, to enter into relationship with him. Like Job, we can acknowledge God's greatness and our smallness as we respond to his coming to us. Like John, we can fall down before the crucified one. As we worship, we will find that worship is actually something needed for recovery, because we need to reconnect to God in order to reconnect to ourselves and to the world. As I recognize the different fragments in myself, I can learn to direct each one to God: unifying their direction develops a unity of being, and can be the route towards enabling the parts to be reconciled to one another rather than warring with one another.

Further, worship puts life into perspective: it enables us to take the focus off the traumatized self, and to focus on the wounded Messiah.[25] As we face our ongoing vulnerability and the fact that we will never be the same again, we recognize the scars that remained after the resurrection and into heaven. Those scars tell us that Jesus's trauma accomplished something – that he is now our Safe Place.

And that brings us back to mission. Why was the Messiah wounded? To ransom not only us, but also people from every tribe and language and people and nation (Rev 5:9). It is this that provokes the worship of heaven. Let us, then, end with the instructions given by the Master as he faced his own coming trauma, and prepared his disciples for theirs.

Matthew 24 gives the basics:

- Watch out; be ready (vv. 4, 42–44)
- Don't be alarmed (v. 6)
- Keep loving (v. 12)
- Stand firm (v. 13)
- Don't be deceived (vv. 4, 23–26)

---

25. The LXX uses the verb *traumatizo* in its translation of Isa 53:5: "He was *wounded* for our transgressions."

- At the right time, flee (vv. 16–18)
- Pray (v. 20)

Expect traumatic events, says our Lord. Be ready for them, so that you can take your part in God's mission to his world of pain. If we face traumatic events in this way, will we be spared the wounding? Perhaps not, but we can be sure of our place in the kingdom of God. "But not a hair of your head will perish. By your endurance you will gain your lives" (Luke 21:18–19).

Postlude: Towards an Ordered World

I had not realized how deeply I have been seeking for order throughout this PTSD experience. During the final editing of this paper, I have also been working on a commentary on Genesis 1:1 – 2:3. How much I need this vision of the beautiful ordering of God's creation, with its hope of the final new creation! No need to edit God's perfect work!

Genesis 1 has its own beautiful ordering, with its repeated patterns of words and seven-fold groupings.[26] *The perfect number seven is emphasizing the focus on the seventh day. We began with God and the* tohu wa bohu – *the formless chaos – of 1:2, and we finish with God and the blessing and holiness of his completed, organized creation. We imagine God contemplating his work, and the eternal Wisdom rejoicing (Prov 8:30–31). But look! Wisdom is rejoicing not only over what we might term "natural beauty," but also over the children of Adam who inhabit it. The apex of God's order is humanity. And we are called, sabbath by sabbath, to pause, to contemplate that first perfect creation, and to anticipate the coming perfect new creation through living in the way of the wounded and risen Wisdom of God.*

Lord, has your Spirit been hovering over the tohu wa bohu*of my being right from its beginning? And over the* tohu wa bohu *we see and experience across your world? Are you rejoicing in your re-ordering of my being? Help us all to rejoice with you as we walk together towards the new sabbath of the new heavens and the new earth!*

Bibliography

Albright, N. B. "Was David Familiar with the Book of Job: The Enigma of Psalm 139." *Edge Induced Cohesion* (blog), 10 August 2011. https://edgeinducedcohesion.

---

26. For an inspiring literary analysis of Genesis 1:1 – 2:3, see Gordon Wenham's *Rethinking Genesis 1–11: Gateway to the Bible* (Eugene, OR: Cascade Books, 2015), ch. 1.

blog/2011/08/10/was-david-familiar-with-the-book-of-job-the-enigma-of-psalm-139/.

Glaser, Ida. "We Sat Down and Wept: Biblical Resources for Conflict Situations," in *The Round Table: The Commonwealth Journal of International Affairs* 382 (2005): 641–652.

Glaser, Ida, with Hannah Kay. *Thinking Biblically about Islam: Genesis, Transfiguration, Transformation*. Carlisle: Langham, 2016.

Heller, Laurence, and Diane Heller. *Crash Course: Auto Accident Recovery Breakthrough*. Berkeley, CA: North Atlantic Books, 2001.

Herman, Judith. *Trauma and Recovery: The Aftermath of Violence – from Domestic Abuse to Political Terror*. New York: Basic Books, 1992.

Shapiro, Francine, and Margot Silk. *EMDR: The Breakthrough Therapy for Overcoming Anxiety, Stress and Trauma*. New York: Basic Books, 1997.

Spencer, Stephen, ed., *Mission and Migration: Papers Read at the Biennial Conference of the British and Irish Association for Mission Studies at Westminster College, Cambridge, 2nd–5th July 2007*. Sheffield: Cliff College, 2008.

Wenham, Gordon. *Genesis 1–15*. Waco, TX: Word Books, 1987.

———. *Rethinking Genesis 1–11: Gateway to the Bible*. Eugene, OR: Cascade Books, 2015.

5

Heeding Matthew's Voice in the Conflicts and Civil Wars in the DRC

Dr Isaac K. Mbabazi

Background

This article has emerged from my personal experience as a Congolese from Bunia, the headquarters of the Ituri Province, in the northeastern Congo. Ituri is one of the Congolese regions torn severely by conflicts and civil wars, and I am writing this article as a victim of these atrocities.

The political crisis in the Congo, which began in 1997, has given rise to an ethnic conflict, particularly between two ethnic groups: the Hemas (a minority ethnic group formed essentially, but not exclusively, of shepherds) and the Lendus (a majority ethnic group formed essentially, but not exclusively, of cultivators). My family belongs to one of these two groups. On both sides, the political turmoil and ethnic conflict has caused inestimable losses of both human lives and property damage.

The situation reached its climax on 6 March 2003 when a militia band entered the town of Bunia. This eruption quickly turned to a manhunt, and many people were killed. My family and I narrowly escaped as others were killed and houses and shops were systematically looted and burned down. Our house and all our belongings were plundered and wrecked. Only my books, which I kept in my office on the seminary campus, were spared.

Fortunately, just a day before the tragedy, I had evacuated my family, taking refuge on the seminary campus. We carried with us only our Bibles, certificates, and a few small belongings. Later, I learned that the assailants came several times to my house, looking for me by my name. They wanted to kill me and my family because we belong to the rival tribe.

When I consider the evil that people did to one another during those days, tears run from my eyes. The following passage from Nahum 1:7 came to me at that time and was a tremendous consolation:

> The LORD is good,
> a stronghold in a day of trouble;
> he protects those who take refuge in him,
> even in a rushing flood. (NRSV)

This promise of the Lord was true for us on 6 March, for as bullets resounded throughout the town, and assailants entered houses one after another, we were safe in hiding on the seminary campus. This promise was also true on 21 March 2003, when a seminary staff member and her mother were killed on the seminary campus by the same militia group. We had left one hiding place on the campus for another; and so, remained safe.

As the situation worsened, we took refuge in Kampala, Uganda, which at that time was the only safe place to be for the survivors from one of the above-mentioned ethnic groups.

The depth of trauma that my family and I went through caused us to ask God to show us clearly what he had in store for us. As a result, God opened doors for us to further our studies in Kenya, an English speaking country, which had been one of my dreams. Indeed, God surprised us! My wife and I were admitted to Nairobi Evangelical Graduate School of Theology (NEGST), currently Africa International University (AIU), to complete a diploma and masters degree, respectively. More than this, by grace, God provided for all our needs as family.

In spite of the tragedy our family has been through, we continue to give glory to God, for we know and believe firmly that in him and him alone, we can be freed from bitterness against those who wronged us. We remember what Paul says in Romans about the action that God takes in such situations: "Vengeance is mine, I will repay, says the Lord" (12:19 NRSV).

Conflicts and Civil Wars in the DRC

A recent report described Africa as "a major site for civil violence in recent decades" and also recognized Africa as having "much at stake and much to offer for those who want to learn more about the barriers and pathways to conflict resolution and social reconstruction."[1] What has been said of Africa as a continent can also be said of the Democratic Republic of Congo (DRC), which has been at war for a generation. The country is facing many problems due to a succession of civil wars and armed revolutions. Until very recently, it has been at the center of what is called "Africa's world war." These wars and armed revolutions have claimed thousands of lives. Fighting has been fuelled by the country's vast mineral wealth, with all sides taking advantage of the anarchy to plunder natural resources.[2]

The war in eastern Congo to separate from the rest of the country is complex and confusing, with an intertwined web of actors pursuing a multiplicity of agendas. Over thirty armed groups have been identified in eastern Congo, where they operate with a dreadful impact on the people of that part of the country. Significant groups include: the Forces Démocratiques de Libération du Rwanda (FDLR), Maï Maï groups,[3] Raia Mutomboki, Local Defence Forces Busumba (LDF), Front de Défense du Congo (FDC), Mouvement Populaire d'Autodéfense (MPA), Allied Democratic Forces (ADF), Lord's Resistance Army (LRA), Alliance des Patriotes pour un Congo Libre et Souverain (APCLS), Forces de Resistance Patriotique en Ituri (FRPI) and Kata Katanga. An overview of the groups is provided by the Integrated Regional Information Networks (IRIN), a humanitarian news agency covering sub-Sarahan Africa.[4]

The first actual Congo civil war began when a regional coalition succeeded in overthrowing Mobutu Sese Seko and replaced him with Laurent-Désiré Kabila in 1997. Some foreign governments participated in supporting this regime change. In little more than a year, Kabila was accused by his former allies of assuming dictatorial power. As a result, the alliance that had formed to depose Mobutu began to split; while some backed the Kabila government, others supported the rebel groups based in the eastern part of the country. Separate from the war in the rest of the country, a smaller conflict between

---

1. J. Carpenter and N. Kooistra, *Engaging Africa: Prospects for Project Funding in Selected Fields* (Nagel Institute, 2015), 64.

2. O. Das, "Natural Resources, Conflict and Investment: Conflict Minerals in the Democratic Republic of Congo and the Challenges to Sustainable Investment," in *International Natural Resources Law, Investment and Sustainability*, ed. S. Alam, J. H. Bhuiyan and J. Razzaque. Routledge, 2017. Available at http://eprints.uwe.ac.uk/31423.

3. These include: Maï Maï Hilaire, Maï Maï Sheka, Maï Maï Kifuafua, Maï Maï Morgan, Maï Maï Simba, Maï Maï Yakutumba and Maï Maï Nyatura.

4. IRIN, "Armed Groups in Eastern DRC," 2013, np. http://www.irinnews.org/report/99037/briefing-armed-groups-eastern-drc. See also "The Networks of Eastern Congo's Two Most Powerful Armed Actors," http://enoughproject.org/files/CongoArmed Actors_Table_August2013.pdf.

two ethnic groups in the Ituri Province in northeastern Congo escalated into a violent war, a fact which has been well documented.[5]

The abundance of lucrative natural resources in the Ituri region ignited ethnic tensions and escalated the level of bloodshed. The consequence of these conflicts on the people of the northeastern Congo has been a terrible loss of human life. The nature of this violence escalates as follows: (1) a person kills a member of the family of a rival tribe; (2) the family members of the victim seek revenge by killing two people in the murderer's family; (3) the inhabitants of a village then burn a village belonging to people of the rival tribe; (4) the inhabitants of the victimized village burn more than a village.

Since October 2014, the rebel groups listed above have unleashed a wave of civilian massacres on Beni and its surroundings. More recently, on 13 August 2016, over fifty people were murdered in Beni, presumably by ADF-NALU rebels.[6] On 20 August 2016, there was a bloody conflict between the Yira and the Hutu communities in the Rutsuru.[7] These atrocities have claimed hundreds of civilian lives – more than seven hundred, according to the United Nations, and up to thirteen hundred, according to NGOs.

As can be seen, the Congolese have been experiencing unbearable atrocities and are hurting deeply. They have been wronged in every area of their lives, causing the spirit of retaliation to grow as a response to the violence, thereby creating a circle of violence. Sometimes the violent reactions to the atrocities are conducted without a system of justice or any degree of accountability. As Christians who have been offended, how should we respond in light of the wrongs we have suffered? How should perpetrators respond after we have hurt others? What is the gospel message for both sides? What is an appropriate Christian theological discourse?

---

5. Important works and reports include those by: (1) J. Pottier, "Roadblock Ethnography," *Africa* 76, no. 2 (2006): 151–179; (2) K. Drake, "Gold and Ethnic Conflict in the Ituri Region of the Democratic Republic of the Congo"; (3) H. Boshoff, "Tension in Ituri," *Institute for Security Studies* (2003): 1–9; (4) T. Heller, S. Krasner and J. McMillan, "A Trust Fund for Ituri," http://faculty- gsb.stanford.edu/mcmillan/personal_page/documents/ Ituri.pdf; (5) "Ituri: A Need for Protection, a Thirst for Justice," available at http://www.amnesty.org/en/library/asset/AFR62/032/2003/en/dom-AFR620322003en.pdf; (6) "The War within the War," available at http://www.hrw.org/reports/2002/drc/Congo 0602.pdf; (7) "Maintaining Momentum in the Congo," available at http://www.crisisgroup.org/home/index.cfm?id=1174.

6. ADF-NALU stands for Allied Democratic Forces-National Army for the Liberation of Uganda. It is a Ugandan-led Islamist rebel group operating northwest of the Rwenzori Mountains around the DRC's Beni Territory in North Kivu Province. It was founded in 1995. Available at http://www.irinnews.org/report/ 99037/briefing-armed-groups-eastern-drc.

7. Available at http://m.leparisien.fr/faits-divers/noel-sanglant-au-congo-22-civils-massacres-au-nord-kivu-25-12-2016-6494250.php.

The Gospel Message

As a country torn by conflicts, violence and civil wars, forgiveness and reconciliation have become common themes in preaching and teaching in eastern Congo. However, the Christian theological discourse about forgiveness and reconciliation in a contemporary Congolese context is poor because it has failed to heed Matthew's voice on the subject. Yet these texts, with their primary focus on the responsibility of the offended person towards the offender, can greatly enrich this theological discourse. A discourse well informed by Matthew's voice will seek to highlight the following: (1) promote a culture of non-retaliation; (2) distinguish between the responsibility of the offender and the offended; (3) not insist on reparation as a prerequisite for forgiveness; (4) consider the place of repentance in a forgiveness and reconciliation praxis; (5) consider the place of justice in a forgiveness and reconciliation praxis; (6) identify motivations underlying forgiveness. Each of these themes will be discussed more fully below.

The words "forgiveness" and "reconciliation" are used loosely nowadays and bear a range of overlapping meanings.[8] For our purposes, "forgiveness" means giving up or letting go of resentment for an injury, wrongdoing, or failure to meet one's obligation. When we forgive, we move past someone else's transgression or failure by ceasing to harbour bitterness and by refraining from taking revenge. The ultimate aim is to restore a disrupted or a broken relationship between a wrongdoer and a wronged person. Forgiveness is offered by the victims, who recognize that they have been wronged but do not hold to account those who have wronged them. Reconciliation "is part of a process that moves those suffering the disabling consequences of possibly violent conflict, harm, or injustice towards a situation that delivers them to live together sustainably."[9] Quite clearly, forgiveness and reconciliation have something in common: both seek to put right relationships that have gone wrong; both resist holding onto grudges; both move away from being trapped in the past.

Promoting a Culture of Non-retaliation

Matthew 5:39 contains one of the key commandments that Jesus proclaimed in the Sermon of the Mount: "But I say to you, Do not resist an evildoer. But

8. A. Bash, "Forgiveness, Reconciliation and Spirituality: A Theological Perspective," *Journal for the Study of Spirituality* 4, no. 1 (2014): 58.

9. J. Haers et al., eds., *Reconciliation: Empowering Grace* (London: SCM Press, 2013), 7–8.

if anyone strikes you on the right cheek, turn the other also" (NRSV). This commandment is also reflected in Romans 12:17–21: "Repay not anyone evil for evil." Similar injunctions appear in 1 Thessalonians 5:15[10] and 1 Peter 3:9.[11] R. Appressyan states that "the inner ethical meaning of this commandment and its immediate context both in the Sermon on the Mount (albeit implicitly) and in the Apostles (especially Paul), show its direct connection with the commandment of love, and are thus to a large extent explained by it."[12] Indeed, Matthew links the idea of non-retaliation to loving enemies and peacemaking, thereby contrasting the *lex talionis*[13] principle (Matt 5:21, 38)[14] with the love commandment, which follows. We see this in verses 38–48 (NRSV):

> You have heard that it was said, "An eye for an eye and a tooth for a tooth." But I say to you, do not resist an evildoer. But if anyone strikes you on the right cheek, turn the other also; and if anyone wants to sue you and take your coat, give your cloak as well; and if anyone forces you to go one mile, go also the second mile. Give to everyone who begs from you, and do not refuse anyone who wants to borrow from you.
>
> You have heard that it was said, "You shall love your neighbor and hate your enemy." But I say to you, love your enemies and pray for those who persecute you, so that you may be children of your Father in heaven; for he makes his sun to rise on the evil and on the good, and sends rain on the righteous and on the unrighteous. For if you love those who love you, what reward do you have? Do not even the tax collectors do the same? And if you greet only your brothers and sisters, what more are you doing than others? Do not even the Gentiles do the same? Be perfect, therefore, as your heavenly Father is perfect.

This passage calls hearers to display a radical attitude towards adversaries and enemies, an attitude that does not respond with retaliation or hatred.

---

10. "See that none of you repays evil for evil" (NRSV).

11. ". . . do not repay evil for evil or abuse for abuse" (NRSV).

12. R. G. Appressyan, "'Revenge Is Mine, I Will Repay,'" *Russian Studies in Philosophy* 48, no. 2 (2009): 9.

13. This Latin term means "law of retaliation" and describes the principle that a punishment should correspond to an offense (i.e., an eye for an eye, a tooth for a tooth).

14. "You have heard that the ancients were told, 'You shall not commit murder' and 'Whoever commits murder shall be liable to the court'" (v. 21). "You have heard that it was said, 'An eye for an eye, and a tooth for a tooth'" (v. 38).

The language of loving enemies in verses 43–48 is used to describe both divine-human and interpersonal relationships. The divine-human relationship is in the background, for the way that the disciples are instructed to relate to (or deal with) one another is supposed to emulate how God deals with both the righteous and unrighteous. By loving enemies, Jesus's disciples reflect the character of God himself, who shows his gracious love and mercy to both the righteous and unrighteous alike (v. 45b). This notion was familiar in the Christian tradition of the first century. Christians are likewise called to love others, including their enemies, just as God loves the righteous as well as the unrighteous; they are called to be merciful as God is merciful, perfect as God is perfect. Although God is God and humans are humans,[15] Matthew suggests that God's gracious love and mercy provide the paradigm for how the Christian community is to understand its vocation as members of the kingdom: they are to imitate God, the heavenly father and king. Thus loving one's enemies and being perfect are aspects of *imitatio Dei.*

Clearly, the call of Matthew 5:39 is to effect love of enemies both within and outside Matthew's community. Matthew 7:12 also alludes to this precept, calling the disciples to reciprocity in dealing with and relating to one another: "In everything you do to others as you would have them do to you; for this is the law and the prophets." This passage connects with Matthew 5:17, "Do not think that I have come to abolish the Law or the Prophets; I have not come to abolish but to fulfill," which introduces a major section of the discourse that outlines the relationships of the disciples with others.

Matthew's teaching takes Jewish teaching on forgiveness and reconciliation a bit further. Although the law of retribution, which was legislated by the conditions described in the Pentateuch,[16] was given to Jewish people, there are several cases of interpersonal forgiveness in Jewish Scriptures. The three examples below may suffice to illustrate this.

First, Genesis 50:15–21 gives an account of an offender/offenders fearing possible revenge from his/their victim for a wrong done in the past. In the story, we note the initiative of the offenders imploring forgiveness from the victim, which can be regarded as an act of repentance.

The text appears in the broader context of relational tension between Joseph and his brothers because of their unfair treatment of him in the past, a tension that is finally resolved. In actual fact, Joseph was ready to be reconciled

15. Cf. Matt 19:26: "But Jesus looked at them and said, 'For mortals it is impossible, but for God all things are possible.'"

16. Cf. Exod 21:24; Lev 24:20; Deut 19:21.

with his brothers, which is clear from his deeds and words in Genesis 45. But his brothers never asked for forgiveness, and so "their feelings of guilt had continued to haunt them."[17] Once their father Jacob dies, they become anxious that their past treatment of Joseph will come back to trouble them. To use G. J. Wenham's words, "they are gripped by fear that all Joseph had done [Gen 45] was motivated by affection for Jacob, not out of real love for them."[18] They decide to plead for forgiveness, but are so worried that they put words into their recently deceased father's mouth, reporting that he instructed Joseph to forgive them. As Reimer correctly notes, "the reader does not have certain knowledge about the truth of this claim, but one is hesitant to accept it at face value."[19] It is pertinent to note that the ultimate aim of their appeal is to avoid potential revenge by Joseph.

Second, 1 Samuel 25:24–28 provides another clear example from Jewish literature for seeking and granting forgiveness. The text gives an account of a tension between David and Nabal, a rich and harsh landowner with a large flock of sheep, who lived near the wilderness region where David and four hundred soldiers were encamped after David spared Saul's life in the cave of Engedi.[20] David was desperately in need of food for his hungry band, and so he sent some men to Nabal to ask for food. Nabal refused, insulting David and his father, and refused to acknowledge the protection that David and his men had offered to Nabal's shepherds (1 Sam 25:14–17). When Abigail was informed of her husband's hostility towards David, she took the risk of trying to solve the matter herself. Verses 26–28 describe the tactics she employed: she sent ahead gifts, abased herself at David's feet and spoke of her servanthood with firmness, asking him to forgive her trespass. But her *words,* "Please take away the trespass of your maidservant" (v. 28), only ask for forgiveness for her own actions. Thus she implicitly acknowledged that she was unwillingly and unwittingly involved in her husband's insult. As it stands in the text, the narrated *action* by Abigail seeks to avert vengeance; the *words* she used seem to refer only to her own action.

---

17. G. J. Wenham, *Genesis*, ed. David A. Hubbard et al., WBC 2 (Nashville: Thomas Nelson, 1994), 489.

18. Wenham, *Genesis*, 489.

19. D. J. Reimer, "Stories of Forgiveness," in *Reflection and Refraction: Studies in Biblical Historiography in Honour of A. Graeme Auld*, ed. Robert Rezetko, Timothy H. Lim and W. Brian Aucker (Leiden: Brill, 2007), 369; see also M. Sternberg, *The Poetics of Biblical Narrative*, Indiana Studies in Biblical Literature (Bloomington: Indiana University Press, 1987), 379.

20. For the broader context of this story, see 1 Samuel 24–25.

With her wisdom, Abigail effectively secured forgiveness for Nabal's behavior and also prevented David from what J. P. Fokkelman describes as "acting on his destructive impulse"[21] and the discredit of "guilt from shedding blood—no matter how justified it might seem to be in this case."[22] But as R. W. Klein also notices, "[T]he real protector of the future king's integrity is Yahweh himself"[23] – not Abigail. In this circumstance, Abigail asked for her trespass to be forgiven – for an end to her wrong – by appealing to David's mercy.

Third, the account in Josephus's *War* describes Abraham's response towards Pharaoh's offense for carrying off Sarah. Abraham chose to handle this situation by refraining from retaliation. He could have taken revenge on the ravisher, given both the number and quality of the people who were with him, but he left the matter with God, relying on God's sovereign power and faithfulness to avenge:

> In old times there was one . . . king of Egypt, who was also called Pharaoh; he came with a prodigious army of soldiers, and seized queen Sarah . . . What did Abraham . . . then do? Did he defend himself from this injurious person by war, although he had three hundred and eighteen captains under him, and an immense army under each of them? Indeed, he deemed them to be no number at all without God's assistance, and only spread out his hands towards this holy place, . . . and reckoned upon him as upon his invincible supporter, instead of his own army. Was not our queen sent back, without any defilement to her husband, the very next evening?—While the king of Egypt fled away, . . . and he also trembled at those visions which he saw in the nightseason, and bestowed both silver and gold on the Hebrews . . . [24]

All three of these teachings on non-retaliation are echoed in Matthew's text,[25] and the passages that call for the love of enemies and peacemaking (Matt 5:43–48), mercy and forgiveness (Matt 5:7; 6:14–15; 18:23–35) and reconciliation (Matt 5:23–24; 18:15–17) should be read in this vein. In Jewish writings, God is sometimes revealed as the God who takes revenge over his

21. J. P. Fokkelman, *Narrative Art and Poetry in the Books of Samuel*, vol. 2, SSN 23 (Assen: Van Gorcum, 1986), 473.

22. R. W. Klein, *1 Samuel*, ed. David A. Hubbard, Glenn W. Barker and John D. W. Watts, WBC 10 (Waco: Word Books, 1983), 250.

23. Klein, *1 Samuel*, 250.

24. Josephus, *War*, 5.379–381.

25. Cf. Rom 12:17–21; Matt 7:12.

enemies and avenges his people. When the notion of vengeance applies to God, it has a positive connotation since God is holy, but it has a negative connotation when applied to humans. Human vengeance rarely achieves anything good and merely attempts to satisfy one's anger.[26]

Matthew's teaching on non-retaliation should be incorporated in the Congolese theological rhetoric of forgiveness and reconciliation. The Congolese victims of atrocities should be challenged and encouraged to eschew revenge. Nelson Mandela is probably the best African example on this point. Commenting on Mandela, Washington A. J. Okumu writes:

> After twenty-seven years of political incarceration – the longest-serving political prisoner in the world – he [Nelson Mandela] emerged unscathed and told his people to forgive their former white oppressors and instead fix their attention on the future: on building a new united nation. In spite of the devastating trauma of apartheid, Mandela chose the path of forgiveness and reconciliation rather than the policy of revenge and vindictiveness.[27]

This attitude is in line with the gospel message and is appropriate for all followers of Jesus. Whether wrongs are specified or unspecified, major or minor, or whether the offender repents or not, Matthew urges followers of Jesus to overcome their bitterness and be ready to forgive. As Okumu states, "bitterness, however justified, will just consume our souls and achieve nothing. We must, therefore, learn to forgive even if we don't forget."[28]

Identifying Responsibility of Offender and Offended

A twofold forgiveness pattern is evident in Matthew: first, there is the responsibility of the offender (*logion* in Greek) for seeking forgiveness; second, there is the responsibility of the offended person (*logia* in Greek) for granting forgiveness. In only *one* occurrence (Matt 5:23–25),[29] the former is in view. In the remaining seven occurrences, the latter is emphasized (Matt 6:12b; 6:14–15;

26. This notion has been well captured and aptly developed by Pontien Ndagijimana Batibuka in his "Laisser la vengeance à Dieu: la vérité de Romains 12, 19," *Mélanges de Science Religieuse* (2017): 31–46.

27. In the foreword of R. T. Kendall, *Total Forgiveness* (London: Hodder & Stoughton, 2001), xi.

28. Cf. Kendall, *Total Forgiveness*, xi.

29. And by implication in 6:12a.

18:12–14, 15[30]–17, 21, 33).[31] Clearly, the members of Matthew's community understood that it was the responsibility of the offended person to grant forgiveness to the offenders.

The fact that Matthew's Gospel gives more space to the responsibility of the offended person in forgiving (seven *logia*) than to the offender (one *logion*) suggests that Matthew is extremely concerned about his community members' reluctance to forgive and be reconciled with their fellow brethren. This fits nicely with the flow of thought in Matthew 18 (and beyond), which is concerned with the preservation of the community.[32] In Matthew 18, the members of this community are portrayed as children of the heavenly Father-King and outlines what their behavior should be as children of such a father.

The issues discussed in Matthew 18 may provide a window into discerning the composition of the community behind the gospel itself. It is possible to imagine that this community was composed of two categories of people with asymmetrical levels of spiritual maturity. The first category is comprised of "little ones" – those of "little faith" who need special care, "the least," the spiritually immature – who might show weakness in their relationships with other members of the community. This is supported by the use of language such as "little ones" and "children" that abounds in Matthew 18. It is also suggested through the exhortations in this chapter not to lead even "one" of the "little ones" astray (vv. 6, 10) and to go after the stray sheep (vv. 2–14).[33] The second category of members is comprised of those who are more spiritually mature, and they are exhorted to "become like children" (v. 3) and to "humble oneself like a child" (v. 4). They are also urged to carry greater duties, which include caring for the "little ones" who need special attention, welcoming "one such a child" (v. 5), making every effort not to lead "one of these little ones" to stumble (vv. 6, 10), going after them to be reconciled with them even if they

30. The textual problem that occurs in this verse is discussed in Isaac K. Mbabazi, *The Significance of Interpersonal Forgiveness in the Gospel of Matthew* (Eugene, OR: Pickwick, 2013), 51, n. 54, where I argued for the εἰς σὲ ("against you") reading because this phrase is attested in all old, important and credible text families, ranging from the Majority text to other codices and various traditions.

31. Note Matt 6:12b and the *protasis* in 6:14–15. In 18:12–14, this responsibility is embodied in the initiative of the shepherd to go after the straying sheep; in 18:15–17 through the initiative of the offended person to go several times after their offender for an eventual reconciliation; in 18:21 through Peter's proposal; in 18:33 through the lord's rebuke to his unmerciful debtor for their failure in showing mercy and granting forgiveness to his fellow slave.

32. The discussion over this issue is provided in Mbabazi, *Significance*, 41.

33. For a detailed discussion, see Mbabazi, 37–41.

are unrepentant (vv. 15–17) just as a shepherd would go after straying sheep (vv. 12–14), and being merciful and forgiving (vv. 21–35).[34]

These demands seem to be primarily – but not exclusively – addressed to the spiritually mature members of the community. (As members of the church and citizens of the kingdom, the spiritually immature are also meant to behave properly with other members of the community and outsiders.) But as Donahue notes, the parable of the lost sheep (vv. 12–14) immediately precedes the juridical approach to failure within the community (vv. 15–17), which shows that "however community discipline is to be applied, order within the community is to be measured against the claims of the weaker members for special care and assistance."[35] The initiative of going to one's offender three times with the aim of restoring them to the community[36] strongly suggests that the injured person understood their responsibility towards the other and was enacting the principle underlying the instruction.

This responsibility needs to be highlighted in the teaching and preaching of forgiveness and reconciliation in churches in the DRC and worldwide. As Christians who have been offended, we first need to understand ourselves as sinners who have been *forgiven*. According to Matthew 18, reluctance or failure to forgive by those who have experienced God's forgiveness and been initiated into God's kingdom is scandalous and virtually unthinkable, as portrayed in the parable of the king who wished to settle accounts with his slaves (vv. 23–33). Yet this virtually unthinkable scandal seems to have occurred within Matthew's church, as the prominence of the forgiveness theme in his gospel suggests. Likewise, a reluctance to forgive others seems to occur among Congolese Christians and Christians in all contexts. In the DRC, this raises the question: Is it possible to forgive people or communities that were actively involved or took part in an attempt to exterminate other people's villages or communities, whether or not the offenders seek forgiveness? Does it make sense to forgive somebody who has not repented, or is not ready to repent?

Regardless of the good reasons we may have to withhold forgiveness, the gospel of Matthew makes it clear that offended people should not focus on whether or not forgiveness makes sense, but on engaging in communal practices of forgiveness that reflect God's forgiving character (Matt 18:23–35; 5:7, 44–45, 48; 6:14; 9:13; 23:23). In situations of persistent abuse and intense violence, such as those observed in the DRC and other parts of the world, offended people

34. Mbabazi, 37–41.

35. J. R. Donahue, *The Gospel in Parable* (Minneapolis: Fortress, 1988), 73.

36. See also Peter's concern in Matt 18:21.

will need to reclaim the significance of loving their enemies (Matt 5:42–48) and renunciating violent revenge (Matt 5:38–41) as an indispensable feature of Christian forgiveness. L. G. Jones has commented that Christians should not confront this perplexing and troubling reality by failing to continue to insist on the precedence of God's forgiveness to our forgiveness and repentance. But if, and insofar as, people fail to respond to forgiveness with repentance, then perhaps the best that can be done is to acknowledge that they are enemies of the cross of Christ – but enemies whom we are nonetheless called to learn to love,[37] to pray for, feed and give something to drink (Rom 12:17–21). Miroslav Volf has suggested that repentance should not be regarded so much as a prerequisite of forgiveness; rather, repentance should be regarded as a result of forgiveness,[38] which should cause the unrepentant person to come to their senses. Based on the Matthean forgiveness teaching, any Christian theological rhetoric of forgiveness and reconciliation in its contemporary Congolese context should seek to distinguish clearly between the responsibilities of both parties involved in conflict and stress the responsibility of the offended party to forgive.

Reparation as a Prerequisite for Forgiveness

Another amazing insight from the gospel of Matthew is the Evangelist's silence on the demand for satisfaction or reparation as a prerequisite for forgiveness.

Rather than insisting on the demand for reparation as a prerequisite for forgiveness, Matthew insists on forgiving the offender (cf. Matt 6:12, 14–15; 18:32–35). He even underscores what will befall a person who is reluctant to forgive others. In terms of background, this teaching probably comes from Sirach 28:1–4 (NRSV), which reads:

> The vengeful person will face the Lord's vengeance,
> for he keeps a strict account of their sins.
> Forgive your neighbor the wrong they have done,
> and then your sins will be pardoned when you pray.
> Does anyone harbor anger against another
> and expect healing from the Lord?
> If one has no mercy toward another like themselves,
> can they then seek pardon for their own sins?

37. L. G. Jones, *Embodying Forgiveness* (Grand Rapids, MI: Eerdmans, 1995), 160.

38. M. Volf, "Forgiveness, Reconciliation, and Justice," *Millennium: Journal of International Studies* 29, no. 3 (2000): 875–876.

This Sirach text is the sole LXX Old Testament text where forgiving is explicitly shown as a condition for both seeking and receiving God's forgiveness. This text demands that we forgive, because of the inevitability of our inclination to evil, which makes our need to secure forgiveness constant. The co-text of this passage (Sir 27:30–28:11) addresses various related issues. Together, these passages are part of a larger literary unit (Sir 27:22–28:26), a series of poems on various topics: first, malice (27:22–27); second, anger and vengeance (27:28–28:1); third, forgiveness (28:2–7); fourth, quarrelling (28:8–11); and fifth, evils of the tongue (28:12–16; 28:17–26). As P. W. Skehan notes, Sirach 28:2–7 (the poem that includes the passage quoted above) addresses the duty of forgiving and not holding grudges.[39]

The notion of reciprocity and the link between mercy and forgiveness is plain in Sirach 28:1–7. Petitioners who forgive others are clearly linked with the Lord who forgives them. Stated rhetorically, an unmerciful person cannot dare to seek God's forgiveness and expect to receive mercy from God. As Reimer states, "Those who lack mercy obstruct forgiveness from God when they seek it."[40] As J. L. Crenshaw observes, verses 2–5 insist that anyone who desires forgiveness from the Lord must first exercise that compassion towards their fellow human beings, including their enemies.[41] This desire for God's forgiveness is interestingly set in the context of prayer.

Some aspects of Sirach's teaching about forgiveness are similar to the teaching in Matthew's gospel (6:12, 14–15; 18:32–35), Mark's gospel (11:25), Luke's gospel (11:4) and James (2:13). Significantly, in Sirach, Matthew (6:12, 14–15), Mark and Luke, the idea of conditionality in divine-human forgiveness emerges in the context of prayer. Further, in Exodus, after Pharaoh sinned against God and God's servants, Moses and Aaron, he acknowledged his sin and implored that this sin be removed from him (10:16–17). His request to Moses and Aaron to plead with God on his behalf anticipates the fact that Moses and Aaron will present his plea to God in prayer. The connection between forgiveness and prayer thus has an obvious Jewish foundation. In Sirach 28:1–7, disgrace, anger and wrath are associated with unforgiving people. The stress of God's vengeance is on those who eventually fail to forgive their fellow humans. This same stress underlies the teaching in Matthew 18:23–35.

---

39. P. W. Skehan and A. Di Lella, *The Wisdom of Ben Sira*, The Anchor Bible 39 (New York: Doubleday, 1995), 362.

40. D. J. Reimer, "The Apocrypha and Biblical Theology," in *After the Exile: Essays in Honour of Rex Mason*, ed. J. Barton and D. J. Reimer (Macon: Mercer University Press, 1996), 276–277.

41. J. L. Crenshaw, "The Book of Sirach," in *NIB* 5 (Nashville: Abingdon, 2006), 772.

Sirach 28:1–4 may help our understanding of the two key Matthean interpersonal forgiveness passages,[42] particularly Matthew's focus on the offended person's obligation towards the person who has sinned against them (Matt 6:12, 14–15; 18:15–17, 21–35). In Sirach 28:1–7, however, nothing definite is said about what will happen to the unforgiving person. Verse 1 says that the actively vengeful will face God's vengeance; this vengeful person can be understood to refer to anybody who fails to forgive their fellow humans. In Matthew's gospel, they will be punished. Punishment is the main concern in Matthew 18:23–35.

In Jewish Scriptures, there is attestation of a penalty for stealing (see Exod 22:1–4). This seems to be echoed in Luke 19:1–10, where Zacchaeus is said to have repaid all those debts he owed to the people he exploited. This verse is sometimes suggested as evidence for the gospel teaching demanding reparation, but this does not find support in Matthew's gospel, and the Lukan text, parallel to this text, has nothing to do with forgiveness. Therefore, to demand reparation or compensation would stand in contrast with Matthew's intended meaning of "forgive debts" (see Matt 6:12; 18:27, 32). In all three of these verses, the expression is best understood to mean something like "forgive a debt" in the sense of cancelling it. This notion of forgiveness in Matthew's gospel drives away any expectation that we can demand reparation or compensation from someone who offends us. A Christian theological rhetoric of forgiveness in the DRC (and beyond) should carefully take note of Matthew's silence on the demand for reparation or compensation from the wrongdoer. This silence distinguishes Matthew's teaching on interpersonal forgiveness and reconciliation and can encourage offended people not to insist too much on their rights in seeking justice for the offences done against them.

Repentance in Forgiveness and Reconciliation Praxis

Is repentance a prerequisite for forgiveness and reconciliation? Current discussions on forgiveness and reconciliation, ranging from popular treatments to theological analyses, take seriously the relationship between forgiveness and repentance in general terms. The discussions tend to focus on whether or not repentance is a prerequisite for forgiveness and, if so, to what extent.

About eight decades ago, J. F. Bethune-Baker noted that in nearly all instances where the idea of forgiveness appears in the Old Testament, the

42. Reimer suggests Sir 28:4 as a possible basis for the parable of Matt 18:23–35 (Reimer, "The Apocrypha and Biblical Theology," 277–279).

context implies repentance for the offence and an intention to avoid its repetition as condition of forgiveness.[43] Two decades later, W. A. Quanbeck argued similarly that in the Old Testament, forgiveness is realized through repentance and the intention to avoid a repetition of the offence.[44] Very recently, A. Bash argued that "Christianity applauds, endorses and promotes forgiveness for the unrepentant" and that this is ". . . theologically misguided – and often pastorally naïve, simplistic and dangerous."[45] These observations indicate the belief that, whether in divine-human or interpersonal forgiveness, repentance is fundamental for forgiveness; that is, something is required on the part of the offender before they can be the beneficiary of forgiveness.

There has also been a tendency in the forgiveness and reconciliation rhetoric to overemphasise the centrality of repentance. Richard Swinburne, for example, extending the logic of Immanuel Kant's argument for the prior requirement of repentance to forgiveness,[46] argues that repentance, along with reparation, apology and penance to victims, are all necessary prerequisites for a person to expunge their guilt and make atonement for the past. Of these elements, he singles out forgiving as belonging to the victim.[47] What Swinburne suggests may be taken as evidence for the common contemporary assumption of a causal priority of repentance for forgiveness. Speaking more broadly, those who give much weight to repentance (and acts attached to it) as a prerequisite for forgiveness seem to do so as a way of compelling the offender to acknowledge their responsibility and accountability for their wrongdoing and thus break potential cycles of violence. There may be good reasons to advocate the causal priority of repentance for forgiveness; it seems to take the gospel as a way of ensuring that people take questions of culpability and accountability seriously.

L. G. Jones proposes the need to recognise the logical and theological "priority" of God's forgiveness in relation to various dimensions of human forgiveness in order to understand the relationship between forgiveness and repentance. This implies that as Christians, we can only understand the relationship between forgiveness and repentance in the dynamics of

---

43. J. F. Bethune-Baker, "Forgiveness," in *Dictionary of the Bible*, ed. James Hastings (Edinburgh: T&T Clark, 1934), 56.

44. W. A. Quanbeck, "Forgiveness," in *The Interpreter's Dictionary of the Bible* 2, ed. George Arthur Buttrich (Nashville: Abingdon, 1962), 316.

45. A. Bash, "Forgiveness: A Re-appraisal," *Studies in Christian Ethics* 24, no. 2 (2011): 137.

46. I. Kant, *Religion within the Limits of Reason Alone*, trans. T. M. Green and H. H. Hudson (New York: Harper & Row, 1960), 106–107.

47. R. Swinburne, *Responsibility and Atonement* (Oxford: Clarendon, 1989), 84.

interpersonal forgiveness if we *first* understand our relationship with God's forgiveness, and God's forgiveness provides the paradigm for how we are to understand our own vocation as a forgiven and forgiving people.[48] In Jones's view, this logical and theological "priority" of God's forgiveness consists of being disposed to forgive without requiring prior repentance, because God in Christ forgave without requiring prior repentance. This position, although open to debate, is supported by Miroslav Volf, who argues that repentance is not so much a prerequisite of forgiveness, especially in the first step in the forgiveness process, where forgiveness is not predicated on repentance or a willingness to redress wrongs. Volf suggests that repentance comes as a result of forgiveness, and the absence of forgiveness amounts to a refusal to see oneself as guilty and therefore a refusal to receive forgiveness as forgiveness.[49]

It is somewhat surprising to observe the lack of a direct reference to repentance in Matthew's forgiveness passages and related texts (6:12, 14–15; 18:15–17 and 18:21–22). Curiously, this issue has not grasped the interest of many scholars. Seeking to understand this lack, especially in a forgiveness rhetoric, may help identify Matthew's overall emphasis and provide a plausible explanation for some of the puzzles in Matthew 18. Referring to these texts, many scholars have suggested that repentance is assumed. Hagner, for example, supports this assumption based on Luke 17:3–4, which parallels Matthew 18:21–22. Commenting on the connection between Matthew 18:15–17 and 21–22, he observes that in the first passage, the sinner lacks repentance, whereas in the second passage, the sinner's repentance is assumed.[50]

This assumption is logical, but it does not consider *why* repentance might be lacking in these texts. One possible explanation is that repentance did not square with Matthew's argument about forgiveness and reconciliation in Matthew 18:15–35, which focuses on the responsibility of his community members to forgive. That is, because Matthew was writing with the responsibility of the offended person in mind, he did not find repentance relevant to his argument in Matthew 6 and Matthew 18.

It has been claimed that one of the crucial differences between Jesus and the Judaism of his day was Jesus's willingness to forgive in God's name without requiring prior repentance – and even more determinatively, his authorization for his disciples to do likewise. E. P. Sanders, for example, states that Jesus

48. Jones, *Embodying Forgiveness*, 153, n. 15.

49. Volf, "Forgiveness, Reconciliation," 875–876.

50. D. J. Hagner, *Matthew 14–28*, ed. Ralph P. Martin, WBC 33B (Dallas: World Books, 1995), 537.

invited sinners into the kingdom without requiring them to repent in the way that repentance was understood within Judaism – that is, without the requirements of restitution, sacrifice and obedience to the law.[51] Jones criticizes Sanders for seeming to imply that Jesus's message abandoned repentance.[52] But rather than suggesting that Jesus's message abandoned repentance, I think Sanders is trying to dismiss the view that Jesus called for conventional rituals of repentance as a precondition for inclusion in the kingdom.[53] Sanders draws from texts in the Synoptics, "[emphasizing] that Jesus has the power to announce the forgiveness of individual's and thus to heal him . . ."[54] He also observes that "[t]he story of the father with two sons (Luke 15:11–32), though it lacks the words, is clearly a story of repentance and forgiveness; and it makes the same point as the related parables in Luke 15:3–10: there is more joy over a repentant sinner than over the righteous who have no need of repentance."[55]

Furthermore, in the Synoptic Gospels, Jesus's ministry is inaugurated with his announcement of the kingdom and his call to repentance. To be sure, Matthew does not overlook repentance, for he stresses repentance as a necessary condition to enter the kingdom of heaven (3:2, 8, 11; 4:17). In Matthew 5:21–26, he highlights the urgency of being reconciled with a "brother/sister" in order to avoid eventual judgement. So it is possible to read from this passage the idea of repentance in the process of seeking reconciliation. The main teaching seems to be a prohibition to offend a "brother/sister," but if an offence takes place, the offender should seek reconciliation as quickly as possible in order to avoid judgement. Of particular significance, this text places the onus on the offender. In this context, one may assume that repentance should be incorporated into reconciliation. Surely, repentance is present in Matthew's thinking, and so it may be in the background in 6:12, 14–15 and 18:21–35. However, the stress is on the responsibility of the offended person to forgive. Both Volf and Jones are in line with the first Evangelist's understanding of the relationship between forgiveness and repentance. A Christian theological rhetoric of forgiveness that is informed by Matthew's voice is one that challenges and encourages people to be disposed to forgive without requiring prior repentance, because God in Christ forgave without requiring prior repentance.

---

51. Sanders, *Jesus and Judaism* (London: SCM, 1985), 207.
52. Jones, *Embodying Forgiveness*, 110.
53. Sanders, *Jesus and Judaism*, 206.
54. Sanders, 207.
55. Sanders, 207.

Justice in Forgiveness and Reconciliation Praxis

Though current discussions about forgiveness and reconciliation connect forgiveness with justice, there is controversy about the approach. Should the victim offer forgiveness after or before the demands of justice have been satisfied? Most scholars tend to favour the principle of "first justice, then forgiveness," whereas a minority argue for "first forgiveness, then justice." Volf is among this minority, but he proposes "forgiveness, justice, then reconciliation."[56] In his discussion, he connects "first justice, then reconciliation" with "first justice, then forgiveness," making it clear that "forgiveness is an element in the process of reconciliation, a process in which the search for justice is an integral and yet subordinate element."[57] He dismisses the view of "justice, then forgiveness" as practically illogical:

> If forgiveness were properly given only after strict justice has been established, then one would not be going beyond one's duty in offering forgiveness; one would indeed wrong the original wrongdoer if one did not offer forgiveness. "The wrong has been fully redressed," an offender could complain if forgiveness were not forthcoming, "and hence you owe me forgiveness." But this is not how we understand forgiveness. It is a gift that the wronged gives to the wrongdoer. If we forgive we are considered magnanimous; if we refuse to forgive, we may be insufficiently virtuous . . .[58]

The "justice, then forgiveness" principle is problematic because it fails to recognise the magnanimous character of forgiveness, a character which is stressed in Matthew 18:22–35. Volf reasons that forgiveness *after* justice is not much different from forgiveness *outside* of justice. He argues that forgiveness *outside* of justice means treating the offender as if they did not commit the offence. Forgiveness *after* justice does the same thing, because demanding justice before forgiveness attempts to redress a situation so that an offended person can treat a wrongdoer as if they did not commit an offence.[59]

Volf proposes six points that illustrate the relationship between forgiveness and justice. First, forgiveness does not stand outside of justice. On the contrary, forgiveness is only possible against the backdrop of a tacit affirmation of justice. Second, forgiveness presupposes that full justice – in the strict sense of the

56. Volf, "Forgiveness, Reconciliation," 861–877.

57. Volf, 876.

58. Volf, 871.

59. Volf, 871.

term – has not been established. If full justice were established, forgiveness would not be necessary, except in the limited and inadequate sense of being vindictive, for the establishment of full justice repays for the wrongdoing. Third, forgiveness entails not only the affirmation of the claims of justice but also their transcendence. Fourth, forgiveness, like any instantiation of grace, involves self-denial and risk; one has let go of a right without the certainty that one's magnanimity will bear fruit, either in one's inner peace or in a restored relationship. Fifth, the first step in the process of forgiveness is unconditional; it is not predicated either on the wrongdoer's repentance or their willingness to redress the wrong. Repentance is not a prerequisite of forgiveness, but a result of forgiveness. The absence of forgiveness amounts to a refusal to see oneself as guilty and thus a refusal to receive forgiveness. Sixth, forgiveness is most complete when both repentance and some form of restitution take place.[60]

These points are presented with such compelling logic that critics may find them difficult to criticize. Yet Volf's final point, that "forgiveness is best received if in addition to repentance there takes place some form of restitution," could be more persuasive,[61] for it raises a question about whether a victim ought to seek compensation or reparation after forgiving an offender. Matthew remains silent on this question. Although Volf's suggestions are supported in Luke (19:1–10), they do not find clear support in Matthew. As discussed earlier, demanding reparation or compensation stands in contrast with Matthew's intended meaning of "forgive debts" (6:12; 18:27, 32), where this expression is best understood as a cancelling of the debt.

Motivations Underlying Forgiveness

Why should we forgive? What are the advantages in forgiving? Congolese often ask these questions during the conflict or post-conflict period. For the purpose of establishing a theological discourse on reconciliation and forgiveness that is informed by the gospel, we will consider how Matthew viewed the ultimate motivations underlying forgiveness.

Research shows that the motivations underlying the decision to forgive are varied. Some forgive out of passive acquiescence, others to avoid conflict, and others because they do not have respect for their integrity as human beings and do not believe they are worthy of being treated well.[62] Motivations tend to

60. Volf, 875–876.

61. Volf, 876.

62. Bash, "Forgiveness: A Re-appraisal," 133–134.

depend on individuals, categories of people (e.g. philosophers, psychologists or theologians) and their worldviews about forgiveness. E. L. Worthington, J. W. Berry and L. Parrott's grouping of these motivations is striking. In general, they suggest that people forgive out of either *warmth-based virtues* (i.e. compassion, empathy and altruism) or *conscientiousness-based virtues* (i.e. responsibility, honesty, accountability and duty).[63] Julie J. Exline and others agree with this proposal, adding that in many situations *warmth-based virtues* and *conscientiousness-based virtues* complement each other.[64]

The grouping formulated by Worthington, Berry and Parrott is in line with a recent study, which claims that individuals who forgive out of love for the injurer, in comparison with those who forgive out of a sense of religious obligation, show less elevation in systolic and diastolic blood pressure when recalling the event.[65] This demonstrates a positive outcome of forgiving for warmth-based reasons. But the conscientiousness-based reasons reflect a significant feature of forgiving that is affirmed in Matthew's gospel: accountability. Yet Worthington, Berry and Parrott (and many others) tend to give the impression that altruistic or warmth-based (other-oriented) reasons for forgiving are more important than conscientiousness-based (self-oriented) reasons.

The motivations for forgiving have been carefully studied by J. W. Younger, R. L. Piferi, R. L. Jobe and K. A. Lawler, who argue that the primary motivations for forgiving are self-focused rather than altruistic.[66] Their conclusions may be useful in studying the themes of forgiveness and reconciliation in Matthew's gospel, where both categories of virtues seem to be present, with the self-focused reasons being predominant.

The theme of forgiveness as a gift emerges in the gospel of Matthew in the context of the divine-human relationship (8:2, 6; 18:27, 32). This echoes the OT teaching about the nature of forgiveness. W. A. Quanbeck observes that in the Bible, forgiveness is primarily God's act and benefit (gift). First, this divine act consists of God graciously taking away the barriers that separate humans from God's presence. Second, forgiveness is a free and sovereign gift from the

63. E. L. Worthington Jr, J. W. Berry and L. Parrott, "Unforgiveness, Forgiveness, Religion, and Health," in *Faith and Health*, ed. T. G. Plante and A. Sherman (New York: Guilford, 2001), 107–138.

64. J. J. Exline et al., "Forgiveness and Justice," *PSPR* 7, no. 4 (2003): 343.

65. S. T. Huang and R. D. Enright, "Forgiveness and Anger-Related Emotions in Taiwan," *Psychotherapy* 37 (2000): 71–79.

66. J. W. Younger et al., "Dimensions of Forgiveness," *Journal of Social and Personal Relationships* 21, no. 6 (2004): 837–855.

loving God. As an act and a gift, forgiveness is an expression of the religious relationship between God and humans.[67] W. C. Morro enforces this twofold meaning of forgiveness, seeing forgiveness as a matter of divine privilege rather than a human right. He argues that it is a privilege because the price of sin must first be paid before the conditions can exist for forgiveness to become a reality.[68]

In Matthew's gospel, forgiveness appears as a moral duty most particularly in interpersonal relationships (6:12b, 14–15; 18:33). A sense of accountability motivates the acts of showing mercy and of forgiving,[69] where the ultimate goal is the merciful person's or forgiver's relationship with the heavenly Father. For Matthew, neglecting an aspect of either relationship has potentially severe consequences.

In Matthew's gospel, the acts of showing mercy and forgiving are motivated by our identity as children who belong to the kingdom. This idea is echoed in Jewish and Graeco-Roman thinking.[70] For Matthew, believers forgive *primarily* for their own benefit – not because of others – as a way of maintaining their relationship and fellowship with their heavenly Father so that they may be blessed by him. On the other hand, they also forgive out of fear of potential punishment. Any Christian theological rhetoric of forgiveness needs to take Matthew's teaching seriously.

Conclusion

The Christian theological discourse about forgiveness and reconciliation in its contemporary Congolese context has been poor and needs to be enriched by Matthew's gospel. Matthew's teaching about forgiveness and reconciliation promotes a culture of nonviolence and peacemaking amidst contexts that have been torn by recurrent conflicts, intense violence and persisting civil wars. Contemporary churches and communities in the DRC and across Congo, Africa and beyond desperately need to hear this message. To do justice to Matthew's understanding of forgiveness, any Christian theological rhetoric of

67. Quanbeck, "Forgiveness," 314–315.

68. W. C. Morro, "Forgiveness," in *The International Standard Bible Encyclopedia*, ed. Geoffrey W. Bromiley (Grand Rapids, MI: Eerdmans, 1982), 340.

69. See Matt 6:12b, 14–15; 7:1–2; 18:33 and 5:7 by implication.

70. For Jewish thinking, see *T. Gad* 6.3–4, 6–7. For Graeco-Roman thinking, see Seneca, *Clem.* 1.9.1–7, 11, which narrates an incident between Augustus and Cinna. In this text, the idea of interpersonal forgiveness is linked with the notions of honour and friendship. For a development of the idea of friendship, see Plutarch, *Moralia: How to Profit by One's Enemies,* 91a–b.

forgiveness and reconciliation needs to enact and incorporate the six themes developed in this paper into the church's teaching and preaching.

Another important implication of this reflection is not only that individuals may forgive one another for interpersonal wrongs experienced and perpetrated as individuals, but also that entire communities may seek to forgive and be forgiven for wrongs that have been perpetrated by communities. Forgiveness and reconciliation are appropriate not only for interpersonal relations in the sphere of personal piety, but are also of great benefit when practised corporately, that is by groups, organizations or entire communities.

Bibliography

Annan, K. A. "Special Report on the Events in Ituri, January 2002-December 2003." No pages. http://www.reliefweb.int/library/documents/2004/unsc-drc-16jul.pdf.

Appressyan, Ruben G. "'Revenge Is Mine, I Will Repay': On the Normative Contexts and Associations of the Commandment 'Resist Not Evil.'" *Russian Studies in Philosophy* 48, no. 2 (2009): 8–27.

Bash, Antony. "Forgiveness: A Re-appraisal." *Studies in Christian Ethics* 24, no. 2 (2011): 133–146.

———. "Forgiveness, Reconciliation and Spirituality: A Theological Perspective." *Journal for the Study of Spirituality* 4, no. 1 (2014): 58–72.

BBC. "The DR Congo Country Profile." No pages. http://www.bbc.com/news/world-africa-13283212.

Bethune-Baker, J. F. "Forgiveness." In *Dictionary of the Bible*, edited by James Hastings. Edinburgh: T&T Clark, 1934.

Boshoff, Henri. "Tension in Ituri: An Update on the Democratic Republic of the Congo." *Institute for Security Studies* (2003): 1–9.

Carpenter, Joel, and Nellie Kooistra. *Engaging Africa: Prospects for Project Funding in Selected Fields*. Nagel Institute, 2015.

Crenshaw, J. L. "The Book of Sirach." In *NIB* 5. Nashville: Abingdon, 2006.

Das, O. "Natural Resources, Conflict and Investment: Conflict Minerals in the Democratic Republic of Congo and the Challenges to Sustainable Investment." In *International Natural Resources Law, Investment and Sustainability*, edited by S. Alam, J. H. Bhuiyan and J. Razzaque. Routledge, 2017. http://eprints.uwe.ac.uk/31423.

Donahue, J. R. *The Gospel in Parable: Metaphor, Narrative, and Theology in the Synoptic Gospels*. Minneapolis: Fortress, 1988.

Drake, K. "Gold and Ethnic Conflict in the Ituri Region of the Democratic Republic of the Congo." No pages. http://www.american.edu/ted/ice/ituri.htm.

The Enough Project, Infographic: "The Networks of Eastern Congo's Two Most Powerful Armed Actors" (2013). No pages. http://enoughproject.org/files/CongoArmed Actors_Table_August2013.pdf.

Exline, Julie J., E. L. Worthington Jr., P. Hill, and M. E. McCullough. "Forgiveness and Justice: A Research Agenda for Social and Personality Psychology." *PSPR* 7, no. 4 (2003): 337–348.

Fokkelman, J. P. *Narrative Art and Poetry in the Books of Samuel: A Full Interpretation Based on Stylistic and Structural Analysis*, vol. 2. *SSN* 23. Assen: Van Gorcum, 1986.

Hagner, Donald J. *Matthew 14–28*, edited by Ralph P. Martin. WBC 33B. Dallas: Word Books, 1995.

Haers, Jacques et al., eds. *Reconciliation: Empowering Grace*. Concilium 2013/1. London: SCM Press, 2013.

Huang, S. T., and R. D. Enright. "Forgiveness and Anger-Related Emotions in Taiwan: Implications for Therapy." *Psychotherapy* 37, no. 1 (2012): 71–79.

Heller, T., S. Krasner, and J. McMillan. "A Trust Fund for Ituri" (2003). No pages. http://faculty-gsb. stanford.edu/mcmillan/personal_page/documents/Ituri.pdf.

IRIN, "Armed groups in Eastern DRC" (2013). No pages. http://www.irinnews.org/report/ 99037/briefing-armed-groups-eastern-drc.

"Ituri: A Need for Protection, a Thirst for Justice." No pages. http://www.amnesty.org/en/library/asset/AFR62/032/2003/en/dom-AFR620322003en.pdf.

Jones, L. Gregory. *Embodying Forgiveness: A Theological Analysis*. Grand Rapids, MI: Eerdmans, 1995.

Kant, Immanuel. *Religion within the Limits of Reason Alone*, translated by T. M. Green and H. H. Hudson. New York: Harper & Row, 1960.

Kendall, R. T. *Total Forgiveness: Achieving God's Greatest Challenge*. London: Hodder & Stoughton, 2001.

Klein, R. W. *1 Samuel*, edited by David A. Hubbard, Glenn W. Barker and John D. W. Watts. WBC 10. Waco: Word Books, 1983.

"Maintaining Momentum in the Congo." No pages. http://www.crisisgroup.org/home/index.cfm?id=1174.

Mbabazi, Isaac K. *The Significance of Interpersonal Forgiveness in the Gospel of Matthew*. Eugene, OR: Pickwick, 2013.

Morro, W. C. "Forgiveness." In *The International Standard Bible Encyclopedia*, edited by Geoffrey W. Bromiley, 340–344. Grand Rapids, MI: Eerdmans, 1982.

Ndagijimana, Batibuka Pontien. "Laisser la vengeance à Dieu: la vérité de Romains 12, 19."

Mélanges de Science Religieuse (2017): 31–46.

Pottier, Johan. "Roadblock Ethnography: Negotiating Humanitarian Access in Ituri, Eastern DR Congo, 1999–2004." *Africa* 76, no. 2 (2006): 151–179.

Quanbeck, W. A. "Forgiveness." In *The Interpreter's Dictionary of the Bible* 2, edited by George Arthur Buttrick, 314–319. New York: Abingdon, 1962.

Reimer, David J. "The Apocrypha and Biblical Theology: The Case of Interpersonal Forgiveness." In *After the Exile: Essays in Honour of Rex Mason*, edited by John Barton and David J. Reimer, 259–282. Macon: Mercer University Press, 1996.

___________. "Stories of Forgiveness: Narrative Ethics and the Old Testament." In *Reflection and Refraction: Studies in Biblical Historiography in Honour of A. Graeme Auld*, edited by Robert Rezetko, Timothy H. Lim and W. Brian Aucker, 359–378. Leiden: Brill, 2007.

Sanders, E. P. *Jesus and Judaism*. London: SCM, 1985.

Skehan, P. W., and A. Di Lella. *The Wisdom of Ben Sira*. The Anchor Bible 39. New York: Doubleday, 1995.

Sternberg, M. *The Poetics of Biblical Narrative: Ideological Literature and the Drama of Reading*. Indiana Studies in Biblical Literature. Bloomington: Indiana University Press, 1987.

Swinburne, Richard. *Responsibility and Atonement*. Oxford: Clarendon, 1989. "UN Must Take Urgent Steps." No pages. http://www.genocideprevention.org/ituri_dr_congo_2003.htm.

Volf, Miroslav. "Forgiveness, Reconciliation, and Justice: A Theological Contribution to a More Peaceful Social Environment." *Millennium: Journal of International Studies* 29, no. 3 (2000): 861–877.

"The War within the War." No pages. http://www.hrw.org/reports/2002/drc/Congo 0602.pdf.

Wenham, Gordon J. *Genesis*, edited by David A. Hubbard et al. WBC 2. Nashville: Thomas Nelson, 1994.

Worthington Jr., E. L., J. W. Berry, and L. Parrott. "Unforgiveness, Forgiveness, Religion, and Health." In *Faith and Health*, edited by T. G. Plante and A. Sherman, 107–138. New York: Guilford, 2001.

Younger, Jarred W. et al. "Dimensions of Forgiveness: The Views of Laypersons." *Journal of Social and Personal Relationships* 21, no. 6 (2004): 837–855.

6

Vulnerability and a Vision of Hope

Engaging Creation's Groaning in Romans 8 and Disasters in the Philippines

Rev Rolex M. Cailing

Introduction

Natural disasters often visit the Philippines, bringing staggering destruction, displacement, death, pain, trauma and prolonged suffering. Like all other countries hit by natural disasters, the Philippines groans and hopes for its deliverance. Reflecting from a sociopsychological perspective, V. Villaroman-Bautista writes, "Like all other kinds of extreme human experiences, even disasters have their silver linings. While they bring suffering, they also become catalyst for marshaling the resources and altruistic instincts of Filipinos."[1] From the notion of "everyday theology," K. J. Vanhoozer remarks that theology and understanding (a grasp of what is going on in ordinary situations and why) are short-circuited when we fail to discern "how our faith is affected by the world we live in" and "how we are to embody our faith in shapes of everyday life."[2] Indeed, a responsible theology can only be attained when the Christian faith

1. V. Villaroman-Baustista, "Urabayan: Bringing Wellness and Wholeness to Communities Under Crisis," in *The Church and Poverty in Asia*, ed. Lee Wanak (Manila: OMF/ATS, 2008), 197.

2. K. J. Vanhoozer, C. A. Anderson and M. J. Sleasman, eds., *Everyday Theology: How to Read Cultural Texts and Interpret Trends* (Grand Rapids: Baker, 2007), 16.

is interpreted in conscious relationship with the fundamental "groanings" of human life and the rest of creation. Hence, the theological and hermeneutical task in the Philippine setting lies in the direction of interpreting the human meaning (without ignoring the divine) along with the social content of the Christian faith. With the series of "groanings" in Romans 8 that reconnect the earth, humanity and the Spirit, Paul constructs a vision of hope that awaits the emergence of a liberator who will conquer the ultimate enemy. The echoes of lament in Romans 8 will be interpreted against the background of disasters in the Philippines, specifically typhoon Yolanda, and the Filipinos' expectation of hope and deliverance, which embraces transcendence over the worst of circumstances.

Echoes of Lament in Romans 8

Those who lament often make assertions or requests related to potential or real disappointments, which stem from the tension between hoping in what God has promised and one's actual experience. A lamenter's pain stems from the fundamental disappointment that a prior promise has either been threatened or is not yet realized. There are numerous examples of such laments in the Psalms (e.g. 21:5–6; 30:2; 70:1–2). The following discussion covers the status of creation in Romans 8, the lament of creation, and the liberation of creation.

The Status of Creation

It is difficult to determine the role and status Paul assigns to "creation" in this portion of his letter for the following three reasons: first, his key words are ambiguous; second, his reference is brief and allusive; third, the relevance of potential OT background is uncertain (e.g. Gen 3; Isa 24–27; Ps 43; Joel 1). Reflecting on this difficult task, B. Byrne observes that this passage is "one of the most singular and evocative texts in the whole Pauline corpus."[3] By employing a well-known biblical concept (the mourning creation motif) in Romans 8:22, Paul argues that the entire creation is groaning in lament because of the history of ongoing human sin and the accompanying divine judgment.

In Romans 8:20 (ISV), Paul claims that creation "was subject to futility [*mataiotēs*]." Despite disagreements among scholars about the subjecting agent, the passive verbs *hupetagē* and *hupotaxanta* (both meaning "subjected") within the context point to God, especially if Genesis 3 is perceived in the background.

3. B. Byrne, *Romans*, SP 6 (Collegeville: Liturgical, 1996), 255.

The difficulty of this construction, however, probably stems from Paul's attempt "to convey too briefly a quite complicated point: that God subjected all things to Adam, and that included subjecting creation to fallen Adam, to share in his fallenness."[4] This idea echoes the role of human beings as described in Psalm 8:5–8. But what does Paul mean by subjection?

As noted above, I suggest that Paul is echoing Genesis 3, not only through the link with Romans 5, but also by his use of the aorist *hupetagē* ("subjected") which possibly implies (within the context of present suffering, groaning, and expectant waiting for future freedom) a particular past event in which creation was placed under subjection.[5] The divine curses in Genesis 3 (e.g. the pain of childbirth, the difficulty of toil and the altered productivity of the earth) have been noted by some interpreters as explanations for what Paul means by subjection. Clear enough, creation and humans are bound up together, both in suffering and in hope. Whatever the nuance in Paul's mind might be, echoes of lament are discernible in manifestations of hope.

The Lament of Creation

Romans 8 provides the background story about why creation, God's children and the Spirit are involved in a collective lament in which they "groan" for the resurrection of the dead. I offer three observations about the subjects of this groaning. First, creation (*ktisis*) *groans* (8:19–22). Paul personifies all creation, both human and non-human, as an expectant mother who groans and suffers childbirth pangs with (*sun*) the children of God. Since she is caught between futility and eschatological hope, she cries out like an OT lamenter. Key parts of the OT lament pattern are echoed in Paul's personification, namely, promise, suffering, cry and deliverance. Paul explains that creation eagerly awaits the revelation of God's children because (*gar*) "creation was subjected [*hupetagē*] to futility [*mataiotēs*], not willingly but on account of the one who subjected it, in hope [*eph elpidi*]" (8:20).

Second, God's children *groan* (8:23–25). Paul elaborates, "But not only this, but also we ourselves having the first fruits of the Spirit, we ourselves

---

4. J. D. G. Dunn, *Romans 1–8*, WCC (Nashville: Thomas Nelson, 1988), 471. Cf. B. Byrne, *Romans*, SP (Collegeville: Liturgical, 1996), 260–261, who perceives Adam as the cause of creation's subjection to futility. If Adam subjected creation to futility, it is difficult to understand how he could have subjected it "in hope" (8:20), since he himself was already rendered subject to sin and death.

5. C. E. B. Cranfield, *A Critical and Exegetical Commentary on the Epistle to the Romans* (Edinburgh: T&T Clark, 1979), 413.

groan [*stenazomen*] in ourselves eagerly awaiting [*apekdechomenoi*] adoption, the redemption of our body" (8:23). Paul clearly perceives, as indicated by his use of intensive pronouns and catchwords (*stenazo*; *apekdechomai*), that God's children and creation both participate in the same lament, and both cry out in hope (*elpidi*) (8:24). The substance of their hope is also the same: the resurrection of the dead. Like OT lamenters and creation, God's children struggle with the relationship between the prior promise that they heard (which Paul says is found in the gospel of God) and the pain they are experiencing. For Paul, the message that Jesus was raised from the dead is also a promise that those who believe in him will be raised from the dead (8:11). This promise of inheritance is expressed in Romans 8:17: "But if children, we are also heirs; heirs of God and coheirs with Christ, if indeed we suffer with him [*sumpaschomen*] in order that we might also be glorified with him [*sundoxasthōmen*]." God's children must suffer with Christ, but that suffering comes with the promise of being glorified with Christ, or raised from the dead.

Third, the Spirit *groans* (8:26–27). While the main two participants in lament are the human "I" and the divine "You," here the Spirit takes up the first-person lament of the "I" or "we." Within the context of Romans 8, the Spirit takes up the hopeful cry of creation and God's children and echoes the "lament of the mediator."[6] Paul's narrative revolves around Moses's lament, which is outlined here in summary form: he is weak; he is faced with an impossible task; God helps him through the Spirit; God's word will not fail (cf. Exod 18:22; Num 11:17). Like Moses, God's children cry out, and they are also helped through the work of the Spirit. But far exceeding the experience of Moses and the Israelites, the Spirit will raise God's children from the dead, lead them, put their deeds of sin to death, testify within them that they belong to God, and pray for them (Rom 8:9–17). For Paul, God's children will groan until the resurrection, but they do not know what they ought (*dei*) to pray until that time. Therefore, the Spirit helps (*sunantilambanetai*) and intercedes (*huperentunchanei*) with groaning (*stenagmois*) of its own.

The Hope of Creation: Liberation

Deliverance in OT laments often comes by evoking a prior promise. In Romans 8:28–30, Paul evokes the prior promise of the gospel and then explicates this promise by saying that those who groan will find sovereign deliverance hidden

6. C. Westermann, "The Role of Lament in the Theology of the Old Testament," *Interpretation* 28 (1974): 34.

in their pain and hope. Paul's theological vocabulary is dense: God foreknows, predestines, justifies and glorifies. Yet the final action highlights the fact that creation groans because of the interplay between hope and pain.

When we recognize God as the agent who subjected the earth to futility, our focus alights upon the hope in which creation was subjected. Thus Romans 8:20 has a positive tone rather than a negative one. In other words, creation is not only subjected to decay or death, because it is subjected in hope. This is already made clear from Paul's earlier extended argument on Abraham in Romans 4, which is that in this hope is life itself. The God in whom Abraham trusts is one who has the power to bring life from death. Whereas Abraham's faith brings life, Adam's sin is the cause of death for humankind and also for creation (cf. Gen 3:17–18), for it leads to creation's futility (8:20) and decay (8:21). Romans 8:11–27 reveals the liberating effect that the Christ-event has on humanity, who will be revealed as children of God, and also on creation, which will be liberated from decay.

The liberation of creation from the destructive effects of human sin will happen at the end of history, when Christ-believers will attain their full salvation in the glory of the resurrection (8:21, 23). Since creation's bondage is due to human sin, its liberation must await the cessation of human evil. Hence, it might seem that this passage does not mandate human activity for the relief of creation from the burden of human mistreatment now, in the present age. Clearly, we cannot achieve the eschatological liberation of creation, but we can anticipate it. Therefore, those who are concerned about living according to God's will for his world must avoid and repair damage to creation as much as possible. This accords well with Paul's portrayal of believers as anticipating and already participating in the life of the age to come (8:23). Thus their groaning is not only an expression of suffering, but also a yearning with hope for the redemption yet to come. Averting and helping repair damage caused by natural disasters enacts the hope that believers share with the rest of creation (8:21).

A Different Kind of Hope

My motivation for writing this paper comes from the realities of my daily experiences as a slave of Christ, serving his cause in my own part of the world, the eastern part of Manila, Philippines. Within the Philippine context, our social conventions (*tatak pinoy*) have not only shaped how we sympathize or empathize (*dumamay*, *makiramay*) in times of difficulties, but also how we call upon God (*panalangin para sa kapwa*) for our neighbors, the victims and sufferers. While I am grateful for the significant role that the government has played in facilitating both awareness and concrete responses to disaster-stricken regions, I am concerned with the role of the local church.

In the process of engagement, W. Brueggemann proposes the notion of "prophetic imagination." I am proposing that the church should not only speak and imagine prophetically but also live out its "prophetic vocation." This is not to imply that Brueggemann suggests a kind of static imagination, for prophetic imagination that is grounded in the gospel message should lead us to a firmer commitment of our vocation.

So where has our vocation left us? Or where has the church left itself? Historically, most Philippine churches – and perhaps churches in other parts of the world – are still carrying the aftermath of previous theological debates. For example, my formative years as a theological student were spent in an atmosphere that was conditioned by the fundamentalist-modernist divide, and so the parameter of the church's vocation was defined in this light. Consequently, the church's response to its mission or vocation has been restrained, if not completely blinded. The recent book by Jonathan Leeman, *Political Church*,[7] casts a vision for how the church can fulfill its prophetic vocation within the parameters of God's kingdom message. Leeman perceives the church as an assembly that embodies the radical grace and love of Jesus as well as a vision of transformation for God's creation.

In the following, I will explore how the vision of creation's hope of liberation in Romans 8 is a necessarily critical starting point for fulfilling the church's prophetic vocation. In engaging this discussion, I will also explore the place for hopeful lament within the church. For when Christians embody this vision, two consequences emerge: they gain a deeper awareness of the divine and they gain a vision of human transcendence.

Deeper Awareness of the Divine

The book *Desperately Seeking God's Saving Action: Yolanda Survivors' Hope beyond Heartbreaking Lamentations* by Karl M. Gaspar[8] traces his experiences of living and surviving with the victims of typhoon Haiyan (known as Yolanda). This typhoon "hit the Philippines on 8 November 2013" and "left many people dumbfounded, especially those in the Visayan regions of Samar and Leyte."[9]

7. Jonathan Leeman, *Political Church: The Local Assembly as Embassy of Christ's Rule* (Downers Grove: InterVarsity Press 2016).

8. K. M. Gaspar, *Desperately Seeking God's Saving Action: Yolanda Survivors' Hope Beyond Heartbreaking Lamentations* (Manila: ISA, 2014).

9. Gaspar, *Desperately*, vii.

His book contains seven equally significant chapters, but I will focus on chapter 4, "Presence and Absence of Theologizing in the Context of a Globalized Response to a Localized Catastrophe."[10]

Gaspar describes a three-day missiological conversation that was convened to reflect on the group's "missiological priorities and to discuss how these could be appropriated to the Philippine setting."[11] Typhoon Yolanda arrived midway through this conversation. One of the speakers emphasized the need to reflect on God's love as "vulnerable and contrary to human power," and how God is "active in pain, suffering and ambiguity," which is "contrary to our image of God as powerful, a God who is in charge, who fixes our problems, gives us clear directions and rescues us from crises."[12] Reflecting on this image of a vulnerable God, Gaspar observes the need to look to Jesus as he "finds God's love in rejection, darkness, failure and death."[13] In the aftermath of disaster, Gaspar writes, people learn to theologize. "God's absence as well as God's presence were interpreted a thousand ways as thousands of Yolanda survivors 'theologized.'" Representatives from Tacloban City, where two-thirds of the more than 10,000 people perished in the deluge, learned to theologize. In Gaspar's words, "this landscape became fertile grounds for grassroots people's theologizing as to God's perceived absence and presence."[14] The Philippines' newly elected president (then Mayor of Davao City), Rodrigo Duterte, arrived at the scene of vast devastation, and upon seeing the extent of the tragedy, he "theologized": "God must [have been] somewhere else or he forgot that there's a planet called Earth."[15]

Gaspar describes another workshop where a group bible study focused on K. M. O'Connor's books on Jeremiah and Lamentations, rereading these texts through the lens of contemporary trauma studies. O'Connor posits, "traumatized people often feel that they have lost an important measure of control over circumstances of their own lives and so they are vulnerable."[16] Indeed, in the process of theologizing, survivors ask a set of penetrating questions "as to what disaster was all about, who was responsible for this, why

10. Gaspar, 99–143.

11. Gaspar, 99.

12. Gaspar, 100.

13. Gaspar, 100.

14. Gaspar, 100.

15. Gaspar, 101. To Gaspar, "theologize" refers to "how the people articulated (as well as symbolized) their thoughts about God through words and actions."

16. Kathleen M. O'Connor, *Jeremiah: Pain and Promise* (Minneapolis: Fortress, 2011), quoted in Gaspar, 102.

it happened and what did God have to do with it and is there a way forward for themselves and their loved ones."[17] For survivors who feel betrayed and godforsaken, "disaster can either totally destroy or at least undermine their trust in God as well as with other people and the world."[18] Gaspar observes that, "Beliefs and tradition – interlocking ideas and institutions that once secured them firmly on the earth and kept them grounded in daily life and communal identity – are no longer reliable."[19] Though many survivors often blame God for the catastrophe, many also find the need to keep God alive.

In making sense of the seemingly violent, punitive and absent God of Jeremiah, Kathleen M. O'Connor responds: "At the heart of this book is resilient confidence in God, defense of God – blazing, angry, emotional, muted, weeping, furious, and always yearning for the beloved. Jeremiah's God desires love, gives love, brings new life, and reconceives the nation."[20] A few examples of responses from personal interviews by Gaspar illustrate the peoples' resilient spirit:

> "God took my daughter, because she was still an innocent girl, whereas those of us who survived perhaps need to repent of our sins."
>
> "The people have distanced themselves from God, so Yolanda was God's way of making people aware that they should return to God's fold."
>
> "*Lord tama na po, tama na po. Patawarin mo na po kami kung ano man an gaming nagawang mga kasalanan.*" [Please make the winds stop and forgive us our sins.]

Based on Gaspar's conversations and interviews and my own experiences, the image of a violent, angry, punitive God was not dominant in the minds of the survivors. Though some spoke about God being angry or displeased because of the people's sins as an explanation for Yolanda, the general impression was more affirming – people were drawn to their knees and to a deeper awareness of God being in control. For instance, two examples can be offered here:

> "I lost my husband and daughter because of Yolanda. It was very painful. But I have offered them back to God, hoping that God

---

17. Gaspar, *Desperately*, 103.
18. Gaspar, 103.
19. Gaspar, 106–107.
20. O'Connor, *Jeremiah*, 137.

> would accept them. As for me, I will try my best to be able to survive." (Espina)[21]

> "When the current was very strong, three of my companions let go but were able to swim back to the coast – including my cousin and her five-year-old boy. I told them to hang on to the coconut plant (tree) nearby our fence to be able to survive. Just cling to that plant and trust in the Lord. Say, 'Lord Jesus have mercy on me.'" (Pelies)[22]

More confessions from survivors could be added. Indeed, survivors do not need our theology; rather, they need to be able to theologize within their context. In a similar way, we need to affirm the hopeful lament envisaged from Romans 8 about God's cosmic vision.

Vision of Human Transcendence

In this section I will identify and reflect on short- and long-term acts of rescue, including responding to basic needs, housing, relocation, trauma counseling and livelihood programs. I describe these acts that engage with people in their process of coping with trauma as *human transcendence.*[23] For example, after the disaster, survivors had to "satisfy their need for food, potable water, a roof over their heads and physical safety."[24] This provided an opportunity for the church to help people experience hope in the midst of their lamentations. Comfort, psychological healing and long-term security were also immensely important, but those arose later, after survivors had regained some semblance of stability. No matter how limited, partial or temporary the help provided by the church may seem, it helps to nurture a vision of transcendence. As O'Connor writes:

> Trauma and disaster studies make clear that when lives have been chopped down by sudden and devastating violence, victims have to find an explanation. To resume life, they need to know why. "Why did this happen to us? Who is to blame?" These are ever-

21. Gaspar, *Desperately*, 111.

22. Gaspar, 113.

23. *Human transcendence* refers to people's resilient ability to transcend their traumatic experiences. The traumatized person's faith is at work in the midst of lamenting and desiring to overcome or cope with the situation. The faith of those who are ministering with the victims is also at work, showing the way to a brighter future. Thus *human transcendence* refers both to individual and communal transcendence, which suggests journeying together.

24. Gaspar, *Desperately*, 102.

> present questions for survivors of disaster events. If the world is ever again to be trustworthy, victims need interpretation. For their lives to rest on the most minimal order, they must have meaning, interpretation, explanation, even if the explanation is ephemeral, inadequate, partial, or outright wrong. Explanations put order back into the world.[25]

Two additional concrete examples for nurturing a vision of human transcendence in the Philippine context are the following institutions: the Institute for Studies in Asian Church and Culture (ISACC)[26] and Philippine Psychiatric Association (PPA). Melba Maggay, the chair of ISACC, has helped to fulfill the mission of the institution, which is "Transforming Cultures Through Christ and His Kingdom." Regarding human transcendence for survivors, she writes, "Social support, a sense of transcendence, and meaning making are central to the nature of human beings, and these have been manifest as important to the healing of trauma among disaster survivors. This is corroborated by recent learnings based on our experience of walking with survivors of the biggest typhoon ever to make landfall in human history, Typhoon Haiyan (local name: Yolanda)."[27] The ISACC not only responds to basic needs, but also provides psycho-spiritual training and counseling.

The PPA has also made significant contributions to promoting human transcendence through their services that concentrate on the rehabilitation of survivors. One aspect of their work focuses on psychic numbing, which is an automatic protective measure that isolates and protects people from depression. The PPA provides regional training to develop local leaders who can readily offer psychosocial programs when disaster strikes in their areas of the country. This is a quite a challenge, given the geological and geographical characteristics of the Philippines, which make it particularly vulnerable to disasters on any part of the archipelago.[28] Churches that serve as a base for referrals from these (and other) organizations help to enhance awareness about others' suffering so that believers can embrace and promote a vision for human transcendence.

---

25. O'Connor, *Jeremiah*, 98.

26. The Institute for Studies in Asian Church and Culture (ISACC) is a research and training organization specializing in development, missiology and cross-cultural studies aimed at social transformation within the Asian context.

27. M. P. Maggay, "Trauma Care for Disaster Survivors in Tacloban: Some Spiritual, Psychological, and Cultural Dimensions." ISACC News (27 Nov 2014): 1.

28. See L. Ladrigo-Ignacio, *Ginhawa: Well-being in the Aftermath of Disasters* (Pasig City: PPA, 2011). See the useful work of Bernice Vania N. Landoy et al., "The Application and Adaptation of Psychological First Aid: The Filipino Psychologists' Experience After Typhoon Haiyan," *Philippine Journal of Psychology* 48 (2015): 81–104.

Conclusion

The message of hope embodied in Romans 8 is essential for communities, individuals and all of creation, for it does not ignore the realities of pain and suffering, but confronts them in the light of the death and resurrection of Jesus Christ and the reassuring presence of the Spirit. The historical reality of the crucifixion of Jesus, where our hope resides, "includes both darkness and light, tragedy and transformation, sadness and joy, death and resurrection," and also "embraces not only the future but the present, not only other-worldly realities but this-worldly ones as well."[29] Hence Paul's image of the "groaning of creation" in Roman 8 not only provides assurance by mirroring the sad and alarming situation being experienced in the Philippines and other parts of the world, but also maps the way towards a path that leads us out of this grim situation. The vocation of the church is to engage with this vision, which rests on the truth that God's deliverance is hidden but certain in Christ, the agent of God's new creation, and the hope of all creation.

Bibliography

Byrne, B. *Romans*. SP 6. Collegeville: Liturgical Press, 1996.

Chia, R. *Hope for the World: The Christian Vision*. Leicester: IVP/Langham, 2006.

Cranfield, C. E. B. *A Critical and Exegetical Commentary on the Epistle to the Romans*. Edinburgh: T&T Clark, 1979.

Dunn, J. D. G. *Romans 1–8*. WCC. Nashville: Thomas Nelson, 1988.

Gaspar, K. M. *Desperately Seeking God's Saving Action: Yolanda Survivors' Hope beyond Heartbreaking Lamentations*. Manila: ISA, 2014.

Ladrigo-Ignacio, L. *Ginhawa: Well-Being in the Aftermath of Disasters*. Pasig City: PPA, 2011.

Landoy, Bernice Vania N., et al. "The Application and Adaptation of Psychological First Aid: The Filipino Psychologists' Experience After Typhoon Haiyan." *Philippine Journal of Psychology* 48 (2015): 81–104.

Leeman, Jonathan. *Political Church: The Local Assembly as Embassy of Christ's Rule*. Downers Grove: InterVarsity Press, 2016.

Maggay, M. P. "Trauma Care for Disaster Survivors in Tacloban: Some Spiritual, Psychological, and Cultural Dimensions." ISACC News. 27 November 2014.

O'Connor, Kathleen M. *Jeremiah: Pain and Promise*. Minneapolis: Fortress, 2011.

Vanhoozer, K. J., C. A. Anderson, and M. J. Sleasman, eds. *Everyday Theology: How to Read Cultural Texts and Interpret Trends*. Grand Rapids: Baker, 2007.

---

29. R. Chia, *Hope for the World: The Christian Vision* (Leicester: IVP/Langham, 2006), 27.

Villaroman-Bautista, V. "Urabayan: Bringing Wellness and Wholeness to Communities Under Crisis." In *The Church and Poverty in Asia*, edited by Lee Wanak. Manila: OMF/ATS, 2008.

Westermann, C. "The Role of Lament in the Theology of the Old Testament." *Interpretation* 28 (1974): 20–38.

7

Forgiveness in a Broken World

An Exploration through the Drama of Scripture

Kethoser (Aniu) Kevichusa

The metanarrative of Scripture tells of a world and reality that is created good but fallen, fallen but redeemed, redeemed but not yet fully redeemed. Forgiveness, I suggest, is the most appropriate response to this reality as presented by the drama of Scripture.

Forgiveness as a response to this reality is both divine and human. The drama of Scripture tells the story of God's willingness to continue engaging and working with a world that, though created good, has gone terribly wrong. God's forgiveness communicates that God is not giving up on his project of creation and humanity. Forgiveness, in other words, undergirds God's relationship and engagement with the broken world. Forgiveness is behind God's utter commitment to the world and humanity through his creation, sustenance, redemption and consummation of the world.

The drama of Scripture also makes forgiveness central to human action and conduct in the world. In reading the Bible as a story that is framed by God's creation, sustenance, redemption and consummation, one can detect a moral environment or atmosphere – an *ethos* – about reality. This biblical ethos, which is remarkably consistent with the general human condition and experience, gives rise to an *ethic* that is in consonance with the reality of the world. Appropriate human conduct in the world must act according to the coordinates of the divine story, and this response is best described as "forgiveness."

The overall scheme and structure of the biblical story suggest that in order for humans to live in consonance with reality, and in order for human actions to respond appropriately to broken reality, they must be forgiving. Thus forgiveness is the most appropriate existential posture, mind-set and roadmap for negotiating through life in this world.

Forgiveness in a Good but Fallen World

The biblical metanarrative begins with creation, which recognizes and insists that there *is* a created reality and order. From this beginning point, we can infer that forgiveness is an ethic that assumes the following: first, there is a good, divinely ordained moral order that governs relations among God's creatures; second, this order confers a good, divinely ordained moral worth on each of God's creatures. Two corollaries emerge from these assumptions: first, there is a divinely created moral order that can be disrupted; second, divinely ordained creatures can be wronged.

The ethic of forgiveness presumes not only that reality *can* be disrupted and wronged, but also that reality *is* indeed disrupted and wronged. Forgiveness does not presume that the present world is Edenic. Rather, forgiveness arises from the recognition that there has been disruption and confusion in the natural order, including the moral order, because of the fall. Thus forgiveness is an ethic of realism that takes into account the reality of living in a fallen and broken world. This accommodating ethic takes human imperfection, wrongdoing and evil seriously as well as the broken reality of all creatures and situations. Though reality is created good, it is broken and imperfect. Moreover, it is also imperfectible. This understanding of reality provides the basis for several constituent elements of forgiveness: forbearance, tolerance, restraint and patience.

The imperfection of reality includes the imperfection of those who are forgiving as well as their imperfect perceptions of reality. Thus a forgiveness ethic not only perceives the imperfection in the other, but is also imbued with an acute self-awareness of one's own imperfections, failings and sinfulness as well as one's imperfect perceptions and assumptions about the moral order, good and evil, right and wrong. Because the fall affects both the forgiving self and all other reality, we can discern another element of forgiveness: empathy.

Empathy, on the part of the forgiver, connotes a sensitive understanding and vicarious experiencing of the feelings, thoughts and experience of the other. This assumes that the epistemological and moral landscape of wrongdoers may be so mangled that they do not even know they are doing wrong, let alone have the capacity to repent and confess. Forgiveness does not mean excusing the actions of wrongdoers, but it takes their reality into consideration. Empathy suggests that the victims are aware that they also stand as sinners in need of forgiveness before God.

Moreover, the forgiving self recognizes that in a broken reality forgiveness itself will be imperfect. In extremely traumatic experiences, some people may not be able to recognize or appreciate forgiveness because they are looking for pure or perfect forgiveness. In these circumstances, we need to learn to pray not only, "Forgive us our trespasses," or "Forgive us our unforgiveness," but also, "Forgive us our imperfect and incomplete forgiveness." Even our most noble acts of forgiveness can be so flawed and feeble that they need God's grace and forgiveness. For example, it is not uncommon for victims who have been traumatized by grave evils to remain, perhaps for a lifetime, emotionally and psychologically scarred so that they continue to struggle with flames of resentment even after they have forgiven their perpetrators.

Yet forgiveness is not another form of postmodern relativism, liberal tolerance or quietistic escapism. Rather, forgiveness is a moral protest that assumes both an objective created order and the existence of divinely ordained moral absolutes. Judgement and condemnation are implicit in and intrinsic to forgiveness. To forgive is to judge certain actions as wrong, to identify perpetrators as wrongdoers and to condemn the circumstances that their wrong actions have caused as unacceptable.

Yet forgiveness is not only about judging and condemning wrongdoing, but also redeeming wrongdoing. This is predicated on the fact that the world, as presented by the drama of Scripture, is redeemed in Christ. Though the present world is not without sin, nor is it a world without redemption.

Forgiveness in a Not Fully Redeemed World

The story of the Bible talks about creation and new creation. For Christians, the new creation was inaugurated by the life, death and resurrection of Jesus, but it will not be consummated until the *parousia* (second coming) of the Lord. This new creation that was inaugurated in the person and work of Christ does not suggest a return to the Edenic situation of the original creation. Rather, the movement of the biblical drama is towards the renewal of all things, which is neither determined by the past nor completely disjointed from it.

These truths regarding the new creation have several implications for the biblical practice of forgiveness. First, forgiveness is the epistemological clue and ontological core of the new creation. Thus forgiveness is a response to the biblical summons to live in God's new world, which is not circumscribed by the law of revenge that regulates the violent order of the fallen world.

Second, forgiveness is not just a backward-looking, retroactive action that seeks to return a relationship (intrapersonal, interpersonal, social or political) to a *status quo ante* or some original state of moral equilibrium before a wrongdoing. Rather, the new creation as inaugurated in Christ suggests that the end result of forgiveness is an invitation to an even better relationship, a restored state of reconciliation. For reconciliation to take place, however, the invitation to this better relationship has to be accepted, which usually happens through confession, apology, repentance, remorse, restitution and restoration. The drama of Scripture provides a blueprint for understanding reconciliation. In the Bible, redemption is not merely about the final *shalom* – the reconciliation of all things – nor simply about the restoration of the world to its original state. Rather, the book of Revelation paints a picture of a world that incorporates both the work of God (the garden in Genesis) and the work of humans (the city): the garden-city (Rev 21 – 22:1–5).

Like the new creation, forgiveness involves both continuity and discontinuity with the past. The future to which forgiveness invites us will neither be totally disjointed from nor completely determined by the past. Forgiveness does not suggest that we "act as if it never happened," or "undo the past" or "forget the past," for forgiveness continues to bear the marks of the past, just as the resurrected Christ continues to bears the scars and marks of evil even after his glorious resurrection. Rather, forgiveness frees the future from being determined, dominated and shackled by the past by offering a truly free, unprecedented, radically new and creative future hope in reconciliation.

Third, the drama of Scripture reveals that the new creation will be consummated only in the eschaton. Forgiveness, as a biblical ethic of engaging with broken reality, will seek and claim neither too much nor too little of its transforming power. Because of the reality of the fallen world, forgiveness assumes both the imperfection of the world and the imperfectability of forgiveness – at least until the consummation of new creation. Thus complete healing and reconciliation are not fully possible on this side of reality. It is only at the end of the drama of Scripture that it is promised: "He will wipe away every tear from their eyes, and death shall be no more, neither shall there be mourning, nor crying, nor pain anymore" (Rev 21:4).

8

Christian Discipleship in a Traumatized Society

Rachel C. Mutai

Background

The Democratic Republic of Congo (DRC) is rich in natural and human resources, including fertile soils, ample rainfall, the second largest rain forest in the world and half of all of Africa's forests, along with considerable and varied mineral resources. These rich resources could make the country the most prosperous nation on the continent, but for most people they have proved to be more of a curse than a blessing.

The Great Lakes region in Africa has experienced violent civil wars at varying magnitudes for quite a while, causing death, displacement, rape, destruction of property, poverty and trauma. At least seventy armed groups are believed to be operating in the eastern region of the country. Despite the signing of a peace deal and the formation of a transitional government in 2003, weak governance and institutions, along with corruption and an absence of the rule of law, have contributed to the ongoing violence against civilians in the eastern region.[1] Since 1993, conflict and violence has ranged from ethnic and tribal to political liberation, to cross-border violence, to rebel-led attacks.[2] More

1. Global Conflict Tracker, "Violence in the Democratic Republic of Congo," accessed February 2017, http://www.cfr.org/global/global-conflict-tracker/p32137#!/conflict/violence-in-the-democratic-republic-of-congo.

2. Focus group response, 2017. The focus group was selected from participants in a trauma healing conference that ALARM facilitated in Goma, DRC, in 2016, with a follow-up in 2017. Focus group members included pastors, women and youth leaders.

particularly, the cycles of violent conflict in the eastern part of the Democratic Republic of Congo (DRC) have pushed people to develop survival mechanisms.

In the midst of such ongoing violence and while living as internally displaced persons, how can the church live out the mandate of Christ to "make disciples of all nations" (Matt 28:19)? In the quest to understand Christian discipleship in a traumatized society, I will consider the following: (1) the political, sociocultural and religious context in the first century when Jesus gave his followers the mandate to make disciples; (2) the need for discipleship in traumatized communities, with a specific focus on the church in North Kivu Province, DRC; (3) biblical principles that can guide the church in responding to traumatic events within their communities; (4) community resilience principles or models that the church can adopt to carry out the ministry of discipleship in traumatized communities; (5) the cost of Christian discipleship in a war-torn context.

Those who live in the wake of human-made or natural disasters are traumatized, and so the church needs to respond both to spiritual and psychosocial issues as it seeks to nurture faith and share the gospel within these communities. It is also important to reach out to pastors and church leaders as the shepherds of the flock so that they can better disciple their congregants. Spiritualizing or denying that traumatic events exist is like icing a rotten cake. Pastors and ministry leaders can function more effectively by acknowledging the trauma, focusing on recovery from the effects of trauma, acquiring skills for supporting others' healing and building resilience.

Overview of First-Century Context for the Discipleship Mandate

Political Context

For thousands of years, the Jewish people were subject to foreign rule (Egyptian, Syrian, Babylonian, Persian, Greek, Roman), with only brief periods of independence. In the first century, Romans ruled the Mediterranean area known as Palestine (modern-day Israel), where Jesus was born and lived his life.[3] By the time of Jesus, Palestine had been a Roman colony for more than half a century. The Roman Empire developed by gradually taking over more and more territories in the eastern Mediterranean and progressively moving east (North Africa, Egypt, Asia Minor, modern-day Turkey, Syria). In time, they also conquered Judea. Some of the conquered territories were governed

3. James Tabor, "The Roman World of Jesus," https://pages.uncc.edu/james-tabor/the-roman-world-of-jesus-an-overview/.

as provinces and others as client kingdoms. Judea was a client kingdom and had its own semi-independent king, Herod the Great (who reigned from 37–4 BC). In the hierarchy of power, the Jewish self-government reported to the authority of the local Roman government (King Herod), which reported to Rome, Emperor Caesar.[4] Rome was the source of both the wealth and problems that occurred in the Jewish state.

When Romans ruled Palestine through King Herod, tributes to Caesar were required, and there was severe economic pressure on the people. The peasants could not make a living from their land, and the Israelite family began to disintegrate from hunger and indebtedness.[5] Thus the Jews distrusted and hated the Roman Empire.[6] Jesus addressed all of these problems in his preaching (Luke 6:20–49; 12:22–31; Mark 10:2–31).

In summarizing the context of the New Testament, Howard-Brook and Ringe indicate that "the discontent and social disintegration that resulted from the oppressive structures imposed by the Roman and the exploitative political-economic practices of the multiple layers of rulers – Roman, Herodian, and the high priest – provided conditions for periodic protests, renewal movements, and massive popular revolts."[7] After the death of Herod the Great in 4 BC, the revolts in every major district, as well as movements that attacked royal fortresses and established effective popular control of their areas, took the form of messianic movements, with the people acclaiming their leader as "king."[8] This explains the inscription on Jesus's cross, "King of the JEWS."

Sociocultural Context

Long before the Roman Empire (which was established by Augustus in 27 BC), the reign of Alexander the Great (from 336–323 BC) introduced Greek culture to all the nations that he conquered, influencing their language, values, education and government. Though the Jews already had their own culture and language, the Greek language was imposed on the Jewish nation and eventually became the *lingua franca* of the entire NT world. However, during the first century it was still common for Jews to use Hebrew, Aramaic and Latin.

---

4. E. P. Sanders, "Jesus in Historical Context," *Sage Journal* 50, no. 3 (1993): 429–448.

5. Wes Howard-Brook and Sharon Ringe, eds., *The New Testament: Introducing the Way of Discipleship* (Maryknoll: Orbis, 2002), 4.

6. Asbury Bible Commentary, "Historical context of the NT," https://www.biblegateway.com/resources/asbury-bible-commentary/toc/.

7. Howard-Brook and Ringe, *New Testament*, 5.

8. Howard-Brook and Ringe, 5.

Jesus's everyday language was Aramaic, and the NT was written in Greek. The process of Hellenization, whether deliberate or coincidental, created cultural identity issues for the Jews of Judea, where they were in the majority, as well as for the Jewish diaspora.[9]

The Jews' participation in the governance of Palestine during the first century was limited, since policy only granted full citizenship to Greeks (by birth, language and education). The Greeks only accepted Jews as citizens if they first became Greeks by adopting the language and culture.[10] This was problematic for the Jews, because they understood the world to be divided into Jews and Gentiles (non-Jews), and so they worked hard to disassociate themselves from the Gentiles.[11]

E. Sanders discusses the socio and economic injustices that were present in Palestine during the first century:

> Palestine's small landholders were in a tightening noose of institutionalized injustices such as double taxation, heavy indebtedness, and loss of land. Peasant families fell ever more heavily into debt under the steady economic pressures of double taxation. The wealthy lent them money that they could not repay, charged very high rates of interest, and then foreclosed on the property, so that estates became larger and larger while more and more people were forced off the land. There was rising indebtedness and a declining peasantry, the social-economic infrastructure was in decline and poverty was worsening.[12]

Religious Context

The Roman Empire granted limited religious freedom to its territories. Though the Jews believed in one God, they were divided into sects over variations of the Jewish law (Pharisees, Scribes, Sadducees and Essenes), with the Pharisees controlling the religious opinion. Other factions and subgroups, such as the Zealots, Samaritans, Galileans, Hellenists, tax collectors, God-fearers and

---

9. Donald Gerardi, "Jesus and the Christian Tradition," http://academic.brooklyn.cuny.edu/history/dfg/jesu/topic2.htm.

10. Watson Mills, *New Testament and Background* (Lewiston, NY; Lampeter, Wales: Edwin Mellen, 2002), 20–26.

11. Luke T. Johnson, *The Writings of the New Testament: An Interpretation* (Philadelphia: Fortress, 1986).

12. Sanders, "Jesus in Historical Context," 430–432.

proselytes, played background roles in the NT story.[13] Amidst these various Jewish groups, two underlying institutions formed the foundation for Jewish self-identification: the Torah and the Temple. For most Jews, Jerusalem was the central place of worship. The calendar of religious festivals was another unifying factor for Jewish identity, which continues to be true today.

Because of the centuries of oppression by various foreign powers (see "Political Context" above), the Jews were constantly looking forward to a messiah or savior who would bring spiritual renewal and political freedom. During the time of Jesus, Palestine faced numerous traumatic events that left the people longing for deliverance. This longing for a messiah is shown in the NT gospels (Luke 2:26, 38). Thus many people were disappointed when Jesus, who grew up within the Jewish religion, was not the kind of king they were anticipating.

Despite the ongoing oppression, there was spiritual hunger in the Greco-Roman world, as illustrated in the stories of the Ethiopian eunuch (Acts 8), Cornelius the centurion (Acts 10) and in the number of "God-fearers" who attended Jewish synagogues throughout the empire, many of whom responded readily to the gospel and thereby formed the nucleus of the churches planted through the missionary activities of Paul and others.[14] Spiritual hunger fueled the rapid growth of the Christian church, which began at Pentecost in the first century and then spread throughout Judea (see Acts 21:20), Samaria (Acts 8:4–25; 9:31) and "to the ends of the earth" (Acts 1:8; see Rom 15:23–24). The reception of the gospel among so many diverse ethnic backgrounds and social classes was due in part to widespread spiritual need.[15]

By 66 AD, Jewish discontent with Rome had escalated. At first, the priests tried to suppress the rebellion and even called upon the Pharisees for help. After the Roman garrison failed to stop Hellenists from desecrating a synagogue in Caesarea, however, the high priest suspended the tribute payment, which inaugurated the Great Jewish Revolt. The destruction of the Second Temple by the Romans in 70 AD not only put an end to the revolt, but was also a profoundly traumatic experience for the Jews and marked the end of an era.[16]

By the end of the NT era, Christianity, which had been born in the womb of Judaism, had established itself as an independent religion. Christianity, due

13. Gerardi, "Jesus and the Christian." Online article.

14. Johnson, *Writings*.

15. Asbury Bible Commentary. Online.

16. Watson, *New Testament*, 25–26.

in part to external forces, began to break the shackles of Judaism and move more freely into the Gentile world.[17]

In the next section, I will explore Jesus's first-century mandate for discipleship within the modern-day violence, trauma and displacement in east and central Africa. In the background for this section is a question about how the political, sociocultural and religious context of the Great Lakes region in Africa is similar to or different from that of first-century Palestine.

Need for Discipleship in a Traumatized Community

The ongoing violence in east and central Africa has caused millions of deaths, rape, stigmatization, poverty, separation of families, ethnic hatred and discrimination, poor education and medical facilities, illegal possession of firearms, among many other consequences. According to the Enough Project, rape as a weapon of war in the DRC is quite high. Though it is difficult to get reliable data in the DRC, Heal Africa, one of the Hospitals in Goma that receives victims of rape, reported that there was an 84 percent increase in rape between 2013 and 2016.[18] In the United Nation's estimations, 15,000 women were raped in eastern Congo during 2009 alone and between January 2010 and December 2013, there were 3,645 reported victims of sexual violence; at least 2.7 million persons were internally displaced in the DRC and approximately 450,000 DRC refugees were living in other nations.[19]

In any violent and protracted conflict, Fuertes observes, civilians bear the most brutal effects: communities are disrupted and devastated; people are forced to live as refugees for fear of getting killed; some have lost their relatives; others bear the marks of violence physically, mentally, emotionally and spiritually.[20] Along with meeting basic needs, survivors of war need to get through trauma so they can recover and rebuild their lives and communities.

Trauma also affects the caregivers of those who have been impacted directly by violence. Caregivers range from counselors, pastors, teachers, community social workers, nurses, and in some cases family members of those experiencing trauma. Depending on the magnitude of their engagement with victims of trauma, the caregivers, if unattended to, will begin to demonstrate

17. Sanders, "Jesus in Historical Context."

18. Healafrica.org.

19. Global Conflict Tracker, "Violence."

20. Al B. Fuertes, "In Their Own Words: Contextualizing Discourse of (War) Trauma and Healing," *Conflict Resolution Quarterly* 21, no. 4 (Summer 2004): 491.

their own symptoms of trauma. Therefore discipleship is necessary not only for those who have experienced traumatic events, but also for those who attend to the traumatized people.

The church has also felt the impact of the conflicts and wars. Some regions are currently unreachable due to insecurity. Because of tribalism, some churches have divided along tribal lines, and pastors from certain tribes cannot go to certain areas. Due to poverty, the prosperity gospel is on the rise. Christians, especially those living in camps for internally displaced persons, are asking where the loving God is amidst all the violence and trauma. This has negatively affected the church's ministry of evangelism and discipleship.[21]

African Leadership and Reconciliation Ministries (ALARM) is a nonprofit Christian organization that reaches out to communities affected by violent conflicts in different parts of east and central Africa. In the DRC, particularly North Kivu Province, ALARM has sought to provide alternative conflict resolution skills by training Christian lawyers, police and prison wardens, pastors and church leaders. One ALARM focus group identified trauma as the most severe effect of the years of conflict and violence in the DRC.[22]

Mental health practitioners acknowledge trauma as "a wide range of intensely stressful experiences that involve exposure to levels of danger and fear that exceeds normal capacity to cope."[23] Trauma encompasses a range of "debilitating symptoms that many suffer from in the aftermath of perceived or real life threatening or overwhelming experiences."[24] Yet trauma is one of the most avoided, ignored, denied, misunderstood, untreated causes of human suffering. Words cannot accurately convey the anguish of a traumatized person. Following are statements from an ALARM trauma conference that was held in Goma, DRC in 2016:

> During the war of M23,[25] young people were forcibly taken by the rebels. I was also taken by force with three other youth of our

---

21. Focus group response, 2017.

22. Focus group response, 2017.

23. Priscilla Dass-Brailsford, ed., *Crisis and Disaster Counselling: Lessons Learned from Hurricane Katrina and Other Disasters* (Los Angeles: Sage Publications, 2010), 132.

24. Dass-Brailsford, *Crisis and Disaster*, 7.

25. M23 was a rebel group formed after the desertion of the faction of the Congrès National pour la Défense du Peuple (CNDP, National Congress for the Defence of the People) rebel group, who had integrated overnight into the Congolese military after a peace accord with the government, formally signed on 23 March 2009. Taking their name from this accord, M23 group claimed that the Congolese government has failed to live up to its terms. In various offensives from April onwards, the M23 quickly occupied substantial parts of Rutshuru territory in North Kivu, but the armed group was defeated in November 2013.

> village. The rebels kept us for two days in a hole and the third day we were taken to the field of battle in Rutshuru. Because of lack of food, two of my friends were no longer able to walk and were shot. When I saw my friends fall even before the war began, I was too scared and decided to run away. I managed to escape despite the bullets that were fired behind me to keep me from going away into the bush. There, I experienced a lot of difficulties to reach Uganda . . . [26]
>
> At that time and even today, I have no desire to live. I always preferred to die than to live because my life has no meaning. These lessons we are following here make me bleed heart and remind me of all ills, problems, atrocities and situations I have traversed since my youth. I even feel sick. May God helps me to forgive all those who have contributed to my misfortunes.[27]

These statements reveal how trauma overwhelms an individual's psychological, emotional and spiritual inner resources. Religious leaders are not only affected by traumatic events,[28] but also find themselves serving as caregivers and often end up with compassion fatigue and secondary trauma. Along with social workers, health care workers and counsellors, religious leaders show symptoms of traumatization, which may include: changes in one's worldview and spiritual orientation, challenges to one's meaning and purpose for life, questions about the ultimate meaning of life, despair and loss of hope, lower tolerance for frustration, increased outbursts of anger and sometimes rage, projection of one's own feelings onto those they are serving, dread of working with certain people, among others.[29]

The church in North Kivu Province of the DRC has witnessed their youth abandon the church for the army or armed groups, a decrease in church giving, early marriages, either hypervigilance or laziness among people. The women who have been raped "feel a deep sense of shame, they feel dirty, ruined, and are developing hatred against God and all men."[30]

---

26. Participant, ALARM Trauma Conference held in Goma, DRC, in 2016.

27. Participant, ALARM Trauma Conference held in Goma, DRC, in 2016.

28. "Traumatic event" here is used to refer to threats to lives or bodies that produce terror and feelings of helplessness, overwhelm an individual's or group's ability to cope or respond to the threat, lead to a sense of loss of control, or challenge a person's or group's sense that life is meaningful and orderly (Carolyn Yoder, *The Little Book of Trauma Healing: When Violence Strikes and Community Security Is Threatened* [Intercourse, PA: Good Books, 2005], 10).

29. Edward Wimberly, "Story Telling and Managing Trauma: Health and Spirituality at Work," *Journal of Health Care for the Poor and Underserved* 22, no. 3 (2011): 48.

30. Focus group response, 2017.

In the next section, I will explore biblical principles that can guide the church as they respond to traumatic events within their communities.

Biblical Principles for Responding to Traumatic Events

Since the first century, Christianity has faced different kinds of challenges, ranging from doctrinal differences to martyrdom. Yet at the height of its persecution, the church has continued to share the gospel and disciple believers in the faith. The opposition and violence witnessed in our context today come from political and social rivalry as well as cultural and spiritual beliefs and practices.

The church is a people and a community of believers that has a high calling and a noble mission to accomplish. So can a Christian explain horrible events? When the innocent are harmed? When an unexpected incident results in destruction and death? Responses to these questions range from, "Where is God?" or "Why didn't God prevent this?" to a life of helplessness and hopelessness, which can result in some believers abandoning the Christian faith.

In trying to understand the world as created by a God who is good and powerful, we also need to understand why horrible things happen. In the very goodness of God, we have been given the will to make decisions. These decisions can be based on God's law to serve the good of humankind. But some people take the law upon themselves and decide to do evil.

Following are important biblical teachings that can help us explain the horrible things and traumatic events that are happening in our society.

First, we need to acknowledge and expose the sinful actions of evil men. The greed in human hearts leads some to rape the poor of the little they have, use faulty scales, murder a business competitor or political rival and violate human rights. These things are not of God.

Second, we need to know our enemy: "Our struggle is not against flesh and blood, but against the rulers, against the authorities, against the powers of this dark world and against the spiritual forces of evil in the heavenly realms" (Eph 6:12 NIV). People who see each other as enemies forget that they have a common enemy in Satan and should fight together against evil. Since Lucifer was thrown out of heaven, he has not stopped fighting God's people, and so Peter warns: "Be alert and of sober mind. Your enemy the devil prowls about like a roaring lion, looking for someone to devour" (1 Pet 5:8 NIV).

Third, we must remain confident about God's power to overcome the enemy. The God who told the Israelites, "Be still, and know that I am God" (Ps 46:10 NIV), is the same God who was with David when he fought the Philistines and with Stephen when he said, "Look . . . I see heaven open and the Son of Man standing at the right hand of God" (Acts 7:56 NIV). The evil in this world does not render God powerless.

Fourth, God is not punishing us or angry with us when we are facing terrible things. Some things happen that are not caused by human actions, and we should not take the blame. On the other hand, we need to discern when God allows certain circumstances to demonstrate his power and glory to mankind (John 9:3).

Fifth, lament is biblical. Many biblical characters have conversations with God and talk to God about how they feel, as evidenced by David, Job and Habakkuk. Remaining open with God facilitates honesty as we respond to traumatic events and will also replenish us for the ongoing journey.

Sixth, keep the Sabbath. Sabbath rest is important not only spiritually but also emotionally, physically and relationally. Those who have been affected by traumatic events, along with their caregivers, must take periods of rest. When caregivers experience Sabbath rest, they recognize their limitations, which reminds them that they are human and vulnerable. We are not super-human. Sabbath rest is essential for self-care and for recovering from compassion fatigue, vicarious traumatization, burnout and exhaustion.

Seventh, the ALARM focus group in Goma, DRC, pointed out that responding to trauma was difficult because of recurring violence. In the words of one respondent, "once people are healed a bit, then another conflict or war starts and again the scars are wounded and the trauma becomes worse than it was in the past."[31] However, the group also indicated that the training they had received in trauma healing along with the teachings on forgiveness were very helpful. Discipleship should be understood as a process, particularly when working with traumatized believers.

In the next section, I will explore how the church can disciple the community of believers in order to foster recovery from trauma and build resilience.

Fundamentals of Discipleship for the Traumatized Community

As Paul admonishes, discipleship is about presenting every believer as fully mature in Christ: "He is the one we proclaim, admonishing and teaching everyone with all wisdom, so that we may present everyone fully mature in Christ" (Col 1:28 NIV). Paul continues:

> So then, just as you received Christ Jesus as Lord, continue to live your lives in him, rooted and built up in him, strengthened in the

31. Focus group response, 2017.

> faith as you were taught, and overflowing with thankfulness. See to it that no one takes you captive through hollow and deceptive philosophy, which depends on human tradition and the elemental spiritual forces of this world rather than on Christ. (Col 2:6–8 NIV)

The Christian call to discipleship does not imply that life will be free of problems and challenges of varying degrees. But neither should Christians blindly accept social, political and economic injustices without doing anything about them. Some of our society's structures and systems propagate evil, whether intentionally or unintentionally. Our mandate as the church is to walk with Jesus and be formed in him. Following are community resilience principles that the church can adopt as they seek to carry out the ministry of discipleship in traumatized communities.

First, provide an understanding of purpose and meaning of life. Traumatic events shatter dreams, established concepts about life and purpose for living. Through discipleship, we can provide an environment for finding meaning, relief from grief, emptiness and the struggle of making sense of traumatic events. When those who are affected by trauma can find personal meaning in the event, they can redefine their hopes and goals and find inspiration to move on.

Second, address suffering in a real way by acknowledging people's pain and questions and by listening to their venting and anger. Trauma affects our spiritual thoughts (such as life after death), our motivations (such as the virtue of being good), our feelings about human nature, as well as our relationships with others. Christian discipleship should seek to understand the suffering in the world and focus on enabling traumatized people to rise above the evils in society. The effects of trauma are painful, and so discipleship should also provide a safe space to acknowledge and unearth the trauma that people have faced. In societies that have experienced mass killings, there is the pain of losing loved ones, discouragement about lost property and the despair of living as a refugee or internally displaced person in a camp.

Third, provide an opening to explore spiritual interpretations for a traumatic event. It is difficult to function when deeply held beliefs and values are shaken and when traumatic events caused by human greed or negligence are regarded as acts of God. Thus it is important to remember that God created us because he loves us and never intended there to be tragedy, prejudice, wars, hatred, lust, greed, jealousy or pride. God meant for the earth to be a paradise, a place where there would be no death.

Fourth, affirm the traumatized person's spirituality. When we accept a personal relationship with God through Jesus Christ, we accept Jesus Christ as the owner of our whole life, physically and spiritually, and acknowledge his authority. In fact, the most ancient Christian declaration of faith was simply, "Jesus is Lord!" When foundations are shaken, our identity in Christ clarifies our walk with him (John 1:12; Col 2:9–10; 1 Pet 2:9).

Fifth, transform the sites of violence into sites of grace. When faced with violent conflicts, we need to challenge the urge to fight back or seek revenge by remembering what Jesus did to the people who spat and hit him. Grace, when understood as undeserved favour, enables us to extend that favour to others, just as in Christ we have freely received it. Discipleship should plant the seeds of love, forgiveness and reconciliation.

Sixth, address the issue of trust. Traumatic events can cause complete helplessness and threaten one's sense of self, one's loved ones, one's body, as well as one's sanity. Trauma produces extreme confusion and insecurity and challenges a person's sense of fitting in the world as well as one's reliance on institutions that buffer people from disaster. Thus it is important to deepen a traumatized person's reliance on God.

Seventh, incorporate the whole person. Some explain trauma as an emotional response to extraordinary events that exceed a body's functionality. However, trauma not only affects one's emotions, but the whole person. Levine highlights the importance of wholeness – mind, body, emotions, primitive instincts, intellect and spirituality.[32]

Eighth, explore coping skills and resources. Our spirituality plays a central role in our ability to cope with devastating events. After the 11 September 2001 attacks in the USA, 90 percent of survey respondents indicated that they coped by turning to their faith. Dass-Brailsford notes, "people with a strong spiritual orientation though they may experience a level of spiritual distress, hold on to the source of hope for recovery, wholeness and reconnection with life."[33]

Ninth, build resilience. At the individual or group level, the church community requires resilience. Those who are traumatized need to have the capacity to survive violence and loss as well as the ability to remain flexible over the course of a lifetime.[34] Thus war survivors and refugees need to be given opportunities to name their sense of reality while also being supported in their coping strategies.

Tenth, connect to a support network. Spiritual communities possess resources for understanding and interpreting traumatic stories, spiritual struggles, God's role in traumatic events and also recovery. Reconnecting to

32. Levine and Frederick, *Waking the Tiger*, 10.

33. Dass-Brailsford, *Crisis and Disaster*, 137.

34. Fuertes, "In Their Own," 492.

important people, places and values is a key link in the recovery process. Through shared narratives from the Scriptures, such as the life, death and resurrection of Christ, traumatized people can find hope and inspiration.

Finally, equip the body of Christ to be the voice of justice and agents of reconciliation. In addition to being the salt of the earth and light of the world, Christians are to demonstrate their devotion to God by "loosening the chains of injustice, untying the cords of the yoke . . . sharing food with the hungry, clothing the naked . . . (Isa 58:6–9; Matt 25:31–46; 2 Cor 5:17–20).

The Cost of Christian Discipleship in a War-torn Context

The Cost of Following Christ

Jesus himself said:

> If anyone comes to me and does not hate his own father and mother and wife and children and brothers and sisters, yes, and even his own life, he cannot be my disciple. Whoever does not bear his own cross and come after me cannot be my disciple . . . So therefore, any one of you who does not renounce all that he has cannot be my disciple. (Luke 14:26–27, 33)

Jesus lays out two of the costs of discipleship: hating our life and bearing our cross (vv. 26–27). Then he tells two parables – one about building a tower (vv. 28–30) and the other about a king making a battle plan (vv. 31–32) – that both make the same overall point, which is that a person must give careful consideration to the costs before rashly jumping into a project. Then he states a third cost of discipleship: giving up all our possessions (14:33).

The martyr Dietrich Bonhoeffer (1906–1945) explores these themes in *The Cost of Discipleship*, observing that:

> Costly grace is the gospel which must be sought again and again and again, the gift which must be asked for, the door at which a man must knock. Such grace is costly because it calls us to follow, and it is grace because it calls us to follow Jesus Christ. It is costly because it costs a man his life, and it is grace because it gives a man the only true life. It is costly because it condemns sin, and grace because it justifies the sinner. Above all, it is costly because it cost God the life of his Son: "Ye were bought at a price," and what has cost God much cannot be cheap for us. Above all, it is grace because God did not reckon his Son too dear a price to

> pay for our life, but delivered him up for us. Costly grace is the Incarnation of God.[35]

Whatever our context, as Christians we are called to a costly grace. As Bonhoeffer puts it, "When Christ calls a man, he bids him come and die. But it is the same death every time – death in Jesus Christ, the death of the old man at his call."[36] Jesus's summons to the rich young man was a call to die, because we must be dead to our own will in order to follow Christ. In fact, every command of Jesus is a call to die.

The Cost of Not Following Jesus

> Salt is good, but if salt has lost its taste, how shall its saltiness be restored? It is of no use either for the soil or for the manure pile. It is thrown away. He who has ears to hear, let him hear. (Luke 14:34–35)

In these next two verses in Luke's account, Jesus gives an illustration about salt to illustrate the cost of *not truly* following him. The salt in Jesus's day was often corrupted with other substances. If moisture hit the salt, it would evaporate and leave behind other impure minerals, and so the salt lost its saltiness and became worthless and had to be thrown away. In this metaphor, Jesus is saying that if a follower of his doesn't live as he ought to live, he becomes useless to God. The point is, we need to put Jesus above everything else in life so that we can be useful to God. Jesus concludes the parable with a warning: "He who has ears to hear, let him hear" (v. 35).

When Jesus prays to his Father that the cup may pass from him, his Father hears his prayer, for the cup of suffering passes from Christ – but only as he drinks it.

As Bonhoeffer explains it, "Discipleship means allegiance to the suffering Christ . . . It is a joy and token of his grace . . . To bear the cross proves to be the only way of triumphing over suffering."[37]

Discipleship, from a Christian perspective, is concerned with authentic Christian living. When we carefully consider how Jesus lived among us in the flesh, we can learn how we are meant to live as we are empowered by him who is with us always, even to the end of the age (Matt 28:20). In this way, we begin

---

35. Dietrich Bonhoeffer, *The Cost of Discipleship* (Solon, OH: Playaway, 2009), 5.
36. Bonhoeffer, 99.
37. Bonhoeffer, 45.

to live an intentional *imitatio Christi* (imitation of Christ), not in some slavish or literal fashion, but by catching the spirit and power in which he lived and learning to "follow in his steps" (1 Pet 2:21).[38]

In seeking to strengthen the disciples and encourage them to continue in the faith, Paul and Barnabas offer the following admonition: "We must go through many hardships to enter the kingdom of God" (Acts 14:22).

Conclusion

As followers of Jesus, we continually walk with him and are being formed in him. Paul's prayer for the church in Colossae is an appropriate call for followers of Jesus who are living amidst cycles of conflict, war and trauma:

> We continually ask God to fill you with the knowledge of his will through all the wisdom and understanding that the Spirit gives, so that you may live a life worthy of the Lord and please him in every way: bearing fruit in every good work, growing in the knowledge of God, being strengthened with all power according to his glorious might so that you may have great endurance and patience, and giving joyful thanks to the Father, who has qualified you to share in the inheritance of his holy people in the kingdom of light. For he has rescued us from the dominion of darkness and brought us into the kingdom of the Son he loves, in whom we have redemption, the forgiveness of sins. (Col 1:9b–14 NIV)

The task of the church is to build up believers in any context. When Jesus gave the mandate to make disciples of all nations, Palestine was under the authority of the Roman government. We have received the gospel today because the disciples dared to be bold and faithful to Christ's great commission amidst political and religious persecution, violence, prejudice and oppression. We can do the same and much more through him who strengthens us (Phil 4:13).

Bibliography

Asbury Bible Commentary, Online. "Historical context of the New Testament." https://www.biblegateway.com/resources/asbury-bible-commentary/toc/.

Bonhoeffer, Dietrich. *Life Together: The Classic Exploration of Faith in Community*. New York: Harper One, 2009.

38. Richard J. Foster, *Streams of Living Water* (Harper Collins Publishers: San Francisco, 1998), 3.

———. *The Cost of Discipleship*. Solon, OH: Playaway, 2009.

CFR Experts. "Violence in the Democratic Republic of Congo." October 17, 2016. http://www.cirsd.org/en/cirsd-recommends/violence-in-the-democratic-republic-of-congo.

Dass-Brailsford, Priscilla, ed. *Crisis and Disaster Counselling: Lessons Learned from Hurricane Katrina and Other Disasters*. Los Angeles: Sage Publications, 2010.

Foster, Richard. *Streams of Living Water*. San Francisco: Harper Collins Publishers, 1998.

Fuertes, Al B. "In Their Own Words: Contextualizing Discourse of (War) Trauma and Healing." *Conflict Resolution Quarterly* 21, no. 4 (Summer 2004): 491–501.

Gerardi, Donald. "Jesus and the Christian Tradition." Online article. http://academic.brooklyn.cuny.edu/history/dfg/jesu/topic2.htm.

Gingrich, Heather Davediuk. *Restoring the Shattered Self: A Christian Counsellor's Guide to Complex Trauma*. Downers Grove: InterVarsity Press, 2013. http://globalchristiancenter.com/christian-living/bible-studies/895-discipleship-in-the-gospel-of-mark.

Global Conflict Tracker. "Violence in the democratic republic of Congo." Accessed February 2017. http://www.cfr.org/global/global-conflict-tracker/p32137#!/conflict/violence-in-the-democratic-republic-of-congo.

Howard-Brook, Wes, and Sharon Ringe, eds. *The New Testament: Introducing the Way of Discipleship*. Maryknoll: Orbis, 2002.

International Coalition for the Responsibility to Protect. "Crisis in DRC." Accessed February 2017. http://www.responsibilitytoprotect.org/index.php/crises/crisis-in-drc#humanrights.

Johnson, Luke T. *The Writings of the New Testament: An Interpretation*. Philadelphia: Fortress Press, 1986.

Levine, Peter A., and Ann Frederick. *Waking the Tiger: Healing Trauma*. Berkeley, CA: North Atlantic Books, 1997.

Mills, Watson E. *New Testament History and Background*. Lewiston, NY; Lampeter, Wales: Edwin Mellen, 2002.

Rocky Mountain Christian Institute. *New Testament History*. 2008. https://studyres.com/doc/3380026/new-testament-history---rocky-mountain-christian.

Sanders, E. P. "Jesus in Historical Context." *Sage Journal* 50, no. 3 (October 1993): 429–448.

Tabor, James. "The Jewish Roman World of Jesus." https://clas-pages.uncc.edu/james-tabor/the-roman-world-of-jesus-an-overview/.

Weller, Dough, John Ortberg, Mark Foreman, Scott Dudley eds. *First Century Context of NT*. Retrieved from: http://www.jesuscentral.com/ji/historical-jesus/jesus-firstcenturycontext.php.

Wimberly, Edward. "Story Telling and Managing Trauma: Health and Spirituality at Work." *Journal of Health Care for the Poor and Underserved* 22, no. 3 (2011): 48–57.

Yoder, Carolyn. *The Little Book of Trauma Healing: When Violence Strikes and Community Security Is Threatened*. Intercourse, PA: Good Books, 2005.

9

The Bad, the Ugly, the Worst

A Reflection on Christian Forgiveness towards Perpetrators of Traumatic Experiences

Amos Winarto Oei

Forgiveness is the most distinctive characteristic of Christian faith. Huston Smith, the great scholar of religious studies, has made a list of what he considered to be the unique, distinctive characteristics of the various faiths. When he got to Christianity, Smith simply said, "Forgiveness. Forgiveness of enemies. This is the very strange notion that makes the teaching of Jesus distinctive."[1] Forgiveness is central to the gospel of Jesus Christ because the gospel tells the good news about God's forgiveness to us and commands us to forgive one another. Forgiveness is closely related to the themes of sin, repentance and new life and is perhaps the most essential task of Christian living. Nevertheless, forgiving and being forgiven are not simple but rather extremely complex practices. Therefore, while recognizing the complexity of forgiveness, I will argue that Christian forgiveness is "love practiced among people who love poorly,"[2] which should be distinguished from pardoning, condoning or forgetting.

1. Quoted in William H. Willimon, "Matthew 5:43–48," *Interpretation* 57, no. 1 (January 2003): 63.

2. Philip Yancey, *What's So Amazing about Grace?* (Grand Rapids: Zondervan, 1997), 92.

The Challenge of Forgiveness

What makes forgiveness so complex? While the idea of forgiveness may seem simple in itself and a matter of common experience, forgiveness has always confronted Christians with a host of existential and pastoral difficulties. Questions frequently arise about whether, under certain circumstances, it is even right to forgive. What preconditions may or may not be required to prevent forgiveness from becoming cheap grace, a cowardly way of avoiding the hard edge of truth? When is it appropriate to forgive? When should forgiveness be withheld, if ever? When others have wronged us, how can we get past our desire for punishment, revenge or righteous anger to forgive from the heart? These questions about forgiveness are so troublesome that many books have been dedicated to the topic.[3]

Our era has witnessed human violence on a scale that was unknown in biblical antiquity, including the holocaust and other genocides and cruelties. Such evil has run rampant in the earth's history. We can feel the anguished sentiment of individuals suffering personal tragedy and victimization when we hear the petition that Elie Wiesel made to God in 1995 at ceremonies marking the fiftieth anniversary of the end of the World War II and the liberation of Auschwitz: "God of forgiveness, do not forgive those who created this place. God of mercy, have no mercy on those who killed here Jewish children."[4] Such a prayer makes people uncomfortable. However, the prayer shows how difficult it is for people to forgive and be forgiven. As the German poet Heine said, "It is not that hard to forgive one's enemy – but only after they have all been hanged!"[5] Even Nietzsche dismissed talk of enemy love as "weak and dishonest."[6] What contributions does Christianity give to the discussion of forgiveness?

---

3. To mention some of them: E. L. Worthington Jr, ed., *Dimensions of Forgiveness: Psychological Research and Theological Perspectives* (Philadelphia: Templeton Foundation Press, 1998); Geiko Muller-Fahrenholz, *The Art of Forgiveness: Theological Reflection on Healing and Reconciliation* (Geneva: World Council of Churches Publication, 1997); Lewis B. Smedes, *The Art of Forgiving: When You Need to Forgive and Don't Know How* (New York: Ballantine Books, 1996); Martha Alken, *The Healing Power of Forgiving* (New York: Crossroad, 1997); Michael E. McCullough, Kenneth I. Pargament, and Carl E. Thoresen, eds., *Forgiveness: Theory, Research, and Practice* (New York: Guilford Press, 2000); Robert J. Schreiter, *Reconciliation: Mission and Ministry in a Changing Social Order* (Maryknoll: Orbis, 1997).

4. Daniel P. Moloney, "Getting Even: Forgiveness and Its Limits," *First Things* 140 (February 2004): 45, https://www.firstthings.com/article/2004/02/getting-even-forgiveness-and-its-limits.

5. Quoted in Willimon, "Matthew 5:43–48," 61.

6. Quoted in Willimon, 61.

Christian Forgiveness

Christian forgiveness should be distinguished from pardoning, condoning or forgetting. *Pardoning* is the act of tolerating a wrongdoing without demanding a penalty. When we pardon people, we allow an offense to pass without punishment. Christian forgiveness should not be defined as pardoning because if we forgive too easily, we will ignore the genuine damage that has been done. People might argue that we should not cultivate hatred and that we should let go of our hatred by "forgiving" (i.e. pardoning) the offender. It is true that we should not let our hatred consume us, but the argument can be dangerous if it encourages us to lower our guard and allow ourselves to be victimized again.

Moreover, when someone unjustly attacks us, we ought not to like it and should not easily pardon it. Indeed, to give pardon so easily shows an inappropriate sense of justice. As human beings, we should be concerned, perhaps even angry, with the injustice that has been done. Aristotle made a similar point in the *Nicomachean Ethics* that there is a certain sort of anger that we ought to have towards violations of the good, provided our passions and desires are correctly ordered.[7] Therefore, pardoning is not Christian forgiveness because easily letting go of an offense without the demand of justice demonstrates an inadequate love of the good.

God's forgiveness for our sins is not a pardon either. There is a price to pay for the forgiveness of sins. Hebrews 9:22 says, "Without the shedding of blood there is no forgiveness of sins." The context of the text argues, as Lane points out, that this kind of forgiveness signals a definitive putting away of defilement or a decisive purgation.[8] Blood must be shed for our sins, but the good news is that God pays the price through Jesus Christ, his Son, rather than through us. In this way, justice is served. God does not pardon us but forgives us by paying the price, which as human beings we cannot pay.

Condoning can be defined as an attitude that treats something wrong, destructive and evil as acceptable. While pardoning demonstrates a lack of love toward justice, condoning demonstrates excessive tolerance toward injustice as we passively sit by while destruction is taking place. Condoning disregards authentic compassion for the emotional and spiritual pain that has been caused by unjust treatment. God has given human beings a sense of compassion for others that wants to fight against injustice. Suppressing authentic compassion by condoning an evil action is not Christian forgiveness,

7. Quoted in Daniel P. Moloney, "Getting Even: Forgiveness and its Limits," 46.

8. William L. Lane, *Hebrews 9–13*, Word Biblical Commentary 47B (Dallas: Word, 1998), 246–247.

because hastily condoning a wrongdoer may endorse the immoral message that the wrongdoer did no wrong.

God forgives our sins but he does not condone them. Genesis 3 testifies how God deals with sinful humans. He does not say, "It is okay, you're good," but he condemns them and sends them out from the garden. Even though God does not condone sin, he promises a solution for the problem: "I will put enmity between you and the woman, and between your offspring and her offspring; he shall bruise your head, and you shall bruise his heel" (Gen 3:15). K. A. Matthews says that "Christian tradition has referred to 3:15 as the *protevangelium* since it has been taken as the prototype for the Christian gospel."[9] Paul identifies Christ as the "seed" ultimately intended in the promissory blessing to Abraham (Gal 3:16). The Apostle John affirms this when Jesus indicted the Pharisees as children of the "devil" because of their spiritual apostasy (John 8:44), contrary to their claims to be the offspring of righteous Abraham (8:39). John also uses similar imagery when he contrasts God's "seed" and those who are "of the devil" (1 John 3:7–10).

Finally, Christian forgiveness does not suggest *forgetting* about the wrong that has been done. If we define forgiveness as the act of "letting bygones be bygones," we have not dealt with our past adequately. When malice and wrong occur, we become upset, and if we try to forget the wrongs, our hurt will continue to recur and will relentlessly consume us. As philosopher George Santayana poignantly puts it, "those who forget the past are doomed to repeat it."[10]

Thus forgiveness in Christianity does not mean forgetting the horrors of the past, nor that we transform the memory of the horrors into grudges that should be avenged. Rather, Christian forgiveness involves "surveying the damage one incurred through the harmful action of another and eventually remembering it differently rather than trying to erase it from memory."[11] We should not forget but remember the horrors of the past because they have contributed to our identity in the present. It is important to remember because "we should not let such atrocities happen again . . . It means taking what happened seriously and not minimizing it; drawing out the sting in the memory that threatens

9. K. A. Mathews, *Genesis 1–11:26*, The New American Commentary 1A (Nashville: Broadman & Holman, 1996), 247.

10. Quoted by Desmond Tutu, *No Future without Forgiveness* (New York: Image Doubleday, 1999), 29.

11. F. LeRon Shults and Steven J. Sandage, *The Faces of Forgiveness: Searching for Wholeness and Salvation* (Grand Rapids: Baker Academic, 2003), 22.

to poison our entire existence."[12] One benefit of forgiving rather than trying to forget is that it helps us to grow in the process of Christian sanctification.

Does God "forget" our sins? Isaiah 43:25 seems to suggest this, but the context reveals that God does not forget but rather deals adequately with our sins. God requires justice, but when God forgives, he never opens up old sore points. Thus Isaiah 43:25 begins with the sentence: "I, I am he who blots out your transgressions for my own sake." Lange observes that "He says He will do it for His own sake. There is that in Himself that impels Him to this: It is love. It does not rest till it has found the ways and means of gratifying itself without trenching on justice."[13] God does not forget our sins, because he cannot tolerate sin and thereby undermine justice. But when he forgives our sins, he does not accuse us with the sins over and over again.

So far we have distinguished Christian forgiveness from pardoning, condoning and forgetting. We have defined Christian forgiveness, with Yancey, as "love practiced among people who love poorly." This definition needs further elaboration so that we can understand Christian forgiveness properly.

Henri Nouwen eloquently describes Christian forgiveness as the practice of divine love in daily life:

> I have often said, "I forgive you," but even as I said these words my heart remained angry or resentful. I still wanted to hear the story that tells me that I was right after all; I still wanted to hear apologies and excuses; I still wanted the satisfaction of receiving some praises in return – if only the praise for being so forgiving.
>
> But God's forgiveness is unconditional; it comes from a heart that does not demand anything for itself, a heart that is completely empty of self-seeking. It is this divine forgiveness that I have to practice in my daily life. It calls me to keep stepping over all my arguments that say forgiveness is unwise, unhealthy, and impractical. It challenges me to step over all my needs for gratitude and compliments. Finally, it demands of me that I step over that wounded part of my heart that feels hurt and wronged and that wants to stay in control and put a few conditions between me and the one whom I am asked to forgive.[14]

---

12. Desmond Tutu, *No Future*, 271.

13. John Peter Lange et al., *A Commentary on the Holy Scriptures: Isaiah* (Bellingham, WA: Logos Bible Software, 2008), 472.

14. Quoted by Yancey, *What's So Amazing*, 92.

Nouwen's description identifies the divine nature of Christian forgiveness. The source of Christian forgiveness is God himself. Because God loves us first, we practice love toward others through forgiveness.

The Lord's Prayer helps us to understand the divine nature of Christian forgiveness: "forgive our sins as we forgive those who sin against us" (Matt 6:12). It is not that our forgiveness of others earns us the right to be forgiven. Rather, because God loves us so much, he allows himself to forgive us. As God's forgiven people, we should imitate him by practicing love through forgiveness. Christians live out love through forgiveness because this practice reflects God. Bonhoeffer says that he made every effort to practice love by forgiving his enemies and praying for his persecutors because "God loves his enemies – that is the glory of his love, as every follower of Jesus knows."[15]

Christian forgiveness as the practice of divine love recognizes human beings as made in the image of God. As Desmond Tutu describes, forgiveness seeks "to rehabilitate and affirm the dignity and personhood"[16] of humans as being made in God's image, even for the worst criminal. Tutu's book *No Future without Forgiveness* outlines the core of Tutu's personal theology and social philosophy, which can be summed up by the term *ubuntu,* which originally refers to the African expression that "a person is a person through other persons."[17] This relational philosophy is then understood in theological terms as indicating the oneness that is brought through the new human, Jesus the Christ. Forgiveness is the means of overcoming the division – exemplified by apartheid – between people and races and restoring the image of God through a new humanity in Christ, when "enemies might become friends again, when the dehumanized perpetrator might be helped to recover his lost humanity."[18]

Forgiveness as divine "love practiced among people"[19] is the way that Christians participate in the grand movement through which God intends to bring all things in heaven and on earth to a unity in Christ. Teilhard de Chardin, quoted by Tutu, explains this movement toward unity in Christ:

> May the time come when men (and women) having been awakened to the close bond linking all the movements of this world in the single all-embracing work of the Incarnation, shall be unable to give themselves to any one of their tasks without illuminating it

15. Quoted by Yancey, 89.
16. Tutu, *No Future*, 30.
17. Tutu, 35.
18. Tutu, 158.
19. Yancey, *What's So Amazing*, 92.

> with the clear vision that their work, however elementary it may be, is received and put to good use by a Centre of the Universe.[20]

One important observation from de Chardin's explanation is that a new historical situation was created for humanity by Christ through his incarnation. Humanity can only be a part of this new creation in Christ through God's love. As Lewis Smedes argues, "to make a discovery that one is in Christ is, at the same time and with the same wonder, to confess that one is in Christ because God's love freely desired a new creation in Christ."[21] Thus people may experience Christian forgiveness because they realize that hostility can be brought to an end only by practicing the kind of love that is made possible within the new humanity, which has been created through union with Christ, who loved us first and gave his life for us.

Our common sense, however, struggles to admit forgiveness. At least, it is unlikely for us to let go wrongs that have been done to us without seeing justice imposed on the perpetrator. We all too often drift back into "a tit-for-tat struggle," a term that Yancey coins, which closes the door on forgiveness.[22] As human beings, Yancey explains, we "nurse sores, go to elaborate lengths to rationalize our behavior, perpetuate family feuds, punish ourselves, and punish others"[23] in order to avoid this one practice of love: forgiveness.

In our world, which runs by laws of reciprocity and retribution, Christian forgiveness meets the demand of justice in a unique way. As divine "love practiced among people who love poorly,"[24] Christian forgiveness assumes that God is a better justice maker than human beings. By forgiving, we surrender our own right to get even and leave all concerns about fairness for God to work out. We leave the scales in God's hands, which must weigh justice and mercy in balance. Though the atrocities do not disappear when we forgive, they lose their hold on us and are taken over by God. This means that God may not deal with a perpetrator as we wish. This is another unique feature of Christian forgiveness: in the personal realm, we allow God to be the judge instead of ourselves.

Furthermore, Christian forgiveness involves an act of faith. By forgiving, we are "declaring our faith in the future of a relationship and in the capacity of the wrongdoer to make a new beginning on a course that will be different from

---

20. Tutu, *No Future*, 267.
21. Lewis B. Smedes, *Union with Christ* (Grand Rapids: Zondervan, 1983), 90.
22. Yancey, *What's So Amazing*, 92.
23. Yancey, 86.
24. Yancey, 92.

the one that caused us the wrong . . . it is an act of faith that the wrongdoer can change."[25] Christian forgiveness meets the demand of justice through restoration rather than retribution.

Christian forgiveness as "love practiced among people who love poorly"[26] recognizes the fallen state of human beings, whose every intention of the heart "was only evil continually" (Gen 6:5). Our capacity and ability to love as fallen human beings has been severely damaged. Because of our flawed ability to love, we need divine assistance in order to love others well. Christian forgiveness is not merely "pie in the sky," because it gets its character and style from the controlling and liberating Spirit, who is working continuously in the lives of Christians. Though non-Christians may recognize the value of forgiveness because of its physical and psychological benefits, such as health, stress release and peace of mind,[27] Christians are motivated to forgive because they have been united to Christ by the Spirit. If we forgive because we want to have good health, release stress and have peace of mind, then we should consider the question that Jesus asks his disciples, "What more are you doing *than others*? Do not even the Gentiles do the same?" (Matt 5:47). As Christians, we practice divine love through forgiveness because we are Christ's disciples and children of God, who "walk not according to the flesh but according to the Spirit" (Rom 8:4). The benefits from Christian forgiveness are the effects of our obedience to this practice of love rather than our motivations.

As "love practiced among people who love poorly,"[28] Christian forgiveness acknowledges both parties, the one who forgives as well as the one who receives forgiveness. As Tutu observes, it admits that "confession, forgiveness, and reparation, wherever feasible, form part of a continuum."[29] Ideally, both parties will experience confession, forgiveness and reparation, but there are other possibilities along this continuum since we are still living in a broken world. For example, one may forgive without hearing any confession or receiving reparation from others. Or one may seek forgiveness and never obtain it from others, even if there is an attempt to make reparations. Because of the brokenness of our world and the deep fallenness of human nature, forgiveness may or may not lead to reconciliation and reparation. However, this does not mean that Christian forgiveness is impossible. Rather, the divine nature of

25. Tutu, *No Future*, 273.

26. Yancey, *What's So Amazing*, 92.

27. Debbie Robinson, "Forgiving the Unrepentant," *Christianity Today* (March 2005): 78.

28. Yancey, *What's So Amazing*, 92.

29. Tutu, *No Future*, 273.

Christian forgiveness compels Christians, who are empowered by the Holy Spirit, to forgive and seek forgiveness because there is always the hope for reconciliation and restoration – if not in this life, in the life to come.

Conclusion

Christianity revolutionizes our assumptions about forgiveness. It teaches that all humans are fallen and recognizes that even criminals are loved by God. It also reminds us that the universe is providentially ordered and that God, as the supreme judge, will bring justice to every crime and atrocity in this world. If we think that we alone can or must make everything right, then we risk taking on a kind of self-importance that makes forgiveness of others difficult, if not impossible. Trusting in God's providence, on the other hand, guards us against such overreaching.

When we receive or extend Christian forgiveness, we become our true selves and are set free from the bondage of estranged relationship and strengthened for a new life of love, care and right relating. Christian forgiveness is a profound and subtle form of transformation that is made possible by the work of the Holy Spirit, which reaches into the depths of our souls. The basis of Christian forgiveness is God's love. The motivation for Christian forgiveness is to live according to the Spirit. Consequently, Christian forgiveness transforms our relationships by reflecting divine love as it is "practiced among people who love poorly."[30]

Bibliography

Alken, Martha. *The Healing Power of Forgiving*. New York: Crossroad, 1997.

Lane, William L. *Hebrews 9–13*. Word Biblical Commentary 47B. Dallas: Word, 1998.

Lange, John Peter, et al. *A Commentary on the Holy Scriptures: Isaiah*. Bellingham, WA: Logos Bible Software, 2008.

Mathews, K. A. *Genesis 1–11:26*. The New American Commentary 1A. Nashville: Broadman & Holman, 1996.

McCullough, Michael E., Kenneth I. Pargament, and Carl E. Thoresen, eds. *Forgiveness: Theory, Research, and Practice*. New York: Guilford Press, 2000.

Moloney, Daniel P. "Getting Even: Forgiveness and Its Limits." *First Things* 140 (February 2004): 45. https://www.firstthings.com/article/2004/02/getting-even-forgiveness-and-its-limits.

30. Yancey, *What's So Amazing*, 92.

Muller-Fahrenholz, Geiko. *The Art of Forgiveness: Theological Reflection on Healing and Reconciliation*. Geneva: World Council of Churches Publication, 1997.

Robinson, Debbie. "Forgiving the Unrepentant." *Christianity Today* 49, no. 3 (March 2005): 78.

Schreiter, Robert J. *Reconciliation: Mission and Ministry in a Changing Social Order*. Maryknoll: Orbis, 1997.

Shults, F. LeRon, and Steven J. Sandage. *The Faces of Forgiveness: Searching for Wholeness and Salvation*. Grand Rapids: Baker Academic, 2003.

Smedes, Lewis B. *The Art of Forgiving: When You Need to Forgive and Don't Know How*. New York: Ballantine Books, 1996.

———. *Union With Christ*. Grand Rapids: Zondervan, 1983.

Tutu, Desmond. *No Future without Forgiveness*. New York: Image Doubleday, 1999.

Willimon, William H. "Matthew 5:43–48." *Interpretation* 57, no. 1 (January 2003).

Worthington Jr, E. L., ed. *Dimensions of Forgiveness: Psychological Research and Theological Perspectives*. Philadelphia: Templeton Foundation Press, 1998.

Yancey, Philip. *What's So Amazing about Grace?* Grand Rapids: Zondervan, 1997.

10

Pastoral and Spiritual Response to Trauma and Tragedy

Naji Abi-Hashem

Introduction

Trauma is a very broad and rich concept with many layers and dimensions. It cannot be easily defined in one simple line or compact sentence. Though the term *trauma* is quite popular these days, it can mean different things to different people, depending on their psychological awareness, life experience, emotional tendency and cultural background.

The subjects related to trauma, such as traumatic stress, secondary trauma, acute stress disorder, vicarious trauma, posttraumatic stress disorder, complex trauma, traumatic grief or bereavement and cultural aspects of trauma, are on the front lines of many helping professions and healthcare disciplines, especially for cross-cultural workers and humanitarian caregivers. Many academic fields and people-helping services, including pastoral psychology and counseling, are trying to incorporate some form of trauma awareness and healing into their courses of study, practical training and research curriculum. Therefore there is an increased need, both locally and globally, to understand the nature, causes, types, manifestations, impacts and treatments of trauma and other related tragic events.

Defining Terminologies

Trauma can be described as a force that disturbs the functioning of a person, organism, group or given system, which can cause serious malfunction and personal-communal damage. Usually, trauma fragments the internal mind, unsettles the emotions and wounds the soul. Trauma also affects social behavior, existential outlook, sense of stability and interpersonal relationships.

Tragedy can be similarly perceived as a major calamity, dreadful incident, serious misfortune, strong adversity, deeply sad and fatal event, grave moral failure (as an ethical downfall), horrible occurrence, distressing loss causing significant grief, social dilemma resulting in shame or agony, or an invading event that shatters the reality of survivors.

Disaster is a sudden, hazardous, unfavorable, and catastrophic happening that brings great physical destruction and psychological harm to a family or community. Disaster can be natural (volcano, earthquake, storm, flood, fire) or human-made (attack, riot, explosion, fighting, plague, killing, war). Either kind leaves behind ruins and material damages, and depending on the magnitude of the catastrophe, the damaged society is typically unable to recover on its own or by using its limited resources.

Though the definitions of terms related to trauma can range widely, terminologies have been used in the literature interchangeably, without significant technical distinction among them. Generally speaking, a *traumatic event* is perceived as a major shock or a powerful invader that shakes the stability of the private lives of individuals and communities alike and removes the familiar aspects of daily routine and normal functioning.

Effects of Trauma and Tragedy

Devastating accidents, violent crimes, sudden illnesses, unexpected deaths, severe abuses, forceful separations, natural disasters, religious persecutions, bomb explosions and armed conflicts all generate strong feelings of horror, debilitation and helplessness. These traumatic feelings affect all aspects of life: mental-emotional, biological-physical, interpersonal-behavioral, religious-spiritual, social-communal, existential-philosophical and traditional-cultural. After any tragic event, the victims who are deeply impacted at both personal-individual and collective-communal levels often struggle with aftermath consequences for weeks, months or years to come.

When some researchers evaluated people who survived a trauma, they discovered three time-related effects or responses: the instant-immediate reactions (pressing effect), the intermediate-transitional reactions (integrated effect) and the long-term-chronic reactions (unresolved effect).[1]

Experiences of acute stress and tragic occurrences affect all people, each in their own way, regardless of age or status. Several factors greatly affect how people interpret, experience and express tragedies and traumas, which include ethnic, social, cultural, religious, psychological and existential factors. Interestingly, communities and nations tend to react, struggle, cope, process, survive or recover from calamities and disasters in a fashion that is similar to an individual self or a single person.

Responding to Trauma

Emotionally struggling people and victims of tragic disturbances normally seek their spiritual leaders, friends, teachers, local pastors or religious mentors before seeking other professionals, such as a counselor, nurse, therapist, physician or healthcare provider. Mainly, distressed and troubled people are looking for soothing affirmation, supportive presence and calming assurance. Following any crisis or trauma, people need to restore a sense of stability and security along with a balanced worldview while they process their sense of loss, grief, shock, trauma and bereavement. Those who have been traumatized have an existential need to gain a better perspective, seek comfort and become anchored in a larger reality than their diminished circle of existence or shattered world,

1. Abi-Hashem, "Clinical Trauma Psychology," in *Encyclopedia of Trauma: An Interdisciplinary Guide*, ed. C. R. Figley (Thousand Oaks, CA: Sage, 2012), 98–100; "Religious and Pastoral Responses to Trauma," *Encyclopedia*, 542–544; "Trauma, Coping, and Resiliency among Syrian Refugees in Lebanon and Beyond: A Profile of a Nation at War," in *Human Strengths and Resilience: Developmental, Cross-Cultural, and International Perspectives*, ed. G. Rich and J. Sirikantraporn (Lanham, MD: Lexington Books, 2018), 105–130; Beck and Sloan, *The Oxford Handbook of Traumatic Stress Disorders* (Oxford: Oxford University Press, 2012); Collins and Long, "Working with the Psychological Effects of Trauma: Consequences for Mental HealthCare Workers – a Literature Review," *Journal of Psychiatric and Mental Health Nursing* 10, no. 4 (2003): 417–424; Gingrich, *Restoring the Shattered Self: A Christian Counselor's Guide to Complex Trauma* (Downers Grove: InterVarsity Press, 2013); Joseph and Linley, *Trauma, Recovery, and Growth: Positive Psychological Perspectives on Posttraumatic Stress* (Hoboken, NJ: Wiley, 2006); Meichenbaum, *A Clinical Handbook/Practical Therapist Manual for Assessing and Treating Adults with PTSD* (Waterloo, ON: Institute Press, 1994); Murray, *Understanding Loss: A Guide for Caring for Those Facing Adversity* (New York: Routledge, 2016); SAMHSA, "Trauma-informed Care in Behavioral Health Services," *Treatment Improvement Protocol Series* 57 (Rockville, MD: Substance Abuse and Mental Health Services Administration, 2014); Van der Kolk, "Clinical Implications of Neuroscience Research in PTSD," *Annals of the New York Academy of Science* 1, no. 2 (2006): 1–17; *The Body Keeps the Score: Brain, Mind, and Body in the Healing of Trauma* (New York: Penguin Books, 2015).

and so they seek a deep connection that transcends the disturbing physical event and the emotional field of pain.

Religious thought and spiritual experience are vital parts of the human journey. Most people in warm cultures (closely bonded communities and tight-knit societies) are openly religious and devout practitioners of some type of spirituality, at least on the traditional level. Religious identity is part of our social identity, and so the social is religious, and the religious is cultural, and the cultural is political-existential, and the existential is psychological, and so on. Because our spheres of life and the dimensions of our personality are all interconnected, a strong experience (either pleasant or unpleasant) in one realm affects the functions in other realms as well.[2]

Most religious groups and communities of faith mobilize their resources to serve those who are hurting, underserved and traumatized in their neighborhoods. Clergy and church leaders are among the first to respond to major crises, horrific accidents, social turmoil, sudden tragedies, natural disasters and war conflicts. Most religious organizations set aside a budget for humanitarian aid and compassionate funds. In addition, many pastors have shown great interest in gaining some counseling skills in order to help those who are struggling and suffering emotionally or mentally. The fields of pastoral care and counseling, as well as the programs in chaplaincy and soul care, have gained a lot of attention in recent decades. Such disciplines integrate active listening and empathy skills with sound principles of psychology and healthy living, along with the depth of faith and the richness of spiritual life, into caring for the human mind and soul and the wellbeing of both individuals and families.

---

2. Abi-Hashem, "Cross-Cultural Psychology," in *Baker Encyclopedia of Psychology and Counseling*, 2nd ed., ed. D. G. Benner and P. C. Hill (Grand Rapids: Baker,1999), 294–298; "On Cultural Resiliency," *The Australian Community Psychologist* 23 (2011): 23–31; "Counseling," in *Encyclopedia of Cross-cultural Psychology*, ed. K. D. Keith (Malden, MA: Wiley-Blackwell, 2013), 257–260; "Religion and Spirituality," in *Encyclopedia of Cross-Cultural Psychology*, ed. K. D. Keith (Malden, MA: Wiley-Blackwell, 2013), 1091–1094; "Revisiting Cultural Awareness and Cultural Relevancy," *American Psychologist* 70 (2015): 660–661; "Worldview, the Concept of," in *Encyclopedia of Psychology and Religion*, ed. D. A. Leeming (Springer Online Living Reference, 2017), 1–6; Augsburger, *Pastoral Counseling across Cultures* (Philadelphia: Westminster John Knox, 1986); Dueck and Johnson, "Cultural Psychology of Religion: Spiritual Transformation," *Pastoral Psychology* 65 (2016): 299–328; Shaw, Joseph and Linley, "Religion, Spirituality, and Posttraumatic Growth: A Systematic Review," *Mental Health, Religion & Culture* 8, no. 1 (2005): 1–11; Smelser, "Psychological Trauma and Cultural Trauma," in *Cultural Trauma and Collective Identity*, ed. J. C. Alexander, R. Eyerman, B. Giesen, N. J. Smelser and P. Sztompka (Berkeley: University of California Press, 2004), 31–59; Tillich, *Theology of Culture* (New York: Oxford University Press, 1959).

Pastors, ministers and lay workers have long been called upon to help in times of serious crisis, calamity and death and are increasingly called upon to respond to tragedies and to serve on the front lines of trauma and disasters.[3] They are expected to be spiritually present and fully ready to intervene in times of loss, grief and adversity. Through active listening and bonding, reading selected Scriptures, leading therapeutic prayers, facilitating reflection and sharing, showing support and compassionate care and simply being present either in silence or with a few spoken words, they can be of tremendous help and healing to victims and survivors. Though pastoral counselors have an important role to play in stressful times and during the dark nights of the human soul, they can become at risk of trauma-induced conditions, such as *burnout* and *compassion fatigue*, as well as *secondary trauma* (also known as *vicarious trauma*) from hearing graphic stories or being tangibly exposed to drastic circumstances, troubled populations and unexpected catastrophes. Therefore, pastoral counselors and spiritual caregivers must know their limited abilities, learn healthy coping skills and seek coaching and debriefing periods from qualified counselors when they feel overwhelmed and depleted. Examples would be when caregivers become drained, stressed out, exhausted, irritable, depressed, self-doubting, sleepless, highly anxious, lose the desire to serve, resentful and so on.[4]

Responding to Grief after Trauma

When acute grief is connected with a tragedy or traumatic event, normal grief symptoms mingle together with traumatic reactions, intensifying survivors' emotions and confusing their minds. These combined emotions may include depression, anxiety, grief, loss, trauma, disaster, physical ailment and psychological adjustment and may affect the survivors individually, as a family or as a community.

As a result, the way toward healing and recovery becomes longer and more demanding, especially if the causes of traumatic stress and the experience of mourning both continue for an extended period of time. This is often the case with open-ended wars, when people have no space to breathe, mourn or reflect

---

3. Aten and Boan, *Disaster Ministry Handbook* (Downers Grove: InterVarsity Press, 2016); Wright, *The Complete Guide to Crisis and Trauma Counseling: What to Do and Say When It Matters Most* (Ventura, CA: Regal Books, 2011).

4. Ashley and Lockwood, "The Role of Religious Leaders in Crisis Response: Caring for the Soul," 2007; Benner, *Care of Souls: Revisioning Christian Nurture and Counsel* (Grand Rapids: Baker Books, 1998).

on the chaos around them because their main concern is daily survival. Thus it is important to address both conditions simultaneously by alternating between grief and healing, on the one hand, and trauma recovery, on the other hand.

Since most of the world's population live in collective societies, tight-knit communities and warm cultures, healing and recovery must consider both the individual and collective aspects of trauma, loss and grief. Healing must move beyond the personal scope of a single trauma to the concept of *social trauma* and beyond individual grief to the concept of *collective grief*.

After a trauma, disaster or tragedy, a community normally reacts, suffers and recovers much like a single person. Thus pastors and spiritual leaders can respond well to the collective nature of suffering and comfort, sorrow and joy, failure and triumph, turmoil and peace, agony and blessing. They can lead, teach, preach and conduct services in a therapeutic way that brings a sense of communal solidarity, restoration, insight, consolation and recovery to their communities of faith. Effective Scriptures include those that portray mercy to the afflicted, peace in times of trouble, empathy with the sufferer, hearing the cries of the broken-hearted, grace for the weak, solace to the distraught, divine presence in the dark shadows and hope for the future days.

Responding to Existential Disorientation

Following any major loss, trauma or tragedy, survivors usually struggle not only with emotional devastation but also with existential disorientation and philosophical wondering. Many begin to question the meaning of life, the purpose of existence, the theological sovereignty of God, the usefulness of piety or faith, the place and role of worship or church along with many other basic religious tenets, beliefs and practices. Bereaved or traumatized people often struggle with crises of faith and show significant doubts toward God, and they may display resentment toward religious organizations and establishments or avoid religious gatherings and spiritual activities. They often isolate themselves and may engage in unhealthy behaviors as a coping strategy, even ones that are totally uncharacteristic of their personality and previous lifestyle (e.g. drinking alcohol, smoking, gambling, etc.). This may be because they have a low tolerance for stress or a weak resilience for survival, or they may hold unrealistic expectations about life, others, God and the world in general. Those who refuse to reconcile the dark side with the bright side of existence are unable or unwilling to accept that problems are part of life and that hardships are an integral part of the human journey. These victims struggle to integrate the badness that they just experienced with the goodness that they previously enjoyed.

The role of the pastor or spiritual mentor is not to defend God or correct the theological doctrines with which the victim is struggling, as this will shut down the person who is suffering and keep him or her from opening up and sharing from a place of emotional depth. Though negative feelings and expressions will emerge, the pastoral counselor should not become defensive or feel an obligation to correct the victim's belief system or present the best model of the true faith. People in pain have unconventional questions because their minds are disoriented and their hearts are in agony, so it is natural for them to verbalize shocking, angry or resentful statements, including unkind accusations toward God and the church, as well as apathy, resignation and a loss of zeal for life and faith, including ideas about suicide and multiple wishes to die.

As survivors of tragic events struggle to make sense of their experiences, they often ask "why" questions and usually need an object, real or abstract, onto which they can vent their frustration and project their internal turmoil – be it society, life, others, God, fate, destiny, evil or any other entity (including you as their caregiver). Instead of fighting these philosophical questions, the wise pastor and spiritual counselor can listen to the confusion and anguish of those who have endured calamities and allow them to express their struggles within a safe environment. Counselors can encourage the free expression of intense feelings, raw emotions and painful memories that are boiling inside the survivors without entering into debates or arguing about the appropriateness of their logic, especially in the early stages of the helping process. Blaise Pascal observed that the heart has its own reason, which reason itself cannot know or understand. Engaging in mere intellectual discourse or giving quick answers or solutions without listening and providing a safe and warm environment will interrupt both the healing of those who are suffering as well as the therapeutic relationship.[5] Accomplished teachers and preachers usually have a hard time adjusting their styles to become good listening counselors. Over time, struggling people begin to discover that God has remained with them and has

---

5. Abi-Hashem, "Cross Cultural Psychology," "Grief, Loss, and Bereavement: An Overview," *Journal of Psychology and Christianity* 18 (1999): 309–329; "Caregiving and Counseling in an Age of Globalization, Secularization, and Radicalization," unpublished manuscript, 2010; Ashley and Lockwood, "Role of Religious Leaders"; Benner, *Care of Souls*, 2008; Capretto, "Empathy and Silence in Pastoral Care for Traumatic Grief and Loss," *Journal of Religion and Health* 54 (2015): 339–357; Collins, *How to Be a People Helper,* 2nd ed. (Wheaton, IL: Tyndale House 1995); *Christian Counseling: A Comprehensive Guide,* 3rd ed. (Nashville: Thomas Nelson, 2007); Pascal, *Pensées*, rev. ed., trans. A. J. Krailsheimer (London: Penguin Classics, 1995).

never abandoned them. Hopefully, they will also come to realize that the Spirit has been guiding them and comforting them, and so they have never been left completely alone but have been partaking in divine suffering.

Identifying Psycho-Emotional Trauma

Following a tragedy, time seems to stand still, and the sense of shock and perplexity can seem to become frozen in the memory. Trauma can alter one's sense of routine and normality and can throw a person or group into a state of confusion and restlessness. If an individual or group cannot restore what has been lost or damaged, they will develop ways to cope with the devastation, either in positive-constructive ways or negative-destructive ways, depending on the severity of the event and on the tolerance and emotional health of those involved.

Acute Stress Disorder (ASD) is a condition that is characterized by severe anxiety and other related symptoms that appear after witnessing a tragic shock or horrific event. It is normally a short-term impact – approximately a few days to a few weeks in length – but could include serious psychological conditions, such as intense fears, splitting, phobias and dissociation. This syndrome is also called *Acute Stress Reaction* and overlaps with adjustment disorders, which ultimately show the degree to which a person or a group adapts to disturbing and highly stressful situations. Normally, the acute symptoms and emotional struggles begin to decrease with time as most people eventually recover well with minimum residuals.

Posttraumatic Stress Disorder (PTSD) tends to be a long-term condition. It is a well-established diagnosis with specific signs, criteria, research and a firm base in scientific literature. However, according to many observers and professionals, PTSD tends to be overly used and overly diagnosed. A few other diagnoses have created similar debate and controversy. This raises two questions: what constitutes a psycho-emotional trauma? to what degree do social and cultural factors determine the meaning of trauma and its condition and classification?

Since not all traumatic experiences are the same, and not all people's reactions are the same, we have to be very careful about how, what and when to label someone or some experience as PTSD. Not all crises, stressors, hardships, losses or adversities are severely traumatic or tragic in nature and therefore do not generate enough trauma responses or qualify for clinical diagnoses. Besides, as many anthropologists have noticed, people who live in poor conditions often expect hardships to be part of life, while those who live in more affluent societies with a high level of comfort develop higher expectations for a trouble-free living and thus have a lower tolerance for uncertainty, dilemmas, misfortunes and pain.

Technically, PTSD uses a cluster of symptoms to describe the major responses to trauma, which include: re-experiencing the fears, remembering and reliving certain aspects of the assault or horrific event, recurrent intrusive thoughts and flashbacks, persistent avoidance of any triggers or reminders associated with the event, an inability to recall many important details of what really happened, psychic numbness, flat or restricted emotions, sleep disturbances, increased arousal and hyper vigilance, recurring nightmares and exaggerated responses to any situation that barely resembles the traumatic event. Some other major crimes, severe maltreatments and war atrocities can similarly generate intense feelings of injustice, substantial anger, marked helplessness and a wide range of cognitive-behavioral symptoms.

Typical symptoms of PTSD include signs of disorientation, impairment and humiliation. Initial disbelief, anxiety, confusion, denial, resentment, hurt and hopelessness may engulf the whole person, family or community. Traumatic experiences can cause lasting effects in every sphere of life: mental (nervous breakdown), emotional (depression and anxiety), physical (somatic complaints, such as aches and pains), social (detachment or withdrawal), personality (obsessions or compulsions), behavioral (addictions and acting out) and philosophical (apathy or under/over spiritualization).

The DSM-5 of the American Psychiatric Association[6] has reorganized the criteria for PTSD and classified it under "Trauma and Stressor-Related Disorders" rather than under "Anxiety Disorders." The new descriptions focus more on the tangible impacts of the shocking and painful event and the behavioral symptoms that result (as impairment to human functions), regardless of the root causes, triggers, types or natures of trauma.

The changes from DSM-IV to DSM-5 include the elimination of subjective definitions of trauma, the explication and tightening of the elements and exposures and the rearrangement of the symptoms criteria with various specifications. In addition, the changes include a repeated exposure to aversive details of the traumatic event as well as negative alterations in cognition and mood associated with that event. Learning that a traumatic event has occurred to a close friend or a family member can also trigger a significant reaction. In addition, a sudden tragic death of a public figure/leader or a militant/

6. APA, *Diagnostic and Statistical Manual of Mental Disorders*, 5th ed. (Washington, DC: American Psychiatric Association, 2013).

terrorist attack on a certain location can similarly generate major traumatic-bereavement reactions at the individual, communal and national level.

Impact of Trauma on the Brain

Much research has been done lately on the human brain and its wiring and network of nerves to determine the impact of general habits, behaviors and life experiences on human neurophysiology. It has been observed that a significant traumatic event can alter the wiring and the synaptic operations of the brain and its related nervous system functions. For instance, after a traumatic event, a person may spend a lot of emotional energy on being watchful and awake, as if on high alert, preparing oneself for the worst. The mind and the body seem to "keep score" of what has happened in terms of unpleasant experiences, crises, maltreatments and tragedies.[7] If a person or a group does not receive help in an adequate and timely manner or does not process the crisis with good interventions, the negative memories and distorted influences will remain stored in his or her system, and the effects will become engraved deeper into his or her subconscious and organism.[8]

Socially and culturally, this storing of negative memories and distorted influences is also true for a tribe, community or nation. People groups develop a collective memory that helps keep their history and heritage alive, deep in their psyche and oral tradition.[9] Honors, victories, accomplishments and glories as well as tragedies, failures, shames and genocides become engraved in the collective memory for generations or even centuries to come. For this reason, the whole population engages in therapeutic practices and rituals, both to relive and celebrate the glorious past and also to mourn and grieve the painful past – and at times to do both. Some examples include erecting monuments and shrines, recalling the memories together, conducting feasts, seeking closure and recovery and exchanging comfort and solidarity in order

7. Van der Kolk, *The Body Keeps the Score: Brain, Mind, and Body in the Healing of Trauma* (New York: Penguin Books, 2015).

8. Van der Kolk, "Clinical Implications"; *Body Keeps Score*.

9. Abi-Hashem, "Cross-Cultural Psychology"; "Worldview, the Concept of"; "Trauma, Coping, and Resiliency"; Assmann, "Communicative and Cultural Memory"; Cole, *Cultural Psychology: A Once and Future Discipline* (Cambridge: Harvard University Press, 1996); Dueck and Johnson, "Cultural Psychology"; Rubin, "Oral Traditions as Collective Memories: Implications for a General Theory of Individual and Collective Memory," in *Memory in Mind and Culture*, ed. P. Boyer and J. V. Wertsch (Cambridge: Cambridge University Press, 2009), 273–287; Tillich, *Theology of Culture*; Triandis, "Collectivism and Individualism as Cultural Syndromes," *Cross-Cultural Research* 27 (1993): 155–180; *Individualism & Collectivism* (New York: Westview Press, 1995).

to ensure that the healing touches their historical wounds and reaches deep to bind and soothe their communal roots. Vivid models and instances of these practices occur both in ancient history and in our modern times.

Survival after Trauma

Responses and coping styles differ a great deal among victims and survivors of trauma, depending on several factors and influences, such as the nature and severity of the trauma, loss or tragic event as well as the background and history of those involved. Influencing factors include: age, gender, previous exposures, emotional stability, degree of tolerance, preexisting conditions, stage of development, experience in handling previous crises, support system during and after the tragedy, available resources within the community, mental outlook and existential hope, spiritual faith and religious involvement, general potential for survival and degree of resiliency.[10]

For example, when a major trauma or tragedy hits a community, children and teenagers will be affected differently than middle-aged adults or older adults. Those who are able to maneuver their way through calamities and benefit from warm and supportive relationships will fare better than those who suffer alone, have prior vulnerabilities or lack adequate social assets and internal resiliency. Many practitioners and researchers have established that people who have a strong faith and active spiritual/prayer life and who display a positive attitude and existential hope generally survive better than those who do not.[11] They tend to endure sickness (be better patients), recover from illness (get healthier) and even transition better into death (smooth passing and inspiring deathbed countenance). Those who do not possess any faith, have never been active spiritually or do not enjoy the benefits of a supernatural hope seem to be at a lesser advantage. Thus faith is an essential factor in cultivating a general sense of well-being for humans and is a vital dynamic influence in

---

10. Abi-Hashem, "Grief, Loss, and Bereavement" and "On Cultural Resiliency"; Bonanno, "Loss, Trauma, and Human Resilience: Have We Underestimated the Human Capacity to Thrive after Extremely Aversive Events?" *American Psychologist* 59 (2004): 20–28; Joseph and Linley, *Trauma, Recovery, and Growth*; Worden, *Grief Counseling and Grief Therapy: A Handbook for the Mental Health Practitioner*, 4th ed. (New York: Springer, 2009); Wright, *Recovering from Losses in Life* (Grand Rapids: Revell, 2006); Wright, *Complete Guide to Crisis*.

11. Abi-Hashem, "On Cultural Resiliency" and "Religion and Spirituality"; Koenig, and Larson, "Religion and Mental Health: Evidence for an Association," *International Review of Psychiatry* 13 (2001): 67–78; Shaw, Joseph and Linley, "Religion"; Wong and Wong, *Handbook of Multicultural Perspectives on Stress and Coping* (New York: Springer, 2006); Wortmann and Park, "Religion and Spirituality in Adjustment Following Bereavement: An Integrative Review," *Death Studies* 32 (2008): 703–736.

generating peace, harmony, affirmation, confidence, congruence, strength and serenity even in the midst of troubles, traumas and tribulations.

Unfortunately, not everyone handles trauma and tragedy well or survives crises and adversities in a creative way. Rather some people develop unhealthy, even destructive, coping styles to deal with the uncertainties of life and intrusive pain. For those with an active religious faith, a belief system may become part of the problem instead of part of the solution, since an inflexible faith and narrow religious views may cause confusion, disappointment and bitterness in times of adversity instead of providing inner strength, emotional healing, supportive community, and mental peace, clarity, and restoration.[12]

Armed conflicts, military invasions and intense wars are more difficult to manage on the social and psychological levels. Wars are devastating for individuals, families, societies and cultures, as they severely disturb community cohesiveness, continuity between generations and a sense of rootedness in the land. Those who are exposed to the stresses and tragedies of war not only face psycho-emotional trauma but also have to deal with multiple losses, displacement, physical injuries, stories of bloodshed, family separations, constant fear of death, ruined history and heritage, eroded identity and difficult sociocultural adjustments. War victims eventually become war survivors as they carry multiple scars and later struggle to reconstruct their shattered lives, usually in a different setting and under difficult circumstances.[13]

Unhealthy Coping Styles

Following are some examples of unhealthy coping styles. Some traumatized people may show reluctance to face daily life-demands and employ prolonged avoidance. Resignation and isolation can lead to further immobilization and mental paralysis. Some victims become embarrassed due to physical injuries or material losses, so they shut themselves out. Taking action and creating new meaningful connections are essential to resume some normal routines and break the cycle of helplessness and passivity.

Some people may complain, blame others, lash out and persistently display a high level of negative frustration and irritation. Some may become angry and display aggressive behavior, such as yelling, fighting, hitting, breaking things,

---

12. Abi-Hashem, "Cross-Cultural Psychology" and "Worldview, the Concept"; Oman and Thoresen, "Does Religion Cause Health?: Differing Interpretations and Diverse Meanings," *Journal of Health Psychology* 7 (2002): 365–380.

13. Abi-Hashem, "Trauma, Coping, and Resiliency."

intimidating others and becoming increasingly involved in multiple conflicts, family maltreatment, domestic violence and abusive behaviors.

Others may display excessive involvements and behaviors, such as overworking, over-studying, over-exercising, over-volunteering, over-playing, over-spending, over-spiritualizing, over-socializing, over-sexualizing and so forth.

Another coping strategy is to become chemically dependent or addicted to drugs. Following a major loss or tragedy, especially during the stress of war, some people begin to rely on all sorts of drugs and alcohol to numb their pain and help them manage their acute anxieties. They tend to overuse or abuse many legal or illegal medicines and other calming substances as external agents for the sake of better sleeping, relaxing and tranquilizing their agitated nerves, bodies and souls.

Others may develop a pessimistic and cynical attitude. It is easy to become negative, apathetic and irresponsible regardless of the situation. Cynicism and pessimism are powerful tendencies that can lead individuals to believe that the worst is going to happen anyway. They exaggerate every crisis and amplify every problem to the level of an insurmountable catastrophe.

Another common response to social turmoil, major crisis, local unrest, natural disaster or the outbreak of war is to move residence, travel away or migrate to another country. However, a quick decision to uproot oneself or the family and completely leave everything behind for good (or quickly replace a significant loss with another substitute) has negative psychological consequences and presents the survivor(s) with a host of new stresses, perplexities, disorientations, challenges and adjustment difficulties.

Accompanying Survivors Toward Healing and Recovery

Counseling and treatment for the victims of traumas and tragedies depend largely on the training, experience, networking, expertise and orientation of the caregiver or counselor. Following are some basic guidelines for sound intervention that can apply to all survivors and victims of severe traumatic stress and tragic events.

It is important to establish a warm connection and a welcoming relationship so that each person with whom you are working feels safe and secure. Such an inviting atmosphere can be nurtured by providing solidarity through emotional reassurance and empathy through comforting statements at the beginning of each visit. You can also help to ensure distressed people's survival by providing physical provision, if needed, whenever possible.

As you get to know each other, ask gently about the general details of what happened, without pushing as if you are conducting an interrogation interview. If there have been multiple tragedies and victimizations, start with the most pressing. Be particularly careful when uncovering memories, as some aspects of recollection can be unconsciously expanded and reconstructed. Research has shown that basic memories of abuse or trauma may not always be accurate or reflect the original events. With time, story facts and experiences can become vague, develop new dimensions or take different versions due to the accumulation of negative emotions and unpleasant memories stored in the human physiology, which may result in rewiring of certain brain functions and its nervous system. For those who are traumatized and significantly bereaved, it may be necessary to conduct grief therapy in order to facilitate the mourning process.

As you educate those who are suffering about the nature of common psychological struggles, such as loss, grief, trauma, tragedy, severe stress, anxiety and depression, address target symptoms while also teaching them tools and techniques about how to reduce their inner tension and anxiety and manage their ongoing stress. Assure them that some of their reactions are measures for self-protection in order to avoid intense pain and that this coping strategy is common in the beginning phases of recovery, but they will need to move toward deeper recovery and healing. Teach them to desensitize strong reactions and check irrational thoughts so that they don't exaggerate their fears and worries. Teach them also to reframe their perceptions into more realistic assumptions and ways of thinking. Gently encourage them to reverse unhealthy coping mechanisms.

Help them to shift their identity from being victims to survivors by commending their positive abilities and the strength they are gaining day by day. In order to avoid setbacks or major lapses in the future, discuss recovery plans and network collaboratively with other caregivers to connect them with resources in the surrounding cultural centers, communities of faith and society at large. These may include human resources – such as mentors, support systems, and spiritual care – as well as tangible resources – such as basic supplies, physical commodities, and paying jobs.

In order to encourage spiritual vitality and health, find out whether faith is part of the problem or a solution in their lives. Spiritual inventories and religious assessment tools can help evaluate people's spiritual commitment, pious background, religious practice, and general worldview.

Guide them to establish new and meaningful relationships, set new goals and reinvest their mental and emotional energy (which is currently spent on dealing with hurt, fear and anxiety) into broader endeavors, people and projects. Inspire them to get involved in helping others who are struggling with similar conditions and agonies, based on the well-known principle that by helping others, you help yourself twice. Promote resiliency by encouraging them to begin to transfer their "pain" into "purpose," their "crippling" into "creativity," their "misery" into "mission" and their "tragedies" into "treasures."

Finally, remain available for continual support, feedback, consultation, accountability, evaluation and encouragement.

Cross-Cultural Counseling

As the world becomes smaller through global travel and mass migration, most societies host a mixture of traditions, mentalities, languages, heritages, norms and faiths. Since clergy and pastors are often called upon to minister to people from various backgrounds, educations, ethnicities, mindsets, traditions, religious beliefs and socio-economic levels, those who want to provide appropriate service and effective soul care for distressed people in crisis will need basic training in cross-cultural counseling, intercultural communications, customs understanding, interfaith and interdenominational dialogue, worldview sensitivity and spiritual competency.[14]

Technical and Ethical Limitations

Pastoral counselors should recognize their limits in handling difficult emotional cases and serious mental conditions and impairments (psychopathology). At times, technical issues and medical symptoms can be severe and complicated that are beyond the basic training or ability of a regular pastor and an average counselor/caregiver, regardless of their good intention and availability. So, referring such individuals to more specialized care, psychological evaluation,

---

14. Abi-Hashem, "Cross-Cultural Psychology"; "Caregiving and Counseling"; "Working with Middle Eastern Immigrant Families," in *Working with Immigrant Families: A Practical Guide for Counselors,* ed. A. Zagelbaum and J. Carlson (New York: Routledge, 2011), 151–180; "Religious and Pastoral Responses"; "Counseling"; "Worldview, the Concept"; "Trauma, Coping, and Resiliency"; Augsburger, *Pastoral Counseling*; Cole, *Cultural Psychology*; Gerstein, et al., *International Handbook of Cross-Cultural Counseling: Cultural Assumptions and Practices Worldwide* (Thousand Oaks, CA: Sage, 2009); Hesselgrave, *Counseling Cross-Culturally: An Introduction to Theory and Practice for Christians* (Grand Rapids: Baker, 1984); Lingenfelter and Mayers, *Ministering Cross-Culturally: A Model for Effective Personal Relationships* (Grand Rapids: Baker, 2016); Marsella, "Toward a Global-Community Psychology: Meeting the Needs of a Changing World," *American Psychologist* 53 (1998): 1282–1291; Palmer, *Multicultural Counselling: A Reader* (London: Sage, 2002); Wong and Wong, *Handbook of Multicultural Perspectives.*

and medical treatment is essential. Incidentally, each pastor should have a list of other medical specialists and mental health experts in his or her neighborhood. Developing a good relationship with community leaders, educators, human services personnel, and healthcare providers will allow the clergy, pastors, and spiritual advisors to collaborate together and enjoy the benefits of mutual referral, consultation, and the sharing of valuable expertise.

In addition, all caregivers should be aware of the sensitive nature of their work. Obviously, they are working with humans and not with machines. Therefore, they always should conduct themselves in full personal integrity, increase their skills and competency, and strive to be guided by sound moral values and spiritual ideals. They attempt to provide the best care possible and avoid any questionable behavior. They would subscribe to the historic and well-known basic caring motto, "*To Do No Harm!*"

Presently, every major profession or association has developed some kind of guidelines for its practitioners in the form of ethical codes and legal policies. These codes and regulations cover a wide range of topics, such as the following. First, stay up to date with your career and occupation. Receive more training when the opportunity arises so you acquire better insights, tools, and perspectives. Second, consult with others and seek supervision and coaching especially for difficult situations and complicated cases. Third, practice healthy self-care and good maintenance of your life, personal matters and finances so that your mind will remain alert and able to focus clearly on the tasks ahead and the people who are entrusted to your care. Fourth, avoid getting involved in disputes, conflicts and problematic behaviors, which greatly disrupt the flow of service and affect the harmony of the team and your sensitive work. Fifth, watch for the areas of your weaknesses, vulnerabilities, and temptations, as these commonly lead to excessive control and abuse of power, financial greed and misuse of funds, or inappropriate physical intimacies and sexual misconducts. All of these behaviors can easily cause unnecessary harm to others, especially those who are at-risk and emotionally vulnerable. Also, they can ruin the reputation of the religious organization or the humanitarian agency that provides such services and can ultimately hurt the cause of the healing ministry itself.

Working with people who are distressed, needy, and emotionally at-risk puts extra responsibility on the part of general providers, spiritual directors, and humanitarian aids. Therefore, it would be wise for all caregivers to remind themselves of the seriousness of the work at hand and to realize that their duty involves both privileges and responsibilities, rewards and challenges as well as stress and satisfaction. This is the nature of all helping professions, including pastors and ministers, who consider their work not only as a *career* but as a *calling*, and thus they care about their character as much as their career. They try to serve with a clear conscience and compassion in order to present themselves with high morality, good virtues, sound integrity, and clean reputation.

Soul Care for the Helper

In closing, caregivers who are involved in a demanding and stressful work need to remember the importance of self-care. Although helping those who are suffering is rewarding, there are also many psychosocial challenges to this work.

Helpers often become fatigued, drained and depleted after devoting their attention to those who are struggling, distressed and troubled for an extended period of time. Those who tend to over-invest and over-empathize with others are particularly at-risk. Symptoms of acute stress, burnout, anxiety and depression are common among the helping professionals in general, particularly among those who are serving under pressure or on the front lines. This raises an important concern about who will help the helpers, guard the guards, pastor the pastors and care for the caregivers.

Those who want to be effective in service and ministry need to be careful to take breaks and take proper care of themselves by seeking help for themselves and cultivating healthy soul care and a balanced lifestyle.[15] Caregivers are also encouraged to develop both self-awareness and peer-awareness by keeping an eye on one another and offering graceful yet honest feedback when noticing early symptoms of burnout, depression, depletion or other unhealthy behaviors. Such colleague support can be cultivated through mutual team-monitoring and group supervision.

Signs of burnout and acute stress include headaches, poor concentration, mild anxiety, low tolerance, high irritation, feeling overwhelmed, resentment, heart palpitations, constant exhaustion, insomnia, hypertension or blood pressure, loss of interest in regular activities, low or sad mood, lack of motivation and fulfillment in previous occupation, lack of productivity, desire to withdraw or isolate and a sense of helplessness.

Living and working under severe stress for a long period of time will create chronic conditions that are psychologically damaging to the human mind, body, and soul. Chronic or prolonged stress is also known to affect many areas of social functioning, such as communal and interpersonal relationships,

---

15. Benner, *Care of Souls*; Collins and Long, "Working with the Psychological."

everyday routine and family life and the purpose and success of the mission itself. The stress hormone *cortisol* has been proven to be damaging to our health. Because chronic stress can affect us physically, psychologically, morally and spiritually, it is counterproductive to continue working under the same intensity when a person or team becomes significantly drained and exhausted.

Following are some guidelines and suggestions for encouraging proper self-care and team-care. First, learn to identify and manage stress. To avoid stress, start your day with some type of exercise and a relaxing meditative activity. Try to remain mobile and active throughout the day, looking for small sanctuaries along the way. Practice deep and slow breathing. Pay attention to your heart palpitations and watch for the buildup of inner tensions. Adopt healthy eating habits, drink plenty of fluids and get enough sleep on a regular basis. Take short breaks or go for short walks during stressful days. Invest time in appreciating arts, beauty, nature and music. Memorize proverbs, wisdom sayings and sacred Scriptures. Remember Christ's invitation to his disciples "go off . . . to a quiet place and rest for a while" (Mark 6:31).

Second, develop healthy self-awareness. Pay attention to your conscious behaviors and unconscious responses, acknowledging the negatives but dwelling on the positives. Listen to the thoughts that run through your head, focusing on how you can develop healthy self-talk by replacing defeating thoughts with constructive messages and inner dialogue. Affirm and encourage other colleagues and team members, agreeing to give each other honest feedback when needed in a spirit of grace. Develop a positive attitude and a heart of gratitude, remembering that "in quietness and confidence is your strength" (Isa 30:15).

Third, develop good time-management and efficacy skills. Try not to allow small intrusions and distractions to interfere with your passion for service. Practice letting go quickly of small frictions, irritations, and conflicts around your workplace. Stop in your tracks, reflect on your steps and the direction you're heading and pray often. Work on having realistic assumptions and reasonable expectations of yourself, others, life and God. When desiring a change of habits, take slow and gradual steps, intentionally targeting one behavior at a time.

Fourth, increase your resiliency. Avoid the stress-distress cycle and subsequent emotional impairment by learning to differentiate between denial and endurance. Remember your strengths and weaknesses as well as areas of temptation and vulnerability. Naturally, we are most tempted when we are tired, susceptible and weak. Watch for any symptoms of burnout, exhaustion or compassion fatigue. Remind yourself that it is both moral and ethical to care properly for yourself so that you can help those whom you are seeking to serve.

These stress management, self-awareness, efficacy- and resiliency-building tools also promote well-being and healing among trauma survivors and those who are grieving or considerably stressed. As the American philosopher and theologian Reinhold Niebuhr (1892–1971) once wrote: "God, grant me the serenity to accept the things I cannot change, the courage to change the things I can, and the wisdom to know the difference."

Bibliography

Abi-Hashem, N. "Caregiving and Counseling in an Age of Globalization, Secularization, and Radicalization." Unpublished manuscript, 2010.

———. "Clinical Trauma Psychology." In *Encyclopedia of Trauma: An Interdisciplinary Guide*, edited by C. R. Figley, 98–100. Thousand Oaks, CA: Sage, 2012. Online version. http://knowledge.sagepub.com/view/trauma/n32.xml.

———. "Counseling." In *Encyclopedia of Cross-Cultural Psychology*, ed. K. D. Keith, 257–260. Malden, MA: Wiley-Blackwell, 2013. Online version. http://onlinelibrary.wiley.com/doi/10.1002/9781118339893.wbeccp109/abstract.

———. "Cross-Cultural Psychology." In *Baker Encyclopedia of Psychology and Counseling*, 2nd edition, ed. D. G. Benner and P. C. Hill, 294–298. Grand Rapids: Baker, 1999.

———. "Grief, Loss, and Bereavement: An Overview." *Journal of Psychology and Christianity* 18 (1999): 309–329. Online version. https://www.academia.edu/28011457/_Grief_Loss_and_Bereavement_An_Overview.

———. "On Cultural Resiliency." *The Australian Community Psychologist* 23 (2011): 23–31. Retrieved from: https://groups.psychology.org.au/Assets/Files/Abi-Hashem-ACP-2-11.pdf.

———. "Religion and Spirituality." In *Encyclopedia of Cross-Cultural Psychology*, ed. K. D. Keith, 1091–1094. Malden, MA: Wiley-Blackwell, 2013. Online version. http://onlinelibrary.wiley.com/doi/10.1002/9781118339893.wbeccp453/abstract.

———. "Religious and Pastoral Responses to Trauma." In *Encyclopedia of Trauma: An Interdisciplinary Guide*, ed. C. R. Figley, 542–544. Thousand Oaks, CA: Sage, 2012. Online version. http://knowledge.sagepub.com/view/trauma/n183.xml?rskey=0yXGp6&row=1.

———. "Revisiting Cultural Awareness and Cultural Relevancy. *American Psychologist* 70, 660–661. Online version. http://psycnet.apa.org/journals/amp/70/7/660.

———. "Trauma, Coping, and Resiliency among Syrian Refugees in Lebanon and Beyond: A Profile of a Nation at War." In *Human Strengths and Resilience: Developmental, Cross-Cultural, and International Perspectives*, ed. G. Rich and J. Sirikantraporn, 105–130. Lanham, MD: Lexington Books, 2018.

———. "Working with Middle Eastern Immigrant Families." In *Working with Immigrant Families: A Practical Guide for Counselors*, ed. A. Zagelbaum and J. Carlson, 151–180. New York: Routledge, 2011.

———. "Worldview, the Concept Of." In *Encyclopedia of Psychology and Religion*, ed. D. A. Leeming, 1–6. Springer Online Living Reference, 2017. Retrieved from: https://link.springer.com/referenceworkentry/10.1007/978-3-642-27771-9_9357-6.

APA. *Diagnostic and Statistical Manual of Mental Disorders*, 5th edition. Washington, DC: American Psychiatric Association, 2013.

Ashley, W., and S. Lockwood. "The Role of Religious Leaders in Crisis Response: Caring for the Soul." 2007. Retrieved from: http://www.nydis.org/nydis/downloads/manual/NYDIS_Disaster_SC-MH_Manual_SectionII-Chapter7.pdf.

Assmann, J. "Communicative and Cultural Memory." 2011. Retrieved from: https://link.springer.com/chapter/10.1007/978-90-481-8945-8_2.

Aten, J. D., and D. M. Boan. *Disaster Ministry Handbook*. Downers Grove: InterVarsity Press, 2016.

Augsburger, D. W. *Pastoral Counseling across Cultures*. Philadelphia: Westminster, 1986.

Beck, J. G., and D. M. Sloan, eds. *The Oxford Handbook of Traumatic Stress Disorders*. Oxford: Oxford University Press, 2012.

Benner, D. G. P. *Care of Souls: Revisioning Christian Nurture and Counsel*. Grand Rapids: Baker Books, 1998.

———. *Strategic Pastoral Counseling: A Short-Term Structured Model*, 2nd edition. Grand Rapids: Baker Academic, 2003.

Bonanno, G. A. "Loss, Trauma, and Human Resilience: Have We Underestimated the Human Capacity to Thrive after Extremely Aversive Events?" *American Psychologist* 59 (2004): 20–28.

Capretto, P. "Empathy and Silence in Pastoral Care for Traumatic Grief and Loss." *Journal of Religion and Health* 54 (2015): 339–357.

Cole, M. *Cultural Psychology: A Once and Future Discipline*. Cambridge: Harvard University Press, 1996.

Collins, G. R. *Christian Counseling: A Comprehensive Guide*, 3rd ed. Nashville: Thomas Nelson, 2007.

———. *How to Be a People Helper.* 2nd edition. Wheaton, IL: Tyndale House, 1995.

Collins, S., and A. Long. "Working with the Psychological Effects of Trauma: Consequences for Mental Health-Care Workers – A Literature Review." *Journal of Psychiatric and Mental Health Nursing* 10, no. 4 (2003): 417–424.

Dueck, A., and A. Johnson. "Cultural Psychology of Religion: Spiritual Transformation." *Pastoral Psychology* 65 (2016): 299–328. Retrieved from: https://link.springer.com/article/10.1007/s11089-016-0690-8.

Gerstein, L. H., P. P. Heppner, S. Aegisdottir, S. M. A. Leung, and K. L. Norsworthy, eds. *International Handbook of Cross-Cultural Counseling: Cultural Assumptions and Practices Worldwide*. Thousand Oaks, CA: Sage, 2009.

Gingrich, H. D. *Restoring the Shattered Self: A Christian Counselor's Guide to Complex Trauma*. Downers Grove: InterVarsity Press, 2013.

Hesselgrave, D. J. *Counseling Cross-Culturally: An Introduction to Theory and Practice for Christians*. Grand Rapids: Baker, 1984.

Joseph, S., and P. A. Linley, eds. *Trauma, Recovery, and Growth: Positive Psychological Perspectives on Posttraumatic Stress*. Hoboken, NJ: Wiley, 2006.

Koenig, H. G., and D. B. Larson. "Religion and Mental Health: Evidence for an Association." *International Review of Psychiatry* 13 (2001): 67–78.

Lingenfelter, S. G., and M. K. Mayers. *Ministering Cross-Culturally: A Model for Effective Personal Relationships*. Grand Rapids: Baker, 2016.

Marsella, A. J. "Toward a Global-Community Psychology: Meeting the Needs of a Changing World." *American Psychologist* 53 (1998): 1282–1291.

Meichenbaum, D. *A Clinical Handbook/Practical Therapist Manual for Assessing and Treating Adults with PTSD*. Waterloo, ON: Institute Press, 1994.

Murray, J. *Understanding Loss: A Guide for Caring for Those Facing Adversity*. New York: Routledge, 2016.

Oman, D., and C. E. Thoresen. "'Does Religion Cause Health?': Differing Interpretations and Diverse Meanings." *Journal of Health Psychology* 7 (2002): 365–380.

Palmer, S., ed. *Multicultural Counselling: A Reader*. London: Sage, 2002.

Pascal, B. *Pensées*, rev. ed. Translated by A. J. Krailsheimer. London: Penguin Classics, 1995.

Rubin, D. C. "Oral Traditions as Collective Memories: Implications for a General Theory of Individual and Collective Memory." In *Memory in Mind and Culture*, edited by P. Boyer and J. V. Wertsch, 273–287. Cambridge: Cambridge University Press, 2009.

SAMHSA. *Trauma-Informed Care in Behavioral Health Services*. Treatment Improvement Protocol Series 57. Rockville, MD: Substance Abuse and Mental Health Services Administration, 2014. Retrieved from: https://www.ncbi.nlm.nih.gov/books/NBK207201/.

Shaw, A., S. Joseph, and P. A. Linley. "Religion, Spirituality, and Posttraumatic Growth: A Systematic Review." *Mental Health, Religion & Culture* 8, no. 1 (2005): 1–11.

Smelser, N. J. "Psychological Trauma and Cultural Trauma." In *Cultural Trauma and Collective Identity*, edited by J. C. Alexander, R. Eyerman, B. Giesen, N. J. Smelser, and P. Sztompka, 31–59. Berkeley: University of California Press, 2004.

Tillich, P. *Theology of Culture*. New York: Oxford University, 1959.

Triandis, H. C. "Collectivism and Individualism as Cultural Syndromes." *Cross-Cultural Research* 27 (1993): 155–180.

———. *Individualism & Collectivism*. New York: Westview Press, 1995.

Van der Kolk, B. A. *The Body Keeps the Score: Brain, Mind, and Body in the Healing of Trauma*. New York: Penguin Books, 2015.

———. "Clinical Implications of Neuroscience Research in PTSD." *Annals of the New York Academy of Science* 1, no. 2 (2006): 1–17.

Wong, P. T. P., and L. C. J. Wong, eds. *Handbook of Multicultural Perspectives on Stress and Coping*. New York: Springer, 2006.

Worden, J. W. *Grief Counseling and Grief Therapy: A Handbook for the Mental Health Practitioner*, 4th edition. New York: Springer, 2009.

Wortmann, J. H., and C. L. Park. "Religion and Spirituality in Adjustment Following Bereavement: An Integrative Review." *Death Studies* 32 (2008): 703–736.

Wright, H. N. *Recovering from Losses in Life*. Grand Rapids: Revell, 2006.

———. *The Complete Guide to Crisis and Trauma Counseling: What to Do and Say When It Matters Most*. Ventura, CA: Regal Books, 2011.

11

Trauma Care for Disaster Survivors in Tacloban

Spiritual, Psychological and Cultural Dimensions

Melba Padilla Maggay

Social support, a sense of transcendence, and meaning making are central to the nature of human beings. Globally, there is now a body of literature on studies that establish a link between spirituality and mental health.[1] All these have been manifest as important to the healing of trauma among disaster survivors. This has been corroborated by recent learnings, based on our experience of walking with survivors of the biggest typhoon to make landfall in human history: Typhoon Haiyan (local name: Yolanda), which hit the Philippines on 8 November 2013.

1. See, for instance, C. M. Hall, "Crisis as Opportunity for Spiritual Growth," *Journal of Religion and Health* 25, no. 1 (1986): 8–17. A longitudinal life history of two hundred families in crisis and two hundred in non-crisis situations studied the influence of crisis conditions on spiritual growth. Results indicated that the most substantial impact of crisis interventions occurred in families where one or more members reoriented their lives according to spiritual values or shifted in focus from the previous perception that they were victims of social or emotional circumstances. Transcendent realities provided a frame of reference that allowed them to cope objectively with difficult empirical conditions. Also, a study has correlated core spiritual experiences, such as: (a) a distinct event and a cognitive appraisal of that event, which resulted in a personal conviction of God's existence and (b) a perception of the internal relationship between God and the person, e.g. feeling of closeness, with: (1) increase in life purpose and satisfaction, (2) increase in health-promoting attitudes, (3) decrease in frequency of medical symptoms. The measure used is now known as Index of Spiritual Experience (INSPIRIT). See J. D. Kass, R. Friedman, J. Leserman, P. C. Zuttermeister, and H. Benson, "Health Outcomes and a New Index of Spiritual Experience," *Journal for the Scientific Study of Religion* 30, no. 2 (1991): 203–211.

Our organization, the Institute for Studies in Asian Church and Culture (ISACC), has been accompanying Barangay 89 in San Jose, Tacloban City in its journey to recovery. This barangay has been one of the hardest hit in terms of the number of dead and missing and the extent of the devastation. Barangay 89 had a population of about fifteen hundred households, which has now swelled to eighteen hundred families, or about 7,200 people, with the arrival of other disaster survivors who migrated to the area.[2]

As a first response, ISACC initiated a psychospiritual approach to healing the trauma of the survivors. To be able to offer a more wholistic response, ISACC cobbled together a partnership with at least six organizations – *Kabalikat Para sa Maunlad na Buhay Inc.* (KMBI) for micro-loans and livelihood, Operation Blessing for relief and housing, *Talete King Panyulung Kapampangan Foundation Inc.* (TPKI) for technical assistance in housing, Center for Community Transformation for skills training and Samaritana Transformation Ministries along with Care and Counsel for psychospiritual interventions.

The following learnings focus on ISACC and its partners' early psychospiritual intervention work, distilling insights based on narratives from the people of Barangay 89 along with participants in the retreats and capacity-building workshops on administering psychological first aid for various sectors from multiple barangays in Tacloban over a period of one year.

Initial Psycho-Spiritual Interventions

Three weeks after the typhoon, ISACC started its interventions, beginning with a rapid appraisal of the extent of the devastation and a sense of the people's psychospiritual needs.

ISACC immediately designed and conducted seven training workshops on psychological first aid. The participants consisted of faculties from two universities (Eastern Visayas State University and Leyte Normal University), disaster workers from church and faith-based organizations, preschool teachers, health workers and grassroots leaders across multiple barangays, nurses and medical students. Altogether, they comprised more than two hundred participants. A consultant clinical psychologist assessed the extent of trauma

2. Barangay 89 is adjacent to Barangay 90, which was completely leveled and so was informally counted as part of Barangay 89. There are four "Puroks" or sub-areas in Barangay 89: Mamsa, Balanak, Lapu-Lapu, Tawa-ay. About five hundred have been reported dead, excluding those missing. The people of this seaside community are mostly fishermen, pedicab drivers, carpenters, vendors and small store owners.

among these participants.[3] A team of theater and visual artists conducted art and play therapy for children.[4]

In March of 2014, another round of psychological first aid and therapeutic workshops were conducted for roughly one hundred church workers and pastors.[5]

Faced with massive trauma, ISACC, together with our partner Samaritana, experimented with community healing rituals to build on what was already culturally present, such as a procession and candle lighting for the dead. We also conducted a series of community consultations to listen to the heartbeat of the people about where they were and what they wished for themselves.

During Holy Week in April 2014, ISACC conducted a retreat for barangay leaders, theater and ukulele workshops for the children and another round of community consultations. We innovated on the existing spiritual infrastructure – the *siete palabras, the cenaculo, salubong, Pasko ng Pagkabuhay* and other such reenactments of the Passion of Christ – as a way to help the entire community symbolically express communal grief through familiar rituals.

In November 2014, one year after the typhoon, the Monsigñor of Tacloban invited ISACC to conduct three one-day retreat-cum-workshops among 130 basic ecclesial community leaders, tricycle drivers and leaders of various barangays who were all part of the city's Sto. Niño Parish.

All these interventions, which were initially aimed at building capacity for doing psychological first aid among the communities where the participants served, proved to be therapeutic for the participants as well, strengthening their spiritual and emotional resources in coping with their communities' lingering trauma and grief.

Explorations in Trauma Care

Spiritual care can be viewed as a category within integrative medicine. When blended with public health and group psychology, it forms an integrative psychosocial resilience, or IPR.[6]

3. Dr Christian Chan from the University of Hong Kong.

4. This was led by the Manila Playback Theater and Ms Sabana Lluch Dalena.

5. These were offered with the added help of Care and Counsel's Dr Violeta Bautista.

6. See Siddharth Ashvin Shah, "'To Do No Harm,' Staff Care, and Ethnomedical Competence: Four Spiritual Care Examples of Psychosocial Trauma Recovery after the 2004 Tsunami and 2005 Earthquake in South Asia," in *Creating Spiritual and Psychological Resilience:*

To pave the way for understanding spirituality as an integral part of trauma care, let me clarify some concepts as tools for getting a handle on this.

Distinguishing between Religion and Spirituality

"Spirituality" has been defined as "an attempt to seek meaning, purpose and a direction of life in relation to a higher power, universal spirit or God."[7] In another study, it is described as "a diverse construct referring to existential concerns as life and death, personal wellbeing, life direction, comfort and inner peace."[8] Viktor Frankl, a holocaust survivor, understands "religion" as belief in a "final meaning." The psychologist Virgilio Enriquez, pioneer of what is now known as *Sikolohiyang Pilipino* (Filipino Psychology), sees spirituality as a human faculty, an organ for sensing the transcendent, just like one of the five senses – seeing, hearing, tasting, smelling, feeling.

For conceptual clarity, we use the term "spirituality" to refer to the human sense for the numinous, the feeling for the divine presence and the quest for ultimate meaning and purpose. "Religion," on the other hand, is the institutional expression of spirituality in time and social space, as expressed in a community that defines itself by its beliefs, practices, symbols and rituals. Spirituality tends to be borderless and universal, while religion is culture-bound and made distinct by its particular symbols, rituals and creeds. Hence, one can be spiritual without being religious, or one can be uncommitted to any particular set of institutional expressions but appropriate ritual practices in a rather eclectic way, such as combining Christian practices with meditation techniques from eastern religious traditions.

Psycho-Spiritual as Distinguished from Psycho-Social Approach

The term "psychosocial" was popularized by the psychologist Erik Erikson, who defined it as the combination of the psychological (which relates to the mind or personality) and the social (which relates to one's external relationships and environment).

Integrating Care in Disaster Relief Work, eds. Grant H. Brenner, Daniel H. Bush, and Joshua Moses (New York: Routledge, 2010).

7. Donald Meichenbaum, "Trauma, Spirituality and Recovery: Toward a Spiritually-Integrated Psychotherapy," www.melissainstitute.org, 5.

8. H. G. Koenig, "Research on Religion, Spirituality and Mental Health: A Review," *The Canadian Journal of Psychiatry* 54, no. 5 (2009): 283–291.

Based on ISACC's experience, a Psycho-Spiritual approach differs from the usual Mental Health and Psycho-Social Support (MHPSS) approach in the following ways: 1) it is sensitive to people's spiritual cosmology and the way this frames mental distress; 2) it intentionally draws from spiritual resources for inner healing; 3) it uses traditional rituals and cultural practices to facilitate communal release from grief and trauma after disaster.

Spiritual Dimensions in Trauma Care

Consistent with findings elsewhere, spirituality served as a positive resource in helping Taclobanons cope with the trauma of disaster.

Emerging from the rubble of her home, Roselyn despaired at the sight of the devastation everywhere and the collapse of all the institutions that could be counted on for help. "There was no one to call, except God," she said. Badly shaken at first, her faith grew as she found herself receiving sacrificial kindness from friends and neighbors. A friend walked through debris all the way from Samar just to bring some bananas. A neighbor from Palo shared one kilo of rice at a time when there was absolutely nothing to eat. She also found herself being taught by her own child's naïve faith. When she went to see the condition of the Bible bookstore that her husband managed, it was flooded and all the books were wet and in shambles. Her child was hungry and asked for food. "There is no food here," she told the child, "just books." The child replied, *"Nay, mali ka. Di ba sabi mo may Bread of Life dito?"* ["Mom, you are wrong. Didn't you say there is Bread of Life here?"]

Stories of starvation and looting abounded, but so did the sense of miraculous provision. Though many children and elderly died from lack of food and medicine, an elderly couple who had medicines that had been looted from a drugstore asked a family if they needed any. They gave the family two bottles, and the house help who received them trembled and cried, for they were exactly the medicine that a child in their household badly needed.

The sea and the waves that destroyed the coastal city of Tacloban created in the people a fear of nature and a constant threat about what it could do. But to Medith, the rainbow restored her sense of stability in the processes of nature: "When I saw the devastation of Tacloban, it looked hopeless . . . But after the storm, I saw a rainbow. It reminded me of his promise. The steadfast love of the Lord never ceases."

The people's faith helped to frame the disaster in a bigger, more coherent narrative that placed God at the center. In the face of sheer helplessness and dysfunction at the centers of power, the sense that God was in control and continued to be a source of goodness and stability helped the people cope with the devastating consequences of nature gone awry.

However, there were also signs of some ambiguities. Participants from churches and faith-based organizations were observed to be more reticent in telling trauma stories than those from secular organizations. When they did tell stories, a flood of tears and anger emerged. One survivor spoke of her resentment at those who thoughtlessly threw Bible verses at her: "They said, 'God has a purpose for it.'" *"Mabuti pa sila,"* she said, *"alam nila ang purpose; bakit ako hindi?"* ["Good for them," she said, "they know his purpose; how come I don't know it?"]

Some of these believers were experiencing a dissonance between what they knew of God and the grim realities that they were facing. In theological terms, they were disabled by the mystery of theodicy, which is the perplexity that God allows bad things to happen.

Adding stress to this group of believers was the fact that they had been damaged as a community, but they had to go and serve their own people while also organizing and housing the predominantly foreign aid agencies within their ruined churches and shelters.

This reveals how the pressure to help others because of a religious commitment can serve as a negative factor when coping with trauma. Of the two pastors in this group, one was found to have signs of posttraumatic stress disorder (PTSD), and the other felt useless in spite of his busyness in doing relief work. Because his entire congregation had disappeared, having died or gone missing or been evacuated to other places, he felt lost, robbed of a job and his pastoral routine, and he suffered a form of identity crisis: *"Pastor ba ako, o ano? Kalaban ko ang sarili ko . . ."* ["Am I a pastor, or what? My own worst enemy is myself . . ."]

Inappropriate pietism, in an attempt to salve wounds, may in fact cause the opening up of traumatic memories without necessarily healing them. For instance, some barangay leaders felt some vexation over the song, *"Natutulog ba ang Diyos?"* ["Is God slumbering?"], which was sung at a performance in the city hall by a faith-based group. They felt annoyed and perturbed, because the song preyed on their raw emotions and offered comfort prematurely.

Unwittingly, a religious approach can deepen people's sense of spiritual deficit. The people of Tacloban were already struggling with a deep sense that they might be suffering because of some misdeed that they had done.

"What did we do wrong?" Manang Precy, a city government employee, cried as she sat on the stone steps, bemoaning the destruction of the city, "Tacloban was moving up." She shared how difficult it was for her to go to work every day after the storm, after seeing her friends, relatives and neighbors dead on the streets. She was thankful that she and her elderly mother had survived, but she could not help crying every day on her way to work.

Along with the feeling of God's judgment, the people of Tacloban carried a lingering sense of guilt for participating in the looting. One male confessed to having looted a department store to hunt for food. "Our children were starving," he said, his hands trembling as he spoke. The shame of the looting riled the people. "It's those strangers who looted appliances," a bedraggled woman kept saying while holding an equally ragged baby on her hip, as if trying to wipe away the shame, "we Taclobanons just took food."

Survivors who could process the traumatic experience within a bigger, cosmic world centered on a benevolent force that is fully in control received cognitive comfort. The practice of silence, which is a rich resource in Asian religious traditions, helped to relax survivors' tensions and relieve their anxieties. Focusing on *how* to cope rather than *why* the disaster happened further enhanced the survivors' ability to help themselves.

The community healing rituals provided a kind of "Wailing Wall," a space for grief and remembrance. The retreats provided a safe space for expressing troubled feelings and questions about God.

Such recourse to the healing power of lamentation and questioning has a long history, from the story of Job to the harrowing experience of survivors of the Holocaust. In his book *Night*, Elie Weisel describes how God was put on trial by prisoners in a concentration camp. God was found guilty as charged; then the prisoners went on to pray anyway.[9]

The Psychological Dimensions

Like many others, the massive trauma we encountered moved us to find a way to address it with the psychological tools that were available to us.

"The entire city was full of 'walking zombies' right after the storm surge," recounted Nedde, a Tacloban resident who was able to evacuate with her family. "Some people were just running around and screaming. Others were just picking up anything they find on the streets, even it was in truth only trash. It seemed like they just wanted to hold on to something."

As we moved through the city to make a rapid appraisal of the people's needs, the government officials at the mayor's office and the city hall seemed like robots. Though visibly battered and worn out, they could not stop and

9. As quoted by Donald Meichenbaum, "Trauma, Spirituality and Recovery," 6.

grieve because they needed to function. Aside from the obvious need for food and emergency relief, the people were groping about for a meaning to the bewildering desolation brought by the storm.

Our intervention built on a recent shift in therapeutic paradigm, from an emphasis on reducing risks and vulnerability to enhancing competency and resilience.

Consistent with the stepped-care model, or the scientific finding that most survivors will manage through psychological first aid and self-help, and only 7 percent on average will experience mental discomposure, we did trainings on psychosocial first aid and administered a screener. Among the early batch of ISACC's workshop participants, 10 percent showed signs of PTSD, and the majority of these, 84 percent, were in the faith-based group. This suggests that these participants were especially experiencing a cognitive dissonance between their idea of God and their own devastating experience of loss.

Learnings from the Field

ISACC's field experiences in Tacloban yielded practical insights as well as theoretical challenges to current approaches to healing trauma. The following are reflections on some of these.

Cognitive behavior therapy (CBT)

This approach, we found, helps reframe reality for survivors, but it is important to recognize that culture is embedded in the making of meaning for disaster or illness. Filipinos, for instance, see God and the spirit world as a major frame of reference in understanding reality, yet mental health assistance is often framed within secularist premises. Alison Schafer makes a similar observation in a study of the responses following Haiti's Earthquake:

> . . . western psychology may emphasize knowledge and understanding to elicit changes in perception, but in Islam, knowledge is often perceived as pointless unless it can be translated into practical action . . . Whereas Buddhists may perceive catastrophe as part of their karma, and believe they require spiritual endurance to faithfully cope during difficult times.[10]

---

10. Alison Schafer, "Spirituality and Mental Health in Humanitarian Contexts: An Exploration Based on World Vision's Haiti Earthquake Response," War Trauma Foundation.

Critical Incidents (Storytelling) Approach

Many well-meaning groups of mental health professionals trooped to Tacloban to encourage storytelling, consistent with the Critical Incidents Debriefing approach. While helpful in some cases, this exacerbated the people's already fragile psychological state. A local Department of Social Work and Development (DSWD) officer complained that some groups doing debriefings simply opened up fresh wounds and then left the people twisting in the wind, causing even more mental disturbance, particularly in children. A year later, one person said that the people were tired of debriefings because they made them relive the painful memories all over again without any real healing.

We have found that there is a difference between stress-engendering storytelling and the need for emotional expression as a form of relief. The faculty of the two universities who were our earliest participants in the Psychological First Aid seminars – Eastern Visayas State University and Leyte Normal University – opened up freely without prompting, an exercise that seemed to bring immediate release.

Similarly, a year after the storm, a barangay leader shared his need to be able to tell his story of having to bury his wife alone. "I went to the funeral parlor, and there was nobody there. My friends and neighbors disappeared or were buried in the wreckage. There was no church nor priest. In the end I dug a grave by myself and buried my wife alone." The man had felt unhealed even after a year because he hadn't had a venue to surface his grief over this very sad story.

The critical incidents debriefing approach seemed most helpful for those whose psychological dislocation was transient. However, recounting traumatic experiences without the presence of a trained professional and the necessary follow-up is not considered compliant with international standards.[11] Following are some practices that we found helpful.

First, receive people's stories as a gift. Take their stories at face value, without probing beyond what they are prepared to share. This provides space to help people verbalize and thus objectify their experiences, which can help them cope better.

Second, train survivors to listen to one another. The simple exercise of listening among survivors leading Basic Ecclessial Communities in the city had enabled them to embark on an "each one, heal one" community healing

---

11. See the "Do No Harm" Inter-Agency Standing Committee (IASC) Guidelines on Mental Health and Psychosocial Support in Emergency Settings, 2007.

process. Mutual and careful listening helps people feel valued and that their grief has been honored.

Psychological First Aid

Psychological first aid proved to be a useful tool for restoring calm and competence, but it requires supportive structures to work. In a context such as the aftermath of Yolanda, where structures do not exist so that survivors can feel safe, secure or stable (a necessary condition of psychological first aid), trauma can become prolonged. The lack of a referral system on the ground for those needing professional help also hinders the capacity for moving on.

Despair, like hope, is a projection of the imagination. During the typhoon, two mothers related their sense of despair when it seemed that their small children were already dead, swept away by the floodtide. One tried to commit suicide by drinking the filthy water, and the other let go of the log she was holding onto, hoping to drown herself. Miraculously, they both survived, and so did their children, except one.

On the other hand, some participants in ISACC's workshops reported more despair in the aftermath of the typhoon. Faced with the task of having to rebuild without any resources, a participant confessed that he felt depressed and saw the future as utterly bleak.

To encourage people to rise up and hope, it is important to put people in a situation where their actual condition holds out a real promise of recovery and restoration.

Without concrete signs that things will get better, posttraumatic stress graduates into deep and prolonged depression. Unfortunately, signs of improvement in the condition of the majority of survivors in Tacloban were scant, except for those who had the resources to rebuild and reopen their businesses. Some months after the storm, there were reports of survivors who had lost their hold on life and died because of depression.

Culture and Community-Based Healing

Because the massive trauma could not be addressed by one-on-one counselling or psychosocial support as framed by western paradigms, ISACC innovated community-based healing rituals, drawing from the spiritual infrastructure that was already in place within the culture.

In December, just a month after the typhoon, ISACC helped the people of Barangay 89 walk through their grief by facilitating a procession around the community, which culminated in candle lighting for the dead. A volunteer team of visual and theater artists conducted art and play therapy for children, which became a focal point of joy and recovery for the children. One child, who showed early signs of PTSD and was refusing to eat and isolating himself, began to join and eventually looked forward eagerly to the art and music workshops, gaining friends and normalcy in the process.

During Holy Week, ISACC trained the youth to perform the traditional *cenaculo,* which reenacts the Passion of Christ. We also conducted a psychospiritual retreat for the barangay leaders, which proved to be decisive in moving them towards healing and recovery. A team of pastors and theologians offered reflections on the *Siete Palabras,* the Seven Last Words of Christ from the cross. On Easter Sunday, the community staged a *Salubong*, where men and women segregated into groups and walked from opposite directions, meeting at the midpoint of the barangay shoreline, reenacting the meeting between Mary Magdalene and the risen Christ.

To address the people's fear of the sea, which is a constant reminder of traumatic memories, ISACC performed a cleansing of the sea ritual. At the end of the ceremony, water from the sea was symbolically purified and then used to sprinkle and bless the people, an intentional reminder of the Catholic practice of blessing the faithful with holy water. As a climax to the Easter celebrations, people threw flowers to the sea, a symbolic way of saying farewell to the dead and those who had been swallowed by the sea and were still missing. Instead of the usual prayers for the dead, we composed a prayer that the people recited as they released and committed their loved ones to the hand of God.

These and other rituals were so moving that the impact exceeded our expectations. Many of the people stood in silence for a long time before the sea, praying and weeping, mourning and remembering their dead. Even the children remained quiet. At dusk, the children lighted candles for their families and relatives. At the end, the people reported a sense of release. The surrounding communities who witnessed these events expressed the wish that they, too, could take part in similar rituals in their communities.

From these community-based healing rituals, we have learned the following:

First, the power of poetics was evident in the community rituals, which served as public expressions of collective grief and a communal way of addressing the Almighty. They fostered solidarity and connectedness, what the Apostle Paul calls the "fellowship of His sufferings" (Phil 3:10 NASB).

Second, while prayer can have ambiguous results,[12] the support of a community is important to healing. Culturally, the Filipino can face almost anything as long as she has a *kasama*, a companion for the journey. Besides the need for a set of beliefs that lend coherence to experiences of crisis or set people on their way toward right practices and helpful habits, community rituals are powerful resources for healing that boost community spirit and massify interventions that facilitate coping.

Third, the recourse to a community's existing store of healing rituals should be intentional and deliberate. There is now international consensus to encourage traditional healing rituals, rather than just translating western methodologies into local idioms and languages.[13]

Fourth, memory markers for the dead are especially important for traumatized communities. During the rituals commemorating the day the typhoon hit, which happened to coincide with the celebration of All Souls' Day, the people of Tacloban quite spontaneously built little makeshift altars on the sites where many people had died.

The Filipino culture is particularly concerned with what to do about the dead, which is evidenced by the numerous rituals and artifacts that have to do with honoring or appeasing the dead. This is poignantly revealed in the lament of Tonya, who lost her husband during the typhoon and whose body was never found. She shared the pain of not having any burial rites for him, no tomb to go to and offer flowers on All Souls' Day.

Trauma is not healed by obliterating memory, but by putting up memorials that serve as bridges from the past to the present and future. We need to help people "move towards memory," not "beyond memory."[14]

This raises a question about the *galang kaluluwa* (literally "wandering soul"), the souls of people who are believed to be roaming around because they died suddenly and were not able to leave their attachments on earth. Immediately after the typhoon, ghost stories proliferated, and they continue to be told, causing persistent fear among the people. However, this area of inquiry has been largely ignored or glossed over because of the largely secularist and

12. Frequency of prayer has been correlated with improved mental health, but it has also been found that the more ritualistic and prescribed the prayers become, the greater the loneliness, depression, tension, and the sense of distance from God (Masters and Spielmans, 2007). However, there is overwhelming support for the power of community to foster mental health.

13. Inter-Agency Standing Committee (IASC) Guidelines, 2010.

14. Meichenbaum, "Trauma, Spirituality and Recovery," 9.

naturalistic paradigm of aid agencies from the North and their institutional proxies in the South.

Yet addressing this question is crucial to the people's healing. During the memorial mass commemorating the day Typhoon Yolanda hit, a man suddenly crumpled up before a little wooden cross in the midst of the rows and rows of white crosses without names that the local government had put up in remembrance of those who had died in the Typhoon. When asked what had happened, he said he had asked for a sign that his five-year-old granddaughter would make *paramdam* (her presence felt) if she were one of the unidentified bodies buried in the mass grave. He said that she had appeared, skipping along the rows of crosses with no names, and he had broken down in tears, mingled with both grief and relief.

The cosmos is far bigger than the part of the natural world that lends itself to empirical investigation, for it includes both the seen and unseen, and it assumes unbroken continuity between this life and the next and constant traffic between the living and the dead.

The Filipino belief in the reality of the spirit world and the way it impinges on our mental health needs a therapeutic response that is sensitive to the cultural and spiritual dimensions of psychological discomposure.[15] In the old days, this seemed to be assuaged by ritual sacrifice and other ways of easing cosmic anxieties and dread. Today, we need to reinvent healing rituals that are cogent within the cosmology and faith traditions of various peoples.

Political Dimensions

Following most disaster situations, people can usually tap into stable institutions or humanitarian agencies on the ground, such as the local government, schools, churches or hospitals. But during Typhoon Yolanda, all these institutions were destroyed or impaired and could not function.

In Tacloban, the trauma was so massive that it demobilized the entire population – from the mayor to the lowest functionary in the barangays. In the National Disaster Risk Reduction Management Center's April report of casualties, the body count was 6,193 dead and 1,061 missing, but only one

---

15. A possible tool for this is the Cultural Formulation framework of the American Psychiatric Association (2000), a guide to clinicians in probing various ways that culture is embedded in diagnosis and treatment. Yet even this needs to be re-evaluated in the light of the clinical experiences of those operating in non-western contexts.

person on the death list and one on the missing list were from Tacloban![16] Yet in Barangay 89 alone, one of 138 barangays in Tacloban City, there were at least five hundred reported dead, excluding those missing.

From this, we saw how government dysfunction and partisan politics greatly hindered rehabilitation and recovery of survivors.

A year after Typhoon Yolanda hit, people were still in need of food, safe shelter and livelihood opportunities. The ongoing instability made people insecure, uncertain of the future and unable to move on. Many people still remain in a state of debilitation and depression because of the sheer inability of the local and national government to coordinate rehabilitation efforts.

The clan war between the Aquinos, on one side, and the Romualdezes and Marcoses, on the other side (as represented by the then president, Benigno Aquino III, and the then Tacloban mayor, Alfred Romualdez) has hindered government decisiveness in delivering relief and other forms of assistance. Medical professionals say that thousands of lives could have been saved if help had come within the first five days. Many of those who could have survived died because of lack of food, water and medicines, especially the children and the elderly.

The destructive impact of Yolanda could have been mitigated by competent and decisive leadership, but the fractures dating back to the authoritarianism of the Marcos years resurfaced. The nation's trauma from this tragic history will continue to remain an undercurrent until the unhealed wounds of the past are redressed. This in itself demands closure and healing.

From this, we have learned how systemic dysfunction prolongs trauma. Our people have been extraordinarily resilient in the face of calamities, both natural and political, but there is a limit to our carrying capacity for suffering.

Bibliography

Ashvin Shah, Siddharth. "'To Do No Harm,' Staff Care, and Ethnomedical Competence: Four Spiritual Care Examples of Psychosocial Trauma Recovery after the 2004 Tsunami and 2005 Earthquake in South Asia." In *Creating Spiritual and Psychological Resilience: Integrating Care in Disaster Relief Work*, edited by Grant H. Brenner, Daniel H. Bush, Joshua Moses, 157–179. New York: Routledge, 2010.

Hall, C. M. "Crisis as Opportunity for Spiritual Growth." *Journal of Religion and Health* 25, no. 1 (1986): 8–17.

16. http://www.gov.ph/crisis-response/updates-typhoon-yolanda/casualties/, accessed 25 November 2014.

Kass, J. D., R. Friedman, J. Leserman, P. C. Zuttermeister, and H. Benson. "Health Outcomes and a New Index of Spiritual Experience." *Journal for the Scientific Study of Religion* 30, no. 2 (1991): 203–211.

Koenig, H. G. "Research on Religion, Spirituality and Mental Health: A Review." *The Canadian Journal of Psychiatry* 54, no. 5 (2009): 283–291.

Meichenbaum, Donald. "Trauma, Spirituality and Recovery: Toward a Spiritually-Integrated Psychotherapy." www.melissainstitute.org.

Schafer, Alison. "Spirituality and Mental Health in Humanitarian Contexts: An Exploration Based on World Vision's Haiti Earthquake Response." War Trauma Foundation. http://www.gov.ph/crisis-response/updates-typhoon-yolanda/casualties/. Accessed 25 November 2014.

12

Strengthening Resilience of Disaster Survivors

Integrating Psychospiritual Support in Mental Health and Psychosocial Support Response[1]

Annabel Manzanilla-Manalo

On 8 November 2013, Super-Typhoon Yolanda (international name Haiyan) hit different regions of the Philippines, wreaking widespread devastation throughout these regions and bringing unprecedented suffering into the experience of millions of people. Haiyan claimed more than 6,300 lives (with a further 1,062 reported still missing), injured 28,688, disrupted community support structures and livelihood sources in forty-four provinces, damaged 1,140,332 houses and left more than three million homeless.[2]

The individual stories of survivors of Super-Typhoon Haiyan dramatize how disaster impacts the total person – body, mind, spirit and relationships. However, most post-disaster recovery interventions focus only on the visible physical and social effects of disaster rather than the invisible psychological, spiritual and existential impact. Also, most conceptualizations of post-disaster experiences tend to focus on survivors' vulnerability to psychopathology and

1. This article was originally published in *Why, O God?: Disaster, Resiliency, and the People of God*, eds. Athena Gorospe, Charles Ringma and Karen Hollenbeck-Wuest (Mandaluyong City, Metro Manila: OMF Literature Inc. and Asian Theological Seminary, 2017).

2. National Disaster Risk Reduction and Management Council, "Final Report re Effects of Typhoon 'Yolanda' (Haiyan)," 3, http://ndrrmc.gov.ph/attachments/article/1329/FINAL_REPORT_re_Effects_of_Typhoon_YOLANDA_(HAIYAN)_06-09NOV2013.pdf.

dysfunction. Yet these conceptualizations do not give a complete picture of survivors' experiences, since the majority of survivors have amazing survival skills and have already demonstrated a tremendous capacity for effective coping. In the case of Haiyan, within a month after the disaster many survivors had already started rebuilding their lives, their homes and their communities.

Resilience is the capacity to adapt well and recover from adversity, trauma or tragedy. In the context of multiple losses and traumas, resilience does not mean readily getting closure and moving on, since post-disaster recovery is a process that may take a long time. Rather, resilience is the condition of being able to "bounce back" after a disaster to a "new normal." The new term for this is "building back better."

Typhoon Haiyan: A Survivor Story

Understanding the particular impact and meaning of a traumatic experience provides insight into the uniqueness of each survivor's suffering and how resilience can be strengthened. Following is one survivor's account of inner wounding and the struggle to make sense of traumatic loss.

Marina[3] was in tears as she recounted the ordeal of watching her seven children get snatched by the waves and strong wind. Five of her children survived, but the two youngest ones did not. Marina herself almost drowned. For several weeks, she and her husband tried hard to locate the remains of their missing children, but their bodies were never found. Marina's husband started drinking alcohol as a way of dealing with his grief and guilt over his failure to save his children. He was angry at God and blamed him for the death of his children.

> *Maybe there is no God. If there is, why did he allow this to happen to my children? They are innocent!*

As a believer, Marina struggled to make sense of how a good God could allow the violent death of her children. In the depths of her suffering, she perceived God as one inflicting punishment unfairly.

> *It is so painful, I always remember them. I'm confused and have so many questions. Why is God punishing us? They are good children, why them and not the bad ones?*

3. Not her real name.

For Marina, having a safe space to tell her story and talk about faith issues and questions of meaning facilitated a shift from anger and protest to a deeper sense of God as an ever-present help in times of distress.

> *I can feel God's help. At least we are able to survive each day, with food on the table we can eat three times a day, and my children are now back in school. Help comes in times of severe need, and I know it is from God.*

This encounter raises questions about how trauma and suffering can be transformed and meaningfully integrated into one's life story. How can resilience be supported and nurtured? These questions guided the content and process of the Asian Theological Seminary (ATS) response to Haiyan survivors.

The ATS response, categorized as mental health and psychosocial support (MHPSS), is an integrated, multi-component intervention comprising community outreach, psychoeducation, training, capacity building and psychospiritual support. MHPSS refers to "any type of local or outside support that aims to protect or promote psychosocial well-being and/or to prevent or treat mental disorders."[4] It addresses both psychological (cognitive and emotional) and social (relationships and family/community networks) dimensions of individual functioning. Psychospiritual support is a core component of the ATS response and involves a supportive, compassionate presence that draws on survivors' strengths and inner resources and facilitates shifts to more hopeful narratives.

ATS Mental Health and Psychosocial Support Response

Responding to the psychosocial and spiritual needs of survivors is particularly important when the usual support structures in a community have been temporarily demobilized. The majority of survivors will return to normal psychosocial functioning once they have basic services and security needs met and are reconnected with family/communal support. However, those who have been more severely affected may suffer from ongoing emotional distress, such as depression, grief, anxiety and other spiritual and existential issues triggered by trauma exposure. While these are normal reactions, depending on the severity and magnitude of the disaster's impact, some individuals or specific

---

4. Inter-Agency Standing Committee (IASC), *Inter-Agency Standing Committee Guidelines on Mental Health and Psychosocial Support in Emergency Settings* (Geneva: IASC, 2007), 1, https://interagencystandingcommittee.org/system/files/legacy_files/guidelines_iasc_mental_health_psychosocial_june_2007.pdf.

groups will need further support in order to manage their stress reactions and restore their sense of well-being. In such cases, lack of support in addressing emotional and social distress may undermine long-term mental health and coping resources.[5]

The ATS response abided by the guidelines issued by the United Nations' Inter-Agency Standing Committee (IASC) on the minimum responses to protect and promote the mental health and psychosocial well-being of people. One of the guidelines is that in non-Western societies, where survivors usually experience suffering in spiritual, religious, family or community terms, there is a need for interventions that facilitate conditions for appropriate communal, cultural, spiritual and religious healing practices.[6] Thus we employed an integrated and culturally sensitive community-based psychosocial response.

Outreach to Affected Communities

During the first phase of our work (which was conducted between three weeks and two months after the disaster), ATS organized, trained and deployed volunteer counselors to Leyte (Tacloban City, Ormoc, Dulag, Carigara), Samar (Basey), Aklan and Capiz. ATS deployed ten teams in seven batches, each consisting of sixty-six volunteers from ATS faculty, staff, students and alumni. We made therapeutic visits to homes, evacuation centers and local churches. We provided psychospiritual support to survivors (adults and children), using informal *kumustahan and kwentuhan* (storytelling sessions). We facilitated group and family-centered activities using a variety of creative approaches, such as art, music, liturgy, community rituals, storytelling and play activities for children. Recognizing the importance of timing, we planned our community outreach to take place after the initial period of chaos was over, once people were starting to take stock of the disaster's impact and ready to process their feelings and reactions.

Mindful of the core principle of "doing no harm" in humanitarian emergency situations,[7] we ensured adequate preparations for volunteers by facilitating preparatory trainings on disaster mental health, the psychosocial impact of disaster and psychospiritual support for children and adults. We also provided volunteers with clear guidelines so that they would be able to work effectively while avoiding further harm to survivors. Recognizing the potential damage caused by inappropriate theology, we discussed various theological

---

5. IASC, *Guidelines on Mental Health*, 1.
6. IASC, 106.
7. IASC, 10.

perspectives on suffering as well as the appropriate responses to questions about faith and other existential issues raised by survivors. Because most of the volunteers did not have experience in disaster response, each team was headed by a lead counselor, who provided field supervision and coaching to ensure that our approach would be grounded in the realities of the survivors.

Because ATS values partnership, we coordinated with local churches, NGOs, local government units and other knowledgeable groups in the community. This minimized confusion, overlapping of services and competition while also ensuring a psychological climate that would be conducive to our activities.

To monitor the impact of these experiences on the volunteers, we conducted post-deployment debriefing, conversation/reflection sessions and a retreat. These sessions enabled volunteers to discuss questions about faith and the theology of suffering, such as God's providence and God's presence or absence. In the context of a retreat, volunteers struggled to make sense of these issues while also nurturing space to bring their laments collectively before God.

Psychoeducation on Disaster Mental Health

Another important dimension of our community outreach was to raise awareness among survivors about their mental health and the psychological aspects of disasters. We provided psychoeducation on the common stress reactions to disasters in order to help survivors understand the psychological mechanisms behind their anxieties and difficulties. We also discussed effective ways to help survivors cope with these anxieties and difficulties.

Training and Capacity Building

During the second phase of our work (which was conducted between four and seven months later), we made home visits and provided psychospiritual support to the communities we had visited during the first phase. In preparation for this second phase, the counseling interns received a series of trainings before they were deployed. In order to situate our work in broader context, they were oriented in disaster risk reduction management by resource persons from the Center for Disaster Preparedness and the University of the Philippines College of Social Work and Community Development.

To ensure the long-term sustainability of a psychosocial support response to disasters, we conducted trainings on psychological first aid and community mobilization with community workers/*barangay* service point officers in Tacloban City, Leyte and with pastors and church workers in Ormoc City, Southern Leyte. ATS also provided trainings in crisis and trauma care, grief support, disaster preparedness and psychospiritual support to churches and organizations that were involved in disaster response work or the formation of disaster response teams.

In disaster prone areas, we coordinated with different ministerial associations so that we could work together to provide psychosocial training opportunities. Through this partnering, we developed the "Community-based Psychosocial Support in Times of Disaster" certificate training program, which is designed for pastors, church leaders, community workers and NGOs who are interested in starting a disaster response ministry to the community.[8] The program consists of ten modular courses that aim to develop participants' psychosocial support skills, along with the theological and biblical perspectives necessary to enhance survivors' capacities to overcome the vulnerabilities caused by disasters. The training program also integrates self-care and lay counseling skills.

Psychospiritual Support

At the core of the ATS response is a commitment to providing psychospiritual support for disaster survivors. Because people are affected by disaster in such different ways, they need different kinds of support in the aftermath of a disaster. Although the first priority after a disaster is to respond to survivors' needs for basic services and security, survivors also need to address the mental, emotional and spiritual distress caused by disasters.

Because a person is an integrated whole, rather than a collection of fragmented parts, each individual has bio-psychospiritual-social dimensions that can be harnessed together to support resiliency in times of disaster.[9] Psychospiritual support harmonizes with the goals of psychological first aid, which are to reduce initial distress and to foster long-term adaptive functioning and coping.[10] Psychospiritual support also draws on mass trauma intervention

---

8. The ATS Counseling Center is now implementing the certificate program in partnership with three ministerial associations. In Haiyan-affected communities, our partners are Ormoc City Evangelical Ministerial Association (OCEMA) and Tacloban Evangelical Association of Ministers and Churches (TEAMC). We are also implementing the same program with Onesimo Church-Based Ministry. Each training site has an average of thirty trainees, who are committed to apply their learning to their ministries.

9. See also Violeta V. Bautista, *Urabayan: Bringing Wholeness to Children and Families in Crisis through Community-Based Family Counseling* (Quezon City, Philippines: World Vision, 2006).

10. Cf. World Health Organization (WHO), *Psychological First Aid: Guide for Field Workers* (Geneva: WHO, 2011).

principles, which are to promote safety, calming, connectedness to others, a sense of self-efficacy and community-efficacy and hope.[11]

The ATS model of psychospiritual support employs culturally sensitive processes that draw from the experiences, practices and healing resources of the community. It also taps into spiritual coping resources – such as people's beliefs, values and virtues – that will support survivors on their healing journeys and anchor their resilience. Psychospiritual support helps survivors connect with themselves, others, God and nature in ways that allow them to find meaning, transcend tragedies and foster healing and posttraumatic growth.[12]

One core component of psychospiritual support is to engage the survivor in a therapeutic conversation that facilitates storytelling, validates feelings and reactions and highlights narratives of survival, resilience and growth.

In such a therapeutic conversation, the survivor tells his or her story to a compassionate listener, sharing experiences and feelings at his or her own pace and comfort level. Because therapeutic storytelling is non-intrusive, the listener does not probe into the details of the person's experience, as that might cause the survivor to relive memories of the event, causing further trauma. Instead, the listener becomes attuned to the survivor's inner world, listening to the narrative, observing body language and identifying what it would be like to be that person.

To validate a survivor's feelings and reactions, the listener acknowledges the profound grief and "soul wounds" caused by the disaster. The listener makes space for survivors to express their deepest pain, grief, anguish, anger and protest to God. The listener accepts, values and respects all emotions.

While attending to a story, the listener draws on the survivor's strengths and coping skills by asking questions, such as, "Where do you draw strength to rise above the tragedy?" or "What has sustained you during this time?" The therapeutic conversation ends with pastoral words of comfort, using language that conveys God's comforting presence, God as a refuge and strength, God as source of peace and security and God's invitation to come and rest. This invites survivors to move toward a hopeful perspective for the future.

Listeners need to be very sensitive as they highlight the spiritual/faith dimension in survivors' stories without necessarily using religious language.

---

11. Cf. Stevan E. Hobfoll, Patricia Watson, Carl C. Bell, Richard A. Bryant, Melissa J. Brymer, Matthew J. Friedman, Merle Friedman, et al., "Five Essential Elements of Immediate and Mid-term Mass Trauma Intervention: Empirical Evidence," *Psychiatry* 70, no. 4 (2007): 283–315.

12. Cf. Annabel Manzanilla-Manalo, "Phenomenology of Posttraumatic Growth in Survivors of Political Violence," paper presented at the 49th Annual Convention of the Psychological Association of the Philippines, August 2012.

This may involve helping survivors become aware of their inner resources or of God's presence in the midst of their suffering. These conversations facilitate healing and help the survivor construct hopeful narratives.

Facilitating Shifts in Survivors' Narratives

Sensitive and caring psychospiritual support can facilitate shifts in survivors' perspectives about their traumatic experiences. The following two scenarios illustrate these narrative shifts at several different stages of a survivor's healing journey.

From Despair to Hope

Jeffrey[13] was part of a group of five survivors who joined the informal *kwentuhan* (storytelling) session that I facilitated in his community a month after the disaster. Jeffrey's family lived in one of the hardest-hit coastal communities in Tacloban, where several cargo ships were washed ashore, flattening several houses and killing many people. For several months after the disaster, the ships remained there, reminding the community dwellers of the tragedy that had hit them. Despite many losses, Jeffrey and his surviving family members managed to build a temporary shelter across from their damaged house.

In tears, Jeffrey recounted the loss of his wife, mother, and two siblings. He shared about his struggle to survive, the pain of his loss and how his faith had sustained him.

> At the height of the storm my wife told me to hang on to our two children. I braved the raging waters and struggled to bring them to a higher, safer place. I almost gave up but my children's cries would bring me back to my senses, emboldening me to fight for our lives . . . I can still imagine and feel those events . . . I feel intense pain whenever I remember her [wife] and the life we have shared. It's hard to accept life without her. Even now when my youngest cries, I just pat him on the back. I try to be strong and hold back my tears so he might not feel discouraged . . . I always pray for inner strength for my children.

At the close of the group session, Jeffrey expressed curiosity and appreciation.

> Why do you take time to come here? We are happy that there are people who come to talk and listen to us. We hope that you will

13. Not his real name.

> visit us again maybe after three years, and by then we would have recovered already. Our only request is that when you visit us, you will bring us a prayer book as a sign of our conversation.

Jeffrey was pleasantly surprised to see me during my next visit, four months after the disaster. He shared about lingering feelings of grief and how our previous conversation had been helpful in reminding him to hold onto God during difficult times. He expressed gratitude that he could provide for the family's daily needs through the financial assistance he had received from an NGO and the support of other survivors.

> It was a very sad Christmas, not like before . . . But the small income from the store helps meet our daily needs. At least even with the barest we have, we manage to survive . . . I draw strength from my children, from the support of other survivors and from God.

Seven months after the disaster, Jeffrey's narratives reflect how our previous conversations were crucial in helping him cope with grief. He shared that in times of distress, he had found peace and comfort in God. He had started reading the Bible and could best resonate with the stories of Jesus healing the sick. His youngest son had begun attending Sunday school in a newly built local church in the community. Jeffrey called my attention to a miniature boat that he and other survivors were constructing, which they planned to parade in the town fiesta celebration:

> This is a symbol of what we went through with Haiyan. There are many painful memories, but as the boat sails away we are reminded that life must go on.

During my fourth home visit, fourteen months after the disaster, Jeffrey told me about his relocation to a safer place. His narrative reflects signs of healing and growth, revealing his acceptance of how his life has changed as a result of the disaster. He was also able to hold the tension between living with his grief as well as his gratitude for having survived the tragedy.

> My life has changed. I can no longer bring back the past, but I realized we can still be happy in the midst of tragedy. There is both sadness and joy . . . While there is life there is hope.

From Lament to Hope

With members of a local church that was completely destroyed by Haiyan, I facilitated a liturgy to create space for the congregation to bring their lament to God. The congregation of about one hundred members was shocked that their church had not been spared and that many members had lost their homes, properties and livelihoods. Because the church was from a triumphalist tradition that celebrates expressions of faith even when going through dark times, there wasn't space for an honest expression of despair, loss and grief. Members struggled to make sense of their belief in a good and loving God and their experience of suffering. They grieved not only their physical losses, but also their sense of security and invulnerability. Their church tradition had not prepared them to deal with suffering and could not provide them with a way to bring their heart cries collectively before God.

The liturgy included silence, meditation, prayer and biblical reflection on the theme of "lament and hope." During the communal prayer of lament, many participants stayed with their grief and cried silently. For them, it was not just a cathartic moment, but an expression of an honest faith as they dared to bring their pain, perplexities, questions and disappointments before God.

The church pastor later disclosed that the liturgy had been a therapeutic experience for him personally as it enabled him to resonate with other church members' experiences. The prayer of lament connected them to one another in a new way. They collectively experienced a deeper sense of God's healing presence, making it easier for hope to spring forth.

> I was healed by the worship service as I was able to relate with the message you shared with us. It was exactly what I experienced. In my personal prayer, I asked, "Why Lord? Didn't You foresee how this will affect the members? Aren't You pleased with my ministry? How can we move on from here?" I realized it is okay to pray this way. I felt God's presence even stronger. Now I feel more ready to resume ministry to my church members.

Lessons Learned in Psychospiritual Support after Disaster

Reflecting on our experiences in providing psychospiritual support, I have been able to identify good practices and draw several conclusions.

Building on Strengths and Coping Resources

Psychospiritual support requires listeners to attend to stories of trauma, loss and grief as well as stories of survival, strength and hope. Traumatic experiences tend to narrow a person's focus on their pain and emotional distress or what is pathological and dysfunctional. Yet there is always something positive in people's narratives that needs to be recognized and affirmed. Recognizing people's strengths and focusing on what is working in their lives helps them build coping resources.

Nurturing Spirituality

Conversations that nurture spirituality can strengthen survivors' resolve to engage life. Helping survivors focus on their beliefs, values, virtues, skills and abilities will strengthen their coping resources. We can help broaden and build these strengths by affirming narratives of faith, hope, courage, love, caring for others, generosity and self-giving.

Using Culturally Sensitive Processes

Psychospiritual support draws on positive healing elements of the Filipino culture. This means doing things in the spirit of *pakikipagkapwa* (recognition of shared identity), *pakikiisa* (being in solidarity with), *pakikidama* (shared inner perception or feeling with another), *pakikiramay* (sharing in one's grief or loss) and *malasakit* (showing compassion). When we act as neighbors to one another, we relate not only as fellow Filipinos, but as fellow humans *(kapwa)*, deeply aware of our shared humanity and our common experience of vulnerability and suffering.

Relabeling Counseling

In providing psychospiritual support, it is better to present oneself in a less formal way and to avoid stigmatizing jargon or labels. Rather than using the term "counseling," we might talk about *pakikipag-kuwentuhan* (sharing of experiences), which is a form of therapeutic conversation that involves *pagbubukas ng loob* (opening up one's heart). By nature, Filipinos are storytellers and should be given space to share their stories.

Utilizing Creative Reflective Activities

Disaster survivors often find it difficult to put their experiences of trauma and suffering into words. Creative reflective activities – such as art, music, metaphors, liturgy, community rituals, meditative prayer, storytelling and play activities for children – can help survivors express their inner feelings. Getting in touch with these feelings of pain and grief can facilitate the healing journey.

Facilitating Family and Group Support

Family or group-centered processes help to strengthen social resources, such as *damayan* (looking after and caring for one another). Group-centered processes also nurture safe spaces for family or group members to grieve together. Through these gatherings, members feel less isolated and begin to build deeper emotional connections as they grow in intimacy and learn how to care for one another.

Enhancing Local Capacities

Training those in the frontline, such as church and community workers, ensures the sustainability of disaster response services. Being equipped with a sufficient understanding of disaster-related stress, trauma and grief reactions, along with skills in psychospiritual support, empowers local volunteers to work in an efficient and effective manner. Those who are working in the frontline also need to be able to integrate psychospiritual support with existing services and structures in the local community.

Care for Volunteers

Because working in disaster response can impact the mental health and well-being of volunteers, it is important to provide them with adequate training, team support and supervision both before and throughout the time of deployment. Hearing stories of trauma and suffering can cause vicarious trauma, existential dilemmas and faith crises, raising questions about providence, God's presence or absence and social justice. To help volunteers process their own disaster response experiences, debriefing sessions, retreats and spiritual direction should be made available.

Exploring a Community-Based Psychosocial Program

Psychospiritual support needs to be fully integrated into community-based psychosocial support programs. In the aftermath of widespread devastation and the displacement of thousands of people, a community-based psychosocial approach addresses mental health issues while strengthening individual and community resilience. This empowers affected communities to return to a "new normal," while also strengthening their resolve to participate in larger disaster risk reduction and community rehabilitation initiatives by creating systems that will eventually become part of the community's healing, caring and development systems.[14] A community-based psychosocial program ensures responsiveness, accessibility and sustainability of psychospiritual support services through support group formation, training, capacity building, advocacy and collaboration with existing efforts in the community.

---

14. See Annabel Manzanilla-Manalo and Fermin P. Manalo Jr., "Bringing Psychology to the Marginalized: Exploring the Role of Community-Based Counseling," *Journal of Psychology and Christianity* 33, no. 2 (2014): 121–126.

Upholding Rights-Based Approach

It is important for psychosocial services to be framed as citizen entitlement or state obligation so that survivors do not see themselves as recipients of outside interventions. Affected communities need to be informed about their rights to multiple layers of support, protection and participation in disaster-related response and planning. In addition to raising awareness about these rights, programs should help the community build their capacity for asserting those rights.[15]

Pastoral Response: Challenges to Churches

Reflecting on the lessons learned in providing psychospiritual support, I have been able to identify significant challenges to churches and how we can expand ways of doing disaster response ministry.

Being in Solidarity: Compassionate Presence

To nurture a compassionate presence, those who work in disaster areas need to be willing to reach out and stand in solidarity with – or be one with – those who are suffering while accompanying them on the journey of healing and rebuilding. This compassionate solidarity is grounded in God's love for the vulnerable, which is made visible in the life, ministry and teachings of Jesus. The very life of Jesus reveals a self-emptying, downward movement (Phil 2:5–8). Instead of holding on to power, Jesus served those on the margins of society, making himself vulnerable by entering into their lived experiences, listening to and understanding their pain and allowing himself to be moved by their suffering.

Compassion is not just a feeling. As Nouwen, McNeill and Morrison observe in their book *Compassion*, "*compassion* is derived from the Latin words *pati* and *cum*, which together mean 'to suffer with.' Compassion asks us to go where it hurts, to enter into places of pain, to share in brokenness, fear, confusion, and anguish . . . Compassion requires us to be weak with the weak, vulnerable with the vulnerable, and powerless with the powerless. It means full immersion in the condition of being human."[16] Jesus, who came as a poor man and a servant, shows us what it means to live with compassion –

---

15. Fermin Manalo Jr., "Towards Theologizing that Accompanies the Political Struggle of the Poor," *Phronesis* 15, nos. 1–2 (2008): 47–67.

16. Henri Nouwen, Donald P. McNeill, and Douglas A. Morrison, *Compassion: A Reflection on the Christian Life* (New York: Image Books Doubleday, 1982), 4.

sharing our humanity with others and living in deep solidarity in weakness, brokenness and woundedness.

Demonstrating Love of Neighbor

This compassionate engagement is further defined by Jesus's teaching on the love of God and neighbor as the greatest commandment (Matt 22:36–40). Only by loving our neighbors (the poor and vulnerable) and acting in compassion for them can we as a faith community truly demonstrate genuine love for God. This can be inferred from the parable of the Good Samaritan (Luke 10:25–37), which teaches that loving our neighbor is best demonstrated by reaching out to the vulnerable. This is how we work out God's love in people's particular contexts.

The kind of love that we are called to demonstrate is one that does not create dependence or reinforce helplessness, but rather empowers people to realize their human dignity and capacity. When expressed in servanthood, love becomes "a gospel invitation, and consequently, a potent challenge to the status quo when practiced as a lifestyle."[17] Love, in this context, is a redemptive and liberating act.[18]

Building Genuine, Enabling Relationships

This approach to helping involves more than a set of strategies, for it is about building genuine relationships, participating in people's lives and coming alongside them in their healing journeys. In order to move beyond techniques and effective strategies, we will need to use our self as a therapeutic tool so that we can become human beings – compassionate, authentic and fully present to others.

To be able to sustain this kind of engagement, we will need to nurture, energize and empower our inner beings by practicing the disciplines of silence, solitude and prayer.[19] We will also need to be part of a community that nurtures this kind of commitment.

---

17. Lorenzo C. Bautista, "Cristo Hombre es Mas Grande Que Cristo Dios: Appropriating the Humanity of Jesus in Filipino Christology," in *The Gospel in Culture: Contextualization Issues through Asian Eyes,* ed. Melba P. Maggay (Quezon City, Philippines: Institute for Studies in Asian Church and Culture/OMF Literature, 2013), 141.

18. See also Charles Ringma, "Liberation Theologians Speak to Evangelicals: A Theology and Praxis of Serving the Poor," *Phronesis* 15, nos. 1–2 (2008): 7–25 and Manalo, "Towards Theologizing that Accompanies the Political Struggle of the Poor."

19. Cf. Ringma, "Liberation Theologians Speak to Evangelicals."

Conclusion

Psychospiritual support can be meaningfully integrated into any MHPSS program that seeks to strengthen the resilience of disaster survivors. Rather than treating people as helpless and dysfunctional, effective psychospiritual support builds on their strengths and coping resources. This involves listening not only to accounts of trauma, losses and grief, but also survival, strength and hope. When practiced in a culturally-sensitive manner and as a component of a long-term, community-based psychosocial program, psychospiritual support can help survivors find meaning in their suffering, nurture a spirituality that enables them to engage life with a broader view and promote the wellbeing of individuals, families and communities.

Providing psychospiritual support concretizes Jesus's call to love our neighbors and bears witness to God's loving and empowering presence in the midst of devastation and chaos. Psychospiritual support is modeled after Jesus's way of being with people – fully present, caring and compassionate. To follow Jesus in this way, we cannot approach people as if we are mental health "experts," but must stand alongside them in a position of solidarity.

Bibliography

Bautista, Lorenzo C. "Cristo Hombre es Mas Grande Que Cristo Dios: Appropriating the Humanity of Jesus in Filipino Christology." In *The Gospel in Culture: Contextualization Issues through Asian Eyes*, edited by Melba P. Maggay, chapter 5. Quezon City, Philippines: Institute for Studies in Asian Church and Culture/ OMF Literature, 2013.

Bautista, Violeta V. *Urabayan: Bringing Wholeness to Children and Families in Crisis through Community-Based Family Counselling.* Quezon City, Philippines: World Vision, 2006.

Hobfoll, Stevan E., Patricia Watson, Carl C. Bell et al. "Five Essential Elements of Immediate and Mid-term Mass Trauma Intervention: Empirical Evidence." *Psychiatry* 70, no. 4 (2007): 283–315.

Inter-Agency Standing Committee (IASC), *Inter-Agency Standing Committee Guidelines on Mental Health and Psychosocial Support in Emergency Settings*. Geneva: IASC, 2007. https://interagencystandingcommittee.org/system/files/legacy_files/guidelines_iasc_mental_health_psychosocial_june_2007.pdf.

Manalo, Jr., Fermin P. "Towards Theologizing that Accompanies the Political Struggle of the Poor." *Phronesis* 15, nos. 1–2 (2008): 47–67.

Manzanilla-Manalo, Annabel. "Phenomenology of Posttraumatic Growth in Survivors of Political Violence." Paper presented at the 49th Annual Convention of the Psychological Association of the Philippines, August 2012.

Manzanilla-Manalo, Annabel, and Fermin P. Manalo Jr. "Bringing Psychology to the Marginalized: Exploring the Role of Community-Based Counseling." *Journal of Psychology and Christianity* 33, no. 2 (2014): 121–126.

National Disaster Risk Reduction and Management Council. "Final Report re Effects of Typhoon 'Yolanda' (Haiyan)." http://ndrrmc.gov.ph/attachments/article/1329/FINAL_REPORT_re_Effects_of_Typhoon_YOLANDA_(HAIYAN)_06-09NOV2013.pdf.

Nouwen, Henri, Donald P. McNeill, and Douglas A. Morrison. *Compassion: A Reflection on the Christian Life*. New York: Image Books Doubleday, 1982.

Ringma, Charles. "Liberation Theologians Speak to Evangelicals: A Theology and Praxis of Serving the Poor." *Phronesis* 15, nos. 1–2 (2008): 7–25.

World Health Organization (WHO). *Psychological First Aid: Guide for Field Workers*. Geneva: WHO, 2011.

13

Suffering and Mission

Narrative Research from Cambodia

Yuzo Imamura

Introduction: Suffering in Today's World

Every single day, we read stories of suffering in the newspaper. Tsunamis, hurricanes, an Ebola outburst, multiple terrorist attacks all over the world, bombings in Syria, countless mental and psychological collapses and the list goes on. Because the world is so full of suffering, we agonizingly ask, "Lord, can this be your will?" Suffering is so commonplace that a Google search on "theology of suffering" hits 17,400,000 results in 0.46 seconds.[1]

In Cambodia today, more than three decades have passed since the devastation of the Khmer Rouge period, yet scars left by the Pol Pot regime and subsequent civil wars are still tangible. We can observe both physical sufferings such as land-mine victims as well as invisible psychological sufferings such as PTSD/depression. In a 2012 report, between 15 and 35 percent of those who survived the Khmer Rouge and experienced violence associated with armed conflict suffer from PTSD. Even more people among the general Cambodian population suffer due to a wider transmission of Khmer Rouge-associated trauma.[2]

1. Accessed 19 November 2015.

2. Daniel McLaughlin and Elisabeth Wickeri, "Special Report: Mental Health and Human Rights in Cambodia," Leitner Center for International Law and Justice (New York: Fordham Law School, 2012), 12.

Dictionaries define suffering as "the state of undergoing pain, distress, or hardship"[3] and "physical, mental, or emotional pain or anguish."[4] Such definitions do not identify where suffering comes from or whether it is beneficial or totally harmful.

In reality, there are many different views of suffering. For instance, among those living in highly industrialized countries such as Japan, suffering is an unpopular word today. People in these places are often convinced by the mass media that making our lives easier, smoother and barrier-free is an ultimate value. They are constantly advised to eliminate suffering in their lives as much as possible by using high technology or *kaizen* (continuous improvement) spirit.[5] Otherwise, they ignore it or think that it is nonexistent in their lives while they strive to survive in a very fast-paced life. When they encounter suffering, they can seek help from experts such as counselors, psychologists or folk beliefs. The motto is to manage, reduce, and cope with stress, anxiety, or trauma. On top of that, they are prone to blame the sociopolitical and economic system for their suffering. As a result, there is very limited space to consider biblical ideas of persevering, enduring and living with suffering. But once cross-cultural workers from more industrialized countries land in developing countries like Cambodia, they are overwhelmed by the suffering faced by the local people, such as poverty, injustice and the lack of social security.

Persecution (including martyrdom) is another form of suffering. Tieszen comments that "any unfortunate experience befalling a Christian is considered persecution."[6] Of course, persecution comes in various forms and intensities, but it hurts Christians physically, psychologically (mentally or emotionally) and socially. Tieszen rightly says, "We cannot define the event based on the level of pain it might cause, or the level of intensity in which it occurs. Instead, a definition of persecution encompasses actions spanning the full range of hostility."[7]

While suffering can be subjective, some types of suffering – such as natural disasters – are evident for everybody. Rather than reviewing suffering

---

3. "Suffering," Oxford Dictionaries, accessed 19 November 2015, http://www.oxforddictionaries.com/definition/english/suffering.

4. Millard J. Erickson, "Suffering," in *The Concise Dictionary of Christian Theology*, rev. ed. (Wheaton: Crossway, 2001), 192.

5. This is the famous core value of Toyota. The infamous Toyota Production System (TPS) is a corporate decision-making process, which is essential for the success of *kaizen*.

6. C. L. Tieszen, "Redefining Persecution," in *Sorrow & Blood: Christian Mission in Contexts of Suffering, Persecution, and Martyrdom*, eds. William D. Taylor, Antonia van der Meer and Reg Reimer (Pasadena: William Carey, 2012), 43.

7. Tieszen, "Redefining Persecution," 43. On the one hand, extensive hostile actions could include beating, torture, isolation or imprisonment. On the other hand, mildly hostile actions would include ridicule, restriction, certain kinds of harassment or discrimination.

in terms of non-Christian philosophical analyses, whether ancient, medieval or modern,[8] this paper will focus on what the Bible tells us about suffering. Following this discussion, the paper will explore the role of suffering and the mission of the church in the context of Cambodia.

What the Bible Tells Us about Suffering

Countless books and articles have been written on suffering,[9] and so it is not necessary to duplicate these sound biblical teachings here, though I do cite some helpful resources in the bibliography. Instead, I will briefly explore foundational teaching and practical issues surrounding suffering.

Suffering as a Part of the Christian Life

The Bible affirms that Christians will suffer. As Keller rightly says, "The Bible . . . is about suffering as much as it is about anything."[10] It is worth quoting his summary of the biblical view of suffering at length:

> The book of Genesis begins with an account of how evil and death came into the world. The wisdom literature of the Old Testament is largely dedicated to the problem of suffering. The book of Psalms provides a prayer for every possible situation in life, and so it is striking how filled it is with cries of pain and with blunt questions to God about the seeming randomness and injustice of suffering. The books of Job and Ecclesiastes are almost wholly dedicated to deep reflection on unjust suffering and on the frustrating pointlessness that characterizes so much of life. The prophets Jeremiah and Habakkuk give searing expression to the human complaint that evil seems to rule history. New Testament books such as Hebrews and 1 Peter are almost entirely devoted to helping people face relentless sorrows and troubles. And towering over all, the central figure of the whole of Scripture, Jesus Christ, is a man of sorrows. [11]

---

8. Timothy Keller surveys these three eras in *Walking with God through Pain and Suffering* (New York: Random House, 2013), ch. 2.

9. Amazon.com lists 2,941 books on suffering under the category of Christian Books and Bibles, accessed 23 March 2016.

10. Keller, *Walking with God*, 6.

11. Keller, 5–6.

While we try to eliminate suffering, the Bible tells us that suffering can be both beneficial and indispensable to our Christian life. Indeed, suffering is a gracious gift from God (Phil 1:29). From a biblical perspective, suffering gives believers not only sorrow and pain (e.g. Job in the OT) but also joy (e.g. Acts 5:41; Rom 5). Though such an epistemological discussion lies outside the scope of this paper, in the next section I will explore possible meanings of suffering in the Bible.

Possible Meanings of Suffering

Although as humans we instinctively try to understand the purpose or meaning of suffering, the Bible does not give us a clear answer about *why* we face suffering, but only explores *how* we can endure it. Following are some possible meanings for suffering that can be found in the Bible.

Suffering as God's Justice and Judgment

Genesis 1–3 explains that suffering entered the world as a result of the original sin of human beings, who turned away from God. Paul later writes, "For the wages of sin is death, but the free gift of God is eternal life in Christ Jesus our Lord" (Rom 6:23). Adam and Eve's disobedience to the Creator's will and the breakup of the relationship with God filled the world with suffering: spiritual alienation, inner psychological pain, social and interpersonal conflict and cruelty, natural disasters, diseases and death (Gen 3:17–24). In addition, the books of Psalms and Proverbs suggest that suffering can be directly related to transgression (Pss 32:1–5; 38:1–4; Prov 12:21; 13:20–21; 22:3; 27:12).

Suffering as God's Mystery and Good Intention

Trying to understand the reason for evil and suffering drives us to consider the bigger picture, which is that God's planning is far beyond our understanding. There are hard questions in all of our lives. In the Old Testament, though Joseph suffered numerous setbacks, such as when he was sold by his brothers to Egypt, he endured and trusted in God throughout his suffering. In the end he came to understand God's big picture, which was "a great deliverance" for many people (Gen 45:7 NIV). Joseph reveals this broader perspective when he says, "As for you, you meant evil against me, but God meant it for good, to bring it about that many people should be kept alive, as they are today" (Gen 50:20). The books of Job and Ecclesiastes also richly demonstrate that suffering is not directly related to justice and judgment, but rather to God's mystery, which is beyond our understanding (Deut 29:29). Joni Eareckson Tada views her suffering in this way: "My suffering is redeemed for His purpose."[12] This resonates with the teaching in Romans, where Paul writes, "All things work together for good" (8:28). Peter encourages us to entrust our souls to a faithful Creator even when we do not understand our circumstances (1 Pet 4:19).

Suffering as a Way to Strengthen Faith and Holiness

God saves us and shows us the infinite depths of His grace and love through weakness and pain. Dan McCartney writes, "Christ learned humanhood from his suffering (Heb 5:8). [And therefore] we learn Christhood from our suffering."[13] Just as Jesus experienced our humanity through suffering (Heb 2:18; 4:14–15), we are able to grow in Christlikeness and care for others who are suffering when we suffer. Job acquires a deep knowledge and experience of God through his suffering (42:5–6). The psalmist writes that suffering is good for us and leads us to have a better understanding of God (Ps 119:71; see also Jas 1:2–4). Paul writes that God disciplines us through suffering (Heb 12:10–11). Peter says that we will be restored, confirmed, strengthened and established by God in the end (1 Pet 5:10; 4:12–14). Likewise, Paul encourages us to be prepared for "an eternal weight of glory beyond all comparison" (2 Cor 4:17) and argues that "the sufferings of this present time are not worthy to be compared with the glory that is to be revealed to us" (Rom 8:18 NASB).

Suffering as God's Glory

God came to us and suffered for us chiefly through his death on the cross, as Isaiah prophesies (ch. 53). John Piper and Justin Taylor summarize the achievements of Jesus Christ through his suffering as follows:[14] (1) Christ absorbed the wrath of God on our behalf (Gal 3:13); (2) Christ bore our sins and purchased our forgiveness (1 Pet 2:24; Isa 53:5); (3) Christ provided a perfect righteousness for us that becomes ours in him (Phil 2:7–8; Rom 5:19); (4) Christ defeated death (Heb 2:14–15); (5) Christ disarmed Satan (Col 2:14–15); (6) Christ purchased perfect, final healing for all his people (Isa 53:5; Rev 7:17); (7) Christ will bring us finally to God (1 Pet 3:18). Ultimately, suffering exists in the universe so that Christ might display the great glory of the grace of God by enduring suffering himself and thereby overcoming our suffering.

---

12. Joni Eareckson Tada, "Theology of Suffering," recorded 11 February 2009 in Dallas Theological Seminary chapel, accessed 17 November 2015, http://www.dts.edu/media/play/theology-of-suffering-joni-eareckson-tada/.

13. Dan McCartney, *Why Does It Have to Hurt?: The Meaning of Christian Suffering* (Phillipsburg, NJ: P&R, 1998), 60. Quoted in Keller, *Walking with God*, 152.

14. John Piper and Justin Taylor, *Suffering and the Sovereignty of God* (Wheaton: Crossway, 2006), 87–89.

Suffering as a Challenge to the Character of God

While an atheist is free from the problem of evil, religious people, including Christians from ancient times, have developed the study of theodicy, which is "an attempt to show that God is not responsible for evil,"[15] or "the justification of a deity's justice and goodness in light of suffering and evil."[16] There is no space to describe all ideas of theodicy here, but there are five practical challenges in considering suffering and God: (1) a suspicion about God's omnipotence; (2) a suspicion about God's sovereign control of the future; (3) a suspicion about God's goodness; (4) a suspicion about God's love and presence with us; and (5) a rejection of the idea of evil and suffering. Some might conclude that if there is a good god, there should be no evil. But since there is evil in this world, a god who is both good and powerful cannot exist. This perspective misses the great teaching of suffering and leads to a very myopic understanding of the gospel. Instead, Christians need to develop a biblically sound understanding of God's character by studying the whole Bible and then seeking to live out the word of God.

Suffering in Cambodia and Her Church

Since the first Protestant missionaries with the Church and Missionary Alliance (CMA) arrived in Cambodia in 1923, the gospel has not been received well and the Cambodian church has suffered. In 1946, after the Second World War, the political vacuum gave rise to the nationalistic movement called the Khmer Issarak Movement, which was an anti-French nationalist movement.[17] They hated the Khmer Christians seeing them as spies and sympathizers of the French. As a result, many Christians were persecuted, and the first Cambodian Christian was martyred by members of the movement.[18]

By the 1960s, forty years after the first CMA missionaries arrived, there were only 734 baptized believers in good standing in the Khmer Evangelical Church that was started by the CMA. Ellison estimates that there were roughly

15. Millard J. Erickson, "Theodicy," in *Concise Dictionary*, 198.

16. Donald K. McKim, "Theodicy," in *Westminster Dictionary of Theological Terms*, ed. Donald K. McKim (Louisville: Westminster John Knox, 1996), 279.

17. John Tully, *A Short History of Cambodia: From Empire to Survival* (Chiang Mai, Thailand: Silkworm, 2006), 119–121; "Khmer Issarak," *Encyclopaedia Britannica*, accessed 25 December 2015, http://www.britannica.com/event/Khmer-Issarak.

18. Don Cormack, *Killing Fields Living Fields* (Crowborough, UK: MARC, 1997), 75–79.

two thousand "Christians" in Cambodia.[19] In 1965, King Sihanouk expelled all missionaries, and evangelical church leaders were ordered to close their churches when diplomatic relations with the West were terminated.

Before the civil war broke out in 1970, there were only three congregations in Phnom Penh.[20] Then during the years of the civil war, from 1970 to 1975, missionaries were allowed to return to Cambodia with the rise of a pro-American regime. In 1972 the Khmer Evangelical Church held two evangelistic campaigns in Phnom Penh. Dr Mooneyham of World Vision was the guest speaker, with music provided by the Palermo Brothers and also by the Danibelles. In these two campaigns more than three thousand people made public decisions to accept Christ.

One Cambodian Christian, Mr Taing Chhirc – who was a high-ranking military officer, a major in the nation's armed forces, a strong Christian leader and the General Secretary of the Cambodian Evangelical Church – spoke at the Keswick Convention in England in the summer of 1973, issuing a challenging call to raise awareness and prayer for his country.[21] On the way back to Cambodia, he stopped in Singapore and talked with the directors of the Overseas Missionary Fellowship who were assembled in General Council, inviting them to follow him into Cambodia, where the harvest was great and the laborers few. The mission directors concluded that God was indeed calling them to preach the gospel to the people of Cambodia. By early 1974, the first missionaries of an eventual band of five from OMF entered Cambodia, wading into a harvest for which they had not labored but were now privileged to help reap.[22]

Just a few days after the fall of Phnom Penh to Pol Pot in April 1975, Major Chhirc was standing on the roadside just beyond the city with a colleague, sharing the gospel to all the people who were on their way to the provinces. Chhirc did not hide his identity but continued boldly to proclaim Christ to his countrymen, whom he dearly loved, and consequently was taken by a martyr's death.[23] Before the fall of Phnom Penh, he had told a missionary friend: "Communists are willing to die for what they believe. Is not Jesus worth

---

19. J. Paul Ellison, "A short history of the Cambodian Evangelical Church known in Cambodia as the Khmer Evangelical Church with particular attention being given to people movements and some factors related to church growth," paper presented at Cambodian Christian Services Conference, San Jose, California, 1991.

20. OMF International, "Cambodia Profile," accessed 20 January 2016, https://omf.org/cambodia/cambodia-profile/.

21. Cormack, *Killing Fields*, 130–133.

22. Cormack, 133.

23. Cormack, 169–171.

more than all these things?"[24] In writing of Bonhoeffer, Fernando could equally have been referring to Chhirc when he commented, "Many people thought his death was the waste of a great resource for the church. But Bonhoeffer himself remained close to God and knew that his death would only bring him nearer to God."[25]

More than one million people were massacred during the Pol Pot regime from 1975–1979. These four years were the darkest period in the history of Cambodia, and its effects are still fresh and can be observed in daily life. Almost every household lost loved ones during that period. Because of Pol Pot's systematic elimination of national leaders and intellectuals, poverty and poor education have been major problems in Cambodia since the 1980s. The situation is improving very slowly, and Cambodia has recently escaped from its "poor country" status and joined the "low-income country" category.[26] Today many tourists visit S-21, a former torture center converted from a high school in Phnom Penh, the killing fields across Cambodia, as well as the Angkor Wat complex, a World Heritage site.

When Pol Pot's notorious regime took control of Cambodia in 1975, there were ten thousand believers in thirty congregations in Phnom Penh.[27] By the time the Vietnamese army invaded Phnom Penh on 7 January 1979, there were only a few hundred Christians still alive on that "liberation day."[28] Ellison describes a list of thirty-three pastors and church leaders and found that twenty-seven of them were martyred or died as part of the policy of enforced starvation. By the end of 1979, 80 percent of Cambodia's believers had been martyred. But even after the horrors of Pol Pot's Killing Fields, difficult situations continued for Cambodian believers. Following the fall of Pol Pot's regime in 1979, the Vietnamese government continued to persecute the church, confiscating Bibles, refusing to allow church meetings and keeping known Christians under surveillance.

This practice continued until the Vietnamese withdrew in 1989, and then in 1990 the Cambodian Protestant Church was officially recognized by the new

---

24. Cormack, 326.

25. Ajith Fernando, *The Call to Joy and Pain: Embracing Suffering in Your Ministry* (Wheaton: Crossway, 2007), 178.

26. The Minister of Commerce announced that the General National Income (GNI) for 2015 would be estimated as US $1096. The definition of a "low income country" according to the World Bank was a GNI of US $1046 in 1985.

27. OMF International, *Pray for Cambodia* (Littleton, CO: OMF International, 2012), 12.

28. Some sources say that there were two hundred Christians. For instance, Veritas College International, accessed 20 January 2016, http://www.veritascollege.org/countries/cambodia/cambodia-religions.

government. In the early 1990s, there were only about thirty small churches across the country.[29] Over the last twenty-five years, the number of believers has grown significantly, and it is now estimated that there are more than 250,000 believers in over two thousand churches.[30]

Suffering in the Life Stories of Cambodian Christians

I have chosen a narrative research method since the suffering that the Cambodian people faced is likely very different from the suffering I have experienced. Moreover, the experience of suffering varies between different Cambodian Christians. In addition, I am curious about their interpretation of their life experiences as Christians.

I am also using qualitative research methods, which allows us "to examine people's experiences in detail by using a specific set of research methods such as in-depth interviews, focus group discussions, life histories, etc."[31] This approach gathers complex textual descriptions about how people experience a given research issue to provide information about the human side, such as contradictory behaviors, beliefs, opinions, emotions and relationships. Qualitative methods are also effective in identifying intangible factors – such as social norms, socioeconomic status, gender roles, ethnicity and religion – whose role in the research may not be readily apparent in order to interpret and better understand the complex reality of a given situation and the implications of quantitative data.[32] Nowadays, qualitative research methods are used in social science, medicine and anthropology, among other disciplines. For the

---

29. Interserve New Zealand, "The Cambodian Church: From 30 Churches to 5,000 in Only 20 Years," Go Magazine (2012): 18, accessed 20 January 2016, http://www.interserve.org.nz/RESOURCES/PUBLICATIONS/GO+MAGAZINE/The+Cambodian+Ch urch.html.

30. This number of churches is from Keith Carey, ed., *Global Prayer Digest* (Pasadena: US Center for World Mission, 2011), 9. Others cite different numbers of churches. Some say there are 750 churches (e.g. OMF International), others mention five to seven thousand congregations (e.g. Interserve) or 1,224 Protestant churches (e.g. the 2010 International Religious Freedom Report published by the U.S. Department of State, accessed 28 March 2016, http://www.state.gov/j/drl/rls/irf/2010/148861.htm). In a 2012 report, Steve Hyde suggests that the different numbers of churches is caused by "different definitions of what a church is or incomplete research." A nationwide statistics research by MK2021 is now ongoing. As of 25 August 2017, 2,920 churches were registered.

31. M. Hennink, I. Hutter and A. Bailey, *Qualitative Research Methods* (London: SAGE, 2011), 8–9.

32. N. Mack et al., *Qualitative Research Methods: A Data Collector's Field Guide* (Durham, NC: Family Health International, 2005), 1–2, accessed 20 January 2016, http://www.fhi360.org/sites/default/files/media/documents/Qualitative%20Research%20Methods %20-%20A%20Data%20Collector%27s%20Field%20Guide.pdf.

purposes of this paper, qualitative research methods can help us learn both from the interviewees' experiences as well as their perspectives about suffering, in particular how the Pol Pot genocide continues to affect their life.

I have conducted life story interviews with Cambodian Christians using the Khmer language even though this is a time-consuming research method that further challenges my linguistic ability of analysis. The interviews were recorded with the interviewees' permission. After each interview, the transcripts were typed verbatim, and the abstracted stories are summarized below.[33] I have changed or withheld the interviewee's name, ethnicity and place names in order to protect their identity.

Story 1

Story 1 is about a Khmer man in his fifties who lost his parents during the Pol Pot era. His family background is mainland Chinese, as his grandparents had migrated from China to Cambodia. Before losing his parents, his father taught Chinese at a Chinese school, and his family followed Taoism, Buddhism and any gods that provided merit for their lives. After his parents died, he went to a refugee camp in Thailand with a friend when they heard that they might be able to get some means to earn a living. His four brothers and sisters were separated from each other while traveling from Phnom Penh. When he heard the gospel for the first time, he was a teenager at the refugee camp, where he started attending a church on Sundays and joined a youth group activity because his friends went. Many people also said that the Christians helped their daily life more than others, including government organizations. After a couple of months, when many people were getting baptized, he thought that he could gain some benefits too, so he also got baptized. He looks back on this event later and concludes that he neither had faith in Jesus nor experienced any spiritual transformation.

In the early 1990s, the UN encouraged people in the refugee camps in Thailand to go back to Cambodia. When he returned to Phnom Penh, he was reunited with his brothers and sisters and stayed with his uncle and aunt. But he and his siblings were not welcomed by his uncle and aunt due to the shortage of food. In addition, he had to work hard to take care of them while he started studying English to get a better job. Then he got married and moved to his wife's province and started to work with a Christian NGO.

Through his work with missionaries, he became convinced that Jesus was the only Savior and so got baptized a second time after a sincere conversion.

---

33. In this method, the relationship between the interviewer and interviewee is affected by the way the interviewee is interpreted.

Looking back on his life, he said that he did not feel miserable during the Pol Pot regime and his life in the refugee camp because everyone was in the same situation, and everyone felt equally hungry due to the lack of food. He felt he suffered more after he became a Christian and was baptized a second time than during the Pol Pot era. He was dejected after his good friends suddenly changed their attitudes towards him, and the termination of their friendship hurt him very much. His siblings and relatives also discontinued warm relationships with him because of his refusal to join them to drink alcohol, smoke and gamble. They also considered him a traitor to Buddhism. He has been able to stay with Jesus because he has received much better benefits from Jesus. He mentioned a couple of passages from the Bible that helped him to go through his suffering. For him, the greatest news is that he understands his future destiny (John 14:1–3; Rom 8:31–39; Rev 21:3–4), living with the true God forever with eternal life and the incomparable peace from God. He understands God's purpose in his life and has no more fear of death. This is the good news he needed in order to live his life at that time.

Story 2

Story 2 is about a minority tribal man in his twenties whose family was not affected during the Pol Pot time. He never heard of anyone being killed by Pol Pot's soldiers. The first time he heard of Jesus was from his uncle. It scared him because he heard that he would go to hell if he did not believe in Jesus Christ. His family and he believed in many gods, both Buddhist and animistic. Ten years later, he got into trouble when his motorbike was stolen. He was so ashamed and lost face with his family and community. He was helpless and had no more hope to restore his face among them. Suddenly he remembered his uncle sharing that Jesus took his shame on the cross and he could restore him by the power of the cross. He asked his uncle for more teaching on this good news. Later, he got baptized. Since then, he has felt no more shame. Moreover, he has an unshakable hope and peace in Jesus and is always thankful to Jesus for his goodness. He boldly shares the good news with people in his community. When he shares the good news, he is intimidated by others who do not believe in Jesus, but he does not feel lonely at all. Rather, he gives thanks to the Lord that he belongs to the community of believers.

Story 3

Story 3 is about a minority tribal man in his twenties. His family also had a normal life during the Pol Pot era. The first time he heard of Jesus was when evangelists came to his village. One year later, he joined a church conference at a district town far from his village because he wanted to see the town. At the conference he clearly understood that he was a sinner and received Jesus as his Savior. Immediately afterward, he started to suffer from an unknown disease, which affected the right side of his whole body, causing numbness and pain. He got medical help from missionaries and stayed in a mission hospital in Phnom Penh for one month. After he got sick, his family offered pigs and chickens to the forest gods repeatedly, but his disease was not healed. He resisted joining their "satanic worship" because he believed Jesus would heal him because he is love. When discharged from the hospital, his numbness and pain were almost healed except for on the right side of his abdomen. His family were amazed that his disease was healed without any help from their gods, and all of them decided to believe in Jesus as their Savior. He is happy that all his family came to Christ Jesus and wants to serve him forever.

Story 4

Story 4 is about a Khmer man in his forties who was born in a poor family and used to work for the military.[34] Years ago he heard about the salvation Jesus brings through a Bible school student who came from Phnom Penh to share the good news in his city. After he became a Christian, he resigned from military service and started serving a church while working as a night guard for an NGO office. He has a beautiful wife and two children. His family has faced many challenges, especially in the last decade. First, he has had a difficult relationship with his wife, as he was too busy at church and with ministries, and their relationship became sour and tense. After reducing his time in church and ministries, their relationship improved. Second, shortly after his relationship with his wife improved, he was taking a shower from the well outside his house when a coconut fell and hit his head. He was almost killed, but God saved his life without any aftereffects. Later, his wife got a strange illness that lasted many months. Local doctors could not help her so she traveled to a neighboring country a couple of times, but her symptoms did not improve. She ended up unconscious, and they rushed her to one of the most expensive private hospitals in Phnom Penh without thinking of the medical fee. She was diagnosed with an autoimmune disease and slowly improved. Every time she visited the hospital after her discharge, she had to pay an expensive bill, but God provided for them through many miraculous ways. During the same year, his daughter started tumbling and was later diagnosed with brain tuberculosis. By God's grace, she received medical treatment and was healed a year later. Very recently his workplace which had formerly been an NGO

34. His story was published in a different form in EMQ, January 2016 (online).

was put under government control, and his salary was cut by more than half. His family is struggling to live and send two children to a middle school, but he and his family continue to serve the Lord faithfully.

Insightful Findings from the Stories

These interviews show how the interviewees' life events vary from person to person, generation to generation and tribe to tribe. The overall life stories focus on each person's faith, probably since the interviewer was a missionary. Although these stories are still in the process of analysis by the author, following are some prominent findings.

There are a couple of key words used regarding faith in Christ Jesus, suffering and how to endure sufferings. First, socioeconomic, physical, emotional and/or spiritual crises and sufferings are observed as experiences that prompted interviewees to seek Christ Jesus. Because many communities in Cambodia are based on a "shame" culture, it is a good opportunity to seek the ultimate solution from a Savior rather than within their community, particularly when they face trouble with family members, close friends or the community. Suffering prepares our hearts and minds to look for the truth.

Second, the experience of suffering is not stereotypically linked to the Pol Pot time or refugee experience. On the contrary, relationship issues (which also trigger the seeking after Jesus Christ) are the foremost causes of suffering. Because of the interviewees' faith in Christ, they suffered from bitter and broken relationships with family, relatives and close friends and were sometimes ostracized by the community. In addition, many mentioned dealing with feelings of "loneliness."

It is interesting to see that the suffering in their lives is related to their faith. It is also curious that they did not feel sorry or poor when they experienced the same situation as others during the Pol Pot era. As outsiders, we tend to feel sorry for the locals when we see that their lives are hard or more devastated than ours. When we are involved in a development project, it would be helpful to get an insider perspective in order to prevent over-aid or inappropriate aid, which might lead to dependency. However, this unexpected finding related to the interviewees' experiences during the Pol Pot era might result from the lack of depth in the interviewer's relationship with them. It is rare in Cambodia for people to share about the suffering they experienced under the Pol Pot regime with someone they do not yet trust, as they might end up being caught up in troubles, such as gossip, in the community. Subsequent interviews following a more developed relationship will address this point more clearly.

Third, the interviewees share key biblical truths about enduring suffering by faith, which includes their eternal relationship with God, the power of the resurrection, God's protection, God's indescribable eternal love, eternal life and a clear destination. In listening to their sharing, I think it could be helpful for them to understand the nature of the Trinitarian God, the work of the Holy Spirit, the theology of suffering and their belonging to the new community of believers since their community is a shame- and relationship-oriented culture.

Fourth, the interviewees in Story 3 and Story 4 both accepted Jesus Christ as Savior prior to sufferings. Though it would be impossible to generalize this, they could look back on their sufferings as God's way to strengthen their faith and holiness (see the section "Suffering as a Way to Strengthen Faith and Holiness" above). Even though they did not stand calmly in the midst of suffering, they clung to God's faithfulness and goodness through faith and prayers and waited for his glory ahead. On the other hand, the interviewee in Story 2 came to know Jesus after his experience of suffering. Those who experience suffering and then come to Jesus could think that their suffering drove them to thank God's good intention to them and their family (see the section "Suffering as God's Mystery and Good Intention" above).

Fifth, musing upon the Cambodian church history (see the section "Suffering in Cambodia and her Church" above and "Suffering and Church Growth" below), quite a few people came to Christ in Cambodia and in refugee camps at a revival, yet some of their conversions might have been insincere (as cited in Story 1 above). I think it would be instructive to pay attention to a rapid increase of the number of Christians in arduous situations. This would necessitate a careful follow-up study of those who came to Christ in refugee camps, focusing on the long-term relationship between revival and trauma.

Finally, it would be helpful for more interviews to be analyzed from different backgrounds such as gender (female or male), ethnicity (Khmer or other minorities) and religion (folk Buddhism, animism, Islam or others).

Implications for Missions and the Church

Suffering and Church Growth

Tertullian, the second-century church father, wrote, "The blood of martyrs is the seed of the Church."[35] It is a well-known belief among Christians that suffering helps churches grow. We see many examples in church history. For

35. Tertullian, 50.13, quoted in J. M. Boice, *Romans Vol. 3: God and History* (Grand Rapids: Baker, 1991), 1323.

example, nobody would have imagined fifty years ago that there would be more than seventy-five million Christians in China today.[36] Cambodia is no exception. According to Cormack, Cambodia twice experienced a revival: from 1970–1975 in Cambodia and from 1975–1981 in the refugee camps.[37] As reported in the section "Suffering in Cambodia and her Church" above, there were only three congregations in Phnom Penh before 1970, yet more than three thousand people accepted Christ as a result of the 1972 evangelistic campaigns. More people were added to Christ through other evangelistic efforts, such as Brother Chhirc.

Cormack reports:

> The year 1973 ended with about one thousand two hundred Christians in Phnom Penh celebrating the Savior's birth in their various and sundry meeting places. This represented a near one hundred per cent annual increase from the three hundred souls to be found four years earlier in 1970 . . . 1974 was going to be an even more abundantly fruitful year than 1973 . . . By mid-year the church in the capital had increased to upwards of 3,000. A growth rate in those six months alone outstripping the entire growth of the church throughout its fifty year history.[38]

It was also reported that fewer than one thousand Christians survived the end of the Pol Pot time, but many people came to Christ in the refugee camps until the early 1980s.

Looking back on Cambodian church history, we can also see another period of rapid numerical growth between 1990–2010 (see Figure 1).[39] Since 1996 the Protestant church has doubled in size every two years until 2010.[40]

---

36. Jason Mandryk, *Operation World*, 7th ed. (Downers Grove: InterVarsity Press, 2010), 216.

37. Cormack, *Killing Fields*, 371.

38. Cormack, 135–136.

39. Evangelical Fellowship of Cambodia, "Mission Kampuchea 2021," unpublished Occasional Report (Cambodia, 2012).

40. The updated statistics from 2011 onwards are not available yet.

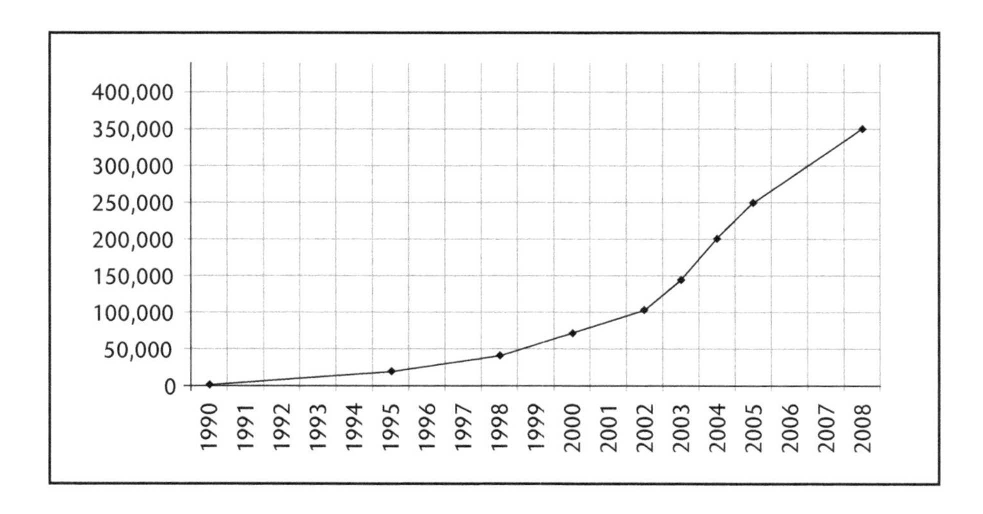

Figure 1: Christians in Cambodia

There are now estimated to be more than 250,000 Protestant Christians in Cambodia in more than two thousand churches. The fact that Cambodia has "the modest two percent annual growth of Christianity from 1910–2010 masks the impact of Pol Pot's genocide in the 1970s."[41] Cambodia's Christian growth rate, at 7.28 percent between 2000–2010, is the fastest in Southeast Asia, followed by 4.8 percent in Timor.[42]

So can we apply Tertullian's phrase to Cambodian church history? Although there are few analyses of why so many people came to Christ, suffering is one of the key factors that contributed to church growth. In addition to suffering, other factors boosted church growth in Cambodia. First, through the supreme work of the Holy Spirit, God prepared Cambodia between 1970–1975 for the next decade's suffering, since the Cambodian church grew just before the Pol Pot regime took over. Many people sought God when they sensed a very ambiguous and unstable political situation. The church growth in refugee camps between 1975–1981 could be explained by the suffering and devastating life situations that stirred many hearts to look for God. As Cormack honestly shares, "In the context of the dull and uninspiring refugee camps, Christianity was very attractive."[43] The brother mentioned in Story 1 above reported that his first baptism when he did not have faith was part of a joyous event at a

41. Todd Johnson and Kenneth Ross, eds., *Atlas of Global Christianity* (Edinburgh: Edinburgh University Press, 2009), 148.

42. Johnson and Kenneth, *Atlas*, 147, 149.

43. Cormack, *Killing Fields*, 317.

refugee camp. Regarding the latest church growth, Cormack observes, "The direct correlation between the level of Christian philanthropic aid and church growth cannot be allowed to escape our attention here."[44] In fact, prior to 1993, the church in Cambodia consisted of a handful of isolated, small, underground groups, but from 1993 onwards, every major denomination, large Christian NGOs, and many missionaries arrived in Cambodia.[45] In the later 1990s, many young people attended the churches where a Western missionary worked in order to get free English and/or computer-skill instruction so they could seek a better job.[46]

Another interesting phenomenon can be observed in the latter part of the first decade of the twenty-first century. According to the Evangelical Fellowship of Cambodia, the number of new church plants started to decrease after 2008 (see Figure 2).[47]

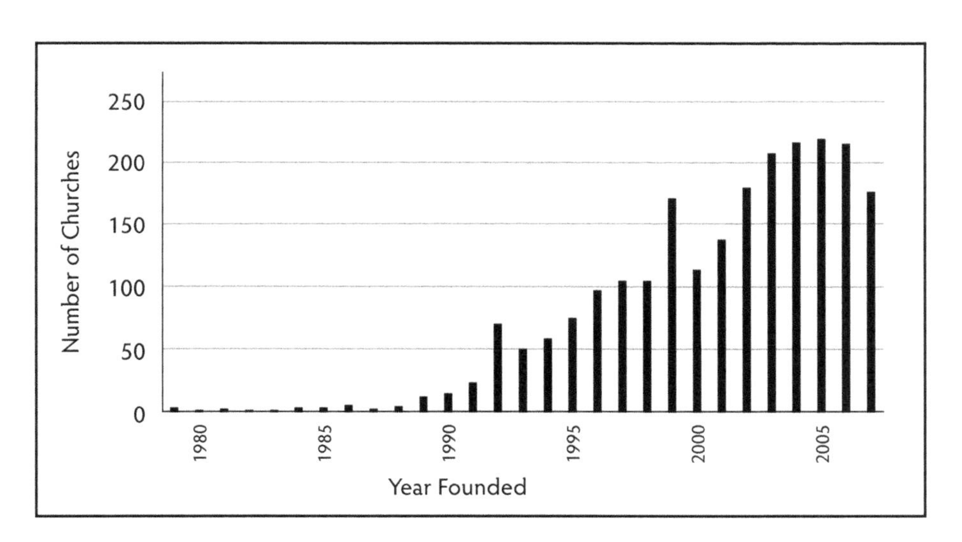

Figure 2: The Number of Newly Planted Churches in Cambodia

44. Cormack, 137.

45. It is interesting to look at the number of missionaries per capita in Cambodia. For East Asia as a whole (excluding China, North Korea, Laos, and Vietnam due to lack of information), the average is twenty-five missionaries per one million people. But Cambodia has thirty missionaries per million people. Yuzo Imamura, "Approach to the Buddhist and Animist in Cambodia," unpublished paper presented at OMF Cambodia Training Session, Cambodia, 2007.

46. Personal communication with Rev Sho Sugaya (OMF worker), 2003.

47. Evangelical Fellowship of Cambodia.

They analyze various reasons, but one strong suggestion is materialism.[48] Cambodia enjoys relative peace and a stable society, which promotes more economic activities. As the growth of the Gross Domestic Product (GDP) shows (see Figure 3), Cambodia's economy has steadily grown since the last coup d'état in 1999.[49] At the same time, Cambodian people have started losing their interest in Christianity. This leads to the next point related to the prosperity gospel.

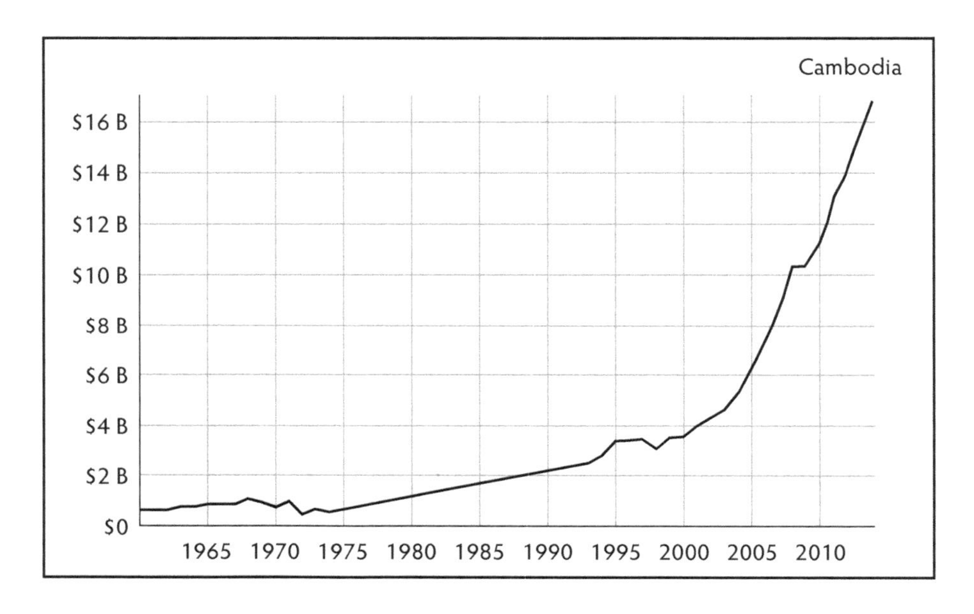

Figure 3: Gross Domestic Product of Cambodia

Suffering and the Prosperity Gospel

The "prosperity gospel" is one of the biggest challenges in mission today, which the Cape Town Commitment of the Lausanne Movement defines as "the teaching that believers have a right to the blessings of health and wealth

48. Rev Heng Cheng (the then General Secretary), personal communication with author at the Annual Congress of the Evangelical Fellowship of Cambodia, 24 February 2011.

49. World Bank, "Gross Domestic Product," accessed 18 February 2016, https://www.google.com/publicdata/explore?ds=d5bncppjof8f9_&met_y=ny_gdp_mktp_cd&idim=%20country:KHM:LAO&hl=en&dl=en#!ctype=l&strail=false&bcs=d&nselm=h&met_y=ny_gdp_mktp_c%20d&scale_y=lin&ind_y=false&rdim=region&idim=country:KHM&ifdim=region&hl=en_US&dl=en&in%20d=false).

and that they can obtain these blessings through positive confessions of faith and the 'sowing of seeds' through financial or material gift."[50] If we say that we have a right to the blessings, we reject suffering. If we then experience suffering, we face problems in our faith.

In Story 2 above, when a brother shares the good news with his fellow villagers, he is often asked, "How much a monthly salary I can get if I believe in Jesus?" Literally this means, "What kinds of benefits do I get from the Christian God?" It is a big challenge to share the good news with people who want to get tangible, material benefits. As this man shared, "They always mocked me when I explain Heaven, eternal life, and the Kingdom of God, which are invisible things."

This response is very common in Cambodia, where churches or Christian NGOs that provide a tangible benefit, such as financial support for the poor, are very popular among the community. Many people do not come to a church to hear the gospel but only want to get immediate, tangible blessings. As a result, it is very hard to share the good news. There is a general feeling that many people in Cambodia respond positively toward Christianity, but very few continue to worship God after several years. This surely relates to a lack of discipleship, but the hope of tangible blessings could also be a key factor. In rural areas, many people respond to Christianity after God heals their sicknesses through prayers or contemporary medical services provided by Christian NGOs. One important approach would be to share the good news through healing. The Lausanne Movement rightly addresses the prosperity gospel. Particularly the Akropong Statement produced by African theologians, convened by the Lausanne Theology Working Group, serves as a good starting point to understand the blessings of health and wealth, the biblical teaching on suffering, and the problems of the prosperity gospel.[51]

Suffering and Evangelization

Suffering as a Wake-up Call to Lukewarm Christians

The Bible teaches that suffering is a part of God's discipleship training, but those who come from relatively comfortable countries without tangible persecutions and sufferings may miss out on the great teaching of suffering in their lives. In addition, if we are affected by the secular worldview that comfort and

---

50. "Cape Town Commitment," pt. 2, II.E., 5.t, 2011, https://www.lausanne.org/content/ctc/ctcommitment.

51. The full text of this statement can be found at https://www.lausanne.org/content/a-statement- on-the-prosperity-gospel.

convenience are essential human rights, we will have a skewed perspective on suffering. Suffering cannot contribute to our growth in Christ if we try to ignore or view it as a curse to be avoided.

For example, Japan has enjoyed a peaceful society for more than seventy years. Japanese Christians love religious freedom since it means there is no public persecution of their faith. In accordance with the Japanese value of social harmony, many do not proactively seek opportunities to bear witness to their faith in public, as this might upset harmony. They sneak in and out of church without telling their friends. When encouraged to share the gospel, they think themselves as unworthy to tell the good news and feel shame rather than honor. As a result, their presence is often as the "hidden Christian," for statistics show the number of Christians is less than 1 percent of the population.

Church and mission societies need to address this reality. Interestingly, when faced with unexpected suffering following the 2011 Tohoku earthquake, Japanese Christians took it as a wake-up call to share the gospel. Even though Christians were a bit confused regarding the biblical response to such an unprecedented natural disaster, they have done much good work in the disaster relief area.[52] Preparation for suffering, along with a deep knowledge of the Bible and a strong, vital prayer life are crucial so that we will not be surprised by fiery trials or conclude that something strange is happening to us when we are tested (1 Pet 4:12). Christians need to proclaim "the whole counsel of God" and teach biblical truth to those who are suffering (Acts 20:27).

Suffering as a Threat to Gospel Workers

Second, the failure to develop a theology of suffering may threaten a gospel worker's life. For in most cross-cultural and pastoral settings, gospel workers face numerous challenges, including suffering. If they are unprepared and do not understand the meaning of suffering, they will not survive and often terminate their service prematurely.

John Stott's contemporary classic *The Cross of Christ* is still relevant to us:

> The place of suffering in service and of passion in mission is hardly ever taught today. But the greatest single secret of evangelistic or missionary effectiveness is the willingness to suffer and die. It may be a death to popularity (by faithfully preaching the unpopular biblical gospel), or to pride (by the use of modest methods in

---

52. Disaster Relief Christian Network, "Higashi Nihon Dai Shinsai No Keiken Kara Mananda Koto/ Kongo Heno Shishin" [Lessons from the Great East Japan Earthquake and Suggestions for Future], accessed 14 March 2016, http://drcnet.jp/lessons_from_311_disaster_and_guidelines_for_future/.

> reliance on the Holy Spirit), or to racial and national prejudice (by identification with another culture), or to material comfort (by adopting a simple life style). But the servant must suffer if he is to bring light to the nations, and the seed must die if it is to multiply.[53]

It is important to recognize that we are tempted by such things as popularity, pride, material comfort, and racial and national prejudice. These temptations often challenge us in difficult and stressful situations and become stumbling blocks for the Kingdom of God. If dying to these things is suffering, we should learn to suffer well. Sunquist rightly summarizes: "Mission is from the heart of God, to each context, and it is carried out in suffering in this world for God's eternal glory."[54]

Narrative Research as a Powerful Tool for Mission

While interviewing Christians about their life stories, I came to realize that narrative research is a powerful tool for opening up people's worldviews, particularly their perspectives on suffering. As noted at the beginning of this study, one's perspective on suffering is subjective, and it is never easy to understand each person we evangelize or disciple. While there are many helpful books being published on suffering, we cannot apply these studies and findings uncritically to the people in our contexts. Narrative research provides a strategic tool to help us accomplish our vision and mission by practicing incarnational ministry, which is one of our core values. Though it takes time and requires local language proficiency for cross-cultural settings, it is worth doing for God's glory.

Conclusion

Every Christian today must understand suffering from a biblically sound perspective and live out their faith in the midst of the difficult situations that surround us. By God's grace, the Cambodian church continues to grow through varied sufferings. Narrative research could address questions about the kind of suffering that Cambodian Christians face, how Cambodian Christians recognize their sufferings and how they keep their faith in Christ Jesus through suffering. The battle against the prosperity gospel is before us, and so we not

53. John Stott, *The Cross of Christ* (Downers Grove: InterVarsity Press, 1986), 322.

54. Scott W. Sunquist, *Understanding Christian Mission: Participation in Suffering and Glory* (Grand Rapids: Baker Academic, 2013), xii.

only need to defend the gospel apologetically, but also proclaim the whole gospel effectively in our context. If suffering is our cross, we should live out our suffering well. Indeed, if we obey God's call, God will glorify his name through that cross.

I end with the admonition of Patrick Fung, General Director of OMF International, at Urbana 15:

> Your talents, your gifts, your profession cannot change the lives of people. That cannot bring hope to the people. It's only in Jesus. So my encouragement to you is love the Word of God, the Truth will bring change. Love the Word of God. Study the Word of God. And live out the Word of God by your lives because as you live out the Word of God people see that are attracted to Jesus Christ. That will change people. Let God be using you as a change agent. But in the end it has to be the Truth that brings changes. So let the Word of God be in your life as you study, meditate, and live out the Word.[55]

Bibliography

Bias, Mona P., and Larry J. Waters. *The Book of Job*. Asia Bible Commentary. Manila: Asia Theological Association, 2011.

Boice, J. M. *Romans Vol. 3: God and History*. Grand Rapids: Baker, 1991.

Bonhoeffer, Dietrich. *The Cost of Discipleship*. New York: Touchstone, 1995.

Carey, Keith, ed. *Global Prayer Digest*. Pasadena: US Center for World Mission, 2011.

Carson, D. A. *How Long, O Lord?: Reflections on Suffering and Evil*. Grand Rapids: Baker Academic, 2006.

Cormack, Don. *Killing Fields Living Fields*. Crowborough, UK: MARC, 1997.

Cosby, Brian. *A Christian's Pocket Guide to Suffering: How God Shapes Us through Pain and Tragedy*. Fearn, Ross-shire, UK: Christian Focus Publications, 2015.

Davies, Martin Brett. *Doing a Successful Research Project: Using Qualitative or Quantitative Methods*. Hampshire, UK: Palgrave, 2007.

De Neui, Paul H., ed. *Suffering: Christian Reflections on Buddhist Dukkha*. SEANET Series 8. Pasadena: William Carey, 2011.

Disaster Relief Christian Network. "Higashi Nihon Dai Shinsai No Keiken Kara Mananda Koto/ Kongo Heno Shishin" [Lessons from the Great East Japan Earthquake and Suggestions for Future]. Accessed 14 March 2016. http://drcnet.jp/lessons_from_311_disaster_and_guidelines_for_future/.

---

55. "Dec 30 2015 Interview with Patrick and Jennie Fung," Urbana 15, accessed 16 March 2016, https://www.youtube.com/watch?v=ATintqZnAhQ.

Ellison, J. Paul. "A Short History of the Cambodian Evangelical Church Known in Cambodia as the Khmer Evangelical Church with Particular Attention Being Given to People Movements and Some Factors Related to Church Growth." Paper presented at Cambodian Christian Services Conference, San Jose, California, March, 1991.

Erickson, Millard J., ed. *The Concise Dictionary of Christian Theology*, revised edition. Wheaton: Crossway, 2001.

Evangelical Fellowship of Cambodia. "Mission Kampuchea 2021." Unpublished PDF manuscript, 2012.

Fernando, Ajith. *The Call to Joy and Pain: Embracing Suffering in Your Ministry*. Wheaton: Crossway, 2007.

Hennink, M., I. Hutter, and A. Bailey. *Qualitative Research Methods*. London: SAGE, 2011.

Hicks, Peter. *The Message of Evil and Suffering: Light into Darkness*. The Bible Speaks Today. Downers Grove: InterVarsity Press, 2006.

Hyde, Steve. *Portrait of the Body of Christ in Cambodia*. Cambodia: Antioch Institute, 2012.

Imamura, Yuzo. "Approach to the Buddhist and Animist in Cambodia." Unpublished manuscript, 2007.

———. "#Iwitness: Joyful in the Midst of Sufferings: A Life Devoted to Christ in Cambodia." *Evangelical Missions Quarterly* 52, no. 1 (2016). Accessed 7 April 2016. https://emqonline.com/node/3454#overlay-context=node/3468.

Interserve New Zealand. "The Cambodian Church: From 30 Churches to 5,000 in Only 20 Years." *Go Magazine*, 2012. Accessed 20 January 2016. http://www.interserve.org.nz/RESOURCES/PUBLICATIONS/GO+MAGAZINE/The+Cambodian+Church.html.

Johnson, Todd, and Kenneth Ross, eds. *Atlas of Global Christianity*. Edinburgh: Edinburgh University Press, 2009.

Keller, Timothy. *Walking with God through Pain and Suffering*. New York: Random House, 2013.

The Lausanne Movement. *The Cape Town Commitment: A Confession of Faith and a Call to Action*. Peabody, MA: Hendrickson, 2011.

Lausanne Theology Working Group. "A Statement on the Prosperity Gospel." 2009. Accessed 20 January 2016. https://www.lausanne.org/content/a-statement-on-the-prosperity-gospel.

Lewis, C. S. *The Problem of Pain*. London: William Collins, 1940.

MacArthur Jr., John. *The Power of Suffering: Strengthening Your Faith in the Refiner's Fire*. Colorado Springs: David C. Cook, 2011.

Mack, Natasha, Cynthia Woodsong, Kathleen M. MacQueen, Greg Guest, and Emily Namey. *Qualitative Research Methods: A Data Collector's Field Guide*. Durham, NC: Family Health International, 2005.

Maher, Brian. *Cry of the Gecko: History of the Christian Mission in Cambodia*. Centralia, WA: Gorham Printing, 2012.

Mandryk, Jason. *Operation World*, 7th edition. Downers Grove: InterVarsity Press, 2010.

McCartney, Dan. *Why Does It Have to Hurt?: The Meaning of Christian Suffering.* Phillipsburg, NJ: P&R, 1998.

McKim, Donald K., ed. *Westminster Dictionary of Theological Terms.* Louisville: Westminster John Knox, 1996.

McLaughlin, Daniel, and Elisabeth Wickeri, "Special Report: Mental Health and Human Rights in Cambodia." Leitner Center for International Law and Justice. New York: Fordham Law School, 2012.

Mission Kampuchea 2021. "Country Statistics." Accessed 25 August 2017. https://cambodiachurches.org/harvest/mapping/CP/map.html?displaylang=EN&lang=sec.

Morgan, Christopher W., and Robert A. Peterson, eds. *Suffering and the Goodness of God.* Theology in Community Series. Wheaton: Crossway Books, 2008.

OMF International. *Pray for Cambodia.* Littleton, CO: OMF International, 2012.

Piper, John, and Justin Taylor. *Suffering and the Sovereignty of God.* Wheaton: Crossway, 2006.

Stott, John. *The Cross of Christ.* Downers Grove: InterVarsity Press, 1986.

Sunquist, Scott W. *Understanding Christian Mission: Participation in Suffering and Glory*. Grand Rapids: Baker Academic, 2013.

Tada, Joni Eareckson. "Theology of Suffering." Recorded 11 February 2009, Dallas Theological Seminary Chapel. Accessed 17 November 2015. http://www.dts.edu/media/play/theology-of-suffering-joni-eareckson-tada/.

Taylor, William D., Antonia van der Meer, and Reg Reimer, eds. *Sorrow & Blood: Christian Mission in Contexts of Suffering, Persecution, and Martyrdom*. Pasadena: William Carey, 2012.

Tully, John. *A Short History of Cambodia: From Empire to Survival.* Chiang Mai, Thailand: Silkworm, 2006.

Urbana 15. "Dec 30 2015 Interview with Patrick and Jennie Fung." Accessed 16 March 2016. https://www.youtube.com/watch?v=ATintqZnAhQ.

U.S. Department of State. "Cambodia." 2010 International Religious Freedom Report. Accessed 28 March 2016. http://www.state.gov/j/drl/rls/irf/2010/148861.htm.

14

The Family as a Source of Mental Trauma in the Military Conflict in Ukraine

Svitlana Kravchuk
and
Vacheslav Khalanskyy

Defining the Problem

Until recently in Ukraine, most people had never heard the terms "psychological trauma," "posttraumatic stress disorder" (PTSD) or "acute stress disorder" (ASD). However, the military events in Ukraine prompted many helping profession specialists to turn to the study of psychological trauma. The military conflict in Ukraine is a significant psycho-trauma factor that has affected many Ukrainian families in the twenty-first century. Tragically, there have been numerous victims of the war, and the war has been particularly traumatizing for families living in the territory of military operations.

Because of the military operations in east Ukraine, many men die at the front or return crippled. For those who have been displaced by the conflict, other areas of the country only accept women, old people and children, causing a rupture of family ties.

The military conflict in Ukraine has united both public organizations as well as Christian organizations and churches. In responding to the many new challenges in our time, churches need to consider the following. First, we must consider the role of the church in the context of the military conflict in Ukraine.

Second, we must consider the nature of our contextual theology in the light of the military conflict. Third, we must consider if the church should take a pacifist stance or be social and politically active. Finally, we must consider if theology should take into account the psychological features of a person's mental health in the context of the military conflict in Ukraine.

From the many interviews we have conducted over the past three years, it is clear that adapting to the realities of war has been a complex process for the church and church leaders. Pastors often said that they did not know how to help parishioners who had experienced acute stress disorders after the traumatic events in Donetsk, where military events occurred and continue to happen. Clergymen noted that prayers for these church members "did not work," because they continued to experience depression and grief. Then the pastors began to seek help from Christian psychologists as well as secular specialists. Even though the prevailing paradigm among evangelical churches of Ukraine denies the compatibility of science (psychology) and theology, many pastors have begun to integrate into their service the psychological knowledge they gained at trainings and conferences run by Christian psychologists.[1]

Analyzing the Problem

Long-term military events in Ukraine, which have been unfolding for a long time, have become an all-encompassing source of trauma for people who are not at the forefront of the conflict. Specialists who have been searching for rehabilitation programs for those who have survived traumatic events in Ukraine suggest identifying the family as a resource for overcoming the consequences of trauma, such as insecurity, uncertainty, and so on.[2]

The idea of the "Family Circle" project arose in early March 2014.[3] The project works with groups of adults and children based on age, offering individual counseling in accordance with the stages of grief, spiritual help from pastors, recreational activities to prevent pathological grief processes, and connecting participants with resources and new meanings in life. Usually, activities take place over three or five days, when families join together to grieve, live together and support each other. In daily, three-hour self-help

1. Vyacheslav Khalanskiy, Association of Christian Psychologists and Psychotherapists in Ukraine, http://www.eastwestreport.org/pdfs/ew21-4.pdf.

2. Tatyana Titarenko, "How to Help Witnesses and Participants in Traumatic Events: Horizons of Social-Psychological Rehabilitation," *Actual Problems of Sociology, Psychology, Pedagogy* 29, no. 4 (2015): 163–170.

3. Center for Crisis Psychology in Ukraine, http://www.rodynnekolo.in.ua/en/.

groups, participants listen to one another talk about their pain and their ways of coping with the guidance of a psychologist. Total strangers become close to each other because they know that they will be understood and supported. Hearing an encouraging word and listening to the experience of others often gives participants the strength and faith to move forward into the future. Everyone has the opportunity to work individually with a psychologist and, if necessary, a child psychologist. There are also opportunities for master classes, seminars and quests for adults and children. From experience, we can confirm that the work of psychologists, psychiatrists and pastors with families through these family encounters helps to restore mental and spiritual health.

We participated in helping people from the city of O. (Luhansk region), where a large evangelical church in the city was destroyed. Even though the church was destroyed, the members of the church remained in close contact and interacted with each other. When there were more explosions in the city, members of the church teamed up to help and support each other and to help other affected people. They created free spaces where people could come for food and prayer (spiritual support).

When these families left the war zone, we held a day-long psychological support group for seven families and their children. We wondered what helped them survive in these inhuman conditions, as their homes had been destroyed, and the place where they were living had become occupied by the aggressor. (At that time, husbands could not reach their families to support them.) We also wondered what helped them preserve their human dignity and overcome difficulties. (It should be noted that their emotional reactions changed in the course of the day – crying to laughter, crying to laughter, all day long.)

From this experience, we can highlight several aspects that helped people survive and maintain their psychological and spiritual resources. First, we saw the importance of perceiving another person as someone of value, as one for whose sake it was worth living and helping. Second, all members of the group highlighted the importance of the spiritual aspect of life. Having faith in God and believing that God hears us and protects us helps people make sense of difficult times. Third, people were strengthened and encouraged by having the opportunity to share different emotions with the group – tears and joy, sadness and sorrow, fear and hope. Fourth, we realized that grief requires work and specific treatment. During the group time, participants talked freely about their feelings while crying and laughing, which allowed them to take a new, distant look at their feelings. Fifth, we realized the importance of humor and the development of optimism in situations of extreme tension and despair. As we led the group, we did not see people who were desperate, but rather people who were filled with hope and were capable of mutual support. Sixth, we recognized the importance of understanding that children need psychological help. In an interview, one of the children said about his feelings: "War took my favorite store [it was destroyed], my room and my bed [the house was also destroyed by a shell]. I have nothing left."

This analysis confirms the concept that positive changes can result from traumatic events, which is described by the term "posttraumatic growth."[4] These findings led us to conclude that the rehabilitation potential of the family needs to be revitalized in the context of the military conflict in Ukraine.

Each event occurring within the family is experienced in different ways. Some events are talked about openly and turn into family stories. Other events are hushed up because they are too scary to talk about (a tragic or early death), or because it is a shame to remember them (an act of treason, betrayal, violation of human norms or the foundations of the family), or because they are associated with too much injustice. Events that are not talked about turn into family secrets. The first category of "open" events becomes the property of the group or family consciousness; the second category of "silenced" events belongs to the group or family unconsciousness. The consequences of collective trauma, unprocessed mourning, unspoken feelings and unshed tears can be transmitted from generation to generation.[5]

We can mark out the following types of families that have distorted emotional connections.[6] In *traditional families*, everything is "as it should be." Family members give all their strength to create an external image of a prosperous and wealthy family. Such a family rests on rational foundations. In *emotionally rejected families*, direct interpersonal communication is often absent and contacts are replaced by fierce attacks and accusations behind one's back.[7] In *families of workers*, family members give all their time to work and their own self-realization outside the family without contacting each other for days, weeks or even months. Children in such families are given to the care

---

4. Vitaliy Klimchuk, "Posttraumatic Growth and Ways of Facilitating in the Psychotherapy," Science and Education, *Psychology*, no. 5 (2016): 46–52; Joseph S. Positive, "Changes Following Adversity PTSD Research Quarterly," *Journal of Traumatic Stress* 21, no. 4 (2010): 1–3; Kanako Taku, "The Factor Structure of the Posttraumatic Growth Inventory: A Comparison of Five Models Using Confirmatory Factor Analysis," *Journal of Traumatic Stress* 21, no. 2 (2009): 24–27.

5. Many authors write about this, such as P. F. Kellermann, "Transmission of Holocaust Trauma," *The Israel Journal of Psychiatry and Related Sciences* 4, no. 1 (2001): 55–58; and Anne Ancelin Schutzenberger, *The Ancestor Syndrome: Transgenerational Psychotherapy and the Hidden Links in the Family Tree* (Moscow: Institute of Psychotherapy, 2001), 320–328.

6. Anna Varga, *Systemic Family Psychotherapy* (St Petersburg: Rech, 2001), 144.

7. Varga, *Systemic Family Psychotherapy*, 144.

of boarding schools, babysitters, grandparents and others. In *families with symbiotic connections,* a new member of the family claims primacy in the relationship. In *families with an incomplete parent clan,* a parent tries at any cost to achieve self-realization in the person of his or her own child.

Underlying such relationships is dissatisfaction with the emotional relationship with the offending family member(s), which is veiled by external coldness and accompanied by resentment. At the same time, there is a sense of guilt towards the offended members of the family, which often is either not realized or not fully realized by the offending family member(s). The latter, trying to get rid of guilt, but not daring to recognize this feeling in themselves, use manipulative methods to exert pressure on family members towards whom they feel guilt, trying in this way to evoke a reciprocal feeling towards themselves and thus shift responsibility for the relationship to someone else. The most vulnerable person is the member of the family who assumes the role of a mediator in such relations, since the warring parties do not take the initiative for reconciliation or responsibility for the strained relations, hoping instead that a third party will do everything for them.[8] Thus the mediator finds himself or herself in the role of a "scapegoat" and is compelled to listen to reproaches from both sides.

Studies of "intergenerational trauma" in countries with a communist past are associated with "traumatic memory," which is the return of the past that we have accepted and understood. The events of the past serve as both a subject of memory and a subject of the resistance of memory.[9] These studies cite the stories of Soviet children whose parents went through totalitarian camps and often lacked vocabulary to describe their trauma. As N. I. Kigai notes:

> After the Second World War, psychoanalysts drew attention to the fact that the children of the victims of the Holocaust are poorly adapted. The peculiarities of their behavior and well-being allowed us to talk about the intergenerational trauma created by traumatized parents in children born after the disaster. Trauma creates certain mental conditions that disrupt social and emotional

8. Mikhail Reshetnikov, *Mental Trauma* (St Petersburg: Institute of Psychoanalysis, 2006), 322.

9. Jacob D. Lindy, and Robert J. Lifton, eds., *Beyond Invisible Walls: The Psychological Legacy of Soviet Trauma, East European Therapists and Their Patients* (Philadelphia: Brunner-Routledge, 2001).

> adaptation. The catastrophe, experienced by the parents, resonates in the form of one or another deficit in the generation of children.[10]

We can only phenomenologically describe traumatic experiences under a totalitarian regime, but it is often characterized by the following. First, people are afraid to talk about their feelings. Perhaps that is why in our culture and in churches, the modus is to treat feelings with mistrust and suspicion. Second, because it is considered taboo to express grief and tears, there is a suppression of the suffering experience. Third, there is a fixation on the traumatic experience of the past, a verbal "hanging" on the subject of suffering, which is perceived as a norm of life. Fourth, there is an experience of ontological horror, which undermines the foundations of the existence of the person who is experiencing it.

This horror forms a polar mindset (a system of relations), where there is hostility and distrust towards the world (a mindset defined by *I / the world / strangers* rather than *we / our own / ours*). The focus of such a polar mindset is to leave society and establish a habitual way of life and specific model of self-perception. Futile attempts to formulate acceptable reasons for the unexpected rupture of the fabric of social life cause further trauma. The experience of horror also leaves feelings of emptiness and hopelessness, which are often expressed as a chronic sense of nervousness that can be interpreted as the equivalent of activity, but does not yield results. This experience of horror deprives people of faith in the future, hope for development and the opportunity to live or demonstrate a life-affirming attitude towards reality.

Traumatization also lowers the value of human life among the citizens of society. Thus recognizing trauma and working with it is a condition for the healthy functioning of an individual and society as a whole.

Following are the main features of family mental trauma.[11] First, family mental trauma is personally significant for all members of the family. Second, it affects people who are very close to one another, which determines the emotionality of perception (imbalance, quick temper, depression, etc.). Third, it changes the family members' perception of the events related to the trauma. Fourth, it entails changes in the family members at the personal level. Fifth, it entails a violation of the habitual way of life and the interpersonal relations

---

10. Vladimir Gruzdev and Natalya Kigai. "About the Causes of Social Depression, Cruelty, Crime and Invincible Corruption in the Country," http://portal-nko.ru/dialog/point/325.

11. Anna Varga, *Systemic Family Psychotherapy*, 144; Cohen Judith, Antony Mannarino, Esther Deblinger, *Psychotherapy with Children and Adolescents Who Have Suffered Injury and Loss* (Lviv: Svichado, 2016), 264; Alexander Liders, *Family as a Psychological System* (Moskva: Obnisk, 2004), 296.

that are most important for family members. Sixth, it affects the entire life activity of a person, which can equate to a loss of the meaning of life. Seventh, it causes family members to feel guilty because of the negative reactions they are experiencing towards other family members. The conviction that a close family member cannot be bad puts a person in a dual situation: on the one hand, there is resentment against the family member who committed treachery; on the other hand, there is a sense of guilt for feeling such negative feelings towards someone who is supposed to be close and dear. Eighth, it can affect several generations in the family as it is inherited as a negative family experience through family myths, rituals, legends and family stories. Ninth, it affects the life activity and well-being of all family members. Finally, it destroys the existing legend of the family. The psychological and cultural consequences of permanent trauma are related to the traumacentric culture of society.[12]

The Study

The goal of this study is to analyze the impact of military events in Ukraine on individuals and their families and to identify the dominant factors of individuals' psychological problems following the situation of military conflict in Ukraine.

There were 246 participants in our research study.[13] Among these participants: 33 were living in Donetsk (the zone of military conflict); 21 were students of Kiev University CROC; 10 were students of Kiev University of Culture; 76 were students of Kiev National Linguistic University; 22 were students of Kiev National Taras Shevchenko University; 12 were students of the Ukrainian Evangelical Theological Seminary (Pushcha Voditsa), 38 were living in the city of Kiev (as displaced persons from the conflict zone); and 34 were living in the city of Mariupol (in the direction where military operations were taking place).

To study the influence of military events in Ukraine on personality and people's families, we used the following methods: two author's research

12. Anna Varga and Grazyna Budinayte. "Trauma of the Past in Russia and the Possibility of Using Systemic Family Therapy," http://psyjournal.ru/articles/travma-proshlogo-v-rossii-i-vozmozhnosti-primeneniya-sistemnoy-semeynoy-terapii; Schutzenberger, *Ancestral Syndrome*, 320–328.

13. We would like to thank the ICF Caritas Ukraine for their assistance in conducting surveys.

questionnaires and the "Impact of Event Scale" developed by M. J. Horowitz and N. Wilner.[14] In analyzing the results of the study, we learned the following.

First, 54.2 percent of all participants said that the situation of the military conflict in Ukraine had affected their relationships with their immediate relatives; 45.8 percent said it had not. The displaced persons living in Kiev had the most significant differences regarding the impact of the military conflict on their relationships with their immediate relatives. Of these participants, 70.3 percent answered, "Yes, there is such an influence" and 29.7 percent answered, "No."

In analyzing the exact impact of the military conflict in Ukraine on participants' relationships with their immediate relatives, we learned the following.

Participants currently living in Donetsk said that they had been affected by the military conflict in the following ways: (1) the family had become united; (2) some families had experienced disagreements and quarrels; (3) the family budget had been reduced; (4) the problem of communication with distant relatives had arisen.

The displaced persons living in Kiev indicated that the military conflict had: (1) caused misunderstanding and a deterioration of relations with relatives who remained in the combat zone (e.g. split in the family, no communication, aggression, irritability in communication); (2) affected the parents, their relationship in the family; (3) created difficulties with housing in connection with resettlement; (4) created problems due to cohabitation with parents because of the relocation from the combat zone; (5) made family members unite; (6) caused quarrels in the family.

Participants currently living in Mariupol said that the military conflict had: (1) caused a break in relations with relatives (alienation, misunderstanding); (2) caused conflict with relatives; (3) united the family; (4) caused a deterioration in the financial situation that affected relationships in the family; (5) caused disagreements in the family.

The students of the Ukrainian higher educational institutions indicated that the military conflict had: (1) caused controversy and conflicts with close relatives living in the territory of Russia regarding the ownership of the territories of Ukraine and what was happening in the combat zone; (2) strengthened the relationships between immediate relatives, uniting the family; (3) caused a break in relations with relatives (stopped communicating).

---

14. M. J. Horowitz, N. Wilner, and W. Alvarez, "The Impact of Event Scale: A Measure of Subjective Stress," *Psychosomatic Medicine* 41, no. 3 (1979): 209–218.

Students of the Ukrainian Evangelical Theological Seminary (which included students from different regions of Ukraine, including Kiev, Odessa, Mariupol) noted that the military conflict had caused some disagreement in the family.

Second, 48.0 percent of all participants believed that members of their family had become more aggressive and more prone to conflicts when compared with the period before the military conflict in Ukraine; 52.0 percent did not think so. An increase in aggression and proneness to conflict was observed, however, among the majority of the participants currently living in Mariupol (58.8 percent) and the displaced people living in Kiev (57.9 percent).

Third, 35.1 percent of all participants indicated that the number of conflicts in their family had increased when compared with the period before the military conflict in Ukraine; 64.9 percent noted that there had been no increase in the number of scandals in their families. In comparing the results of different groups of participants, a more significant increase in the number of family conflicts could be observed among those currently living in Mariupol (47.1 percent).

Fourth, 84.4 percent of all participants of the study noted that they had become more anxious in comparison with the period prior to the military conflict in Ukraine. Thus in all groups, there was a significant increase in the level of anxiety and also in people's perception of life events.

The participants of the study living in Donetsk noted that they had: (1) begun to value their lives, their loved ones and all people more; (2) re-evaluated their values; (3) begun to live for the day in constant anxiety; (4) become more easygoing in their attitude towards life in general.

Displaced persons living in Kiev indicated that they had: (1) re-evaluated their values; (2) begun to value life more; (3) developed distrust, uncertainty about the future and begun to perceive life through the prism of despair; (4) become more interested in politics; (5) changed their attitudes towards Russia.

The people living in Mariupol thought that they had: (1) begun to value their relationships and life itself more; (2) re-evaluated their values and come to understand that the most important thing in life was their family; (3) become nervous and more sensitive; (4) begun to be more interested in politics; (5) become less gullible, more careful; (6) come to understand that everything in life is very changeable, unstable, dangerous.

Students of the Ukrainian higher educational institutions noted that they had: (1) begun to think more about family and their loved ones; (2) re-evaluated their values; (3) become more serious and begun to evaluate events more critically, with less confidence; (4) become more skeptical towards the flow of information; (5) come to understand that there is no stability.

Students of the Ukrainian Evangelical Theological Seminary noted that they had: (1) become more serious; (2) come to understand that many things in life are very unstable.

Fifth, 74.6 percent of all participants indicated that the military conflict in Ukraine had been stressful for their family and for them personally. The displaced persons living in Kiev (85.7 percent) and the people currently living in Mariupol (80.0 percent) considered the military conflict especially stressful for their families and for them personally.

Sixth, 63.2 percent of all participants noted that the military conflict in Ukraine had negatively affected the well-being of their family members. The displaced persons living in Kiev (75.0 percent) and the people currently living in Mariupol (74.2 percent) emphasized the negative impact of the military conflict on the well-being of their family members.

Based on the results of factor analysis, we identified three factors that account for the dispersion of the variables (which totals 54.9 percent). The first factor explains the greatest number (31.1 percent) of the dispersion of the variables, which we have interpreted as stress, anxiety and the deterioration of the family members' well-being.

We have interpreted the second factor (which accounts for 13.7 percent of the dispersion of the variables) as aggressiveness, proneness to conflict.

We have interpreted the third factor (which accounts for 10.1 percent of the dispersion of the variables) as family disagreements.

Next we analyzed the results of the study to determine how much the military conflict in Ukraine – as a life event – had exhausted the participants of the study.

First, we found that something that reminded participants about the military conflict in Ukraine caused either "rather strong" or "very strong" feelings among participants who were residing in Donetsk, living in Kiev as displaced persons or living in Mariupol.

Second, when we compared data on the degree of sleep disorders in connection with the military conflict in Ukraine, we observed a "fairly strong" and "very strong" degree of sleep disorders among participants who were residing in Donetsk, living as displaced persons in Kiev or living in Mariupol.

Third, we observed irritation and anger in connection with the military conflict in Ukraine to a "rather strong" and "very strong" degree among the participants who were residing in Donetsk, living as displaced persons in Kiev and living in Mariupol.

Fourth, "rather strong" and "very strong" emotions about the military conflict in Ukraine were expressed by the participants living in Donetsk, the displaced persons living in Kiev and those residing in Mariupol.

Finally, "rather strong" and "very strong" feelings along with a sense of constant "readiness" that something terrible might happen again in connection with the military conflict in Ukraine were expressed by participants living in Donetsk, the students of the Ukrainian Evangelical Theological Seminary, the displaced persons living in Kiev and those residing in Mariupol.

Then we analyzed the results of the study to determine the participants' current understanding of the meaning of life.

The participants of the study living in Donetsk noted that they saw meaning of life in: (1) the family; (2) prosperity and peace; (3) serving people.

Displaced persons living in Kiev indicated that they saw the meaning of life in: (1) living not only for oneself, but loving and being useful to other people, (2) being loved and children; (3) life itself; (4) the salvation of the soul; (5) peace on earth, the health of relatives; (6) bringing benefit to the family and other people; (7) interesting and creative work, self-realization.

Participants residing in Mariupol saw the meaning of life in: (1) being loved and children; (2) peace or a peaceful, stable life; (3) self-realization, favorite or interesting work; (4) love.

Students of the Ukrainian higher educational institutions saw the meaning of life in: (1) self-realization and doing one's thing; (2) the creation of a happy family and love; (3) the course of life; (4) the development of society and one's own spiritual development; (5) benefit people.

Students of the Ukrainian Evangelical Theological Seminary saw the meaning of life in: (1) the service of God, their calling; (2) their care of children; (3) self-realization; (4) being at peace with oneself, with neighbors and with God.

Psychotherapeutic Intervention

The concept of trauma can be used to describe a person's reaction to a difficult day or a brutal violence or murder. However, we must distinguish stress from the deeper shocks that affect the physical, emotional, cognitive, behavioral and spiritual condition of individuals and entire groups. Traumatic events differ from ordinary stress by intensity and/or duration.

Many studies have confirmed the importance of therapeutic intervention as a psychological mechanism that affects the development process of individuals after they experience a traumatic event.[15] Researchers rely on data that shows the connection between intrusive symptoms (as an independent attempt of the psyche to process traumatic experiences from the past) and a person's posttraumatic recovery. They also pay attention to psychotherapeutic interventions in psychotraumatic events in order to help a person live through traumatic memories in order to integrate those traumatic memories into the person's life history.[16]

One program that is effective for responding to psychological trauma is STAR (Strategies for Trauma Awareness and Resilience), which unites traditionally disparate fields of knowledge and activity: traumatology (including neurobiology), human security, restorative justice, conflict transformation and making peace and faith / spirituality.[17] This program has been developed at the Center for Justice and Peacemaking of East Mennonite University.[18] A comprehensive model for responding to trauma is the "Path of Healing Traumas: Interruption of Cycles of Victimization and Violence, which has been developed by the Center for Strategic International Studies in Washington, DC. This program would be effective in the context of the military situation in Ukraine because it examines the consequences of trauma for groups or societies experiencing trauma. This program explores how social groups should perceive and respond to traumatic events – including terrorism – so that they do not fall into vicious cycles of victimization and/or violence (e.g. a "tooth for tooth") and do not perceive themselves as eternal victims.

Problems Faced by Victims of Military Events

When protests first broke out during the Maidan[19] in 2013–2014, we noticed the following problems. First, in some families, there were conflicts between

15. Birgit Wagner and Andreas Maercker, "The Diagnosis of Complicated Grief as a Mental Disorder: A Critical Appraisal," *Psychologica Belgica* 50, nos. 1–2 (2010): 27–48.

16. See Carolyn Yoder, *Little Book of Trauma Healing: When Violence Strikes and Community Security Is Threatened* (Editore: Good Books, 2005); Bessel A. van der Kolk, *The Body Keeps the Score: Brain, Mind, and Body in the Healing of Trauma* (New York: Penguin Books, 2015); Judith Lewis-Herman (April 2003), "The Mental Health of Crime Victims: Impact of Legal Intervention" *Journal of Traumatic Stress* 16, no. 2: 159–166.

17. Carolyn Yoder, *Little Book of Trauma Healing.*

18. Liders, *Family as a Psychological System*, 296.

19. In this case, we use the concept of "Maidan" as a historical event and not as a geographical place located in the center of Kiev. The word "Maidan" became a symbol of Ukraine's struggle for its own freedom, independence and dignity. Mass protests in Ukraine began on 21 November 2013 as a reaction to the decision of the Cabinet of Ministers of Ukraine to suspend the process of preparing to sign an agreement on an association between Ukraine

husband and wife evoked by their political prejudices. For example, the husband supported the advocates of the Maidan, and the wife stood up for the authorities existing at that time. One could see the same kind of disagreements among other relatives as well. Children sometimes could not understand who to believe under conditions of such conflict.

Second, family members often experienced psychological problems. People were afraid to go out into the streets in Kiev, where the main events took place (over a period of one year, this square in the center of Kiev – the Maidan – was permanently occupied by approximately 500,000 people).

Third, we noticed that the children were experiencing psychological problems because of the agitation and fears experienced by the adults. The children were afraid of the explosions on the streets, were afraid to fall asleep and felt themselves to be defenseless. They felt irritation and embarrassment and became absentminded and inattentive. They demonstrated unusual aggressiveness or heightened anxiety. The children were afraid that the events that had taken place earlier could happen again. Knowing that these events were affecting their immediate families, friends and relatives, children got worried and anxious about other people.

In late November 2013, mass protests began in Ukraine. In 2014, a military conflict ensued. During the 2014–2017 period, we noticed the following problems. First, wounded soldiers started coming back from the front lines and desperately needed help, but their families did not know how to deal with them, which created a crisis. According to the military prosecutor's office, between the beginning of the conflict in 2014 and the first days of June 2017, about five hundred soldiers committed suicide after returning from the combat zone. Between 90 and 95 percent of all combatants had medical, social and/or psychological problems. About a third of all combatants were diagnosed with posttraumatic stress disorder.

Second, the families who lost their sons, brothers, fathers or other relatives in the war – and whose relatives continued to die – did not know how to survive the grief, and so they started using alcohol and drugs and separated themselves from society.

---

and the European Union. The Maidan took hold not only of Independence Square and several nearby streets and squares in the center of Kiev, but the whole Ukraine. Approximately eleven million people passed through the Maidan. AutoMaidan was an automobile march of protest in Ukraine. Maidan was a phenomenon of direct democracy, which demonstrated a high level of self-organization, discipline, structure and infrastructure, and included elements of cultural leisure in the form of an open university and the Maidan library.

Providing Assistance to Victims of Military Events

We proposed the following strategies for offering psychological and spiritual help to victims of military events. First, we created centers of help, where people could come for some simple support. In these centers, people could sit in silence with a social psychologist or a priest. The volunteers working in such centers went through special training, usually taking courses on providing initial psychological and medical assistance.

Second, we created a network of organizations that included churches, Christian organizations and many psychological and psychiatric centers that could serve as a good resource for people. Many soldiers, especially from religious regions such as western Ukraine, preferred to seek help from a priest rather than a psychologist. The military personnel who suffered as a result of the war received comprehensive assistance: psychological, medical, psychiatric and spiritual.

Third, we created support groups that united families who had lost their sons in the war. These groups met for one year and became a great support for the families.

Fourth, we established special assistance centers for displaced persons from east Ukraine. These families suffered the most severe shocks because they needed shelter and food. The lack of funding caused these families to experience a severe crisis, and these assistance centers provided them with good support.

Fifth, we offered instruction to volunteers, psychologists and priests on a variety of relevant subjects, including the following: a theological justification of the appearance of evil; what is PTSD; what is loss; how to survive grief, among others. We noticed that this training helped pastors, clergymen and volunteers working with the families of the displaced in many ways.

Sixth, a therapeutic art association[20] conducted instructional and practical trainings in Kiev and Odessa entitled, "Overcoming psychotrauma: art therapy, alternative methods of conflict resolution, pedagogical and therapeutic support under unusual conditions."

Seventh, in our work with children and soldiers, we used art therapy techniques since ordinary psychological counseling did not work. This method enabled people to interpret their feelings through drawings and to talk about themselves and say things that they hadn't been able to speak for a long time.

---

20. This was offered through the support of the German-Ukrainian-Belarusian society, "Europe without Borders."

We also supported children by using games to help them find peace of mind and strength. Free games have a great healing power, providing children with a space for living and mastering reality, particularly dangerous situations that are destructive to the child's soul. We organized games to help children process their experiences and to activate resources to overcome mental trauma, stress and crisis. The games aimed to activate children's imaginations, help remove their emotional and bodily tension, help them safely express their feelings and encourage them to develop friendships and relationships so they could offer mutual assistance to one another.

Eighth, we organized training programs for the chaplaincy that were prepared by Christian educational institutions. Some state universities opened joint programs with Christian educational institutions. The chaplaincy program served as a significant resource for soldiers. Many soldiers spoke about the importance of a chaplain with whom they prayed before battle or who could offer a prayer for them.

Ninth, we did not focus on psychotherapy with soldiers or displaced persons as they needed psychic and medical stabilization.

Conclusion

The military conflict in Ukraine has seriously affected family relationships, and this is most powerfully observed among the displaced persons living in Kiev. Understanding the causes of family trauma makes it possible to provide full and effective psychotherapeutic assistance to individuals. Seeking to understand the determinants of family trauma opens up new possibilities for psychotherapy and provides resources to address difficult problems.

Bibliography

Adler, Alfred W. *Understand the Nature of Man*. St Petersburg: Academic Project, 2000.

American Association of Christian Counselors. http://www.aacc.net/about-us/.

Brown, Joseph H., and Dana N. Qiristensen. *Family Therapy*. St Petersburg: Peter, 2001.

Burlachuk, Leonid, Alexander Kocharyan, and Maxim Zhidko. *Psychotherapy: Textbook for High Schools*. St Petersburg: Peter, 2003.

Center for Crisis Psychology in Ukraine. http://www.rodynnekolo.in.ua/en/.

Center for Justice & Peacebuilding. https://emu.edu/cjp/grad/admission.

Cohen, Judith, Antony Mannarino, and Esther Deblinger. *Psychotherapy with Children and Adolescents Who Have Suffered Injury and Loss*. Lviv: Svichado, 2016.

Dozortseva, Elena. *Psychological Trauma in Adolescents with Problems in Their Behavior: Diagnosis and Correction*. Moskva: Genesis, 2006.

Freud, Sigmund. *Three Essays on the Theory of Sexuality*. Kharkov: Filio, 2005.

———. *Psychology of the Unconscious*. Moskva: Prosveshenie, 1990.

Gruzdev, Vladimir, and Natalya Kigai. "About the Causes of Social Depression, Cruelty, Crime and Invincible Corruption in the Country." http://portal-nko.ru/dialog/point/325.

Horowitz, M. J., N. Wilner, and W. Alvarez. "The Impact of Event Scale: A Measure of Subjective Stress." *Psychosomatic Medicine* 41, no. 3 (1979): 209–218.

Kellermann, Natan P. F. "Transmission of Holocaust Trauma." *The Israel Journal of Psychiatry and Related Sciences* 4, no. 1 (2001): 55–58.

Khalanskiy, Vyacheslav. Association of Christian Psychologists and Psychotherapists in Ukraine. http://www.eastwestreport.org/pdfs/ew21-4.pdf.

Klimchuk, Vitaliy. "Posttraumatic Growth and Ways of Facilitating in the Psychotherapy." *Psychology* 5 (2016): 46–52.

Lewis-Herman, Judith. "The Mental Health of Crime Victims: Impact of Legal Intervention." *Journal of Traumatic Stress* 16, no. 2 (April 2003): 159–166. https://onlinelibrary.wiley.com/doi/abs/10.1023/A%3A1022847223135.

Liders, Alexander. *Family as a Psychological System*. Moskva: Obnisk, 2004.

Lindy, Jacob D., and Robert J. Lifton, eds. *Beyond Invisible Walls: The Psychological Legacy of Soviet Trauma, East European Therapists and Their Patients*. Philadelphia: Brunner-Routledge, 2001.

Positive, Joseph S. "Changes Following Adversity PTSD Research Quarterly." *Journal of Traumatic Stress* 21, no. 4 (2010): 1–3.

Reshetnikov, Mikhail. *Mental Trauma*. St Petersburg: Institute of Psychoanalysis, 2006.

Ripley, Jennifer S., and Everett L. Worthington. *Couple Therapy: A New Hope-Focused Approach*. Downers Grove: InterVarsity Press, 2014.

Schutzenberger, Anne Ancelin. *The Ancestor Syndrome: Transgenerational Psychotherapy and the Hidden Links in the Family Tree*. Moskva: Institute of Psychotherapy, 2001.

Taku, Kanako. "The Factor Structure of the Posttraumatic Growth Inventory: A Comparison of Five Models Using Confirmatory Factor Analysis." *Journal of Traumatic Stress* 21, no. 2 (2009): 24–27.

Tarabrina, Nadegda. *Psychology of Post-Traumatic Stress: Theory and Practice*. Moskva: Institute of Psychology of the Russian Academy of Sciences, 2009.

Titarenko, Tatyana. "How to Help Witnesses and Participants in Traumatic Events: Horizons of Social-psychological Rehabilitation." *Actual Problems of Sociology, Psychology, Pedagogy* 29, no. 4 (2015): 163–170.

———. *Test by the Crisis*. Moskva: Kogito Center, 2010.

Van der Kolk, Bessel A. *The Body Keeps the Score: Brain, Mind, and Body in the Healing of Trauma*. New York: Penguin Books, 2015.

———. *Psychological Trauma*. Washington, DC: American Psychiatric Press, 1987.

Varga, Anna. *Systemic Family Psychotherapy*. St Petersburg: Rech, 2001.

Varga, Anna, and Budinayte Grazyna. "Trauma of the Past in Russia and the Possibility of Using Systemic Family Therapy." http://psyjournal.ru/articles/travma-proshlogo-v-rossii-i-vozmozhnosti-primeneniya-sistemnoy-semeynoy-terapii.

Wade, Nathaniel G., William T. Hoyt, Lem E. M. Kidwell, and Everett L. Worthington. "Efficacy of Psychotherapeutic Interventions to Promote Forgiveness: A Meta-analysis." *Journal of Consulting and Clinical Psychology* 82 (2014): 154–170.

Wagner, Birgit, and Andreas Maercker. "The Diagnosis of Complicated Grief as a Mental Disorder: A Critical Appraisal." *Psychologica Belgica* 50, nos. 1–2 (2010): 27–48.

Worthington, Everett L. *Hope-Focused Marriage Counseling*. Downers Grove: InterVarsity Press, 1999.

Yoder, Carolyn. *Little Book of Trauma Healing: When Violence Strikes and Community Security Is Threatened*. Editore: Good Books, 2005.

15

By His Wounds I Am Healed to Love

Learning from Rwandans

John Steward

Introduction

For over twenty years I have studied the recovery of Rwandans after the terrible genocide in 1994. When I first arrived in the country in March 1997, I took three months to listen, observe and understand. As I enquired and processed what I heard, I became a friend to some brave sisters and brothers and was amazed that human beings could survive as well as they had, but I could see that they were struggling.

The wounds of genocide are diverse and deep. Many whom I met – whether perpetrator, victim, survivor, refugee or returnee – carried trauma in their bodies and troubled minds. I noticed fear and suspicion, poor personal boundaries, general malaise, dysfunction and lack of vision. I could see little signs of healing and recovery.

I was observing people who had lost purpose and seemed to be held in a paralyzing time warp of the terrifying days of chaos that had built up over months and years and eventually engulfed the country in April 1994. Some told me of their guilt about surviving or their shame for failing to protect their departed. Others were haunted by their dreams and nightmares or their inability to locate the bodies of loved ones.

Many weeks after I arrived, I began to hear about stories of change in individuals, and some months later, we began to make systematic efforts to assist people living with trauma. Light began to dawn as we caught a glimpse of hope returning through the healing of wounds, leading these Rwandans to the joy and peace of renewed faith and restored relationships.

Embarking on the Healing Journey

For more than a year before coming to Rwanda in 1997, I went through my own healing journey. This began with an eight-day silent retreat, and then I participated in a weekly men's group for sixteen months. I learned about my need to change, from holding my thoughts and feelings within, to expressing what I was experiencing in the moment openly and truthfully. I recalled how many times my wife had expressed in frustration, "Just tell me what you think and feel, otherwise I do not know how to relate to you."

After months of listening to Rwandans' stories, God guided my Rwandan team to three different approaches, which were all developed on African soil, that invited and enabled people to change. I realized their value when I discovered that all three offered similar content and direction to my own personal healing journey in the very different culture of Australia.

Over time, additional approaches to healing trauma and broken relationships have been introduced in Rwanda, and thousands more people have benefitted. Such work has also spread into other countries of the Great Lakes Region and further afield. One Rwandan group has opened The Rabagirana Institute for Reconciliation near Kigali and runs an International School of Reconciliation.[1] This bears witness to twenty years of dedicated practice, constant faith and rich learning by doing. The Rabagirana Institute is a resource that will benefit anyone who serves among people with trauma.

A central focus for the Rwandan churches in this journey of recovery was learning about God's desire to bring every believer to wholeness, regardless of how challenging that task might be. This goes far beyond a simple concept of personal salvation.

God's Part: Christ's Love for Us

When I started to think about approaches for change, I kept reflecting on the meaning of Isaiah 53:

1. See Rabagirana.org.

> Surely he took up our pain
> and bore our suffering,
> yet we considered him punished by God,
> stricken by him, and afflicted.
> But he was pierced for our transgressions,
> he was crushed for our iniquities;
> the punishment that brought us peace was on him,
> and by his wounds we are healed . . . (vv. 4–5)
>
> Therefore, I will give him a portion among the great,
> and he will divide the spoils with the strong,
> because he poured out his life unto death,
> and was numbered with the transgressors.
> For he bore the sin of many,
> and made intercession for the transgressors. (v. 12 NIV)

These verses are quoted in the New Testament in Matthew 8:16–17, Luke 22:37 and 1 Peter 2:21–25. The phrase, "By his wounds we are healed" (Isa 53:5), means that Jesus accepted what happened to him for our sake and suggests that we will be restored and brought to wholeness.

Easter is a time when we focus our minds and prayers on the physical suffering of the Christ. Words from Isaiah 53, such as *despised, crushed, pierced, bruised, carried,* help us understand that through the Paschal wounding, Christ's surrender on the cross was the vehicle for a mystical achievement: the Lamb of God taking away the sin of the world. The spiritual importance of Isaiah 53:5 is clear: our sin wounds us spiritually and damages us morally, but Christ became our substitute, and through his suffering and death, our sin is covered. For all that we have done wrong, we need God's forgiveness, and this is available at any time.

However, we need to differentiate between *God's responsibility* – the suffering of Christ for our sins, our need of a savior and the gift of God's Spirit – and *our responsibility* – our behavior and its consequences, our need to seek healing for the hurts of everyday life, the pain that we cause each other, the broken relationships that affect our choices and our attitudes.

A web search on Isaiah 53:4–5 suggests that about half of the writers believe this healing covers every part of our being, while the other half believe that there is a role in healing for natural and psychological processes of recovery. Many Rwandans needed the latter.

Our Part: Opening Ourselves to Love

The majority of Rwandans are Christians, and many of them are familiar with Isaiah 53. But after the genocide, the familiar words from verse 5, "the punishment that brought us peace was upon him and, by his wounds, we are healed," did not seem to help; in fact, there was a strong sense of grief and guilt, and sorrow swirled around in heavy hearts. Time was not healing the hurts within, and you could see the pain on people's faces. Such predicaments are not confined to Rwanda, for this painful and persistent heaviness occurs wherever there is trauma, violence, grief and loss.

The wrong that has been done to us by others needs our forgiveness. But we may not be ready to provide that, because we may still be experiencing much grief, pain, resentment and reactive behavior. We may also feel shame and personally responsible for our failures, and we may be unwilling to forgive ourselves. What can change these problems?

Easter normally falls within the month of April, and so is close to the time of the annual Memorial Week to remember the Rwandan genocide. Each year's commemoration brings questions to the surface, "But what about wounds of the heart and their effect on my being? Why do I remain unsettled, edgy, sleepless, aimless, anxious, sick of heart, struggling?"

Many quote the saying, "Time heals all wounds," but this can be misleading because it is not always true. This statement was made in 160 BC by Terentius, an African slave who was freed by his French owner to participate in the cultural life of his adopted country. Terentius had every reason to say his wounds were healed, because he experienced a generous justice and release, and he received a life of freedom where people could appreciate his contributions and skills. He experienced a rare, but true, restitution of which most victims or survivors can only dream.

As humans we often do not know how to heal wounds of heart and mind, and so we tend to deny, minimize or ignore them. In this we need teaching and leading. A saying from Hippocrates in 410 BC echoes this idea: "Healing is a matter of time, but it is sometimes also a matter of opportunity." Based on my experiences in Rwanda and in my own life, I suggest the following version of these ancient ideas: "Time gives perspective, but only healing will heal my deepest wounds."

Physiological Healing: A Natural Process Model

So what does this healing look like? I find insight by considering how our body heals its physical wounds. We are all endowed with an automatic physiological process – a sequence of steps that flow whether we know it or not. Physiologically, healing is not a *choice* we make. Whenever we cut ourselves, our body heals itself by stopping the flow of blood and rebuilding and protecting the area. There is a normal sequence that occurs in the natural healing response in our body, as outlined below.

Initially, *pain* conveys the following signal: "you are hurt, stop what you are doing and pay attention NOW, so that healing may begin." Four steps follow the pain in a sequence, each building on the previous.

First, a *clot* is created. The body reacts to the injury by stopping the bleeding through forming a block, which slows and eventually stops the flow of blood out of the wound.

Second, once the clot is firm, the *blood vessels* near the wound expand, bringing extra blood, warmth and nutrients to enable speedy new growth.

Third, *walls* form in the wound to reconstruct and strengthen the affected area.

Fourth, a *covering* closes over the walls and protects the area, making it strong. This will become the scar.

This summary outlines only the main steps and disguises the complexity of the process of healing, which (with the exception of really big wounds) happens speedily. This orderly process of healing a physical wound offers insight into the healing that we can seek and choose for our hearts and minds.

Psychological Healing: Wounds of Heart and Mind

By "wounds of heart and mind," I mean feelings, memories, hurts, characteristics or attitudes that emerge in our reaction to painful experiences of trauma and suffering. By "healing," I mean that pain is relieved, poison is removed and change begins, but this does not mean that we will be without any memories or scars.

Our emotional wounds heal through a psychological healing process – a sequence of steps that take place in the mind. I must *choose* to do this healing work, and it only begins when I stop denying (running away from or ignoring) my pain and accept my need for help. Often this assistance comes in the form of mature people whom I can trust, who are experienced in this area of healing and are willing to guide and support me through my recovery. This will take time. It is a form of loving myself and honors God in my mind and body.

How does this happen? What does it look like to be healed by the wounds caused by my failures or the actions of another person or group? We can learn from God's model, which happens physiologically in our bodies, as described above.

The four steps of personal healing and change are the inner equivalents of the natural process model, whose steps (*clot, blood vessels, walls* and *covering*) are metaphors for the transformation of heart and mind that can occur when we choose to step onto this path.

The healing process always begins with *pain*. This time, our heart is hurting and bleeding. We have carried the effects of trauma for long enough. Our dysfunction, weakness or purposelessness is telling us that the cost is too great to bear, that we must act now.

When we want to participate in the healing of our heart and mind wounds, we must feel the pain of failure, hurt and loss. Then we can experience a four-part process of change. As John Bradshaw says, "you cannot heal what you cannot feel."[2]

First, a *clot* is created when we stop and accept the feelings of chaos and anger, recognize our swirling emotions of hurt, grief and loss, embrace our wounded heart with all its pain and bruises and prepare to examine the impact of this injury.

The sign that we are ready is when we accept that we need support and know that we cannot continue to carry the weight and distraction of our struggle within. So we ask for help or choose to attend a healing opportunity. "Work with the willing" is the key criterion for recruiting people to participate in a healing event. You can only heal if you want to; it can never be forced.

Second, the *blood vessels* do their work. Our struggle for survival has weakened us. Our spirit lacks nourishment because of the negative emotions flooding us. Now we seek and receive nourishment for our hearts and minds. For example, we might listen to the testimony of others who have begun the journey of change, or we might receive teaching about God's salvation, love and mercy to sinful people – particularly the grace Jesus showed while he was on the cross. In the diagram opposite, this *blood vessel* stage is described as "The Revelation of God's Heart."

Third, the *walls* are openings within our hearts as we begin to talk about the loss and grief, relive or remember the event and describe painful circumstances. Later, I will describe some of the practical approaches that can assist in exposing and removing the poison that comes with the hurt. The chief act is to tell our stories and to listen to the stories of others. In every Healing of Memories workshop that he leads, Michael Lapsley says, "every person has a story, and every story needs a listener."

2. John Bradshaw, *Homecoming* (New York: Bantam Books, 1990), 80.

When we speak about our experiences in a safe and free space (where people listen with acceptance rather than trying to analyze, correct or solve our pasts), we can better face the effects of our pain and begin to understand and grieve our losses. Talking has another benefit, for every time we tell our story, some of our inner pain reduces. As we talk, we gain insight and perspective, and the bitterness begins to be replaced by the hope that things can change. In the diagram below, this *wall* stage is described as "Healing Wounds."

Fourth, the *covering* protects and shelters our changed and vulnerable hearts, strengthening us when we approach the idea of making a confession or receiving apology. This protects the wound from further infection and enables us to resist the poisoning of hateful revenge. With this covering in place, we can offer an apology or extend compassion. In the diagram below, this *covering* stage is described as "Repentance and Forgiveness."

The above diagram[3] summarizes the psychological aspects that reflect the natural process elements (*clot, blood vessels, walls, covering*) and is the foundation of one of the major Rwandan healing workshops, "Healing the Wounds of Ethnic Conflict." The healing of inner wounds can be so profound that some individuals find themselves embracing their former enemies. The sharing process can be so humanizing that some find themselves being freed from the fear and natural dislike for the "other," which has been ingrained through the traditions of their group and community. It is amazing to see these changes, which can be observed in a softening on the face and new attitudes.

3. From R. Lloyd, J. Nyamutera, R. Schudel and K. Bresser, *Healing the Wounds of Ethnic Conflict,* Facilitators Guide (Geneva: Le Rucher Ministries, 2011), 14.

This marks the beginning of transformation, which is an ongoing work of God with our cooperation.

The cross in the center of the diagram reminds us of the wounds of Christ and the healing he tenderly offers us. Though the picture adds "Reconciliation" as a roof, this can be rare, since it only occurs when two parties in a conflict are both healed – the victim/survivor from pain and shame and the perpetrator from violence and guilt.

I knew that the healing workshops in Rwanda were making a difference after hearing the feedback from participants.[4] Following are some comments from individual participants who gave permission to be quoted without being named:

> *I liked this workshop because it helped me know myself and to know how to manage my feelings.*
>
> *Forgiveness can be achieved from these workshops.*
>
> *Those who watch us are amazed and say, "those people are no longer traumatized."*
>
> *Thank God for we have known ourselves.*
>
> *Feelings are a way through which God speaks to me.*
>
> *I am so very grateful that my daughter attended your seminar where she got so changed.*
>
> *After she shared with us, we realized we were lost and repented from our hatred and anger against the other ethnic group.*
>
> *This process has a strong spiritual component giving wounded people a chance to rebuild shattered spirituality and looking again at their faith in God.*

A Way of Loving Others

Returning to the words, "By his wounds we are healed," from Isaiah 53:5, we remember that Jesus accepted what was happening to him *for our sake*. His suffering was redemptive, on behalf of others. More than that, in the act of becoming Savior, he modeled to us the behavior that promotes healing for others. "Christ suffered for you, leaving you an example, that you should follow in his steps" (1 Pet 2:21 NIV).

---

4. Some of the approaches used are described in the first half of my book *From Genocide to Generosity: Hatreds Heal on Rwanda's Hills* (Carlisle: Langham Global Library, 2015).

In the midst of his own pain and desolation, Jesus showed love and care to those who gathered near him during his crucifixion, whether they were friend, onlooker, official or foe. He spoke to the vulnerable and grieving bystanders (Luke 23:28–31). He listened to the stories of the two men being crucified alongside him (Luke 23:39–43). He heard the murmurings of the crowd (Luke 23:35–37). He chose to ask God's forgiveness on those who did not know what they were really doing (Luke 23:34). He did not curse God, but placed himself in God's hands and surrendered his spirit to God (Luke 23:46). The centurion saw no sign of violence in the dying Jesus and declared him to be "a righteous man" (Luke 23:47).

After his resurrection, Jesus walked with two of his followers to Emmaus, listening to their stories of grief and loss and affirming their future by showing them the hope he provided (Luke 24:13–35). In this way, Jesus practiced compassionate listening and thoughtful responding that offered moments of healing for the inner wounds in their lives. The way Christ received his wounds and responded to them suggests how we might respond to the wounds that we receive in our lives.

Jesus showed his wounds to the disciples – he did not hide them (Luke 24:39). The scars became proof of his resurrection life. Healing does not obliterate the evidence of our wounding, but transforms it to something useful. Scars are reminders that we can recover. They are proof that we have been changed. They become a testimony to God's sustaining goodness. As Richard Rohr writes:

> All suffering is potentially redemptive,
> All wounds are potentially sacred wounds.
> It depends on what you do with them.[5]

What are some ways we can serve others in their healing journeys? Once our hearts have begun to heal, when grief and pain have begun to be replaced by hope and love, we can simply respond as each day provides us with opportunities. When we have love in ourselves, we are ready to follow Jesus's example and love others.

Letting Our Love Flow in Daily Life

In Rwanda the need was huge, and people did not have the luxury of one-on-one counseling. But once small group facilitators were trained, it was possible to

5. R. Rohr, *Things Hidden* (Cincinnati: Franciscan Media, 2008), 25.

work with fifty people at a time, with each participant in a small group of four or five others, including a facilitator or guide. This work requires background and skill, and you can read more in *From Genocide to Generosity.*

A healing process can also occur in a small group of two, three or four people, using some basic guidelines. Jesus invites us to start where we are and gives us the following two suggestions.

First, in Luke 10:3–11, Jesus sends out seventy-two followers two-by-two to make a harvest. A harvest is not a time of giving, but receiving. Jesus sends them into possibly hostile situations, and the response they are to give when they arrive is, "a word of peace" (v. 5). Whoever receives this greeting and welcomes them shows the normal sign of hospitality in the culture by offering the gift of food and drink.

While eating, a conversation reveals to the visitors that most of the family is well, but someone is sick. When the meal is over, the visitors offer to pray for the sick, after which they explain, "this is a sign of the kingdom of God coming into our midst" (v. 9).

We cannot pray for the health of those who are hostile to us until we have forgiven them. We can't wish someone, "all the best, God have mercy upon you," if we are bitter. We can only offer this blessing if we first accept them.

Second, in Luke 17:3, Jesus gives a guideline for healing relational disagreements that arise in the flow of daily life and for reconciling individuals: " . . . rebuke . . . repent . . . forgive." The disciples know how difficult this can be to do well once, let alone seven times (v. 4), for they respond, "'Increase our faith!'" (v. 5). Thus this guideline is best carried out when love bathes the interaction.

In this passage (vv. 1–6), Jesus stresses the need for frequent forgiveness, which he illustrates by using the image of the mulberry tree, which grew in that region. The fruit of this tree contains many seeds, suggesting that unforgiveness may easily multiply. By contrast, forgiveness washes away the stains that are so characteristic of mulberry juice.

Some Ways of Loving Ourselves

We are to love others "as we love ourselves." We can use rituals, ceremonies, symbols, dreams, art, spiritual companioning, meditation or contemplative prayer to assist our healing and help us to receive divine love. Each of these plays a different role in healing.

Rituals, Ceremonies, Symbols

Rituals and ceremonies are actions that can help us symbolically release our real grief and loss into the palm of God, whose hands hold us. In the "Nailing of Pains/Wounds to the Cross" ceremony,[6] each person makes a list of their bad experiences of the past or of events that continue to trouble them and reinforce bad feelings about the one(s) who hurt them. Then they share these stories of pain and loss in pairs or a small group. After sharing with at least one other group member, each person prayerfully nails the list to a wooden cross. The cross is then carried outside while participants sing and carry lit candles. The papers are removed and burnt. The rising smoke ensures confidentiality and also symbolizes that the memory that smoldered inside has been surrendered to God.

Other ceremonies include: washing or pouring out water to symbolize a cleansing of bitterness and stain, drawing the name or a picture of the perpetrator and placing a wreath of leaves and flowers around it while praying for him or her, a foot washing ceremony that evokes humility, acceptance, honor, forgiveness and cleansing for the journey.

Dreams

The messages and images in people's dreams in Rwanda after 1994 were often alarming reminders of bad times and filled with fear. Some believed that such dreams were from Satan and meant to harm or haunt them. However, the teaching of Elihu in Job 33:14–18 is a perceptive summary of how we can value our dreams and receive a message from God to help us respond to the bitter times of life so "that the light of life may shine" on us (Job 33:30). Elihu's basic instruction in interpreting dreams can increase our confidence that God is holding us in love and mercy and inviting us to place our concerns into God's hands.

Art

Because art uses a different part of our brain, it can help us feel and express emotions, and it can enable some people to focus on what they need to tell about their trauma. In Rwanda we found it useful to invite youth to express

---

6. This ceremony can be found in chapter 20 of this book.

their trauma through art, dance, drama, music, poetry and public declaration. Following are some of their descriptions about the impact from this approach:

> *. . . this work helps me have a loving and forgiving heart.*
> *Before I had trauma but now I live at peace with myself, as well as with those who oppressed me.*
> *. . . I have let go of my bitterness and my desire for revenge.*[7]

Art is an important way to enable people to illustrate their painful stories by using the side of the brain that is not engaged by words. People whose trauma makes it hard for them to tell their stories can speak for fifteen minutes when they begin to explain their drawings, no matter how chaotic their pictures may seem. When listeners sensitively ask questions to clarify or expand the stories, the speakers will be amazed to find that they have talked for thirty or forty minutes. Clarity often comes with conversation, and art can help us unravel and clarify our thoughts.

Spiritual Companioning

In spiritual companioning (or spiritual direction), a person of mature faith converses with an individual or a small group to ponder prayerfully the challenging experiences of life and to discern the direction God's spirit is moving within someone and within their context. Together, the spiritual companions consider questions such as, "How is God present in the difficult times as well as the good times in my life?" and "As I reflect on my life situation, how am I seeing God at work in the world where I am immersed?"

Through a gentle unfolding, spiritual companionship allows traumatized people to slowly open their hearts and bring tragic experiences into the light. The openness and confidentiality creates a space for honesty. Because this is a slow process of opening our hearts to God's spirit this work takes time. So the companioning sessions are often repeated monthly. Healing and personal change is like a journey of discovery.

Meditation or Contemplative Prayer

The concept of meditation or contemplative prayer is old in mainstream reflective communities of Christians, but it is often new to Christian groups

7. John Steward, *From Genocide to Generosity* (Carlisle: Langham Global Library, 2015), 147–149.

that focus heavily on action, goals and programs. It is important to remember that both doing and being are part of the work of God.

Jesus modeled a contemplative way of being when he retreated to be alone with the Father, fasted in the wilderness, prayed in the garden of Gethsemane and sojourned regularly on the hills around Galilee. These times of silence and quiet helped Jesus discern God's will, while also bringing him into a place of rest and affirming his trust in God.

We taught several colleagues in Rwanda a daily practice in the discipline of sitting in a quiet place and being receptive to the presence of God's Spirit. We also introduced youth to this form of receptive prayer. Contemplative prayer is an extension of this stillness, with a focus on being aware and receptive to the quiet work of God, who leads us to new insights. Following is a prayer that we used during these times of receptive prayer:

> Tender God,
> You have seen my affliction,
> And unbound my eyes;
> You have bereaved me of the burden
> To which I used to cling;
> You have woven my pain
> Into patterns of integrity;
> The wounds I cherished
> You have turned into honors
> And the scars I kept hidden
> Into marks of truth.
> You have touched me gently;
> I have seen your face, and live.[8]

Love Will Make A Way

Hebrews 12:14–15 challenges us to "Strive for peace with every one, and for holiness without which no one will see the Lord. See to it that no one be deprived of the grace of God, that no bitter root spring up and cause trouble, through which many may become defiled." Bitterness flourishes wherever we neglect to face pain because it remains unhealed. Healing keeps bitter roots from growing by helping us to recognize the poison of bitter feelings when they emerge.

---

8. Janet Morley, *All Desires Known* (London: SPCK, 1994), 77.

We must regularly ask ourselves, How did life wound me today? Do I carry within me the hurt of this painful experience? How are these wounds an opportunity to transcend troubles in my life and can they be transformed into stepping stones? Our wounds are an invitation to attend to what God wants to do in us. The promise, "I am the Lord who heals you," was a precious word to Israel (Exod 15:26). As Richard Rohr writes:

> If we cannot find a way to make our wounds into sacred wounds,
> We invariably become negative or bitter – because we are wounded.
> If I don't transform my pain, I transmit it to others.[9]

In seeking to transform our pain, we can remember the natural process of physical healing. Our decision to stop the downwards spiral is equivalent to the clot that stops the wound from bleeding.

To understand and accept who we are as daily recipients of God's love and grace is equivalent to the fresh flow of blood that brings new nutrients to the wound.

Sharing stories with others, sharing our pain with Christ, forgiving ourselves and others is equivalent to forming new walls and supports around the wound.

Shaping our lives differently by seeking to forgive and reconcile with our enemies or to restore something that was lost because of our actions is equivalent to building a protective roof over the wound.

When we choose to follow this process, our scars become marks of honor, hope and morality. They are like seals or stamps that firmly declare our opposition to hatred and violence, signs that grace is at work in us and is producing the healthy fruit of faith, hope and love. Our scars equip us to become peacemakers and thus to fulfill the standard of Jesus: "blessed are the peacemakers, for they will be called children of God" (Matt 5:9 NIV). This is how we become people who love – even our enemies.

Bibliography

Lloyd, R., J. Nyamutera, R. Schudel, and K. Bresser. *Healing the Wounds of Ethnic Conflict,* Facilitators Guide. Geneva: Le Rucher Ministries, 2011.

Morley, J. *All Desires Known.* London: SPCK, 1994.

Rohr, R. *Things Hidden*. Cincinnati: Franciscan Media, 2008.

Steward, J. *From Genocide to Generosity*. Carlisle: Langham Global Library, 2015.

———. *Insights on Dreams and Visions.* Unpublished paper, 1999.

9. R. Rohr, *Things Hidden* (Cincinnati: Franciscan Media, 2008), 25.

16

The Civil War in the DRC and Trauma

Bishop Muhindo Isesomo

Introduction

The Democratic Republic of Congo (DRC) is the second largest country in Africa, with an area of 2,345,000 km^2 and a population of around 70 million from 450 ethnic groups. The DRC was colonized by Belgium and became independent on 30 June 1960. The official language is French and four national languages, which are Lingala, Swahili, Tshiluba and Kikongo. Since 1960 the DRC has been led by the following presidents: Joseph Kasavubu (1961–1965), Mobutu Sese Seko[1] (1965–1997), Laurent Desiré Kabila (1997–2001) and Joseph Kabila Kabange (2001–Jan 2019).

Roots of Trauma

The major root of trauma in the DRC is the ongoing civil war. The first civil war was in 1964, which was led by Pierre Mulele. After that war, the second president Mobutu Sese Seko took power and ruled for more than thirty years as a dictator.

In 1996, the Congolese people were tired of the dictatorial leadership of Mobutu, and there was a rebel movement in the east of the DRC called AFDL (Alliance de Force Democratic pour la Liberation). This movement, which was

1. Full name: Mobutu Sese Seko Koko Ngbendu Wa Za Banga; original name: Joseph-Désiré Mobutu.

led by Laurent Desiré Kabila, fought against Mobutu's power and successfully chased him out of the country on 17 May 1997. From this war of liberation, trauma began in the DRC through the following events.

Constant Gun Violence

War is emotionally painful and distressing because it overwhelms people's ability to cope with life changes. When armed groups are fighting, they use big guns around the poor villages. Many innocent people die because of these attacks, and many others become traumatized by the constant gunfire. They cannot sleep or eat anymore; they are always looking for a way to run away from the village. On top of this, schools close, churches close, and epidemic diseases come to the villages.

Looting of Civilian Property

In many regions in the DRC, especially in the east, when the armed groups are fighting they loot people's properties. When they fight in the villages, they take food, goats and cows; when they fight in cities, they loot shops, vehicles, motor bicycles.

Before 1991, the DRC never experienced this sad looting of people's properties. But from this time onward, many people have suffered because of looting. This very bad situation has left many people poor, to the point that there is not even enough for the people who live in the villages to eat. Even though many people have enough land to dig and grow crops, or keep cattle, or fish, it has become difficult to do so because of insecurity. This is very traumatizing.

Presence of Rebel Groups

In many villages in the east of the DRC, people live with the rebels. There are so many different rebel groups in the region, some coming from other countries, others coming from other tribes and others created from within the tribes. The young people in some villages, wanting to protect their parents and relatives, group themselves and start fighting against other rebel groups or against the loyal army. The population quickly becomes victimized, because when these young people get guns from the dead bodies of other rebels or loyal soldiers, they start asking for taxes from their own people, and this becomes another source of trauma. In 1964 one rebel group lead by Pierre Mulele fought the government, but now there are many rebel groups in different provinces in the country. This causes confusion among the civilians because they don't know who the loyal army is and who the rebels are, because everyone is very well armed.

Displacement of the Population

Because of the civil war, people are not stable in their settlements. In most cases, when the rebels or soldiers occupy a village, they block all the roads so that no one can come in or go out. Because people have no other option, many of them run into the forests, where they are killed by wild animals.

When the loyal army is trying to follow the rebels, they fight even if there are civilians in the village. This pushes the poor population to flee in a hurry, leaving all their property behind for the fighters. These displaced people try to get to the big cities, but they don't have anywhere to sleep or eat. Most are hosted by church members and others live in small camps without any assistance.

Kidnapping by Armed Groups

The practice of kidnapping has come with war in the DRC, not only in villages but also in town where there is little security. Kidnapping has become another way to raise funds for war. When the rebels or soldiers kidnap someone, they fix a price for his or her release, usually somewhere between $1000 and $10,000 USD. If this price is not paid, the kidnapped person will be killed by the kidnappers. Many families have to sell their land to release their children, which leaves them helpless. This practice causes people to travel in fear wherever they go.

Sexual Violence

Most people enrolled in the armed forces and rebel groups are men and boys. If there are women, they have usually been kidnapped, apart from a few who enroll themselves. The army groups rape these women, as do some other men, especially those who are addicted to drugs and alcohol.

Because most Congolese people live by agriculture, they have fields in rural areas where they can plant beans, maize, sweet potatoes, Irish potatoes, bananas, cassava, and so on. When women go to their fields looking for food, the armed people living in the bush appear and do sexual violence against them. This brings a lot of trauma and causes the separation of marriages.

Destruction of Property

The ongoing civil war in the DRC has caused the destruction of many properties. The armed groups have destroyed and looted properties such as schools, churches, hospitals, shops and civilian homes.

During the war, it can be difficult to live together as families in houses because of the fear that when rebels come, they will kill everyone in the family. So sometimes whole villages come to a school and live there. The teaching stops, and people destroy everything in the classrooms for firewood. This also occurs in churches and hospitals in many villages. The victims of these atrocities live in trauma.

Massacre of Innocent People

Massacring people with machetes is a new experience in the region, but thousands of people have lost their lives during the ongoing civil war. There have been machete massacres in Beni territory, which is part of our diocese, and many children have become orphans. Between 2015–2016, more than two thousand people have been killed by armed groups living in the bush. They came into the villages during the night and attacked people and killed them with machetes. Some of the bodies were buried but others were abandoned. This sad situation has caused many people to live in trauma.

Corruption

In villages operated by rebel groups, there are no government services – no police, leaders, schools, hospitals. Everyone must obey the orders of the rebel leader. He fixes the taxes he wants, and people have to obey and pay so that they will not be killed. In towns where the rebels are not in control, all the government leaders, including the police, run away from the villages, and they also fix expensive taxes, making life too hard on the local people.

Injustice

When some people leave their land in the villages, those who don't leave or have a lot of money in the towns, claim that the pieces of abandoned land belong to them. After war stops in some areas, people quarrel because of the land, and the magistrates give the right to the land to those who have money.

In the DRC we have good laws in writing, but they are not applied or used. The laws are only on paper. Because of this, human rights are not respected, which contributes to corruption in the government. Sadly, in some schools, students are buying marks from their teachers, and young girls who don't have money are selling their bodies sexually.

Freedom without Control

Because the country law is not respected, people live without any control. This is the reason we are facing the violent reaction of so many rebel armed groups. Those who are working in political offices do what they want against the loyal leadership. There is no respect for government authorities. This causes the poor civilian people to live in trauma.

Consequences of the Civil War and Trauma

The continual civil war in the DRC has traumatized many people and had the following consequences.

High Poverty Rate

People who were living in villages, growing their own food on their own land, have left their villages and come to live in the cities as displaced people, where they don't have houses, food or jobs. Their village properties have been looted by armed groups, which causes them to live in poverty. In big cities, most families only eat once a day. There is no breakfast or lunch, only something to eat around 9 p.m. before going to bed.

Unemployment

The government is not creating employment for people, and those who are self-employed have to pay very expensive taxes. Many young people are finishing their studies, but there are not jobs for them. This is one of the reasons that young people join the rebel groups because they can get money from people by force. Even those who are working are not paid by the government, which is why corruption is everywhere. This is another source of trauma.

Widows and Orphans

Another cause of the continual civil war is the presence of many widows and orphans, who have no assistance from the government after their husbands or parents are killed by armed people. Most of the widows and orphans don't have shelter, food, clothes, or access to medicines, school, and so on.

Physical Suffering

The continual fighting has created the following results from 2014 to April 2018:

2,459	People killed
1,657	People kidnapped
7,376	Women raped
2,883	Houses burnt
31	Vehicles burnt
39	Schools destroyed
182,800	People displaced

This has brought about high blood pressure and trauma among more than 80 percent of the population in the eastern part of the DRC, which has also caused premature death, as most people die when they are less than fifty years old.

Loss of Hope for the Future

Because of all these atrocities, many people live in fear and do not have hope for the future. Some do not want to plan for the future because they do not expect to live for long, especially since they are surrounded by rebel groups who might attack and kill them at any time. When people go to bed in the evening, they do not know if they will wake up in the morning.

Alcohol and Drug Abuse

Traumatized people, especially the unemployed youth, are becoming addicted to alcohol and drugs, thinking that they will help them forget the problems they are facing. But the addiction only adds problems on top of other problems. Some are dying abruptly when they use alcohol and drugs without having something to eat. The statistics show that the eastern region of the DRC has the highest rate of people with addictions.

Loss of Trust in Political Leaders

When a society sees all these atrocities take place in a country where the government remains silent, the civilians no longer trust the political leaders. Civilians do not understand how a very rich country such as the DRC can continue to suffer in this way. It is very tiresome when the people cry out to the government, but there is no response to their cries.

Doubt within the Church

Since this problem started in 1990, church members have been praying, hoping that God would put an end to the atrocities. But some are getting tired because there is no change at all. Some are saying, "If God does exist, how and why can he allow all those atrocities to happen to us?" The attendance at church services is reducing, and church members are questioning God's protection.

Role of the Church

The local church, though it is traumatized as well, does not keep silent in the midst of this sad situation. Church leaders are continuing to encourage Christians to pray and stand firm in their faith in the Lord Jesus Christ.

The word of God in Romans 12:13–15 (NLT) says, "When God's people are in need, be ready to help them. . . . Bless those who persecute you. . . . Be happy with those who are happy, and weep with those who weep." The local church is very involved in helping needy people through the following activities.

Raising a Prophetic Voice

The word of God in Ezekiel 33:1–7 guides what should be done by Christians when war comes to the land. In the DRC, the population voted for some Christians to be their representatives in parliament. The local church leaders are approaching political leaders to give them advice about how to govern the country under God's fear and control.

Church leaders are calling upon the rebel groups to stop their atrocities and join the loyal army if they want to work as soldiers.

Church leaders are preaching the gospel among the loyal militaries in different camps and also creating a chaplaincy in each military camp. In 2008–2010, we had a gospel campaign among militaries in the east of the DRC and reached 16,340 military personnel, where 7,680 people decided to receive Jesus Christ as their personal Savior and Lord.

Churches are also preaching the gospel in prisons, and many prisoners are repenting and being baptized.

Exercising Hospitality

Church members, including the poor, are hosting displaced people of war in their families, feeding them and providing medicine for their care. Currently, we have 8,240 displaced people living in our city from rural areas: 1,892 women, 1,260 men, 2,298 boys, 2,790 girls, and 54 orphans.

Praying for Persecutors

The local church is praying for persecutors so that the Holy Spirit may touch them, transform them and bring them to true repentance. As a result of these prayers, some rebels are leaving the bush and joining the loyal army.

Challenges for the Church

Even though there is freedom for people to spread the gospel in the DRC, the church is facing many challenges. The many problems identified here are making a roadblock and preventing the church from achieving its mission. Some activities that should be done by the government are being tended by the church, such as building schools, paying school teachers, building hospitals and health centers and taking care of displaced people.

The church is moving ahead to spread the holistic gospel, which will transform people spiritually, physically, morally, socially, economically and intellectually. We hope that through the preaching of the holistic gospel, the DRC will have good roots that will produce good fruits.

Conclusion

The ongoing civil war has split the country and left the population of the DRC helpless. The consequences of the civil war are significant, and they need to be worked upon so that people may recover their normal lifestyles. We thank God for the courage he has given to church ministers and other humanitarian workers, who are working so hard to reduce trauma among the most affected people. We extend thanks to all who have welcomed the displaced people in their homes. May God bless them richly.

17

Trauma Healing and Reconciliation in Sub-Saharan Africa

The Role of the Church

Gladys K. Mwiti

Introduction

Africans believe that the world is like a spider's web. When one part is touched the whole web trembles. Similarly, Christians belong to the Body of Christ, with each one as part of the whole. When one part ails, the rest is affected. Sub-Saharan Africa is part of the worldwide community. Mental health and trauma urgently need attention in society today. World Health Organization (WHO) estimates that one in four people in the world will be affected by mental or neurological disorders at some point in their lives. Around 450 million people currently suffer from such conditions, placing mental disorders among the leading causes of ill-health and disability worldwide, with depression as one of the major leading factors. WHO estimates that more than 300 million people are now living with depression, an increase of more than 18 percent between 2005 and 2015. The trauma of sub-Saharan Africa is in essence the distress of the world, suggesting that the global church should share the burden that this suffering places on the African church.

Africa is a continent at the crossroads. Many perceive her as a sleeping economic giant with masses of unexploited resources. However, layers of psychological trauma weigh down the social capital of her young population, creating hopelessness and threatening progress. On the other hand, the church of Jesus Christ has a massive presence in Africa. As the bearer of sustainable hope and lasting transformation in a world of grief, loss and brokenness, she has the power and mission to declare the presence of God – the healer. Holistic healing involves an active response to distress, encapsulating categories such as diagnosis and treatment, medical and non-medical, religious and culturally indigenous, technological and non-technological, all within the majority and minority world. Indeed, the song of healing is sung in many tongues.

This paper examines the challenge of psychological trauma in sub-Saharan Africa: the impact of layers of grief and loss from the AIDS pandemic, broken promises of colonialism – historical and new – wars and ethnic strife, poverty and economic standstills, terrorism and foreign control and the reality of compromised resiliency among a people who will not, howbeit, be broken. The church, a present and respected voice, should be the healing hope of millions who struggle. We showcase the role played by the church in trauma healing after the 1994 Rwanda genocide and also explore the utility of the Oasis Africa Center for Transformational Psychology Ripple Effect Model® for adapting lessons learned in Rwanda to other disaster situations.

Historical and Socioeconomic Context

Sub-Saharan Africa lies south of the Sahara Desert and comprises forty-seven countries, which have a combined population of over 960 million.[1] The area has experienced significant economic growth and includes some of fastest emergent economies in the world. However, sub-Saharan Africa has also been called a region in transition, with many nations in between conflict and reconciliation, disease and healing, illiteracy and education, stagnation and development, war and peace, poverty and prosperity, hope and despair, a land between the East and the West. On the one hand, the region still has some of the wealthiest natural resources, and most of them are still unexplored. Lawson-Remer and Greenstein[2] argue that although Africa holds 60 percent of the world's platinum deposits, more than 40 percent of the world's gold, and almost 90 percent of the world's diamonds as well as massive oil reserves, it remains the world's poorest continent. Millions live in poverty and lack common resources, tilling land under which *un-extracted* diamonds lie, and

1. The World Bank, 2015.

2. See T. Lawson-Remer and J. Greenstein, "Beating the Resource Curse in Africa:

where the blood of their kindred is constantly poured as a few individuals, local and foreign, seek to control her treasures. Sub-Saharan Africa also faces major economic, social and political challenges due to corruption, misrule, tribalism and poverty.[3]

Religious Context

The sub-Saharan church is alive and growing. There is a throb of hope in every village and a commitment to a faith that is alive, creating optimism for a better tomorrow. Anna Bono observes that Christianity is Africa's first religion, with 46.53 percent Christians, 40.46 percent Muslims and 11.8 percent African traditional religions.[4] Christianity is the predominant religion in thirty-one African countries. Projections indicate that if the current trend continues, African Christians will form the largest continental bloc of the faith in ten years, outgrowing Europe and the Americas. These projections have unfathomable historical, cultural and political significance, outcomes that will change not only Africa but global Christianity as well.

The influence of the church can be tapped to become a channel of healing and reconciliation, with a special focus on care and counsel as mission. The Bible gives us the promise of healing, renewal and restoration. Jesus Christ, the healer who abides with the broken, can bring healing and transformation through the African church, generating a ripple effect of "oaks of righteousness" springing up across Africa (Isa 61:3, 11 NIV). As promised in Isaiah 61, these healed and restored wounded healers can, in turn, rename, reclaim and remember shattered communities for a greater Africa (vv. 3–5). This call to care and counsel should become a new approach to church missions in sub-Saharan Africa in this decade.

Isaiah 61, which was also cited by Jesus Christ (Luke 4:16–21), sums up the role of the church in the healing of the nations. In this context, healing refers to Christ's transforming power that changes the poor, brokenhearted, captives and prisoners into "oaks of righteousness" (v. 3). In my book on Christian counseling from an indigenous perspective, which I co-authored with A.

---

3. A Global Effort, *Africa in Fact: The Journal of Good Governance Africa* 3 (2012): 20–23. Online. See O. N. Awojobi, "Corruption and Underdevelopment in Africa: A Discourse Approach," *International Journal of Economics, Commerce, and Management* 2, no. 10 (2014): 3–10.

4. A. Bono, "The Predicament of Christians in Sub-Saharan Africa: Italian Atlantic Committee," University of Turin, accessed 8 February 2015, http://www.comitatoatlantico.it/?studi=the-predicament-of-christians-in-sub-saharan-africa.

Dueck, we discuss the reality that Africa can be described as a dismembered continent, where the wounded and broken become healers that can rebuild broken walls and renew ruined cities.[5]

The Art of Holistic Healing

Holistic healthcare is an integrated approach that takes care of the whole person, not simply symptoms and disease. Holistic healing recognizes that body, mind, spirit, emotions, relationships, social and societal context are all integrated and inseparable. As complete interdependent systems, when one ails, the whole is affected. Holistic health calls for care practitioners who do more than just identify and treat a specific ailment.

Traditionally, healing from a Western perspective is associated with medicine and the practice of the biomedical model, where physicians prevent, diagnose and cure disease.[6] In essence, *cure* rather than *care*, became the primary intention of medicine, and the physician's responsibility became "curer of disease" rather than "healer of the sick."[7] While the reality of holistic healing far surpasses curative medicine, the former is often not discussed in scientific literature.

Egnew argues that holistic healing can be operationally defined as the personal experience of the transcendence of suffering, which involves wholeness, narrative and spirituality.[8] He defines healing as an intensely personal, subjective experience that involves a reconciliation of the meaning an individual ascribes to distressing events with his or her perception of wholeness as a person. This makes the understanding of healing a personal definition and experience rather than an external prescription or prognosis. The author believes that physicians need to appreciate that beyond recognizing, diagnosing, minimizing and relieving suffering, they also need to help patients transcend suffering.

Transcendence is often perceived as a spiritual term, and many scientifically trained medical practitioners do not perceive themselves as spiritual healers.

---

5. G. K. Mwiti and A. Dueck, *Christian Counseling: An African Indigenous Perspective* (Pasadena, CA: Fuller Seminary Press, 2006).

6. K. M. Ludmerer, *Learning to Heal* (New York: Basic Books, 1985), https://www.mercyships.org/surgeries/mental-health/; S. Toulmin, "On the Nature of the Physician's Understanding," *The Journal of Medicine and Philosophy* 1 (1976): 32–50.

7. S. Hauerwas, *Naming the Silences: God, Medicine, and the Problem of Suffering* (Grand Rapids: Eerdmans, 1990).

8. T. R. Egnew, "The Meaning of Healing: Transcending Suffering," *Annals of Family Medicine* 3 (2005): 255–262. doi:10.1370/afm.313.

However, this paper seeks to point out that one of the greatest failures of Western practitioners is the separation of human faculties rather than integration. Driven by the belief that what matters can be scientifically proven, Western medical practice has claimed a superior role for treating physical ailments at the exclusion of the psychological, spiritual, relational and social. This approach has labeled some practices as "mainline" and less scientific ones as "complementary." With this delineation, holistic health practitioners are supposed to employ complementary methods and alternative approaches to health in their practices.

Africans would object to this demarcation. Awofeso defines health as a dynamic state of well-being exemplified by a physical and mental potential, which gratifies the demands of life corresponding with age, culture and personal responsibility.[9] In traditional African medicine, healthcare services that include training, promoting and practicing health, fall within the principle of *umuntu*, where shared norms, taboos, tradition, culture, other-care, community support and shared wellness are the cornerstones of clinical practice. Healthcare that envelops such inclusive approaches to healing and wholeness finds greater acceptance by the population. Mhame, Busia and Kasilo argue that this kind of philosophical care embedded in African tradition makes traditional medicine practices acceptable and demanded.[10] They add that these approaches include curative services, general traditional healthcare services, mental health care, midwifery, bone setting, rehabilitative and promotional services that increase health awareness and develop positive attitudes and behaviors towards healthier living. Mhame, Busia and Kasilo believe that African philosophical clinical healthcare practice "is the bridge between people's well-being and life. It is the practice that is embedded in the tradition, culture and taboos that are still relevant to the way of life of Africans."[11] This kind of approach calls for interdisciplinary partnerships in healing and wellness as well as the practice of holism in order to maximize healthcare coverage.

Although Awofeso defines health as a dynamic state of well-being exemplified by a physical and mental potential, Africans recognize spirituality as a major contributor to wholeness through belief in God, participation in religious practices and, for Christians, belonging to a church family and

9. N. Awofeso, "In: Re-defining 'Health,'" *Üstün & Jakob* 83 (2005): 802.

10. P. P. Mhame, K. Busia and O. M. J. Kasilo, "Clinical Practices of African Traditional Medicine," *Africa Health Monitor* 13, World Health Organization, Africa Health Observatory (2010). Available at: https://www.aho.afro.who.int/en/ahm/issue/13/reports/clinical-practices-african-traditional-medicine, accessed 5 August 2017.

11. Mhame, Busia and Kasilo, "Clinical Practices."

community.[12] These factors influence individual perceptions about health and illness, healthcare and the sustainability of wellness.

In this regard, Africans do not separate the functions of the body from those of the soul. From a systemic perspective, the one impacts the other. African traditional wholeness is a balance, not only within the individual, but also with others and nature. Others include both the unborn and the departed. Health also includes balance between the spirit world and the realm of matter. Spirituality is not part of life, for all life is spiritual. Healing calls for balance between the visible world and the invisible, between the temporal and spiritual, between humanity and creation. For this reason, the church is the first place to seek healing for African Christians. The pastor and the Christian community are perceived as safe places to seek biblical healing, even before seeking medical help.

Biblical Principles of Holistic Healing

God is interested in wholeness and wellness. He designed the human being in a marvelous way, interlinking the spirit, mind and body to work together perfectly. Such a worldview is more holistic and relational,[13] interrelational and positive in nature.[14] Previous definitions of health were concerned with illness and the body and were considered in terms of isolated physiological systems.[15] A more holistic perspective has transformed the notion of health and wellness, suggesting that there are several principles that undergird wellness and healing.

The first principle of holistic healing begins with healthy spirituality that recognizes the reign of God and his omnibenevolence over humanity and, by extension, over every individual believer. God is not only all good but is absolutely and purely good. This awareness inspires transcendence of life ordered by knowledge of the eternal (John 17:3). Knowledge of God and awareness of his presence provides hope (Heb 11:6), for since God is present, he is interested in wellness: "I am the Lord who heals you" (Exod 15:26 NIV). From a cognitive behavioral perspective, this knowledge informs our thinking and perceptions about illness and wellness, for as we think, so we become

12. Awofeso, "In: Re-defining 'Health,'" 802.

13. J. Larson, "The Conceptualization of Health," *Medical Care Research and Review* 56 (1999): 123–136.

14. C. E. Westgate, "Spiritual Wellness and Depression," *Journal of Counseling & Development* 75 (1996): 26–35, http://dx.doi.org/10.1002/j.1556-6676.1996.tb02311.x.

15. W. McSherry and P. Draper, "The Debates Emerging from the Literature Surrounding the Concept of Spirituality as Applied to Nursing," *Journal of Advanced Nursing* 27 (1998): 683–691.

(Prov 23:7). The psychiatrist Frankl, in writing about his experiences in a Nazi concentration camp, stated that what destroys man is not suffering but suffering without meaning.[16] Transcendence and faith in God help people to find meaning and acceptance in the midst of suffering and chronic illness, making spirituality the basis of meaning and purpose for many people.[17]

There are times when God may not heal or deliver his children from death. Besides hope, transcendence creates trust, which arises from total dependence on the eternal and his will regarding each of his children. Trusting in God during times of illness is not passive resignation but active engagement with him through the process of lament. American theologian Brueggemann notes that when the human heart cries out unreservedly to God, it becomes an opportunity for a healing relationship between the wounded humanity and a caring God.[18] In the Psalms, we have accounts of deep cries in times of despair. Known as laments, individuals and communities offer raw, unrefined cries to God, which remind us that believers do not have to package their pain into tidy bundles before they ask God to intervene with healing. Often, David would cry to God: "Have mercy on me, LORD, for I am faint; heal me, LORD, for my bones are in agony. My soul is in deep anguish. How long, LORD, how long?" (Ps 6:2–3 NIV). After lament, there would either be rejoicing for God's healing or acceptance that God has chosen not to heal. Thanksgiving and trust are therefore major parts of healing.

The second principle of holistic healing has to do with maximizing physical care. Because our bodies are the temple of the Holy Spirit (1 Cor 6:19–20), we seek healing when we are sick and provide care for the ailing (Matt 25:36). The prevention of illness and healing are consistent interdependent realities. As stewards of all that God has given us, we live obediently through self-care in matters of diet, exercise and lifestyle, and this contributes to health and disease prevention.[19]

Disease prevention also includes care of the environment. The WHO is concerned that chronic, non-communicable diseases are rapidly becoming epidemic worldwide. Beyond lifestyle, nutrition and genetics, there is

---

16. V. E. Frankl, *Man's Search for Meaning: An Introduction to Logotherapy* (New York: Simon & Schuster, 1984).

17. J. P. Foglio and H. Brody, "Religion, Faith, and Family Medicine," *Journal of Family Practice* 27 (1988): 473–474.

18. W. Brueggemann, "The Psalms and the Life of Faith: A Suggested Typology of Function," *Journal for the Study of the Old Testament* 17 (1980): 3–32.

19. W. El, "Principles of Disease Prevention from Discovery to Application," *Soz Praventivmed* 39 (1994): 267–272.

growing concern that early life and ongoing exposures to bioaccumulated toxicants may cause chronic disease. This means that holistic healing needs to include prevention policies regarding a reduction of exposure, monitoring environmental pollution and engagement of public health in community education on avoidance of pollutants.[20] Where there is disease, the ability to access medical care when needed is critical, and so the church needs to engage in holistic ministry that includes running healthcare systems as well as partnering with public healthcare institutions.

The third principle of holistic healing entails the relationship between the body and mind, since from a systemic perspective, one affects the other. Poor physical health can lead to an increased risk of developing mental health problems. Similarly, poor mental health can negatively impact physical health, leading to an increased risk of some conditions. The WHO states that schizophrenia, depression, epilepsy, dementia, alcohol dependence and other mental, neurological and substance-use (MNS) disorders constitute 13 percent of the global burden of disease, surpassing both cardiovascular disease and cancer.[21] Depression is the third leading contributor to the global disease burden, and alcohol and illicit drug use account for more than 5 percent.[22] Poverty impacts both physical and mental processes. According to the WHO, the world's most ruthless killer and the greatest cause of suffering on earth is extreme poverty.[23] Abject want encompasses the inability to satisfy basic needs, a deficient control over resources and poor or absent education. Poverty alienates and has indirect effects on the development and maintenance of emotional, behavioral and psychiatric problems.

The fourth principle of holistic healing has to do with emotional care, a reality that is often ignored in wellness and healing. We have already discussed the interlinking of mental health and physical wellbeing. Depression, for example, a clinical status of mental health, may begin with emotional factors such as traumatic stress; if untreated, it can spiral into posttraumatic stress

---

20. M. E. Sears, and S. J. Genuis, "Environmental Determinants of Chronic Disease and Medical Approaches: Recognition, Avoidance, Supportive Therapy, and Detoxification," *Journal of Environmental and Public Health* (2012), article ID 356798, http://dx.doi.org/10.1155/2012/356798.

21. World Health Organization, "The Global Burden of Disease: 2004 Update" (2008), accessed 10 August 2017, http://www.who.int/healthinfo/global_burden_disease/2004_report_update/en.

22. World Health Organization (2010), *Atlas on Substance Use*, accessed 10 August 2017, http://apps.who.int/iris/bitstream/10665/44455/1/9789241500616_eng.pdf.

23. World Health Report, *Bridging the Gaps* (1995), accessed 10 August 2017, http://www.who.int/whr/1995/en/.

disorder (PTSD); if unchecked, it can gravitate into depression. Research indicates that after critical, life-threatening events, there is a relationship between PTSD, major depression, substance abuse and somatic complaints.[24] Many people naturally recover from traumatic stress, but a few may degenerate into PTSD due to various individual factors, such as poor resilience, a high number of prior life-threatening events, paucity of social support and absence of professional trauma counseling.

The fifth principle of holistic healing regards relational wellness. Healthy relationships enhance physical, mental, emotional spiritual and social wellbeing. Umberson and Montez note that social relationships, both in terms of quantity and quality, affect mental health, health behavior, physical health and mortality risk.[25] These effects have short-term as well as long-term effects on health and begin from childhood into adulthood, with cumulative consequences that affect health throughout the lifespan. The Bible teaches that no root of bitterness should be allowed to sprout in relationships because it causes much trouble (Heb 12:15) and if individuals continue to bicker, they will wear each other out (Gal 5:15). Living together in peace and unity is considered as oil on the head (Ps 133:2).

The sixth principle of holistic healing is the practice of a healthy biblical spirituality, which recognizes that spirituality is linked with health, and that caring for a whole person – physical, emotional, mental, relational and social – is inherently a spiritual activity. For the Christian, spiritual health involves the practice of Christian spiritual disciplines that enhance intimacy with God, giving God space to speak to us and guide us, bring us his power and transform us towards wellness.[26] These disciplines include solitude – where we pray, intercede, study and meditate in silence – as well as surrender – where we repent, confess, submit, fast and worship – along with service – where we engage in fellowship and witness.

Regarding meditation, Christians are warned against transcendental meditation, which is a technique for emptying the mind and becoming "one

---

24. C. S. North, A. Kawasaki, E. L. Spitznagel and B. A. Hong, "The Course of PTSD, Major Depression, Substance Abuse, and Somatization after a Natural Disaster," *Journal of Nervous & Mental Disease* 192 (2004): 823–829; D. G. Kilpatrick, K. J. Ruggiero, R. Acierno, B. E. Saunders, H. S. Resnick and C. L. Best, "Violence and Risk of PTSD, Major Depression, Substance Abuse/Dependence, and Comorbidity: Results from the National Survey of Adolescents," *Journal of Consulting and Clinical Psychology* 71 (2003): 692–700.

25. D. Umberson and J. K. Montez, "Social Relationships and Health: A Flashpoint for Health Policy," *Journal of Health and Social Behavior* 51 (2010): S54–S66, doi: 10.1177/0022146510383501.

26. Siang-Yang Tan and D. H. Gregg, *Disciplines of the Holy Spirit: How to Connect to the Spirit's Power and Presence* (Grand Rapids: Zondervan, 1997).

with the universe." It encourages participants to seek the answers to life's difficult questions within their own conscience instead of the word of God and leaves them open to deception from God's enemy, who searches for victims whom he can turn away from God (1 Pet 5:8). For the Christian, meditation centers on the word of God, his attributes, and the beauty of Jesus Christ, the great physician.[27]

When individuals, regardless of their faith, incorporate these powerful biblical principles of the Christian faith into their lives, spirituality and health connect and they tend to enjoy better health and well-being. Dale Fletcher, the founder of Faith and Health Connection, argues that as God's design, if we live according to biblical principles of wellness, we create an environment that favors good health. We maximize this through holistic self-care, remembering that we are stewards of our bodies, which are the temple of the Holy Spirit (1 Cor 6:19–20). This way, even if illness comes, we endure it while seeking peace, joy and hope.

Sub-Saharan Africa's Broken Walls

Memories of repressive colonialism, a legacy of betrayed trust and the weakening of Africa's governance all contribute to sub-Saharan Africa's broken walls. Kimenyi and Datta argue that two aspects have shaped politics in sub-Saharan Africa: politics of external influence and politics of power in the state.[28] The first aspect refers to an extension of colonial practices, where decisions for Africa were made externally, with little consultation of the recipients. This is how colonial governments controlled Africa, and this practice continues today by ignoring governments in the continent who have the capacity to be involved in decision-making. For example, decisions on aid in Africa by the World Bank and the International Monetary Fund often do not involve recipients, nor do they incorporate African views on felt needs and their solutions.

This non-inclusive decision-making has controlled aid and development funds coming to Africa, with the United Nations (UN) and the WTO prescribing conditions that should be followed, or demanding that donor funds

27. D. Fletcher, "The Spirituality-Health Connection: Why It Exists, A Christian Perspective," Annual Meeting of the Society for Spirituality, Theology and Health, Duke University (2009), accessed 16 August 2017, https://spiritualityandhealth.duke.edu/images/pdfs/fletcher.pdf.

28. M. S. Kimenyi and A. Datta, "Think Tanks in Sub-Saharan Africa: How the Political Landscape Has Influenced Their Origins" (London: Overseas Development Institute, 2011), accessed 1 February 2015, http://www.odi.org/sites/odi.org.uk/files/odi-assets/publications-opinion-files/7527.pdf.

be utilized with advisory from foreign experts. For example, in the late 1980s, the World Bank records that in public sectors of forty sub-Saharan nations, there were over 100 thousand donor-funded expatriate advisors utilizing more than $4 billion, nearly 35 percent of development assistance to the region.[29] This in essence marginalized policy making and strategy analysis by local experts and academics.[30]

The second aspect, the politics of power in the state, refers to where political authority is concentrated and how that control is disseminated. From independence, sub-Saharan Africa has moved from military rule (e.g. Uganda during the days of Idi Amin Dada) to single party politics (e.g. Kenya under President Daniel Arap Moi), where one individual controls governance. In these power vacuums, negative ethnicity and corruption have taken center stage, leaving people reeling from unsteady, self-centered leadership. However, a phase has come where with liberalization and new constitutions, decision-making is shifting to regional and county levels. Control that is vested in one person or ethnic group indicates that by handing over governance to local leadership, colonial powers have left unsustainable systems that have been buffeted since independence.

The Church: Paternalism, Moratorium or Partnerships?

As sub-Saharan Africa struggled through non-inclusive decision making in political and development initiatives, the same struggle faced church relations, where paternalism and non-inclusivity colored global missions and church planting. The African church started demanding either recognition as equal partners or the exit of missionaries in cases where mutuality could not be assured. Reverend John Gatu, the Kenyan Moderator of the Presbyterian Church of East Africa, proposed a moratorium on receiving money and missionaries from overseas to Africa. Christians were asked to rethink the nature of relationship between overseas mission agencies and the church in the Third World. To enable African Christians to collectively find their identity, missionaries were asked to withdraw for at least five years.[31] This was not a demand for total withdrawal of the global church from strategic

29. The World Bank, *Sub-Saharan Africa: From Crisis to Sustainable Growth* (Washington, DC: IBRD, 1989).

30. N. Van de Walle, "Economic Reform in a Democratizing Africa," *Comparative Politics* 32 (1999): 21–41.

31. Gerald H. Anderson, "A Moratorium on Missionaries?" *Christian Century* 91 (1974): 43–45.

partnerships and missions for the sub-Saharan church. Instead, the appeal was for an exploration of felt needs, an appreciation of gifts that could be utilized for the whole and for inclusive decision-making on shared partnerships. This would help the church, both local and universal, use her unique gifting to fulfill God's call for missions.[32]

Resource and Brain Drain

While the global church was debating about a moratorium, another factor was contributing to brokenness in Africa: the ongoing drain of human capital and natural resources that has left behind unsustainable economies and perpetuated poverty. Due to poor economies and an inability to sustain professionals in Africa, many choose the easier route of working and living away from home, a brain drain that includes the exodus of both human capital and the resources they would bring home. For example, healthcare professionals left their nations and many did not reinvest their resources back to their nations of origin.[33] Canada has a comparatively higher proportion of foreign-trained physicians from sub-Saharan Africa,[34] and this region as well as the Caribbean represents nine of the twenty locations with the highest emigration rates. This brain drain ends up lowering the number of medical personnel in developing nations.[35] Indeed, in 2005, Canada deliberately set aside $75 million for the recruitment and employment of foreign-trained healthcare professionals.[36]

The continual drain of wealth in sub-Saharan Africa includes the rape of natural resources whose trade does not benefit the nationals. Some companies exploit close links with corrupt political leaders and fuel conflict and civil wars in the region. Le Billon believes that there is a close relationship between natural resources, armed conflicts and sequential outcomes in history.[37] The problem often is not scarcity or abundance, but rather the "lootability" of those resources that links local corrupt leadership to international markets

32. G. Muzorewa, *The Origins and Development of African Theology* (Maryknoll: Orbis, 1985).

33. P. Collier, A. Hoeffler, and C. Pattillo, "Africa's Exodus: Capital Flight and the Brain Drain as Portfolio Decisions," *Journal of African Economies* 13 (2003): ii15–ii54.

34. F. Mullan, "The Metrics of the Physician Brain Drain," *New England Journal of Medicine* 353 (2005): 1810–1818.

35. Mullan, 1810–1818.

36. Labonte, et al., *The Brain Drain of Health Professionals from Sub-Saharan Africa to Canada* (Idasa & Queen's University, Cape Town: Southern African Migration Project, 2006).

37. P. Le Billon, "The Political Ecology of War: Natural Resources and Armed Conflicts," *Political Geography* 20 (2001): 561–584.

that exploit local instability. He argues that due to the fraud attached to this trade, African diamonds were recently labeled as *blood diamonds*, while those from developed nations were called *clean*.[38] His concern is that labels do not change anything. He argues that global partners should look at factors that contribute to the subjugation and poverty of would-be benefactors and take part in the eradication of the anomalies that continue to contribute to poverty in the midst of plenty. Labeling on its own, he believes, has the capacity to close legitimate markets for such products.

How much does the church understand these realities? Is the church in sub-Saharan Africa cognizant of her special mission as a restorer of the wounded and a rebuilder of broken walls? While appreciating the challenges that sub-Saharan Africa faces, the global church also needs to ask: "*Am I really my brother's keeper*?"

Sub-Saharan Africa's Opportunities and Challenges

Population Growth

In the coming decades, sub-Saharan Africa's youthful population will offer a powerful labor force and extensive consumer market to the world. Africa is the only region in the world where the population is projected to keep increasing throughout the twenty-first century. At present there are 1.2 billion people in Africa, more than five times the population in 1950. By 2050, it is estimated that Africa's population will double to 2.4 billion, eventually reaching 4.2 billion by the end of the century. This is roughly equal to the entire world's population in 1977. The same report estimates that by 2050, about 40 percent of all children globally will be in Africa, up from about 10 percent in 1950, and that 20 percent of the population will be young people between the ages of fifteen and twenty-five years.[39]

However, dangers lurk for the African child. The same UNICEF report notes that three in ten African children live in fragile and conflict-affected contexts, implying the need for programs to end conflict, on the one hand, and to protect children, on the other. The world is still reeling from the April 2014 abduction of 276 girls from the government secondary school in the town of Chibok, Borno State, Nigeria.[40] Many of these girls are still missing to

38. P. Le Billon, 580.

39. *Generation 2030/Africa*, UNICEF, 2014.

40. Anne Perkins, "200 Girls Are Missing in Nigeria – So Why Doesn't Anybody Care?" *The Guardian*, retrieved 14 October 2016.

date. This reality has major implications for the role of the church in building resiliency and mobilizing resources for the care and protection of vulnerable at-risk children.

Urbanization

Along with a population burst, Africa is rapidly urbanizing. In 2010, only 36 percent of the African population was urbanized. Projections indicate a rise to 50 percent by 2013 and 60 percent by 2050.[41] This will change the continent's landscape and bring many challenges through the proliferation of slums and urban poverty as well as increased inequality. The implication is that with inequality, there may be a rise in crime and insecurity, which will raise the level of traumatic stress already present among most of the population. The church in sub-Saharan Africa will need to prepare itself for urban ministry that focuses on resilience, poverty eradication, equality and justice.

Natural Resources

Sub-Saharan Africa's extensive natural resources also provide it with a strong advantage. Opportunities abide for agricultural development, especially with the enhancement of irrigation. Already, sub-Saharan Africa is making a mark in traditional and nontraditional agricultural exports, such as cut flowers from Kenya.

As churches serve the rural poor, there are opportunities to bring hope and empowerment in agriculture, especially with an emphasis on environmental stewardship. The message of caring for natural resources should be clear in the church's message of redemption. Rainwater catchment, creation of dams and irrigation can transform Africa into a breadbasket whose potentially irrigable land is 39.4 million hectares, but only 7.1 million, or 18 percent, is under irrigation.[42]

Sijali and Mwago feature a success story of the use of human-powered irrigation water pumps developed in Kenya and sold in the region.[43] Between

41. M. Ncube, *Urbanization in Africa* (Tunis, Tunisia: African Development Bank Group, 2012).

42. IFAD, "Agriculture Development in Republic of Mozambique," *Agriculture Support Programme Formulation Report,* working paper 2 (Rome: International Fund for Agricultural Development, 2005).

43. I. V. Sijali and M. G. Mwago, "Moneymaker Pumps: Creating Wealth in Sub-Saharan Africa," in *Yes Africa Can: Success Stories from a Dynamic Continent*, eds. P. Chuhan-Pole and M. Angwafo (Washington, DC: The World Bank, 2010).

1991 and 2009, these pumps transformed the livelihoods of small-scale farmers with incomes from as little as $100 to more than $10,000 annually. In addition, food in these households was available throughout the year, and the enriched family units were able to invest in other enterprises, such as dairy, poultry and transport, along with school fees for children. They were also able to offer employment to others as well as share the technology with their neighbors. This case study exemplifies the Christian values of environmental stewardship, utilization of resources and talents and being one's brother's keeper. If local churches were connected to such programs already present in their communities, congregations could become centers of training and equipping in agricultural innovation, output and community transformation. These practical actions would alleviate poverty and other related negative social and psychological consequences, thereby enhancing good neighborliness in the community.

Technology and Transformation

Information technology (IT) is another resource that is transforming sub-Saharan Africa. The mobile phone has become a leading communication device in the region's consumer market, with users utilizing the device for activities normally performed on desktops and laptops. In a 2014 report, GSMA, a global association of mobile service providers, revealed that the mobile industry is driving explosive economic growth in sub-Saharan Africa. Over the past five years, the region is the fastest growing area for both connections and unique subscribers. By June 2014, there were 608 million connections, representing the highest proportion of mobile versus fixed line connections in the world.

The IT service is in use by consumers, governments, learning institutions and businesses across Africa. The current forecast is that over the next six years, sub-Saharan Africa will witness the highest growth of any region in the number of smartphone connections, with 525 million links in the region by 2020, growth that will account for more than half of the total global connection base. The GSMA report states that mobile industry growth could also generate a gross domestic product (GDP) increase of $40 billion, representing 0.54 per cent of the total GDP in the region by 2016.

In recent years, many Christians in Kenya have started coming to church carrying their smartphones or iPads instead of print Bibles. This enables them to use their devices to read several translations of the Bible at the same time as well as take notes. Some of the people reaping great profits from IT are Christian music artists, whose songs can be purchased by smartphone users as ring tones. There is also a scramble to sell mobile apps by various designers with government and nongovernmental organizations (NGOs), using the system to take services to poor and rural people. These amenities create opportunities for the church to create holistic psycho-education apps and also to use the available technology to propagate the transforming message of the gospel. Churches have started uploading sermons online a few days after Sunday worship, meaning that intentional communication with suffering masses can become a channel of healing and reconciliation.[44]

Renzenbrink notes that 75 percent of the world's poor do not have bank accounts. They are either impeded by distance or face technical hindrances.[45] For sub-Saharan Africa, the answer has become mobile money. Kenya leads the world in mobile money transactions.[46] *Safaricom*, Kenya's largest mobile network operator, launched M-Pesa (mobile money) in 2007. Currently, this platform is now used by over seventeen million Kenyans, a figure that is equivalent to more than two-thirds of the adult population. About 25 percent of the country's gross national product flows through M-Pesa. Already, Kenyans are using M-Pesa for church offering and tithing, which suggests that there are many opportunities to train church members on ways and means to save money and transact business so as to use the mobile platform to fight poverty.

Sub-Saharan Africa's Threats to Healing and Reconciliation

Bereavement and Loss

Africa has not adequately dealt with the emotional impact of the AIDS pandemic, which has caused a multiplicity of death and loss. Children have lost parents and breadwinners, the continent's health has been compromised and community resiliency has been broken. These losses have taken place along with the ongoing threat of unemployment, poverty, and malnutrition.[47]

---

44. G. Ganiel, "Reconciliation – The Missing Ingredient in Peace and Conflict Resolution Studies?" In *African Christianity, Churches & Reconciliation* (2011), accessed 9 February 2015, http://www.gladysganiel.com/category/zimbabwe/.

45. A. Renzenbrink, "75% of Poor Don't Have Bank Accounts," *CNN* (2012), accessed 22 January 2014, http://edition.cnn.com/2012/04/19/business/poor-bank-accounts/index.html?iref=allsearch.

46. "Why Does Kenya Lead the World in Mobile Money?" *The Economist* (2013), accessed 22 January 2015, http://www.economist.com/blogs/economist-explains/2013/05/economist-explains-18.

47. E. A. Keene Reder, "Grief and Bereavement," in *A Clinical Guide to Supportive and Palliative Care for HIV/AIDS*, eds. L. Gwyther, A. Merriman, L. M. Sebuiya and H. Schietinger (Alexandra, VA: Global Partners in Care, 2006).

Emotional and psychosocial support is often omitted in planning HIV and AIDS interventions for Africa. At the top of such an agenda is mother-child transmission, healthcare, economic development, education, and so on. In 2013 alone, an estimated 1.3 million people died of AIDS-related causes, although the number fell by 39 percent between 2005 and 2013.[48] Every single funeral represents a brokenhearted family and a grieving community as well as the use of precious resources for burial procedures and a concern about caring for orphaned children.

By 2011, of the 16.6 million children (aged 0–17) who had lost one or both parents to AIDS, 14.8 million were in sub-Saharan Africa.[49] Care for this population often omits emotional support, with claims that in some cultures, children cannot understand the permanence of death.[50] However, such omissions may hinder healthy maturation and interfere with children's ability to solve problems.[51] Daniel adds that the failure to mourn effectively can lead children to ruminate about the parent's death and resulting loss.[52] Rumination takes away mental and emotional energy from more gainful enterprises, such as school performance, and may encourage feelings of shame and guilt.[53] The church in sub-Saharan Africa is positioned to become a safe place for the care of orphans and vulnerable children. Christians have Christ's message of love, acceptance, comfort and hope to meet the psychosocial needs of AIDS survivors.

Refugees and Internally Displaced Persons

War, conflict, displacement and the refugee situation are major concerns in sub-Saharan Africa. The Bible recognizes the role of Christians in protecting and caring for refugees and sojourners as well as in fostering the message

---

48. "Fact Sheet," *UNAIDS* (2014), accessed 24 January 2015, http://www.unaids.org/en/resources/campaigns/2014/2014gapreport/factsheet.

49. United Nations, *Uniting for Universal Access,* report of the Secretary General, 28 March 2011.

50. M. Daniel, *Hidden Wounds: Orphanhood, Expediency and Cultural Silence in Botswana* (Norwich: PhD, School of Development Studies, University of East Anglia, 2005), http://hdl.handle.net/1956/3294.

51. M. B. Snipstad, G. T. Lie and D. Winje, "What Do Tanzanian Children Worry About?" *African Journal for AIDS Research* 4 (2005): 183–193.

52. Daniel, *Hidden Wounds.*

53. K. Wood, E. Chase and P. Aggleton, "Telling the Truth Is the Best Thing: Teenage Orphans' Experiences of Parental AIDS-Related Illness and Bereavement in Zimbabwe," *Social Science & Medicine* 63 (2006): 1923–1933.

of peace. Due to loss, grief, trauma and multiple displacements in volatile situations, many displaced people experience breakdown of support systems, hopelessness, depression and abject poverty. Poverty is defined not only as an insufficiency of basic life necessities but also as the fear of having inadequate shelter and not knowing where the next meal will come from.[54]

The 1951 UN refugee convention identified a refugee as someone who, for fear of persecution due to race, religion, nationality, membership of specific social group or political alliance, is outside their home country and places themselves under the protection of the host nation. During World Refugee Day, the United Nations High Commissioner for Refugees (UNHCR), António Guterres, observed that peace is dangerously in deficit today. We are seeing the immense costs of not ending wars and failing to resolve or prevent conflict.[55] His UNHCR report added that by the end of 2013, for the first time since World War II, the number of displaced persons – refugees, asylum-seekers and internally displaced people – exceeded fifty million.

The UNHCR also reports that in the Central African Republic, since the anti-Balaka militia overran the capital of Bangui in December 2013, there are already 425 thousand refugees, most of them in Cameroon and southern Chad, nations that are already receiving thousands of refugees from the violence in Northeastern Nigeria.[56] In 2014, UNHCR and partners appealed for US $210 million to support basic life-saving initiatives – mainly food, medical care and shelter. But these masses have also experienced psychological trauma and grief. They have lost their nationhood, hope and meaning, which has left them broken and mentally challenged. Many arrive with stories of burnt villages, violence, murder and sexual violence. Others carry physical wounds and the pain of bereavement.

The factors that contribute to Africa's refugee and migration problem are political oppression, poor economies and the destruction of the environment, with conflicts and wars contributing to the largest bulk of displaced people.[57] Churches may need to create proactive interventions for refugee ministries along with other departments of the church that focus on the following.

---

54. P. Hammond, *Biblical Principles for Africa* (Howard Place, South Africa: Christian Liberty Books, 2003).

55. "World Refugee Day: Global Forced Displacement Tops 50 Million for First Time in Post-World War II Era," UNHCR (2014), accessed 26 January 2015, http://www.unhcr.org/53a155bc6.html.

56. "UNHCR and Partners Seek US $331 Million to Help Refugees from Central African Republic," *UNHCR* (2015), accessed 23 January 2015, http://www.unhcr.org/54c24f356.html.

57. J. K. Akokpari, "The State, Refugees and Migration in Sub-Saharan Africa," *International Migration* 36 (2002): 211–234.

First, the needs of displaced people call for global and local partnerships to ensure pastoral care and counseling as a mission of the church. Churches can help people make meaning of their situations by adapting their pastoral theology to the cultures and concrete situations of the target population. Pastoral care needs to be inspired by Christ's redemptive concern for humankind and the call of Christians to become bearers of that message to a broken world.[58]

In addition to becoming safe places for aliens, the church also needs to seek to prevent factors that create instability by teaching and modeling environmental stewardship. Environmental stewardship involves encouraging participation, forging partnerships, creating public policies and generating awareness about the preservation of water and natural resources.

Christians in sub-Saharan Africa are seeking a God who will save their souls, still the clamor of poverty, calm the warring, end pandemics, right compromised political leadership and stop the fallacious promises of the prosperity gospel. These needs outline the mission of the church for healing and reconciliation.

Terrorism and Islamization

By 2012, 46.53 percent of the African population was Christian, 40.46 percent was Muslim and 11.8 percent was traditional African religions.[59] Islamic ultra-fundamentalists believe that it is immoral for there to be more Christians than Muslims in Africa, a factor that may determine whether the world will be more Muslim or Christian. This has resulted in *islamization*, an organized religious, economic and cultural movement that has led to war, conflict and terrorism. Camouflaged as religious conflict and given different names in different nations, this well-funded campaign to spread Islam has left many people dead and displaced. The names Boko Haram in West Africa and Al Shabab in Kenya are one and the same thing. Sponsorship of this movement originates from oil-rich Muslim states in the Middle East, the Persian Gulf and North Africa.[60] Saudi Arabia, Kuwait, Qatar and the United Arab Emirates channel funds through heavily supported Islamic NGOs, for example, the

---

58. T. R. Mobie, "The Persistent Traumatic Experience of Poverty among Refugees from Mozambique Living in the Bushbuckridge Area, a Challenge to Pastoral Care," Master's thesis (Pretoria, South Africa: Faculty of Theology, University of Pretoria, 2005), accessed 26 January 2015, http://upetd.up.ac.za/thesis/available/etd-07242008-124610/unrestricted/dissertation.pdf.

59. Bono, "Predicament of Christians."

60. M. Terdman and R. Paz, "Islamization and Da'wah in Contemporary Sub-Saharan Africa: The Case of the African Muslim Agency (AMA)," African Occasional Papers, vol. 1, Global Research in International Affairs (GLORIA) Center: The Project for the Research of

Muslim World League based in Saudi Arabia and World Islamic Call based in Libya, among others.

From 1970 onwards, these Islamic NGOs have concentrated on thwarting and neutralizing the work of West-supported Christian NGOs with activities directed towards rural poor non-Muslims who are willing to convert to Islam. Development is carried out as a form of *da'wah*, which is Arabic for proselytizing or preaching Islam, and is funded through *zakat*, a form of tax that every Muslim must pay. *Zakat* can be utilized for the extension of Islam, military preparedness and payment for religious leaders, as well as *jihad*.[61]

In Africa, *da'wah* initiatives include the construction of schools and mosques as well as training Muslim teachers, imams and legal experts with specialized instruction in universities and seminaries local and abroad. Islamic campaigns in South Sudan, a region considered as a barrier to the southern spread, has caused two million deaths and displaced four million to date.[62]

In sub-Saharan Africa, Kenya in particular is targeted for terrorism because its majority Christian population is perceived as an obstacle for the islamization of eastern Africa and sub-Saharan Africa.[63] In the past, the equator was the boundary between a dominantly Muslim north and a mainly Christian south. Islamization is determined to push southwards into the prime Christian missionary zone. An example of *da'wah* is the primarily Kuwait-sponsored African Muslim Agency (AMA), one of the most effective Islamic charitable organizations, which is based in Angola and has already established itself in Sierra Leone, Mali, Mozambique, Madagascar, Zimbabwe, Angola, the Gambia and South Africa.[64]

Bono observes that the future of Christians in sub-Saharan Africa is dependent on the global willpower to work against radicalism and terrorist groups.[65] The global church will need to understand and appreciate Africa's

---

Islamist Movements (PRISM) (2007), accessed 27 January 2015, http://www.e-prism.org/images/PRISM_African_papers_vol_1_no_2_--_Islamization_and_Dawah_-_July_2007.pdf.

61. Anita M. Weiss, *Islamic Reassertion in Pakistan: The Application of Islamic Laws in a Modern State* (Syracuse: Syracuse University Press, 1986).

62. R. Downing, *Darfur Crisis – Brief History, Analysis, Strategies* (2015), accessed 14 February 2015, http://www.untilall.org/Darfur.htm.

63. Kefa Otiso, "Kenya in the Crosshairs of Global Terrorism: Fighting Terrorism at the Periphery," *Kenya Studies Review* 1 (2009): 107–132.

64. M. Terdman, "Factors Facilitating the Rise of Radical Islamism and Terrorism in Sub-Saharan Africa," African Occasional Papers, vol. 1, Global Research in International Affairs (GLORIA) Center: The Project for the Research of Islamist Movements (PRISM), 2007, accessed 6 February 2015, http://www.terrorism-info.org.il/data/pdf/PDF_07_061_2.pdf.

65. Bono, "Predicament of Christians."

economic, social and political challenges as well as partner with the African church to counter the spread of Islam, religious intolerance and terrorism.

Individual and Community Trauma

Widespread trauma (for example, from terrorist attacks) creates chaos, fosters disorientation, disconnects survivors from lifelines and destabilizes masses of people within a short time.[66] A traumatic impact distorts preexisting schemata of the self and the world, altering an individual's perceptions about personal invincibility and the safety and predictability of the world.[67] Repeated traumas induce chronic stress that leads to a loss of social networks, poor coping and other secondary stress reactions that wear out individuals over time.[68] These outcomes severely compromise resilience and threaten peace.

Various studies define resilience as the ability of an individual or community to normalize after an overwhelming experience or adversity.[69] Resilience is determined by four aspects: the individuals' or community's economic status, level of connectedness or social support, access to information and communication after the incident (such as psycho-education and empathetic media exposure) and ability to establish shared action towards coping with the trauma.[70]

---

66. J. Miguel-Tobal, A. Cano-Vindel, H. Gonzalez-Ordi, I. Irruarrizaga, S. Rudenstine, D. Vlahov and S. Galea, "PTSD and Depression after Madrid March 11 Train Bombings," *Journal of Traumatic Stress* 19 (2006): 69–80.

67. S. D. Solomon and D. M. Johnson, "Psychosocial Treatment of Posttraumatic Stress Disorder: A Practice-Friendly Review of Outcome Research," *Journal of Clinical Psychology* 58 (2002): 947–959.

68. C. L. Parker, D. J. Barnett, G. S. Everley and J. M. Links, "Expanding Disaster Mental Health Response: A Conceptual Training Framework for Public Health Professionals," *International Journal of Emergency Mental Health* 8 (2006): 101–110.

69. W. Adger, "Social and Ecological Resilience: Are They Related?" *Progress in Human Geography* 24 (2000): 347–364; G. Bonanno, "Loss, Trauma, and Human Resilience: Have We Underestimated the Human Capacity to Thrive after Extremely Aversive Events?" *American Psychologist* 59 (2004): 20–28; B. Pfefferbaum, D. Reissman, R. Pfefferbaum, R. Klomp and R. Gurwitch, "Building Resilience to Mass Trauma Events," in *Handbook on Injury and Violence Prevention Interventions*, eds. L. Doll, S. Bonzo, J. Mercy and D. Sleet (New York: Kluwer, 2008), 347–358.

70. F. H. Norris and S. P. Stevens, "Community Resilience and the Principles of Mass Trauma Intervention," *Psychiatry* 70 (2007): 320–328.

Rebuilding Resilience in Sub-Saharan Africa

In August 2014, Al Shabab terrorists attacked Nairobi's prestigious Westgate Mall, a mass rendezvous of the city's cosmopolitan population. Besides the massive loss of property, at least seventy-two people died, over two hundred were wounded and hundreds were traumatized.[71] To respond to the Westgate Mall attack, the Kenya Psychological Association (KPA) mobilized a team of four hundred counselors and psychologists to offer Psychological First Aid (PFA) to survivors. Most of these psychologists are also committed Christians who believe they are serving God through volunteering to serve in trauma interventions. PFA is recommended as the first crisis response after a disaster and uses multidisciplinary teams to link survivors to medical care, social support, psycho-education and religious services. In addition, the KPA desired to build community among people of different faiths.

Before the terrorist attack, Westgate Mall was a well of diversity and tranquility. In the aftermath, the place became associated with anger, confusion, fear, sadness and mistrust. Negative sentiments began to develop among Muslims and Christians due to fear, resentment and negative press narratives. Many Christians preached and modeled acceptance of people from other religions, emphasizing unity in diversity. Moderate Islamic leaders pointed out that not all Muslims are terrorists. Government leaders urged the populace not to retaliate. However, the church could have been more proactive and visible through united deliberate practical support on a wider scale. Whereas Hindus were organized to help through the Visa Oshwal Community Center, Christian assistance was not as coordinated, although individual believers served as much as they could.

Breaking Cycles of Violence

Dominic Ongwen, a Ugandan Lord's Resistance Army (LRA) commander, was brought to the International Criminal Court (ICC) to stand trial for war crimes. At age fourteen, Ongwen was abducted and forced to join the LRA.[72] Abducted children who are forced to become child soldiers are exposed to traumatic experiences that rob them of childhood and leave them with layers of post

---

71. "Kenyans Donate Blood for Westgate Victims," IRIN News (2013), http://www.irinnews.org/report/98814/kenyans-donate-blood-westgate-victims.

72. Aljazeera, "Ugandan Rebel Commander Makes First ICC Appearance," *War and Conflict* (2015), accessed 9 February 2015, http://www.aljazeera.com/news/2015/01/ugandan-rebel-commander-icc-appearance-150126145242754.html.

trauma reactions. Derluyn, Broekaert, Schuyten and Temmerman interviewed 301 former LRA child soldiers.[73] Abducted at a mean age of 12.9 years, almost all the children reported that they had experienced several traumatic events, including seeing people killed and witnessing suicides. Ninety seven percent of the children reported significant posttraumatic stress reactions.

Research indicates that during adulthood, abused children often become perpetrators, especially if the cycle of abuse-perpetration is not broken.[74] They become locked up in destructive tendencies and so identify with the abuser. With millions of orphans in Africa, child abuse, neglect and abductions pose a challenge that calls for church partnerships to create safe places for vulnerable children. There is an urgent need for child psychosocial support in sub-Saharan Africa.[75]

Nurturing Economic Development

Poverty in Africa is a by product of traumatic experiences, such as war, terrorism, displacement, poor leadership and compromised economies. Indeed, trauma is related to underdevelopment. In 2012, the World Bank reported that 501 million people (47% of the population) in sub-Saharan were living in poverty,[76] nations need to seek new methods of rebuilding economies. The cooperative method is providing such solutions. Many players, such as the International Labor Organization (ILO), the UN, International Cooperative Alliance (ICL) and the European Union (EU), agree that the cooperative enterprise can considerably reduce poverty.[77]

Kenya tops Africa in its use of microfinance, savings and credit cooperatives (SACCOs), a movement where the poor have a voice and power to control their own savings. SACCOs have created ownership and control of the sale of products in farming, fishing, transport, microfinance, dairy, fishing, housing,

---

73. I. Derluyn, E. Broekaert, G. Schuyten and E. D. Temmerman, "Post-Traumatic Stress in Former Ugandan Child Soldiers," *Lancet* 363 (2004): 861–863.

74. M. Glasser, I. Kolvin, D. Campbell, I. Leitch, and S. Farrelly. "Cycle of Child Sexual Abuse: Links between Being a Victim and Becoming a Perpetrator," *British Journal of Psychiatry* 179 (2001): 482–494.

75. Daniel, *Hidden Wounds.*

76. The World Bank. Poverty & Equity Data Portal, 2012, http://povertydata.worldbank.org/poverty/home/.

77. N. C. Kuria, "Cooperatives in Social Development. Developing and Promoting Good Practices and Addressing Internal Challenges: The Experience of Cooperative Insurance in Kenya, in Particular and Africa in General," accessed 9 February 2015, http://www.un.org/esa/socdev/social/meetings/egm11/documents/Kuria-Cooperatives.Kenya.pdf.

credit and agro-processing. Kenya's Cooperative Bank, which originated as a cooperative microfinance, is currently the fourth largest among forty-four banks in Kenya. Of Kenya's population of forty million, an estimated 63 percent participate directly or indirectly in the cooperative enterprise, with 80 percent of Kenyans deriving their income from the movement.[78]

Realizing the need to get involved in poverty eradication, many churches in Kenya have SACCOs with growing membership – for example, Methodist SACCO, Anglican SACCO, Catholic SACCO, and so on. One of the SACCOs linked to Deliverance Church is named *Ukombozi* (Deliverance) SACCO and has the tagline, "Overcoming Poverty Together." The church is called to minister to the holistic needs of its people as well as train them in finance management, savings, enterprise development, farming initiatives and tithing out of their increase. Some Kenyan church SACCOs are involved in real estate and buy land and build residential homes. Eradicating poverty encourages development and breaks cycles of helplessness and hopelessness that chain traumatized communities to paucity generation after generation. SACCOs in Kenya contribute to social support and community resiliency.

Healing and Reconciliation in Sub-Saharan Africa

Learning Villages Rather than Silos

Africans believe that it "takes a village to raise a child." In order to raise an army of workers for the healing, reconciliation and restoration of sub-Saharan Africa, Christian professionals must learn to give away their skills through mentoring, coaching and apprenticeships rather than learning more and more within their particular specialty for personal gain. Chan and Collins describe mentoring that will empower people to learn new skills that will provide insight for daily living and help them prepare for times of crisis.[79]

Church departments that work independently without teaming with others for the benefit of the whole body are called *silos*. They compromise the wider vision of the congregation by placing their goals ahead of the shared ministry. Some churches internationally or in sub-Saharan Africa might also be working in disregard of the needs of the whole Christian body. Some factions of Islam are destructive but are nonetheless united in one common purpose, especially

78. Kuria, "Cooperatives in Social Development."

79. S. Chan, *Spiritual Theology: A Systematic Study of the Christian Life* (Downers Grove: InterVarsity Press, 1998); G. R. Collins, *Christian Coaching: Helping Others Turn Potential into Reality* (Colorado Springs: NavPress, 2001).

when it comes to the islamization of Africa. Global Christianity can no longer afford to live in silos because the whole body shares the impact of the "pain or gain" approach.

Seminaries and universities can also function as silos, remaining oblivious to the needs of the world around them. Rather than connecting scholarship with current global or local needs, research is theoretical, and completed projects are filed away in libraries. To connect with reconciliation needs in sub-Saharan Africa, both theology and scholarship need to remain current, practical, relevant, connected and realistic so that graduates can make a difference in their communities. In the same vein, the global church can partner with African seminaries and universities to avail resources – personnel, materials and funds – that will ensure that training is practical, professional and sensitive to indigenous needs, whether modern or postmodern.

The Church: Raising up *Oaks of Righteousness*

Contrary to the warped theology of the prosperity gospel in Africa, churches are not destinations or treasure houses for poor people to seek riches and wealth.[80] Instead, places of worship are equipping stations for community transformation. Any theology that focuses on an individual's blessing and leaves out God-given responsibilities for ministry is open to abuse and ridicule. Similarly, congregations that become destinations easily turn into churches of disconnect that are oblivious to the needs of the poor. As discussed in the "Religious Context" section of the introduction above, churches that are agents of transformation produce "oaks of righteousness" (Isa 61) who carry on the healing and reconciliation work of God. Disconnected churches function *in* the community but are divorced from its pain; connected churches work *with* the community, sensing its pain and suffering and wanting to be part of its healing.

Church's Role in Reconciliation and Peace Building

In order to facilitate reconciliation, some countries have held truth, justice and reconciliation commissions (TJRC) as part of transitional justice, an investigation that helps nations address legacies of past human rights abuses.[81]

80. F. Samen, *The Prosperity Gospel in Africa: The Cultic Activity Promises Worldly Power in Place of the Power of the Cross,* World Real Matters, WNG.Org (2014), accessed 10 February 2015, http://www.worldmag.com/2014/11/the_prosperity_gospel_in_africa.

81. N. Kritz, *Transitional Justice: How Emerging Democracies Reckon with Former Regimes* (Washington, DC: US Institute for Peace, 1995).

The South African church may not have been at the frontline of their nation's Truth and Reconciliation Commission (TRC), but Merwe is convinced that the church there has the unique capacity to ensure that root factors are addressed so that true reconciliation can be realized.[82] Indeed, in South Africa, due to their associations with the faith and structures of the church, nonreligious civil society initiatives recognize the special role that the church should play to enable sustainable reconciliation.

Reconciliation is not an event but a process that should bring about inner healing before making outward commitments to peace. Reconciled people are able to rebuild trust and commit to shared values and norms that undergird the rule of law.[83] Reconciliation, then, is more than a sum total of the impact produced by the implementation of transitional justice, even if it included trials of perpetrators, truth seeking, investigations and compensations. If hearts are not touched and transformed, the shaking of hands by hostile parties will be a synthetic process, and animosities will resume soon after. Peace is not built on a truce but on transformed relationships.

Christians in sub-Saharan Africa come from diverse indigenous cultures that have their own traditional ways of reconciliation, and these should be encouraged if they do not negate biblical doctrine. For example, in rural Angola and Mozambique, war is viewed as pollution, and those who engage in it have to be ritually cleansed of their felonies before they can be embraced by the community.[84] Such locally conducted rituals restore perpetrators back to their communities and facilitate reconciliation and peace. Unless communities own the reconciliation and peace building process, impunity may continue in sub-Saharan Africa, despite the frequency of transitional justice measures.

Church's Role in Mental Health and Trauma

Many people who have watched the movie *Hotel Rwanda* remember the scene in Hotel Mile Coline in Rwanda, when the United Nations was evacuating their

82. Hugo van der Merwe, "The Role of the Church in Promoting Reconciliation: In Post-TRC South Africa," in *Religion and Reconciliation in South Africa*, eds. A. Chapman and B. Spong (Philadelphia: Templeton Foundation Press, 2003), 269–281.

83. P. de Greiff, "The Role of Apologies in National Reconciliation Processes: On Making Trustworthy Institutions Trusted," in *The Age of Apology: Facing Up to the Past*, eds. M. Gibney, R. E. Howard-Hassman, J. M. Coicaud, N. Steiner (Philadelphia: University of Pennsylvania Press, 2008).

84. A. Honwana, "Children of War: Understanding War and War Cleansing in Mozambique and Angola," in *Civilians in War*, ed. S. Chesterman (Boulder, CO: Lynne Rienner Publishers, 2001).

staff into Nairobi. The plane carrying the personnel landed in Nairobi on the night of 10 April, six days after the onset of the genocide. The United Nations asked me and a team of three others to ensure that the staff received debriefing over the next several months, before deployment or the next step to safety.

By September 1994, a deep concern grew inside my heart for the psychological loss and grief experienced by the Rwandans who had survived the genocide. I started asking everyone about the trauma services that the Rwandans were receiving. The major organizations were offering relief services, but no one seemed to have a trauma program in place. Eventually, after much frustration, my husband asked me, "You keep asking everyone what they are doing about trauma in Rwanda. What are you doing yourself?"

"Me!" I responded. "What can I do? I am only an African woman. I have no money. And Oasis Africa is only a small Non-Governmental Organization (NGO). What can I do?"

He responded, "Gladys, I thought that you are a committed Christian before all these other things!"

I did not respond but asked our few staff members to pray with me. I also started preparing to go to Rwanda should God open the door.

My first step was to prepare biblically based and psychologically informed materials to take to Rwanda. By December that year, through funding from Tear Fund, which is supported by churches in the UK, we printed a trauma counseling manual, a Bible study booklet with ten studies on critical topics dealing with healing and transformation and thousands of tracts discussing case studies of hope in times of brokenness and loss.

In February 1995, I was invited to Rwanda to speak about trauma healing to the first pastors' retreat after the genocide. Sixty clergy hosted by the Anglican Church of Rwanda gathered to seek healing from God and to ask what was next for the broken nation. In June 1995, the Anglican Church in Rwanda invited Oasis Africa to return, in partnership with Tear Fund. Over the next three years, we trained over one thousand trauma counselors, who experienced the beginning of their own healing journeys, and then took the training, materials and Bible studies back to their communities in order to replicate the training. Over two thousand copies of our trauma healing book in Kinya-Rwanda were used in this program, along with thousands of other booklets and tracts.

Willow Creek Church and other American churches partner with World Relief in the Democratic Republic of Congo (DRC) on a reconciliation project, offering counseling to many survivors of war and other atrocities. In a 2009 report by World Relief, Lynne Hybels tells stories of Congolese pastors who received training to cross boundaries and bring healing and reconciliation in their warring communities.[85]

All over Africa, individual Christians serve on the frontline in mental health and trauma situations. Since my specialization is mental health and trauma, I have spent many days over the years providing psychosocial support for humanitarian staff working in very difficult situations. On a recent assignment, I spent eleven days with World Vision International staff in Somalia, Puntland and Somaliland. From a logistical perspective, it was not easy to fly into these regions that have experienced recent skirmishes with Al Shabab and ISIS instigators. The region is also arid and drought stricken, with many needy clients. Many individuals serving in these locations are Christians who are supported by churches and Christian organizations in Africa and abroad.

To ensure that holistic mental health and trauma care is achieved in programs such as these, sending organizations first need to ensure that mental health and trauma programs are included in the overall objectives of the organization. For example, Open Doors, an organization that evangelizes unreached regions of Africa, has a trauma unit and are currently writing modules for staff and community trauma intervention training. Second, each organization needs to include staff psychosocial support in their human resource policies. Finally, Bible seminaries should include mandatory mental health and trauma training in their pastors' training curriculum. Indeed, more and more theological seminaries in Africa are beginning to offer training in counseling and counseling psychology. These include St. Paul's University and Africa Leadership University in Kenya, South African Theological Seminary and Africa Theological Seminary, among others. Pastors who understand the need for mental health and counseling in the church can guide the formation of holistic, multi-leveled programs that will serve members and also provide outreach programs for the wider community.

In a previously published article, I explain that church-based counseling programs should have four levels.[86] Level 1 is *encouragement,* where all Christians can serve. Modeling after Barnabas, all Christians can practice the compassion of Jesus Christ by learning to listen to those who are suffering and to offer them hope, comfort and encouragement (Acts 4:36; 2 Cor 1:3–7).

---

85. World Relief Report, 14 Oct 2009, "Lynne Hybels Speaks Out," https://reliefweb.int/report/democratic-republic-congo/congo-war-lynne-hybels-speaks-out.

86. G. K. Mwiti, "The Call of the Church to Care and Counsel as Mission Indigenous Christian Counseling in Africa," in *Global Mental Health and the Church* (Klosbachstr, Zurich: LIT VERLAG GmbH & Co. KG Wien, 2017).

Level 2 is for *paraprofessionals*, where those who serve should have a basic understanding of mental health (a diploma or bachelor's degree), such as counselors or BA psychology majors. These individuals can help administer and coordinate church-based mental health programs as well as train groups in basic psycho-education.

Level 3 is for *professionals* with masters or doctoral degrees in counseling, psychology or clinical psychology. Some Level 3 individuals may offer supervision to Level 1 and 2 individuals as needed. Level 3 professionals may create psycho-education training materials, offer professional leadership for church-based mental health and trauma programs and also offer professional counseling or psychotherapy services as necessary.

Finally, Level 4 *supervisors* offer supervision to Level 3 individuals. All individuals should work under the spiritual authority of the church pastor(s) and be continually trained in the integration of faith and practice. Services at all four levels should be offered as a time tithe ministry and should not be charged to the church account. Working on these four levels, the church can transform mental health and trauma services into missional caring and counseling for the community.

As a channel for healing, the church is a social support microsystem and is the strongest, most protective factor in moderating trauma recovery.[87] It is perceived as the bearer of a message of reconciliation and hope that can positively impact individuals, leadership, governance, politics, cultural networks and international relations. However, in as much as the church is equipped to advocate for the protection of the most vulnerable – children, women, the displaced and refugees – there is a "hole in holistic mission," because mental health issues are often left out of the agenda of the church.[88] Trauma healing is no longer the preserve of mental health professionals. Churches in sub-Saharan Africa can partner with the global community to create multidisciplinary teams to promote trauma healing, peacebuilding and resiliency in traumatized communities. In our book *Christian Counseling*, A. Dueck and I emphasize that such programs should be professionally sound, indigenously sensitive and biblically accurate.[89] Hobfoll and others are convinced that this is the way to

87. M. A. Hoffman and T. Kruczek, "A Bioecological Model of Mass Trauma: Individual, Community and Societal Effects," *The Counseling Psychologist* 20 (2011): 1–41.

88. B. Smith, G. K. Mwiti and S. Cruz, presentation made at Lausanne Leadership Forum, Bangalore, India, 2013, http://conversation.lausanne.org/en/resources/detail/13178#.VOLl7oXx8y4.

89. Mwiti and Dueck, *Christian Counseling*.

promote security, peace and shared effectiveness to empower individuals and communities against hopelessness after traumatic incidents.[90]

Conclusion

In this paper, I have examined factors that contribute to trauma in sub-Saharan Africa, acknowledging that the local and global church share the negative outcomes of this brokenness. However, though sub-Saharan Africa has suffered decades of devastation from wars, terrorism, corruption, the AIDS pandemic and the rape of her natural resources, the region retains a thriving Christian faith, many underdeveloped resources and bustling economies that challenge the odds.

The challenge is for the global church to partner with Christians in sub-Saharan Africa to mobilize resources in order to reclaim, reconcile, rebuild and rename broken communities. Such initiatives will be sustainable if they can tap indigenous resources for healing and transformation as well as utilize educated and trained church members. These initiatives can form church-based think tanks to identify needs and then harness and utilize indigenous resources for rebuilding and reconciliation. This will empower people and give them voice – not as recipients of knowledge, but as contributors and protagonists of their own development.[91]

Klein argues that as bearers of hope, every local church can become a center of healing and transformation through holistic mentorship, coaching and counseling services.[92] The failure of truth and justice commissions and peace initiatives that remain skin-deep indicates that the church has the opportunity to become translators of forgiveness as well as bearers and interpreters of reconciliation.

Equipping the wounded sub-Saharan Africa should never be conceived as the sole responsibility of an external agent. Many capacity-building initiatives assume that the mind of the beneficiaries is a *tabula rasa* or empty space waiting to be filled with externally packaged solutions. To equip suffering communities in Africa, the church must recognize that there is already a wealth

90. Hobfoll, et al., "Five Essential Elements of Immediate and Mid-Term Mass Trauma Intervention: Empirical Evidence," *Psychiatry* 70 (2007): 283–315.

91. World Bank. World Faiths Development Dialogue, 2004, http://siteresources.worldbank.org/DEVDIALOGUE/Resources/WFDD2001.pdf.

92. H. L. Klein, *Equipping Local Churches to Be Centres of Healing: Basic Steps to Develop a Self-Sustainable Local Church-Based Counseling Ministry* (Kempton Park, SA: AcadSA, 2009).

of solutions within these communities that is crying for recognition and needs to be set free to rebuild the broken.

Focused consistency will bring the ultimate success. The Christian idea of persevering in the face of trials will help the church navigate the course of healing for Africa until ripe, bountiful fruit emerges. At the 1987 inauguration of the South Africa Truth and Reconciliation Commission, Mwalimu Julius Nyerere, the former President of Tanzania, cited a story of African wisdom that he had heard from his father:

> *Wakasusu, nihe wagya?*
> *Nagya kwita Wanzugu.*
> *Oragya kutura?*
> *Ndagya Kusaya-sayamu, Ndinukira!*
>
> Rabbit, where are you going?
> I am going to kill the Elephant.
> Can you do it?
> Well, I'll try, and try again.

Bibliography

Adger, W. "Social and Ecological Resilience: Are They Related?" *Progress in Human Geography* 24 (2000): 347–364.

Akokpari, J. K. "The State, Refugees and Migration in Sub-Saharan Africa." *International Migration* 36 (2002): 211–234.

Aljazeera "Ugandan Rebel Commander Makes First ICC Appearance." *War and Conflict*. Accessed 9 February 2015. http://www.aljazeera.com/news/2015/01/ugandan-rebel-commander-icc-appearance-150126145242754.html.

Anderson, Gerald H. "A Moratorium on Missionaries?" *Christian Century* 91 (1974): 43–45.

Awofeso, N. "In: Re-Defining 'Health.'" *Üstün & Jakob* 83 (2005): 802.

Awojobi, O. N. "Corruption and Underdevelopment in Africa: A Discourse Approach." *International Journal of Economics, Commerce, and Management* 2, no. 10 (2014): 3–10.

Bonanno, G. "Loss, Trauma, and Human Resilience: Have We Underestimated the Human Capacity to Thrive after Extremely Aversive Events?" *American Psychologist* 59 (2004): 20–28.

Bono, A. "The Predicament of Christians in Sub-Saharan Africa: Italian Atlantic Committee." University of Turin, 2014. Accessed 8 February 2015. http://www.comitatoatlantico.it/?studi=the-predicament-of-christians-in-sub-saharan-africa.

Brueggemann, W. "The Psalms and the Life of Faith: A Suggested Typology of Function." *Journal for the Study of the Old Testament* 17 (1980): 3–32.

Chan, S. *Spiritual Theology: A Systematic Study of the Christian Life*. Downers Grove: InterVarsity Press, 1998.

Collier, P., A. Hoeffler, and C. Pattillo. "Africa's Exodus: Capital Flight and the Brain Drain as Portfolio Decisions." *Journal of African Economies* 13 (2003): ii15–ii54.

Collins, G. R. *Christian Coaching: Helping Others Turn Potential into Reality*. Colorado Springs: NavPress, 2001.

Daniel, M. "Hidden Wounds: Orphanhood, Expediency and Cultural Silence in Botswana." PhD dissertation, University of East Anglia, 2005. http://hdl.handle.net/1956/3294.

de Greiff, P. "The Role of Apologies in National Reconciliation Processes: On Making Trustworthy Institutions Trusted." In *The Age of Apology: Facing Up to the Past*, edited by M. Gibney, R. E. Howard-Hassmann, J. Coicaud and N. Steiner, 120–136. Philadelphia: University of Pennsylvania Press, 2008.

Derluyn, I., E. Broekaert, G. Schuyten, and E. D. Temmerman. "Post-Traumatic Stress in Former Ugandan Child Soldiers." *Lancet* 363 (2004): 861–863.

Downing, R. "Darfur Crisis: Brief History, Analysis, Strategies." 14 February 2015. http://www.untilall.org/Darfur.htm.

Egnew, T. R. "The Meaning of Healing: Transcending Suffering." *Annals of Family Medicine* 3 (2005): 255–262. doi: 10.1370/afm.313.

El, W. "Principles of Disease Prevention from Discovery to Application." *Soz Praventivmed* 39 (1994): 267–272.

Fletcher, D. "The Spirituality-Health Connection. Why It Exists: A Christian Perspective." Annual Meeting of the Society for Spirituality, Theology and Health. Duke University, 2009. Accessed 16 August 2017. https://spiritualityandhealth.duke.edu/images/pdfs/fletcher.pdf.

Foglio, J. P., and H. Brody. "Religion, Faith, and Family Medicine." *Journal of Family Practice* 27 (1988): 473–474.

Frankl, V. E. *Man's Search for Meaning: An Introduction to Logotherapy*. New York: Simon & Schuster, 1984.

Glasser, M., I. Kolvin, D. Campbell, I. Leitch, and S. Farrelly. "Cycle of Child Sexual Abuse: Links between Being a Victim and Becoming a Perpetrator." *British Journal of Psychiatry* 179 (2001): 482–494.

GSMA. "The Mobile Economy: Sub-Saharan Africa." Accessed 22 January 2013. http://www.gsmamobileeconomyafrica.com/GSMA_ME_SubSaharanAfrica_Web_Singles.pdf.

Hammond, P. *Biblical Principles for Africa*. Howard Place, SA: Christian Liberty Books, 2003.

Hauerwas, S. *Naming the Silences: God, Medicine, and the Problem of Suffering*. Grand Rapids: Eerdmans, 1990.

Hobfoll, S. E., P. Watson, C. C. Bell et al. "Five Essential Elements of Immediate and Mid-Term Mass Trauma Intervention: Empirical Evidence." *Psychiatry* 70 (2007): 283–315.

Hoffman, M. A., and T. Kruczek. "A Bioecological Model of Mass Trauma: Individual, Community and Societal Effects." *The Counseling Psychologist* 20 (2011): 1–41.

Honwana, A. "Children of War: Understanding War and War Cleansing in Mozambique and Angola." In *Civilians in War*, edited by S. Chesterman. Boulder, CO: Lynne Rienner Publishers, 2001.

International Fund for Agricultural Development (IFAD). "Agriculture Development in Republic of Mozambique." *Agriculture Support Programme Formulation Report, Working Paper 2.* Rome: International Fund for Agricultural Development, 2005.

IRIN News. "Kenyans Donate Blood for Westgate Victims," 2013. http://www.irinnews.org/report/98814/kenyans-donate-blood-westgate-victims.

Keene Reder, E. A. "Grief and Bereavement." In *A Clinical Guide to Supportive and Palliative Care for HIV/AIDS*, edited by L. Gwyther, A. Merriman, L. M. Sebuiya and H. Schietinger. Alexandra, VA: Global Partners in Care, 2006.

Kilpatrick, D. G., K. J. Ruggiero, R. Acierno, et al. "Violence and Risk of PTSD, Major Depression, Substance Abuse/Dependence, and Comorbidity: Results from the National Survey of Adolescents." *Journal of Consulting and Clinical Psychology* 71 (2003): 692–700.

Kimenyi, M. S., and A. Datta. "Think Tanks in Sub-Saharan Africa: How the Political Landscape Has Influenced Their Origins." London: Overseas Development Institute, 2011. Accessed 1 February 2015. http://www.odi.org/sites/odi.org.uk/files/odi-assets/publications-opinion-files/7527.pdf.

Klein, H. L. *Equipping Local Churches to Be Centres of Healing. Basic Steps to Develop a Self-Sustainable Local Church-Based Counseling Ministry.* Kempton Park, SA: AcadSA, 2009.

Kritz, N. *Transitional Justice: How Emerging Democracies Reckon with Former Regimes.* Washington, DC: US Institute for Peace, 1995.

Kuria, N. C. "Cooperatives in Social Development. Developing and Promoting Good Practices and Addressing Internal Challenges: The Experience of Cooperative Insurance in Kenya, in Particular and Africa in General." Accessed 9 February 2015. http://www.un.org/esa/socdev/social/meetings/egm11/documents/Kuria-Cooperatives.Kenya.pdf.

Labonte, R., C. Packer, N. Klassen, et al. *The Brain Drain of Health Professionals from Sub-Saharan Africa to Canada.* Idasa & Queen's University, Cape Town, SA: Southern African Migration Project, 2006.

Larson, J. "The Conceptualization of Health." *Medical Care Research and Review* 56 (1999): 123–136.

Lawson-Remer, T., and J. Greenstein. "Beating the Resource Curse in Africa: A Global Effort." *Africa in Fact: The Journal of Good Governance Africa* 3 (2012): 20–23.

Ludmerer, K. M. *Learning to Heal.* New York: Basic Books, 1985. Mercy Ships. https://www.mercyships.org/surgeries/mental-health/.

Le Billon, P. "The Political Ecology of War: Natural Resources and Armed Conflicts." *Political Geography* 20 (2001): 561–584.

McSherry, W., and P. Draper. "The Debates Emerging from the Literature Surrounding the Concept of Spirituality as Applied to Nursing." *Journal of Advanced Nursing* 27 (1998): 683–691.

Mhame, P. P., K. Busia, and O. M. J. Kasilo. "Clinical Practices of African Traditional Medicine." *Africa Health Monitor* 13 (2010). WHO. Africa Health Observatory. Accessed 5 August 2017. https://www.aho.afro.who.int/en/ahm/issue/13/reports/clinical-practices-african-traditional-medicine.

Miguel-Tobal, J., A. Cano-Vindel, H. Gonzalez-Ordi, et al. "PTSD and Depression after Madrid March 11 Train Bombings." *Journal of Traumatic Stress* 19 (2006): 69–80.

Mobie, T. R. "The Persistent Traumatic Experience of Poverty among Refugees from Mozambique Living in the Bushbuckridge Area: A Challenge to Pastoral Care." Master's thesis, Pretoria, SA: Faculty of Theology, University of Pretoria, 2005. Accessed 26 January 2015. http://upetd.up.ac.za/thesis/available/etd-07242008-124610/unrestricted/dissertation.pdf.

Mullan, F. "The Metrics of the Physician Brain Drain. *New England Journal of Medicine* 353 (2005): 1810–1818.

Muzorewa, G. *The Origins and Development of African Theology*. Maryknoll: Orbis, 1985.

Mwiti, Gladys K. "The Call of the Church to Care and Counsel as Mission: Indigenous Christian Counseling in Africa." In *Global Mental Health and the Church*, edited by U. Giesekus, B. M. Smith, and J. Schuster. Zurich: LIT Verlag, 2017.

———. *Trauma Interventions: An Integrated Psychosocial Trauma Program following 2014 Westgate Mall Terror Attack*. Nairobi, Kenya: In Press, 2016.

Mwiti, G. K., and A. Dueck. *Christian Counseling: An African Indigenous Perspective*. Pasadena, CA: Fuller Seminary Press, 2006.

Ncube, M. *Urbanization in Africa*. Tunis, Tunisia: African Development Bank Group, 2012.

Norris, F. H., and S. P. Stevens. "Community Resilience and the Principles of Mass Trauma Intervention." *Psychiatry* 70 (2007): 320–328.

North, C. S., A. Kawasaki, E. L. Spitznagel, and B. A. Hong. "The Course of PTSD: Major Depression, Substance Abuse, and Somatization after a Natural Disaster." *Journal of Nervous & Mental Disease* 192 (2004): 823–829.

Otiso, Kefa. "Kenya in the Crosshairs of Global Terrorism: Fighting Terrorism at the Periphery." *Kenya Studies Review* 1 (2009): 107–132.

Parker, C. L., D. J. Barnett, G. S. Everley, and J. M. Links. "Expanding Disaster Mental Health Response: A Conceptual Training Framework for Public Health Professionals." *International Journal of Emergency Mental Health* 8 (2006): 101–110.

Perkins, Anne. "200 Girls Are Missing in Nigeria: So Why Doesn't Anybody Care?" *The Guardian*, 23 April 2014. Accessed14 October 2016. https://www.theguardian.com/commentisfree/2014/apr/23/200-girls-missing-nigeria-care-sewol-tragedy.

Pfefferbaum, B., D. Reissman, R. Pfefferbaum et al. "Building Resilience to Mass Trauma Events." In *Handbook on Injury and Violence Prevention Interventions*, edited by L. Doll, S. Bonzo, J. Mercy and D. Sleet, 347–358. New York: Kluwer, 2007.

Renzenbrink, A. "World Bank: 75% of Poor Don't Have Bank Accounts." CNN, 2012. Accessed 22 January 2014. http://edition.cnn.com/2012/04/19/business/poor-bank-accounts/index.html?iref=allsearch.

Samen, F. "The Prosperity Gospel in Africa: The Cultic Activity Promises Worldly Power in Place of the Power of the Cross." *World Magazine*, 2014. Accessed 10 February 2015. http://www.worldmag.com/2014/11/the_prosperity_gospel_in_africa.

Sears, M. E., and S. J. Genuis. "Environmental Determinants of Chronic Disease and Medical Approaches: Recognition, Avoidance, Supportive Therapy, and Detoxification." *Journal of Environmental and Public Health* (2012): Article ID 356798. http://dx.doi.org/10.1155/2012/356798.

Sijali. I. V., and M. G. Mwago. "Moneymaker Pumps: Creating Wealth in Sub-Saharan Africa." In *Yes Africa Can: Success Stories from a Dynamic Continent*, edited by P. Chuhan-Pole and M. Angwafo. Washington, DC: The World Bank, 2010.

Smith, B., G. K. Mwiti, and S. Cruz. Presentation made at Lausanne, Leadership Forum, Bangalore, India, 2013. http://conversation.lausanne.org/en/resources/detail/13178#.VOLl7oXx8y4.

Solomon, S. D., and D. M. Johnson. "Psychosocial Treatment of Posttraumatic Stress Disorder: A Practice-Friendly Review of Outcome Research." *Journal of Clinical Psychology* 58 (2002): 947–959.

Snipstad, M. B., G. T. Lie, and D. Winje. "What Do Tanzanian Children Worry About?" *African Journal for AIDS Research* 4 (2005): 183–193.

Tan, Siang-Yang, and D. H. Gregg. *Disciplines of the Holy Spirit. How to Connect to the Spirit's Power and Presence.* Grand Rapids: Zondervan, 1997.

Terdman, M. "Factors Facilitating the Rise of Radical Islamism and Terrorism in Sub-Saharan Africa." In *African Occasional Papers* 1, no. 1 (2007). Global Research in International Affairs (GLORIA) Center: The Project for the Research of Islamist Movements (PRISM). Accessed 6 February 2015. http://www.terrorism-info.org.il/data/pdf/PDF_07_061_2.pdf.

Terdman, M., and R. Paz. "Islamization and Da'wah in Contemporary Sub-Saharan Africa: The Case of the African Muslim Agency (AMA)." In *African Occasional Papers* 1, no. 2 (2007). Global Research in International Affairs (GLORIA) Center: The Project for the Research of Islamist Movements (PRISM). Accessed 27 January 2015. http://www.e-prism.org/images/PRISM_African_papers_vol_1_no_2_--_Islamization_and_Dawah_-_July_2007.pdf.

The Economist. "Why Does Kenya Lead the World in Mobile Money?" 2013. Accessed 22 January 2015. http://www.economist.com/blogs/economist-explains/2013/05/economist-explains-18.

The World Bank. *Sub-Saharan Africa: From Crisis to Sustainable Growth*. Washington, DC: IBRD, 1989.

———. "World Faiths Development Dialogue: Key Issues for Development." *World Development Report 2001*. http://siteresources.worldbank.org/DEVDIALOGUE/Resources/WFDD2001.pdf.

———. Poverty & Equity Data Portal, 2012. http://povertydata.worldbank.org/poverty/home/.

The World Health Report. *Bridging the Gaps*. 1995. Accessed 10 August 2017. http://www.who.int/whr/1995/en/.

Toulmin, S. "On the Nature of the Physician's Understanding." *The Journal of Medicine and Philosophy* 1 (1976): 32–50.

Umberson, D., and J. K. Montez. "Social Relationships and Health: A Flashpoint for Health Policy." *Journal of Health and Social Behavior* 51 (2010): S54–S66. DOI: 10.1177/0022146510383501.

United Nations. "Uniting for Universal Access." Report of the Secretary-General, 28 March 2011.

UNAIDS. *Fact Sheet*. 2014. Accessed 24 January 2015. http://www.unaids.org/en/resources/campaigns/2014/2014gapreport/factsheet.

UNHCR. "World Refugee Day: Global Forced Displacement Tops 50 Million for First Time in Post-World War II Era." 2014. Accessed 26 January 2015. http://www.unhcr.org/53a155bc6.html.

———. "UNHCR and Partners Seek US $331 Million to Help Refugees from Central African Republic." UNHCR. 2015. Accessed 23 January 2015. http://www.unhcr.org/54c24f356.html.

UNICEF. *Generation 2030/Africa*. 2014.

van der Merwe, Hugo. "The Role of the Church in Promoting Reconciliation: In Post-TRC South Africa." In *Religion and Reconciliation in South Africa*, edited by A. Chapman and B. Spong, 269–281. Philadelphia: Templeton Foundation Press, 2003.

Van de Walle, N. "Economic Reform in a Democratizing Africa." *Comparative Politics* 32 (1999): 21–41.

Weiss, Anita M. *Islamic Reassertion in Pakistan: The Application of Islamic Laws in a Modern State*. Syracuse: Syracuse University Press, 1986.

Westgate, C. E. "Spiritual Wellness and Depression." *Journal of Counseling & Development* 75 (1996): 26–35. http://dx.doi.org/10.1002/j.1556-6676.1996.tb02311.x.

Wood, K., E. Chase, and P. Aggleton. "Telling the Truth Is the Best Thing: Teenage Orphans' Experiences of Parental AIDS-Related Illness and Bereavement in Zimbabwe." *Social Science & Medicine* 63 (2006): 1923–1933.

World Health Organization. *The Global Burden of Disease: 2004 Update*. 2008. Accessed 10 August 2017. http://www.who.int/healthinfo/global_burden_disease/2004_report_update/en.

———. *Atlas on Substance Use*. 2010. Accessed 10 August 2017. http://apps.who.int/iris/bitstream/10665/44455/1/9789241500616_eng.pdf.

World Relief Report, 14 Oct 2009, "Lynne Hybels Speaks Out." https://reliefweb.int/report/democratic-republic-congo/congo-war-lynne-hybels-speaks-out.

18

Trauma Healing in Men

William Foute

Background

Between 2007–2016, my wife and I had the privilege of seeing God heal hearts in Nigeria, West Africa. The primary vehicle we were trained to use was *Healing the Wounds of Trauma: How the Church can Help*, an interactive workshop that originated in central Africa and was developed by members of Wycliffe Bible Translators, using sound biblical and mental health practices.[1] Workshop participants wrestle with core questions, which build sequentially in the following order: (1) If God loves us, why do we suffer? (2) How can the wounds of our hearts be healed? (3) What happens when someone is grieving? (4) Response: Taking your pain to the cross. (5) And how can we forgive others? In addition to these five core lessons, there are other optional topics and traumas.

Approximately ninety minutes is given to each discussion, along with time for sharing personal pain with one another and with God and then taking that pain to the cross of Christ. The workshops have expanded to many corners of the world, including Nigeria. Due to the overwhelming demand for this ministry all over the world, the leadership of this movement has passed from Wycliffe to the American Bible Society, Trauma Healing Institute.[2]

Though we began serving in Nigeria in 1982, our trauma healing work began on a very part time basis in 2007 and then became our full time ministry

1. Harriet Hill, Margaret Hill, Richard Bagge and Pat Miersma, *Healing the Wounds of Trauma: How the Church Can Help* (New York: American Bible Society, 2004).

2. See http://thi.americanbible.org.

by 2014. Participants in our workshops shared about heart wounds that included childhood trauma from living in polygamous homes, being rejected because of their Christian conversion from African traditional religion or Islam, experiencing excessive corporal punishment, as well as adult trauma from betrayal and religious persecution from Fulani and Boko Haram terrorists. This last category often involved the loss of property, church burnings and the murder of friends and family. Many saw loved ones killed before their eyes. Some of our participants literally fled for their lives into the bush, sometimes crossing into Cameroon, ending up in refugee camps and not knowing the fate of loved ones for months. In fact, some of the parents of the Chibok girls,[3] are still waiting for their girls after three years.[4]

By God's grace, we were able to partner with several agencies who work with the persecuted church in Nigeria, both to bring healing to victims and to train others to bring healing to their flocks. This training included mentoring as we facilitated workshops together. In our interactive adult learning pedagogy, we replaced lectures with open-ended questions so that participants could learn through processing. Workshop facilitators drew these questions from the training manual, and a handbook guided the facilitators who typically worked in teams of two or three. Though the workshop materials were easy to use, facilitators were required to go through a week of training in order to be certified as an apprentice facilitator. The apprentice facilitator then began to facilitate healing groups. After further training and experience, an apprentice facilitator could qualify to become a master facilitator.

One practical question when leading trauma healing workshops or healing groups is whether to mix genders or separate men from women. Based on our experience, there is no easy or universal answer. However, we often find it helpful to separate men and women during the sharing and prayer part of the workshop, which usually takes place on the last session of each day. Because so much depends on culture, educational level and trust among the group, it is important to ask God for wisdom in planning.

---

3. In April 2014, 276 girls were abducted by Boko Haram terrorists from a government secondary school in Chibok, Borno State, Nigeria.

4. Ibrahim Sawab and Dionne Searcey, "Chibok Girls, 3 Years Later: Anguished Parents Still Wait," *New York Times*, posted on 14 April 2017, https://www.nytimes.com/2017/04/14/world/africa/chibok-girls-nigeria-boko-haram.html?_r=0.

Overcoming Obstacles to Healing in African Men

This paper investigates the way that African men have found healing for heart wounds or trauma. Trauma healing has been a "hard sell" for male leaders in African churches, because men tend to ignore or not understand heart wounds. They acknowledge that women have feelings but have a hard time admitting their own. Thus one of the greatest challenges for men in Africa along with many other cultures is to open up and share, particularly since many men won't cry in public. As Nana Darkoa Sekyiamah observes:

> The ways in which men are socialized in our societies predisposes the creation of a particular type of man. A man who is sexually unfaithful within monogamous relationships, unable to be openly expressive about his deep emotional and interior life to the majority of his male friends, and perhaps even more significantly unable to be emotionally true to himself. I'm thinking here of men from Ghana, but also men from Nigeria. Yet I don't think this is particularly a Ghanaian, Nigerian, West African or even an African problem. There is a part of men's socialization that almost seems universal in a global patriarchal world. And that part of men's socialization privileges being stoic, bottling up one's emotions.[5]

In our "global patriarchal world," sharing from the heart is not seen as strength, but rather a sign of weakness. Thus men hold feelings inside, especially tender feelings of pain and fear. It is okay for women to have and talk about feelings, but not men.

Furthermore, men who might share their pain often hold back because they do not trust other men to accept their pain and support them. Secrets are not always kept safe by others but end up being gossiped all over, to the embarrassment of the man who opened up.

Moreover, men are not as aware of what they feel. They may know when they are angry, but African men are often not able to sense their own fear, hurt, loneliness, grief or other "tender" feelings. They lack names for these feelings and do not even realize that such feelings are in their hearts.

Finally, male pride is threatened by the fear of what others may think. This fear of humiliation drives a man to protect his manliness.

---

5. Nana Darkoa Sekyiamah, "Men Do Not Cry," *This Is Africa*, posted on 17 September 2013, https://thisisafrica.me/men-not-cry/.

In light of these challenges, it is most encouraging to watch men overcome them and find healing for the wounds of their hearts. Following are a few examples of remarkable healing.

One denomination, more than others, has suffered at the hands of Boko Haram. Six hundred of their pastors lost their churches, their members scattered, and the pastors had to live as displaced persons far from home for safety. A leader from this denomination attended a trauma healing group. When it came time for him to share his pain, he bowed his head as he sat in front of the leaders of his denomination, quietly crying as he shared the devastation he and his church had suffered by terrorists. Then another pastor prayed for him.

Another man from the city of Bauchi shared a secret of abuse from his childhood, which he had never shared with another soul. He had the courage to share that painful story tearfully with a group of believers he hardly knew.

Dano lived and served as a pastor in Kano, which is at the heart of the Islamic region in Northern Nigeria. Some years ago he attended a trauma healing group in the Hausa language. At the end of the workshop, when there was an opportunity to share, Dano raised his hand and said, "I thank God for keeping me alive long enough to attend this workshop. I was able to forgive a fellow pastor, whom I said I would never forgive for what he did to me." This was a remarkable statement about the power of forgiveness, but Dano's history made it even more remarkable. On three occasions, his church had been burned by Muslim fanatics. Attackers poured gasoline on him to light him on fire, but then at the last minute decided not to finish him off. During the same attack, one of his sons ended up in the ICU after being beaten almost to death. Yet Dano had found it easier to forgive such atrocities than an offense from a fellow pastor!

In 2015, we met with some of the parents whose girls had been abducted from their secondary school in Chibok in the spring of 2014. Several of the men were resistant to talk about forgiving Boko Haram. They said over and over, "Don't talk to us about forgiveness; we just want our girls back." This was a heart-wrenching and difficult workshop for us to lead. But by the end of our time together, one of the dads, who still did not know if his daughter was alive or dead, said, "When our girls come home I can now see that we will need help."

These examples are true breakthroughs for African men in finding healing, and God's grace working deep in their hearts enabled them to take place. As I consider the defining characteristics of trauma healing workshops, I see three key factors that God has used to help African men with pain-filled hearts take counter cultural steps toward healing. Healing for men is more likely when their pain is: 1) shared, 2) expressed and 3) released.

Sharing Pain

When a group of Christian men, often church leaders or pastors, come together to find healing, they are admitting there is pain in their hearts. This makes it easier to have honest, face-to-face interactions rather than trying to keep up an image or façade. The workshop takes on a feeling of "shared neediness," where one man's vulnerability opens the door for others to share their pain. We see this modeled by Jesus: "And taking with him Peter and the two sons of Zebedee, he began to be sorrowful and troubled. Then he said to them, 'My soul is very sorrowful, even to death; remain here, and watch with me'" (Matt 26:37–38).

Expressing Pain

Pain is expressed in our workshops through corporate sharing and prayer, lamenting and drawing the story of a heart wound or trauma.

Corporate Prayer

One of the first places men can express pain is when we offer a time of sharing and prayer. On a volunteer basis, men come before the rest of the group and share a five-minute summary of their story of pain. If some begin to make prayer requests, we gently remind them that this time is for sharing the story of their heart wounds rather than prayer points. After each man shares, some of the other men surround him and pray for him based on his story.

Laments

Another way to express pain is through laments. We ask workshop participants to write out a lament for their pain, a prayer to God that draws from the lament psalms as a template. As the men read biblical examples of lament, it gives them courage to write their own, and they feel emboldened to "Arise, cry out in the night, at the beginning of the night watches! Pour out your heart like water before the presence of the Lord!" (Lam 2:19a).

Writing laments helps men honestly bring their pain to their heavenly Father because they are private. No one will see what they wrote if they don't wish to share it. Though we invite and encourage participants to share their laments with one other in a small group or even with the whole group, that is strictly optional.

Both writing and sharing can be emotional points of healing. Dominique Gilliard makes the following helpful reflections:

> Why lament? Because, paradoxically, often the best way to cure pain is to engage it. Lamentation prevents us from becoming numb and apathetic to the pain of our world and of those whom we shepherd. Lamentation begets revelation. It opens our eyes to death, injustice and oppression we had not even noticed. It opens our ears to the sounds of torture, anguish and weeping that are the white noise of our world. To live without lament is to live an unexamined life.[6]

One additional benefit of writing laments is that they can ignite a long-term spiritual discipline of journaling prayers to God. When laments are written in the language of the writer and then read aloud, they have even more impact on the heart.

Drawing Stories

Art therapy has long been known to help children after trauma. As Cathy Malchiodi explains:

> Non-verbal modalities such as drawing are effective because of the impact that trauma often has on language. Language, a function of declarative memory, is generally not readily accessible to trauma survivors of any age after a traumatic event. In particular, Broca's area, a section of the brain that controls language, is affected, making it difficult to relate the trauma narrative. In fact, when a trauma survivor attempts to speak, PET scans actually show that Broca's area tends to shut down. Meanwhile, other parts of the brain, including the limbic system, are in overdrive, particularly in individuals with posttraumatic stress symptoms.[7]

We have found the same to be true for adult men in Africa, who experience remarkable healing after drawing their stories. Victims of Boko Haram, for instance, drew pictures of attacks on villages and churches. Another participant drew pictures of being cruelly treated as a young boy in a polygamous

---

6. Dominique D. Gilliard, "Reclaiming the Power of Lament," *Faith and Leadership*, posted on 25 August 2015, https://www.faithandleadership.com/dominique-d-gilliard-reclaiming-power-lament.

7. Cathy Malchiodi, "When Trauma Happens Children Draw: Part I," *Psychology Today*, posted on 7 May 2008, https://www.psychologytoday.com/blog/arts-and-health/200805/when-trauma-happens-children-draw-part-i.

household. Despite the wide range of artistic ability, the men in the workshops do not seem inhibited by drawing as adults, but rather discover great meaning as they draw pictures of their pain. When we invite the men to draw, we emphasize that we will not be comparing or judging anyone's art, since the purpose is to discern what God is doing in their hearts *while* they draw. What are they feeling and thinking? How does drawing help them? Again, we do not require participants to post their drawings on the wall or explain them to someone else, but almost everyone is happy to do both.

Releasing Pain

During the closing ceremony or near the end of the workshop, we invite participants to write out their pain on a piece of paper, nail it to the cross of Christ and then burn the paper and symbolically "release" their pain to God. We ask God's Spirit to bring to mind any pain the men want to release and hand over that pain to God (1 Pet 5:7). We invite the men to surrender to God any people whom they want to forgive. We also invite them to identify sins that they want to ask God to forgive in them. They never have to share what they write with others, so there is safety and freedom to be honest.

When they bring their papers to the cross, we remind them that this is not an animistic ritual, but a reminder of the death of Christ and his willingness to take our pain, suffering and sin upon himself so that we don't have to carry these things ourselves. We also remind them that they do not need a ceremony, paper, cross or matches to do this at any time, since God is always ready to take our pain through a whispered prayer.

Finding Ongoing Help

Of course, some don't find healing during a week-long workshop. We experienced this from time to time, especially when the trauma was very recent. In these cases, follow-up referrals need to take place after the workshop, ideally with a qualified counselor who is available for long-term, one-on-one counseling. In fact, such a center is now under construction outside of Jos, Nigeria, where we lived and worked in trauma healing. This center will work one-on-one with wounded adults and children, many of whom are victims of Boko Haram terrorism.

Conclusion

This paper offers a distillation of all that we experienced during the nine years we spent doing trauma healing among a variety of groups in Nigeria. I hope it provides a picture of both the challenges and the victories we saw as men found healing in their hearts.

Bibliography

Darko Sekyiamah, Nana. "Men Do Not Cry." *This Is Africa.* Posted on 17 September 2013. https://thisisafrica.me/men-not-cry/.

Gilliard, Dominique D. "Reclaiming the Power of Lament." *Faith and Leadership.* Posted on 25 August 2015. https://www.faithandleadership.com/dominique-d-gilliard-reclaiming-power-lament.

Hill, Harriet, Margaret Hill, Richard Bagge and Pat Miersma. *Healing the Wounds of Trauma: How the Church Can Help.* New York: American Bible Society, 2004.

Malchiodi, Cathy. "When Trauma Happens Children Draw: Part I." *Psychology Today.* Posted on 7 May 2008. https://www.psychologytoday.com/blog/arts-and-health/200805/when-trauma-happens-children-draw-part-i.

Sawab, Ibrahim and Dionne Searcey. "Chibok Girls, 3 Years Later: Anguished Parents Still Wait." *New York Times.* Posted on 15 April 2017. https://www.nytimes.com/2017/04/14/world/africa/chibok-girls-nigeria-boko-haram.html?_r=0.

19

Healing Trauma through Art and Drama

Lorraine Foute

Facilitating Healing through Art

Facing pain in the heart takes courage! In our experience, transformation rarely happens when a heart is barricaded or stuck. Sometimes people just avoid what is deep in their heart. Michael Rosenthal describes how "Recent developments in the field of neuroplasticity prove how your brain is hardwired and genetically designed to heal, change and rewire itself after all types of traumas."[1] He argues that experience can change neuron structure in the brain, saying, "Research proves that it takes 10–20 seconds of a positive feeling for the brain to record it into a deeper neural structure."[2]

For nine years, my husband and I saw people experience healing from horrific trauma in Nigeria. We observed that when people were given an opportunity to process their emotions through verbal expression, artistic representation, written expression or acting out their feelings, they experienced heart transformation as their brains were rewired. One recent article states, "it may be possible to carve out a fresh and unworn path for your thoughts to travel upon."[3] After working with victims of terrorist attacks in northern Nigeria, we became more and more convinced that the medium of art – including drawing,

1. Michele Rosenthal, "Neuroplasticity: What You Need to Know in PTSD Recovery," *LinkedIn,* 30 May 2015.

2. Rosenthal, "Neuroplasticity."

3. Christopher Bergland, "How Do Neuroplasticity and Neurogenesis Rewire Your Brain?" *Psychology Today,* posted on 6 February 2017.

drama, journaling, writing laments and using visual object lessons or cultural proverbs – could help facilitate the healing process by providing a comfortable way for people to understand their feelings. This conviction provides great hope for the hurting.

David faced the pain in his heart by expressing to God, "How long, O LORD? Will you forget me forever? How long will you hide your face from me? How long must I wrestle with my thoughts and every day have sorrow in my heart? How long will my enemy triumph over me?" (Ps 13:1–2 NIV). In this psalm of lament, David acknowledges what he is thinking in his mind as well as what he is feeling in his heart.

Art and verbal expression, visual aids and laments seem to have the power to break open a closed and wounded heart. These creative art forms can give people courage to let go of pain, release hurt, have closure or move on to survive the pain. Healing does not usually happen through intellectual discussions or theological debates. Rather, healing seems to happen as the heart opens to God's touch and God's healing word and when other caring individuals listen and offer their presence. Such experiences can build new connections in the brain. Art forms such as drawing, drama and writing laments help us to identify our thoughts and elicit feelings in our hearts. One study concluded that "art therapy was associated with significant positive changes relative to the control group in mental health symptoms in 7 of the 11 studies."[4]

Healing Workshops

In November 2007 I flew to Kenya from Jos, Nigeria, to receive training from the authors of the book *Healing the Wounds of Trauma.*[5] The book has five core lessons and other optional lessons that can be used to provide healing groups for those who are hurting, and the curriculum is designed around participatory learning tasks. The curriculum does not provide – nor does it require – counseling by professionals, but rather offers church leaders ways to bring healing to members of churches and the wider community. Deeper issues may require professional help.

There are usually sixteen to thirty participants in the training workshops, but the smaller healing groups are comprised of three to twelve members.

4. Lesley Uttley, Matt Stevenson, Alison Scope, Andrew Rawdin and Anthea Sutton, "Clinical Effectiveness and Cost Effectiveness of Group Art Therapy for People with Non-Psychotic Mental Health Disorders: A Systematic Review and Cost-effectiveness Analysis," *BioMedCentral Psychiatry* 15 (July 2015), https://bmcpsychiatry.biomedcentral.com/articles/10.1186/s12888-015-0528-4.

5. Harriet Hill, Margaret Hill, Richard Bagge and Pat Miersma, *Healing the Wounds of Trauma: How the Church Can Help* (New York: American Bible Society, 2004).

There are separate materials for children, teens, adults and story-based lessons for those who cannot read or write. The book has been translated into many languages and has also been contextualized for some particular regions.

Between 2007 and 2016, my husband and I facilitated nearly one hundred workshops in Nigeria with victims of terrorism, pastors, internally displaced people, widows and children, and we also trained others to facilitate workshops. Since January 2017 we have facilitated a few workshops in the Middle East, Latin America and the USA. Although we have some training in mental health, we are not licensed therapists or art therapists.

Many Bible societies in different parts of the world are working with churches in their areas to provide training. One Nigerian took the book with him to South Sudan and shared his learning experiences there. In many places, the training has become a way to provide resources to pastors and other lay caregivers who are concerned about the pain of their communities, where few counselors or therapists are available.

Expressing Trauma through Art

Before people can experience healing, they need to become aware of their pain, be willing to acknowledge their feelings and seek deeper understanding and insight. The most traumatic events often happen before a person reaches eighteen years of age, so this process requires the recovery of buried memories.

Art can help bring these memories to the surface. As victims of trauma engage their hearts, minds and bodies in the healing process through various activities, they find it easier to acknowledge, understand and work through their feelings. Art activities help them identify their pain, tell their stories and build their own narratives about what happened. These narratives give meaning to traumatic events, thereby facilitating their healing. Over time, many people are able to let go of the intense pain and suffering attached to a traumatic event. Though healing is a long process, we have seen dramatic changes in people's countenances overnight after some of these activities brought them relief.

We have seen people shed tears as they drew a picture to represent their pain. We have also seen people shed tears as they began to describe their drawings. As Cathy Malchiodi observes, "Individuals reported that art expression helped them to put their emotions and non-verbal experiences into words."[6] During the act of drawing, someone may gain new insights about their

---

6. Cathy Malchiodi, "Why Art Therapy Works," *Psychology Today* 30 (August 2016), https://www.psychologytoday.com/us/blog/arts-and-health/201608/why-art-therapy-works.

pain. Through art, people in pain are given a chance to communicate their stories, even if it is just between them and the Lord.

A lawyer who lives in Guatemala was a participant in a recent workshop. At the end of the workshop, he courageously stood and tearfully talked about his experience of healing. While drawing a picture of his pain, he reflected on his father's death and realized that he had been holding a grudge in his heart against a man who was good friends with his father. The lawyer had called this man to ask him to come visit before his father died, and the man had never come. While the lawyer was drawing, he realized that God had sent two other men to come and comfort his family and show love to them. This reminder helped give the lawyer the grace to forgive the man who had hurt him. He felt free. Perhaps a new pathway was built in his brain as new neuron pathways and connections grew to replace the old ones!

Drawing and art can help us create new narratives to represent painful events. As we describe our pain, we can reflect on what we have learned from our experiences. This helps us find closure and gives meaning to the pain. Art may give us the courage to share our stories with others.

This happened with some young boys who drew pictures of their pain for their teacher. One had not seen his mother for a year, because she had been forced to leave home after she refused to become a Muslim. He and his sister had been held by force and tortured, but were able to escape. When he explained the picture to his teacher, his feelings and words came flowing out, and he felt relieved after expressing his sadness and fear about the night he had been separated from his mother. The teacher had been working with these boys for about four months and had tried to get them to talk, but it was not until they completed their drawings that they were able to talk individually about their trauma and receive comfort.

Art is a powerful medium that can help unlock the fear and shame connected to painful events. Drawing pictures helps us remember the feelings, memories, sounds and smells that we associate with those events. Those memories provide opportunities for growth, understanding and healing. Drawing a picture of our pain may give us words, emotions or meaning to attach to painful experiences, shifting the event from something that we remember with our brain to something that we feel in our heart. Some people are very self-protective and afraid to enter the dark places in their hearts, but artwork and other forms of creative expression help to rewire our brains, bringing hope and joy where there was pain.

A study of women with cancer who were given the opportunity to engage in different types of visual art concluded that the art "helped them focus on positive life experiences . . ., enhanced their self-worth and identity, . . . enabled them to maintain a social identity that resisted being defined by cancer . . . [and] allowed them to express their feelings in a symbolic manner."[7] Another study "found that those who engaged in art making demonstrated statistically significant decreases in symptoms of physical and emotional distress."[8]

In a healing workshop with Muslims and Christians, we saw how making art and sharing stories became vehicles for building trust. We took the participants through the "Tree of Life," a narrative form of therapy that has been used effectively in Nigeria to bring healing and build resilience among traumatized children, youth and adults.

Facilitating Healing through Drama

Drama can also facilitate transformation and healing because it gives participants the opportunity to see examples of good listening, forgiveness and telling the truth about pain and also highlights what happens when people do not effectively process their pain. Those watching dramas may see depictions of themselves as they are, or they may see the kind of reactions they want to have. Role playing gives participants the opportunity to practice listening, showing compassion, asking for and granting forgiveness.

Drama also provides a great opportunity to contextualize materials. The original version of the trauma healing materials includes biblical principles and theology, but through drama, these topics can be applied and adapted to various contexts where crises occur. For example, we contextualized the trauma healing materials by adapting them for use with widows. In the Nigerian context, many widows are mistreated by family members, and so their personal trauma after losing their husbands is sometimes magnified by the cultural practice of relatives coming to take all their possessions. Sometimes widows have more difficulty healing from the pain of family rejection and blame than from a terrorist attack. A drama that portrays the struggle to forgive helps participants identify their own anger, pain and guilt and also helps them see how they can release their hurt, anger and bitterness.

We also adapted materials to use with a denomination that had their church headquarters destroyed. Acting out the pain of a pastor who had lost

7. Heather L. Stuckey and Jeremy Nobel, "The Connection between Art, Healing, and Public Health: A Review of Current Literature," *American Journal of Public Health* 100, no. 2 (February 2010): 254–263.

8. Stuckey and Nobel, "Connection between Art."

everything helped church leaders identify with the challenges that their people were experiencing and enabled them to see beyond their own pain.

A church group attending a workshop in the Middle East acted out a drama about a pastor who was experiencing burnout. The drama used humor and generated laughter, which gave people the freedom to identify with the feeling of being overwhelmed by the needs of others. After an interactive physical activity, in which each participant heard others share their feelings of fear, confusion and forgetfulness, a participant commented that the exercise felt like a "true confession." The communal experience gave a sense of normalcy to the feelings that many experienced in connection with traumatic events.

In 2015, we were asked to help facilitate a trauma healing workshop for forty parents whose daughters had been kidnapped by the Boko Haram terrorist group the previous year. We had heard many stories about the Chibok girls, and we were not sure how to reach these parents. We knew that some would still be depressed, discouraged and have trouble focusing. At the beginning of the workshop, some of the participants said, "We do not want Boko Haram blood in our homes," because they did not want to receive their daughters home if they had babies. Near the end of the workshop, we organized a drama that depicted a mother receiving her daughter home after a year in captivity, where the daughter had to tell her mother she was pregnant. The powerful, dramatic and unscripted portrayal involved two women who did not know each other, but everyone in the room shed tears. At the end of the drama, one father who had been reluctant to enter into the workshop, stood up and said that they needed help to understand their daughters' pain and how to receive them when they returned.

Drama can also help Scripture come alive. We use the story of Tamar, Amnon and Absalom to introduce the topic of rape (2 Sam 13:1–21). The story describes Tamar's pain and grief after being raped by her brother Amnon (v. 19). By dramatizing a conversation between Tamar and her half-brother, Absalom, participants feel more free to discuss rape and its consequences. Seeing that rape is in the Bible opens doors to explore the challenges that come with the difficult topic of rape.

Drama also opens the door for the Holy Spirit to work in creative ways. The person who dramatizes someone who is hurting may develop more compassion for victims. Drama helps participants place their feet in the shoes of another and gives them opportunities to practice responding in a safe place, where everyone is role playing. Practicing how to respond through a role-playing activity encourages participants to choose to do the right thing. We once saw a group of women acting out a drama about how a mother can listen to the needs of her children. One woman acted out the role of a teenage girl who was pregnant out of wedlock and had to tell her mother. The response of the woman who played her mother was gentle, tender, understanding, patient and full of grace. The woman who played the daughter told me later that she had a teenage daughter who was pregnant and that the drama had shown her how she could respond more lovingly to her pregnant daughter. Only the Holy Spirit could have put such a learning opportunity together for her!

Drawing on Creative Comparisons to Facilitate Healing

Creative comparisons such as object lessons, similes, metaphors and cultural proverbs can also help to engage both the heart and the mind. Object lessons help listeners apply what they are learning to their own life situations. Proverbs bring years of tradition and wisdom into the learning environment. Including visual aids brings deeper meaning and significance to these discussions. In one workshop, we saw how a cultural proverb had the power to calm down a very frustrated, angry and impatient Nigerian man.

Conclusion

Medical research supports the value of art for healing. As Rachel Hajar argues, "Studies show that incorporating the arts in our healing strategies can save money and improve well being and experience of both the patient and physician."[9] More studies need to be done to show the power of the arts to bring transformation, for as Stuckey and Nobel write, "The more we understand the relationship between creative expression and healing, the more we will discover the healing power of the arts."[10]

Looking back over the thirty-four years we spent in Nigeria, these opportunities to witness healing through creative art, drama and visual aids were the highlights in ministry. As we entered into the pain that workshop participants had experienced, it was gratifying to see them be transformed by the power of God's healing touch and receive hope for the future.

Those who care for the traumatized need to become like children by being vulnerable, teachable and humble. Each workshop participant brings a gift, and facilitators need to discern what each has to offer to the rest of the group. Our role is to create a place of safety and set the stage for God to touch participants' hearts so that they can experience freedom, healing and release. Art and drama are powerful ways to draw out that healing touch from God.

---

9. Rachel Hajar, "Art and Medicine," *Heart Views* 16, no. 3 (2015): 116–117.
10. Stuckey and Nobel, "Connection between Art."

When participants take their pain to the cross by literally pounding a nail into a piece of paper where they have written their pain, we can all connect with Jesus's choice to carry our pain and sins to the cross.[11] We are free indeed! As we are healed and transformed, we grow to love God and others more, and we can reach out to others who are hurting.

Bibliography

Bergland, Christopher. "How Do Neuroplasticity and Neurogenesis Rewire Your Brain?" *Psychology Today.* Posted on 6 February 2017. https://www.psychologytoday.com/us/blog/the-athletes-way/201702/how-do-neuroplasticity-and-neurogenesis-rewire-your-brain.

Hajar, Rachel. "Art and Medicine." *Heart Views* 16, no. 3 (2015): 116–117. http://www.heartviews.org/text.asp?2015/16/3/116/164456.

Hill, Harriet, Margaret Hill, Richard Bagge, and Pat Miersma. *Healing the Wounds of Trauma: How the Church Can Help.* New York: American Bible Society, 2004.

Malchiodi, Cathy. "Why Art Therapy Works." *Psychology Today,* blog entry posted on 30 August 2016. https://www.psychologytoday.com/us/blog/arts-and-health/201608/why-art-therapy-works.

Rosenthal, Michele. "Neuroplasticity: What You Need to Know in PTSD Recovery." 20 March 2013. https://www.healthyplace.com/blogs/traumaptsdblog/2013/03/neuroplasticity-what-you-need-to-know-in-ptsd-recovery.

Stuckey, Heather L., and Jeremy Nobel. "The Connection between Art, Healing, and Public Health: A Review of Current Literature." *American Journal of Public Health* 100, no. 2 (February 2010): 254–263. https://ajph.aphapublications.org/doi/abs/10.2105/AJPH.2008.156497.

Uttley, Lesley, Matt Stevenson, Alison Scope, Andrew Rawdin and Anthea Sutton. "Clinical Effectiveness and Cost Effectiveness of Group Art Therapy for People with Non-Psychotic Mental Health Disorders: A Systematic Review and Cost-Effectiveness Analysis." *BioMedCentral Psychiatry* 15 (July 2015). https://bmcpsychiatry.biomedcentral.com/articles/10.1186/s12888-015-0528-4.

Helpful Resources for Those Interested in Using Art in Trauma Healing:

thi.americanbible.org

https://dulwichcentre.com.au/the-tree-of-life/

Robin Harris, Director for GIALS Center for Excellence in World Arts, https://www.diu.edu/world-arts-center/about/.

---

11. This concept is explored further in the next chapter.

20

Healing around the Cross Liturgy

John and Sandi Steward

Introduction

We developed this liturgy in Australia after we experienced its value in healing workshops in Rwanda. It owes much to the healing ceremony that is part of a three-day healing workshop known as "Healing the Wounds of Ethnic Conflict" (HWEC).[1] We added our own material to suit our Christian audiences. The following section describes the preparation, process and materials used for this liturgy.

Preparation

The liturgy has the most impact when the context prepares the person or group beforehand. It works well when it is preceded by biblical teaching that relates to aspects of God's grace in human suffering and/or failing in life. This could include teaching on forgiveness, shared pain, grieving loss, the suffering of Christ, the healing of inner wounds or self-examination for correcting or changing personal behavior.

1. To understand more of the content, I strongly recommend reading Rhiannon Lloyd, *Healing the Wounds of Ethnic Conflict,* 3rd ed. (Mercy Ministries International, 2011), 46–50.

Process

In the Rwandan healing workshops (HWEC), the liturgy is used on the evening of the second day. Day 1 is a teaching on the unconditional love of God, who is compassionate towards sinful people. Day 2 is devoted to sharing grief and painful loss in small groups made up of male and female, Hutu and Tutsi.

By holding the liturgy on the evening of the second day, participants have time to consider biblical teaching about the love of God for sinful humans. They've also had the humbling experiencing of telling their own stories of pain and violence and their struggles with repentance, confession, apology and forgiveness. They have also listened to the stories of others in small groups, which opens their hearts to the possibility of giving compassion. The ceremony that closes the second day is deep and engaging for every participant, like light coming into the darkness. During this time of sharing each person writes their list of painful experiences that is brought to be nailed to the cross during the liturgy.

We have used the liturgy in training events, but it is never run as a training exercise. Rather, it is always a personal time for engaging participants in their personal struggles.

It is important not to put time constraints on the liturgy, as tears of repentance, contrition, relief and release need time to flow. During one workshop as we were engaging this liturgy, a pastor came up to us and whispered: "God is at work here – give Him all the time he needs." In contrast, when a time schedule was imposed on the liturgy during another workshop, participants were very frustrated to have to leave with their notes still nailed to the cross, because the bell had rung and they had to go.

When working with a small group, or even with an individual (as in spiritual companioning), the preparatory work can be done over several meetings. Individual participants can invite a supportive friend or partner to be present so that they have someone who understands what occurred and can accompany them in follow up.

On several occasions we have used some of the components of the liturgy in interfaith events with people from four different faith backgrounds. In such contexts, the liturgy needs a more confined version that is based on sharing our story with another person, writing down our pains, participating in a solemn procession and then burning the papers to ensure confidentiality.[2] Even here, truth is at work, and change can begin.

2. You will find this version in the Facilitator's Guide on www.2live4give.org/STUDY GUIDE.

Materials

You will need paper, pens and a candle for each person. You will also need a wooden cross that can be laid on the floor, along with nails and a hammer, matches and a brazier (a receptacle for burning the papers). Suitable music is also recommended.

The Liturgy[3]

Healing the Memories: What Brings Us Together

Leader: As you bring back to the surface the memories of your life, and those who suffered with you, and as you seek help from God, we commit to be with you, to keep all that you share in confidence and to respect what you choose not to share. In faith we expect that God will use this time to help you move forward in your journey.

Remembering Our Context: The God Who Brings Us Together

Each participant responds to the following question: What characteristics of God do I treasure?

Leader: We meet in the presence of this God today – one in whom we live and move and have our being, from whom nothing is hidden, who knows us through and through.

All: We would not be here if we did not know Jesus. Jesus is the one who introduced us to the way of fellowship and unity first experienced in the Trinity.

Leader: This God also created diversity, which often dominates over unity – through customs and habits passed down by our forefathers, family and faith. This shapes our own unique personal experiences.

All: Today, Lord, we take this opportunity in your presence to remember and process our pain – the wounds of grief, disappointment, shame and loss that we carry from our life and service.

3. Each participant in this liturgy will benefit by having a copy of this material. Readers are free to copy and reprint the liturgy in this section of the book for their own use. When doing so, please also include the following credit: "Taken from *Tackling Trauma: Global, Biblical, and Pastoral Perspectives* (Carlisle: Langham Global Library, 2019)."

Binding the Pain in Myself: Bringing Our Wounds to the Light

All: Sinfulness isn't our only problem in life. We are also wounded by the actions of others when they sin against us. They may not have intended it, but their actions hurt us. Or they may have meant to hurt and belittle us. Either way the pain is ours, while they go on, relatively unaffected by – even oblivious to – our inner struggles and suffering.

Leader: I will read two Scriptures about the deep effects on us of pain and hurt feelings.

> The human spirit can endure in sickness, but a crushed spirit who can bear? (Prov 18:14 NIV)
>
> A cheerful heart is good medicine, but a crushed spirit dries up the bones. (Prov 17:22 NIV)

All: If we hold our pain and wounding in our heart, we cannot bring it to Jesus to be healed. These wounds ransom us to our past and hold us back from progressing. Our painful memories are sometimes more present to us than the Lord.

Leader: Friends, what makes it hard for any of us to express our pain is that we have held it in – and it has become part of us. Today is an opportunity to give it up to someone who is greater than you. There are more than two hundred scriptures about grief, weeping and mourning.

In John 11 Jesus asked for the tomb of Lazarus to be opened even though it would be unpleasant for all present. But Jesus had a work of healing to do.

I offer you this assurance from Psalm 34:18 (NIV): "The LORD is close to the brokenhearted and saves those who are crushed in spirit."

I invite you each to talk about the pains and hurts that you choose to share. We will listen with empathy and promise to keep confidentiality.

Participants share their pains, referring to the sheet of paper they have prepared.

Leader: You have summarized your wounds on a sheet of paper with words or pictures that are known and understood between you and God. These tell the painful truth of your story.

The basis for what we are about to do is from Isaiah 53, which is a prophecy about the pain that Jesus bore for us. Isaiah 53 has many connections with the sacrifice and suffering of our Lord, as shown by the fourteen references to it in the four gospels.

All: We note the following key words from Isaiah 53 (NIV): he "*bore our suffering*" (v. 4); "by his *wounds we are healed*" (v. 5); "the LORD has *laid on him the iniquity* of us all" (v. 6); "he *bore the sin* of many" (v. 12).

Nailing Pains to the Cross

Leader: Think for a moment about one of those phrases in italics. Imagine Jesus doing that for you.

Now I invite you to show your acceptance of how Jesus *bore your suffering* on the cross, *healed you*, *received every human iniquity* and *bears your sins* by symbolically nailing your paper to this cross and making some statement of identification with Jesus's act of suffering for the sins that others have committed against you.

Each participant says, "Jesus, in nailing this paper on the cross, I . . ."

Leader: As witnesses to this act of giving your pain to Christ, we will now release these papers and bring them to the place of fire to be burned. The smoke will symbolically rise towards the heavens.

Burning the Papers

Participants sing, "God is so good . . . God took my sin . . . God took their sin . . ."

All: The burning is a slow process in which the substance of the paper is transformed and slowly disappears. This symbolizes our hope that our pains are taken up by Jesus and our wounds will gradually begin to heal. Our attitude will be transformed as our mind is renewed.

Celebrating the Moment

Leader: In the Bible, celebration always follows the healing of a memory.

Participants share what they feel at this moment about Jesus's identification with us and all who believe.

Leader: Joachim Jeremias says that Jesus understood the necessity of his death primarily from Isaiah 53, the chapter about the suffering servant.[4]

4. John Stott, *The Cross of Christ* (Downers Grove: InterVarsity Press, 2006), 145.

In Mark 14:24, Jesus said, "This is my blood of the covenant poured out for many." His death is representative of salvation for many. Jeremias says that "many" is "the inconceivable many, the whole host, all." This term is rare in the Old Testament, but it is used five times in Isaiah 53, where the servant of God goes to his death as the representative of others.

In our context, this term refers to you, dear friends, and all those who hurt you or failed to support you when you needed it.

Jesus speaks of being "a ransom for many" (Mark 10:45), referring to Isaiah 53, where Jesus is a guilt offering for our guilt and others' guilt (vv. 10–12).

When Jesus says, "The son of man must suffer much and be rejected" (Mark 9:12), this also alludes to Isaiah 53: "He was despised and rejected by mankind, a man of sorrows and familiar with pain" (v. 3).

When Jesus is betrayed (Mark 9:31; 14:41), the term implies the description in Isaiah 53: he "was numbered with the transgressors" (v. 12). Though Jesus was not a transgressor, he was treated as one.

Eucharist (optional)

The following liturgy can be used where it is appropriate to celebrate the Eucharist.

Leader: We remember the victory of Jesus and celebrate his deep understanding of your suffering.

All: The grain is pounded, crushed, mixed and baked; the grapes are trampled, squashed, bruised and squeezed. Out of the bruising of both flows life. We celebrate the healing that has come out of the powerlessness of Jesus.

Participant 1: A reading from *Letters from the Desert*:

> *What does Jesus do in the Eucharist?* I have thought about it often. In the Eucharist Jesus is immobilized not in one leg only, but both, and in his hands as well. He is reduced to a little piece of white bread. The world needs him so much and yet he doesn't speak. People need him so much and he doesn't move!
>
> The Eucharist is the silence of God, the weakness of God.[5]

Participant 2: Another reading from *Letters from the Desert*:

> One has to be courageous not to let oneself be carried along by the world's march; one needs faith and will-power to go across the current towards the Eucharist, to stop, to be silent, to worship.

5. Carlo Carretto, *Letters from the Desert* (Orbis, 1972), 130.

> And one needs really strong faith to understand the impotence and defeat which the Eucharist represents.[6]

All: "The Eucharist is today what the impotence and defeat of Calvary was yesterday. And yet this powerless Jesus, nailed down and annihilated, is the God of the impossible."[7]

Leader: We break the bread and drink the cup. Lord, may this Eucharist increase within us the healing power of your love. May it guide and direct our efforts to please you in all things.

Loosing the Grip of Others: Healing Relationships

Leader: In Matthew 16:19, Jesus promises: "I will give you the keys of the kingdom of heaven; whatever you bind on earth will be bound in heaven, and whatever you loose on earth will be loosed in heaven."

All: At times we were crushed – somebody did something and our pain was a response to their actions. While it was *our* problem, somebody else contributed to it, and our relationship with that person was affected.

The first step towards healing our relationships is forgiveness – which begins with letting go of the bitter poison and the right for revenge and payback. This is where the gradual healing *within* us opens the way for a gradual healing *outwards*.

Leader: In Mark 14:25, Jesus makes a vow to abstain from eating this meal again on earth. This echoed the Palestinian habit of fasting on the night of Passover in order to intercede for Israel until the last minute. This reminds us again of Isaiah 53: "The servant makes intercession for the guilty" (v. 12).

Jesus not only forgives and takes the punishment; he also intercedes for the transgressor.

This model was followed in the early church by Stephen (Acts 7:60) and James, the brother of the Lord (in Eusebius), who also pray for their murderers when dying. In so doing, they follow Jesus's example, "Father forgive them, for they do not know what they are doing (Luke 23:34), as well as his instructions, "Love your enemies and pray for those who persecute you" (Matt 5:44).

---

6. Ibid.
7. Carretto, 130–131.

All: It is healthy to recognize those whom we cannot yet forgive – and to understand that while forgiveness takes time, my unforgiveness is not only a hindrance to reconciliation, but it also binds me to the one who hurt me. As Lewis Smedes says, "Forgiveness sets a prisoner free – only to find that the prisoner is me!"

This challenge mirrors the invitation Jesus gives us in the parable of the prodigal son: to move from being like the older brother, who felt his own pain and loss acutely, to becoming like the father, who – despite his loss – was ready to offer grace and forgiveness to his wayward son (Mark 10:21).

Participants read aloud the following poem. One or two persons may do it as delegated by the leader.

It Is Mine, Let it Be

God does not send your pain
    but suffers it with you
    sharing in the bearing of it.
God does not send your pain
    your grief is also God's grief.
    Jesus bore it first.
All the pain and all the grief
    that ever was, or is, or will be
    He has already borne on the cross.
Between you and the hard wood of your cross
    hangs his crucified body
    absorbing all your grief and pain.
"It is mine," Jesus says,
    "I have pain to share in the bearing
    of this very thing."
Jesus does not will your ill
    but invites you to share
    His cross.
This is not easy –
    a cross that doesn't wound
    is not a cross,
He does not will your ill,
    His whole meaning is love.
So why – why is he letting this happen to you?
Well, why not?

God let it happen to Jesus –
all that injustice, grief and pain.
He could have called in
thousands of angels.
But he didn't. He let it be.
That's what crucifixion is –
letting it be.
That's what God is calling you to do –
"Let it be – in Me."
We will never be asked to let it be
as He did
when the terrible "forsaken" words
tore from his throat.
He alone took that medicine,
that ever afterwards
our "let it be"
might be in Him – **never** forsaken.
Suffering passes, but to have suffered never.
For to have companioned with him on his cross
transfigures our lives
and the lives of those around us
by the holy power of His redemptive love.[8]

Leader: Lift before God the names of those you have forgiven and name those you cannot yet forgive, so as to leave them in the hands of God.

Closing: Where to From Here?

Leader: Although we are grafted into Jesus, some things are not yet made new. We feed from the old roots, some of which are buried so deeply we don't even realize they are there.

God intends all our roots to be good, but any wounds which come from our roots produce bad thoughts. I will read two Scriptures about such roots.

> . . . make sure there is no root among you that produces such bitter poison. (Deut 29:18 NIV)

8. Source unknown.

> See to it that no one falls short of the grace of God and that no bitter root grows up to cause trouble and defile many. (Heb 12:15 NIV)

Each participant considers the following questions:

- Can you identify characteristic roots from your family tree, clan or community?
- How have they influenced your thoughts, attitudes, beliefs, habits, behaviors, responses?
- What sinful responses can you see were modeled to you?
- What bitterness is there and what fruit is being produced from these roots?

Leader: If you find negative patterns in your family tree, you may need a special healing prayer or Eucharist to pray for healing and freedom from that part of your life and heritage.

A closing prayer by the leader that takes up the issues that have emerged; conclude with the Lord's Prayer and invite those who wish to have personal prayer and counseling to seek it as a priority.

As we prepare to close please come and talk further with me so you may be further assisted.

Contributors

Naji Abi-Hashem (MA and PhD in Clinical Psychology, Biola University, California; MDiv in Pastoral and Ethnic Studies, Golden Gate Theological Seminary) currently serves as an associate with Member Care International, dividing his time between the US and Lebanon. Alongside this work, he is involved in editing, speaking, and writing on a range of issues for a variety of international organizations, contributing to over ninety published works. Dr Abi-Hashem worked for twelve years (1992–2004) as a staff psychologist with the Minirth-Meier New Life Clinics and affiliated hospital program, and was the featured therapist in *Working with Arab Americans*, a professional training DVD produced by the American Psychological Association in 2008 for multicultural counselling. He has also served on the Board of Directors for multiple national and international agencies.

Paul Barker (PhD) is Assistant Bishop in the Anglican Diocese of Melbourne. Formerly he was Langham Preaching Regional Coordinator for Asia and Langham Scholar Care Coordinator for Asia. He has taught Old Testament and Homiletics in various Asian seminaries and is Adjunct Lecturer at Myanmar Evangelical Graduate School of Theology in Yangon, Myanmar. His PhD was published as *The Triumph of Grace in Deuteronomy* (Paternoster, 2004), and he has since written *Teaching Deuteronomy* (The Good Book Company, 2014), which has been translated into various languages, and *Deuteronomy: The God Who Keeps Promises* (Langham Preaching Resources, 2017).

Rolex M. Cailing (PhD) is the founding and senior pastor of LifeReach Ministries in the Philippines, and has planted and pastored churches in the Philippines and Korea. Having taught at multiple Bible colleges and seminaries across Africa and Asia, he is now teaching New Testament studies at Alliance Graduate School, Quezon City, Philippines, and has particular interest in Pauline theology, the use of the Old Testament in the New, the background of early Christianity and Second Temple Judaism. Rev Cailing has written several works on Paul's use of the Old Testament.

Bill Foute (MDiv in Missions, Talbot School of Theology) served in Nigeria with SIM for thirty-four years (1982–2016) ministering in the Hausa language to equip Nigerian leaders, missionaries and pastors. His ministry while in Nigeria included teaching, field leadership, pastoral counselling, providing libraries for pastors, and trauma healing. Bill and his wife Lorraine returned to the USA in 2016 and currently work worldwide in equipping in trauma healing and pastoral counselling. They have three adult children and three grandchildren.

Lorraine Foute (MSc, Fresno Pacific University) served with SIM in Nigeria for thirty-four years. In Nigeria, she learned the Hausa language and taught Nigerian pastors and missionaries at a Bible school and gave counsel to many Nigerian and missionary women. Lorraine began a special education program at a school for missionary children that lasted for twenty years and also taught special education at Jos ECWA Theological Seminary for ten years. Having returned to the USA with her husband Bill in 2016, she continues to equip others in trauma healing and is a master facilitator in adult, children's and story-based trauma healing under the American Bible Society Trauma Healing Institute. Lorraine and her husband continue to facilitate trauma healing workshops in various countries.

Ida Glaser (PhD) is the International Academic Coordinator for the Centre for Muslim-Christian Studies, Oxford, and an Associate Tutor at Wycliffe Hall, Oxford. Ida has previously taught physics in Muslim girls' schools in Asia, and has taught on Christian-Muslim relations in Birmingham, Edinburgh and Oxford, as well as intensive courses in Africa, Asia and the Americas. She has worked for, and facilitated, church projects in inner-city Muslim communities across the UK, and was employed by the Anglican mission agency, Crosslinks, for twenty-five years. Ida's writing largely focuses on reading the Bible in the context of Islam, and includes *The Bible and Other Faiths: What Does the Lord Require of Us?* (Langham Global Library, 2012) and *Thinking Biblically about Islam: Genesis, Transfiguration, Transformation* (Langham Global Library, 2016). She is co-series editor for *Routledge Biblical Interpretation in Islamic Context* and for the forthcoming Langham Publishing series of Biblical commentaries from Islamic contexts.

Shirley S. Ho (PhD, Trinity Evangelical Divinity School) is Filipino-Chinese, and has lived in Taiwan for the past eleven years. She is currently Assistant Professor of the Old Testament at China Evangelical Seminary, Taipei, Taiwan, and teaches courses on Biblical Hebrew, the Old Testament, and Research and Writing. Shirley is currently writing her post-doctoral project on Proverbs, and has presented her article, "The Journey of a Son: Narrative Reading of Proverbs 1–9," at the 2017 SBL International Meeting, at Humboldt University, Berlin, Germany.

Yuzo Imamura (MD, Dermatology; PhD, Cell Biology) currently serves with his wife, Hitomi, in the Stung Treng province, one of the least reached areas in Cambodia. Having previously gained a medical degree, he felt God call him to be a cross-cultural worker in Cambodia, and so joined OMF International in 2003. Yuzo was involved with medical teaching and training, as well as university student ministry in Phnom Penh, and later he and his wife spent time serving in Kratie province, before arriving in Stung Treng. He has a passion to reach the unreached in villages and train preachers in rural provinces, particularly in the area of expository preaching.

Muhindo Isesomo has been bishop of North Kivu since 2010, and is also currently National Coordinator for Langham Preaching in the Democratic Republic of Congo. He was the parish vicar at Butembo Anglican parish from 1984–1992, and in 1993 he went to Kinshasa for specialization training in Evangelism. Isesomo worked as the National Coordinator of Evangelism for the Anglican Church from 1995–2010, which enabled him to visit many different countries, and transform the lives of many people with the gospel.

Kethoser (Aniu) Kevichusa (PhD, Oxford Centre for Mission Studies) serves as a speaker and trainer with Ravi Zacharias International Ministries in India. Previously he studied theology in India, then in the UK, following his undergraduate degree in English Literature. He was a lecturer at Shalom Bible Seminary from 1996–1997 and again in 2001–2004. Aniu lives with his wife, Ono, and their three sons in Nagaland, India. His primary ministry gifts are expository preaching, Christian apologetics and evangelism.

Vacheslav Khalanskyy works at REALIS Christian Center and is a lecturer in the Department of Psychology at the National Pedagogical University, Ukraine.

Svetlana Kravchuk is candidate of Psychological Sciences, Senior scientific researcher, Institute of Social and Political Psychology, Kiev, Ukraine.

Melba Maggay (PhD, Philippine Studies) is the president of Micah Global. A writer and social anthropologist, Maggay is a consultant on culture and social development issues, particularly the interface of religion, culture and development. She has lectured on the cross-cultural dimensions of development and missiological issues worldwide as a specialist in intercultural communication. She has been involved in initiating and supervising groundbreaking research and grassroots development projects as president of the Institute for Studies in Asian Church and Culture (ISSAC), a training and advocacy organization engaged in development, cross-cultural and political issues. Maggay is also a prolific writer, and is a three-time top-prize winner in the Don Carlos Palanca Memorial Awards, the most prestigious literary prize in the Philippines.

Annabel Manazilla-Manalo (PhD), a licensed psychologist in clinical, counselling and assessment psychology, serves as the Associate Professor and Chair of the Counselling Department at the Asian Theological Seminary (ATS), Quezon City, Philippines. She also currently serves as the Director of the ATS Counselling Centre and heads the Disaster Response and Psychological Training Program. For the past twenty years Annabel has been involved with various NGOs providing psychological services to many different communities, including those displaced by armed conflicts and natural disasters, survivors of torture and enforced disappearance, families of victims of extrajudicial killings, and street children and youth at risk.

Isaac K. Mbabazi (PhD, University of Manchester) is Professor of New Testament Studies at Université Shalom de Bunia, Democratic Republic of Congo, and also currently serves as the university's director of the PhD program. He formerly served as Dean of the School of Theology and was previously the President of a seminary in Burundi. Mbabazi has written several works including *The Significance of Interpersonal Forgiveness in the Gospel of Matthew* (Wipf & Stock, 2013). He is married to Jeanette, and together are blessed with three daughters.

Rachel C. Mutai (MDiv, Africa International University) is currently completing her studies for a graduate certificate in Peacebuilding Leadership from the Eastern Mennonite University, Harrisonburg, Virginia, USA, while also serving as the Coordinator of Curriculum Development at African Leadership and Reconciliation Ministries (ALARM). Through her work with ALARM, Rachel has been involved in developing curricula and training materials for programs in the areas of servant leadership, conflict resolution, peace building, and interfaith dialogues. She has actively participated in the training of church and community leaders in multiple different countries in which ALARM serves. Her passion is to spur and develop people to fulfil their divine purpose and selfless service to humanity.

Gladys Mwiti (PhD, Clinical Psychology) is the founder and CEO of Oasis Africa – Centre for Transformational Psychology and Trauma. Mwiti also currently serves as the Chairperson of both the Kenya Psychological Association and the Kenya Society for Traumatic Stress Studies. She was previously a Member of the Board of Directors for the International Society for Traumatic Stress Studies and Co-chair of the Lausanne Congress for World Evangelization Mental Health and Trauma Advisory Group. She has received several awards for her work including the Scholar-Leader of the Year 2010 (Scholar-Leaders International, USA), Pure and Natural Woman Award 2011 (James R. Jordan Foundation) and the Alumni of the Year Award 2014 (Fuller Seminary's Graduate School of Psychology 50th Anniversary). She is married to Dr Gerhson Mwiti.

John Steward (PhD, Adelaide University) is a spiritual director, speaker and volunteer garden ambassador in Australia. He previously served in Indonesia lecturing in theology, agriculture and community development from 1974–1978. In 1979 John joined World Vision in Jakarta and was involved in initiating leadership training for village development motivators. John then facilitated adult learning processes for indigenous community workers from over fifty countries. In 1997–1998 he was involved in the post-genocide reconstruction in Rwanda and for the next nine years John returned to Rwanda every six months to mentor Rwandan peace and development workers. Through hearing the stories of change from the many people he met he became a mentor in developing *Vanishing Point*, a peace and conflict curriculum for secondary students using the stories of healed Rwandans. John then turned his focus to writing stories of healing and forgiveness after conflict, and in 2015, *From Genocide to Generosity* (Langham Global Library), was published.

Samuel Thielman (PhD) is a clinical and organizational consultant and faculty scholar at Duke University's Centre for Spirituality, Theology and Health. He currently serves as a consultant to Samaritan's Purse, Open Doors, and the Christian Medical and Dental Association. Dr Thielman is a former Director of the Mental Health Service Program of the US Department of State. He has extensive behavioral health experience in East and Central Africa, working for five years as the State Department's regional psychiatrist at the US Embassy in Nairobi, Kenya. He also served as the Senior Advisor for Resilience at the State Department's Foreign Service Institute. Through working with Americans and others affected by trauma in the Majority World, he has written widely on the psychological effects of terrorism, and has appeared in professional publications such as the *American Journal of Psychiatry*, *Psychiatry*, the *British Journal of Psychiatry*, and the *New England Journal of Medicine*.

Amos Winarto (PhD, Calvin Theological Seminary) is an ordained minister of the Synod of the Church of Christ the Lord, Indonesia, for whom he is also the Chairman of the Dogma and Teaching Department. He is the Dean of Students and a lecturer in Ethics and Theology at Aletheia Theological Seminary, Lawang, Indonesia. He has written and published several academic articles and books including *The Perilous Sayings: Interpreting Christ's Call to Obedience in the Sermon on the Mount* (Langham Monographs, 2017).

Langham Literature and its imprints are a ministry of Langham Partnership.

Langham Partnership is a global fellowship working in pursuit of the vision God entrusted to its founder John Stott –

> ***to facilitate the growth of the church in maturity and Christ-likeness through raising the standards of biblical preaching and teaching.***

Our vision is to see churches in the majority world equipped for mission and growing to maturity in Christ through the ministry of pastors and leaders who believe, teach and live by the Word of God.

Our mission is to strengthen the ministry of the Word of God through:

- nurturing national movements for biblical preaching
- fostering the creation and distribution of evangelical literature
- enhancing evangelical theological education

especially in countries where churches are under-resourced.

Our ministry

Langham Preaching partners with national leaders to nurture indigenous biblical preaching movements for pastors and lay preachers all around the world. With the support of a team of trainers from many countries, a multi-level programme of seminars provides practical training, and is followed by a programme for training local facilitators. Local preachers' groups and national and regional networks ensure continuity and ongoing development, seeking to build vigorous movements committed to Bible exposition.

Langham Literature provides majority world preachers, scholars and seminary libraries with evangelical books and electronic resources through publishing and distribution, grants and discounts. The programme also fosters the creation of indigenous evangelical books in many languages, through writer's grants, strengthening local evangelical publishing houses, and investment in major regional literature projects, such as one volume Bible commentaries like *The Africa Bible Commentary* and *The South Asia Bible Commentary*.

Langham Scholars provides financial support for evangelical doctoral students from the majority world so that, when they return home, they may train pastors and other Christian leaders with sound, biblical and theological teaching. This programme equips those who equip others. Langham Scholars also works in partnership with majority world seminaries in strengthening evangelical theological education. A growing number of Langham Scholars study in high quality doctoral programmes in the majority world itself. As well as teaching the next generation of pastors, graduated Langham Scholars exercise significant influence through their writing and leadership.

To learn more about Langham Partnership and the work we do visit **langham.org**

Lightning Source UK Ltd.
Milton Keynes UK
UKHW022357030619
343799UK00008B/762/P